To Know Him
- *The Way*
- *The Truth*
- *The Life*

Paul A. Duffner, O.P.

VOLUME ONE

New Hope Publications

First Printing January 2006

© 2005 Paul A. Duffner, O.P.

ISBN 1-892875-32-2

All rights reserved. No part of this book may be reproduced or transmitted in any form or by any means, electronic or mechanical, including photocopying, recording, or by any information storage or retrieval system, without permission in writing from the publisher.

Cover painting: Mary Rousseau Van Buren
          after *Way to Emmaus* by Robert Zund

TABLE OF CONTENTS

Preface	v
Introduction	viii

Part One
The Make-up of Man

1. The First Sin in Human History 3
2. Conscience, Our Guide: Its Difficulties 12
3. Conscience, Our Guide: Its Formation 20
4. The Human Soul 27
5. Our Free Will 35
6. This Body of Ours 43
7. Why Are We Tempted? 51

Part Two
The Christian Life

8. The Call to Holiness 62
9. Loving is Self-Giving 69
10. Freeing the Heart 77
11. Yes, Father 86
12. Two Kinds of Self-Love 95
13. The Love of Forgiveness 103
14. Blessed are the Meek 111
15. Blessed are the Merciful 120
16. Blessed are the Clean of Heart 128
17. Redemptive Suffering 135
18. Reparation for Sin 143
19. What Has Become of Sin? 151
20. Cafeteria Catholics 160
21. Worldliness 169
22. Is Lent Dead? 178
23. The Vice of Sloth 185

24. The Slaughter of the Innocent	193
25. *Humanae Vitae* Reviewed	201
26. The Fruits of Secularism	209
27. Our Adversary, the Devil	217
28. Envy and Jealousy, Enemies of Charity	226
29. Monica's Wayward Son	235
30. The Truth Will Make You Free	242
31. Today's Crisis of Faith	249
32. Indulgences	258

Part Three
The Church and The Sacraments

33. Sacred Tradition	268
34. Feed My Lambs, Feed My Sheep	277
35. The Holy Eucharist: Part I: A Sacrifice	285
36. The Holy Eucharist: Part II: A Divine Banquet	293
37. Transubstantiation	302
38. The Mass and the Mystical Body of Christ	310
39. Our Encounter with Christ in the Liturgy	318
40. The Millennium and the Eucharist	326
41. The Sacrament of Penance or Reconciliation	335
42. The Priesthood of the Laity	344

Part Four
Prayer

43. The Lord's Prayer	354
44. Ask and You Shall Receive	362
45. Giving Thanks	371
46. Understanding the Rosary	379
47. Some Objections to the Rosary	388
48. St. Dominic and the Rosary	396
49. Weapons from Heaven	406

Preface
by Fr. Basil Cole, OP

This welcome book has some exceedingly clear and interesting things to say about the Christian life. It is about Jesus, ourselves and how the supernatural organism which has been bestowed upon Christians by the sacraments and grace can be exercised and penetrate one's daily life. Father Duffner has diligently worked over and honed these essays for the last twenty years, attempting to give the fruits of his contemplation within the Thomistic tradition.

The main sources of reference for this book are St. Thomas Aquinas, the Angelic and preferred Doctor of the Church, Sacred Scripture and Tradition, and recent Roman Pontiffs. But since these pages are spiritual theology, the reader will also find a great deal taken from human experience to explain some of the many complexities of the spiritual life, which is especially helpful for beginners.

For over twenty years Fr. Duffner was director of the Rosary Confraternity, the purpose of which is to develop prayer and devotion to the Blessed Virgin Mary, and through her to her Son Jesus Christ the Lord, and through him to the Father and the Holy Spirit. Perseverance in prayer is not easy for sinners unless we make an effort to overcome our innate laziness and boredom. And to do this, we need something to think about so that we become inspired. So, what is shared by the author is what has inspired him to continue faithfully his priestly life these many 64 years of service to the people of God in his ministries, from being an associate pastor, novice master, pastor, promotor of Catholic radio in the Portland area, to being twice named director of the Holy Rosary Confraternity. This book brings together all of these sacred activities and ministries in written form since experience shapes us all for better or worse.

One of the many features of this book is that it can be read slowly and not necessarily in any particular order because each essay stands on its own. When certain crosses come in our lives, different articles can be read with much consolation. When new challenges are offered, other articles need to be mulled over. When God seems to be calling us to works beyond the call of duty, several more thought-provoking pieces can help us work through the new calls to excellence and deeper involvement in the life of divine love.

While the spiritual life revolves around prayer life — because in moments of suffering and temptation to despair or any sin we need to pray for grace to rise above ourselves — the heart and soul of the Christian life is charity or divine love. But that same divine love not only needs to be sustained by the worthy reception of the Eucharist, the sacrament of love, but also by the truth of the Catholic faith, articulated and clarified by the light of reason. As Aquinas once wrote in his *Summa* I, 43, 5 ad 2:

> The soul is made like to God by grace. Hence for a divine person to be sent to anyone by grace, there must needs be a likening of the soul to the divine person Who is sent, by some gift of grace. Because the Holy Spirit is Love, the soul is assimilated to the Holy Ghost by the gift of charity: hence the mission of the Holy Ghost is according to the mode of charity. Whereas the Son is the Word, not any sort of word, but one Who breathes forth Love. Hence Augustine says (*De Trin.* ix 10): "The Word we speak of is knowledge with love." Thus the Son is sent not in accordance with every and any kind of intellectual perfection, but according to the intellectual illumination, which breaks forth into the affection of love.

"Faith seeking knowledge" — as St. Anselm once coined the expression describing the work of theology — is a faith that ideally is informed by charity that becomes, under grace, an intellectual fire that leads one to conversion and penance. The more one knows by the light of reason the meaning of faith, the more apt one is to become inflamed with the love of God. So, the many investigations in this book of our faith mysteries are meant to help the reader break forth in the affection of love of God. With these sentiments, the rosary then becomes a continual reference point for all theological thinking by gazing on the Living Son of God. Too often the reason why the rosary appears to be boring is that we lose the sense that the mysteries are veritable diamond mines, inexhaustible treasures of intelligibility of our faith. Failure to get to the meaning of these mysteries makes the rosary seem like a dull repetition of a series of prayers. Father Duffner, then, has helped us get underneath and go deeper than our surface knowledge of the Catholic faith.

Eventually, even our understanding of the faith by the light of human reasoning must yield to an even deeper understanding, called by Thomistic theologians of spirituality "the divine mode of knowing" or "mystical knowledge." This kind of knowledge can only take place when the gifts of the Holy Spirit are actualized by that same Spirit dwelling in our souls.

For most of us, this happens episodically and much of the time, we are not sensitive enough to know that it is happening, but we at least do not resist it. The great saints, however, live by dogmas of the faith as known predominantly by these gifts. So, the rosary for them becomes infused contemplative/meditative prayer whereby God fills them with such an intense growth in charity that they are able to do many heroic actions with great energy day by day, even in great illnesses. But to get to this point in our lives, we need to grow in ordinary virtue and ordinary prayer. Fr. Duffner's studies in faith will be a stepping stone in our journey.

Introduction

The individual chapters of this book were originally published as articles in a small periodical *The Rosary, Light and Life*, for members of the Rosary Confraternity. They appeared bi-monthly under the general title of "Theology for the Laity" between the years 1983 and 2000. There was never the slightest thought during those years that they would some day be published in a volume such as this. The articles were not written in the chronological order in which they appear in this book, but have been arranged according to general categories. Chapters that follow in immediate succession could have been written ten or more years apart. For this reason there will be noticed a repetition of certain basic ideas in the development of the individual chapters, as well as a diversity of format. Yet it was deemed wiser to leave each chapter intact to preserve the completeness of the particular theme developed. One saving thought in this regard is the old axiom that "repetition is the mother of learning."

Since any true devotion must be based on solid doctrine, it has been our aim to stress the doctrinal basis of the topics presented. One must understand his Catholic faith in order to live it, and the better that understanding the fuller one's Catholic life, when one is faithfully attentive to the sources of grace, and conscientious in his concern to follow Christ. For those whose Catholic education has been incomplete, these pages can be a fruitful source of instruction; and for those well instructed in that respect, it is hoped that they will be an added stimulus to Catholic living.

Our special thanks to Fr. Basil Cole, O.P. for his encouragement and suggestions in the publication of this collection of articles; to Cecelia Hoesly and Calvin Smith who are responsible for the page by page layout of this entire book; to Michele Maitland for the laborious task of proofreading, and to all who in various ways have helped to bring this work to completion.

May Our lady of the Rosary, Mother of God, obtain for the readers of these pages a better understanding of the doctrines of our Catholic faith and the grace to give witness by their lives of the truths they believe.

PART ONE
The Make-Up of Man

Chapter 1
The First Sin in Human History

The account of the fall of our first parents in the book of Genesis is well known to most Christians: that God created Adam and Eve the first man and woman of the human race, and endowed them with many gifts both in the order of nature and in the order of grace; that He put them on trial in which they failed. That failure was the first sin in human history, as a result of which they and their descendants were deprived of many of the gifts they had received.

At first glance, it seems unfair that those born today should be punished for something their forebears did thousands of years ago. To give a satisfactory answer to this question we will have to take a look at the state of Adam and Eve before their fall, the fall itself, their condition after the fall, and why we inherit the consequences of their fall.

Before the Fall

A devoted and loving father is not content merely to supply his children with their basic necessities, but will share with them other gifts and advantages that are within his power to give. So too, God the Creator and Father of us all was not content to grant to our first parents all those gifts and faculties of body and soul that pertain to their human nature; He granted them immeasurably more, for He had created them for a happiness that they could never attain by their natural powers alone. Though their human bodies were marvelously designed and their souls wonderfully endowed with intelligence and will, making them creatures after His own image and likeness, still that was not enough. He conferred on them a share in His own divine life. And in addition to this, He granted them other gifts which theologians call "preternatural" that rendered them free from suffering and death and conflict of any kind. We will look at these gifts in detail.

1) Immortality of the Body

The human body is naturally mortal, that is, subject to death and corruption. Yet, by a special gift superadded to human nature the laws of death and corruption were suspended for Adam and Eve in their primitive state. If our first parents had not sinned, they and their descendants would not have had to die. After a time, says the First Vatican Council (No. 386), they would have passed to the face-to-face vision of God without undergoing death.

2) Impassibility

Just as it is natural for man to die, so it is natural for man to suffer pain. Yet by a special gift, our first parents, prior to their fall, were totally immune from suffering and sickness of any kind. This gift too, was not given to them as *individuals*, but was a gift added to their *nature*, and thus was to be inherited by their descendants, on condition of their fidelity to God.

3) Integrity, Perfect Harmony Within Man

Prior to that first sin of Adam and Eve, their *lower nature* (bodily appetites and passions) was completely subject to their *higher nature* (intellect and will). What their *intellect* saw as right in regard to the appetites and desires of the body, their *will* always had the power to carry out. Thus they experienced an inner harmony with no concupiscence of any kind.

4) Sanctifying Grace

God, in His infinite love and goodness, was not content with the gifts mentioned above that were superadded to man's nature. He granted in addition the supernatural gift of sanctifying grace which gives man a new and higher life, a share in the very life of God. With the reception of grace, man's nature is not essentially changed, but is perfected, is elevated to a higher plane, giving man the capacity to merit by his own free acts the supernatural reward of heaven, something utterly beyond his natural capacity to attain.

The Fall of Our First Parents

Without recalling the details of the fall of Adam and Eve as described in the book of Genesis, we will concern ourselves about two things: What was the reason for God's command, and what was the nature of Adam's sin?

God had created the world and placed man in it as lord over all. All the material, vegetative and animal world was at his disposal, for his use. Why, then, did not God let Adam and Eve enjoy all the fruits of the land? Why did He single out one exception?

Adam was indeed lord over the world that God had created for man's purpose; but he was not lord unto himself. He and Eve were still creatures of God, and as such, owed Him worship and obedience to acknowledge their dependence. And to afford Adam and Eve the opportunity to acknowledge their dependence and subjection, God placed one limitation on their freedom; only one pleasure He forbade them.

It was certainly fitting that man, who had received so many wonderful gifts from God, should make some offering, some sacrifice of what he had received, as an acknowledgment of God's right to command, and his own indebtedness and obligation to obey.

What God was asking was not the sacrifice of the *fruit*. That would present no difficulty at all, for their bodily appetites were under perfect control of reason and will. It was the sacrifice of their *will* through obedience that God asked, by accepting this one limitation to their freedom.

We can see the nature of Adam's sin from the nature of the devil's temptation. Recall how Satan, *"the father of lies"* (Jn. 6:44), showed them their great dominion over all the world, how all things were subject to them, and the great dignity that was theirs. Why should their freedom be limited in this way? Be subject to no one.

Throw off this yoke. Eat the fruit and become even greater. *"Your eyes will be opened and you will be like God, knowing good and evil"* (Gen. 3:5). And we know the rest.

Adam's sin was not one of concupiscence, for in his original state he had no disorderly attachments or inclinations of the body. Hence there was nothing to cloud the mind or pressure the will. Intoxicated with his own excellence, Adam rebelled against this subjection, wishing to be independent of God. It was a sin of sheer rebellion of the mind and will against the claims of God. As St. Thomas Aquinas points out, it was essentially a sin of pride, from which flowed disobedience.[1]

Adam sinned, says St. Thomas, deliberately partaking of *"the tree of the knowledge of good and evil,"* seeking, according to the serpent's suggestion, *"that by his own natural power he might decide what was good, and what was evil for him to do."*[2]

How often do the descendants of Adam seek to take into their own hands the determination of what is morally right or wrong, independently of the clear teaching of the Church handing down the revealed word of God.

Adam sinned, St. Thomas points out, because of his attempt to seek his own fulfillment apart from God, that is, by his own natural powers independently of God.[3] How often, too, do many of the descendants of Adam seem to feel they do not need the channels of grace that God has provided through His Church, or its guiding norms, in order to attain their own fulfillment.

We Inherit Fallen Human Nature

Adam's disobedience was not just an isolated sin, but was a failure in a test in which the whole human race was on trial. The supernatural and preternatural gifts he received were not given to him as an individual. They were bestowed on human nature in the person of Adam. For Adam it was a grave *personal* sin. For his descendants it is not a personal sin, but one that infects the nature they inherit. As Pope Paul VI explained in his *Creed of the People of God*:

> We believe that in Adam all have sinned, which means that the original offense committed by him caused human nature, common to all men, to fall to a state in which it bears the consequences of that offense. . . . It is human nature so fallen, stripped of the grace that clothed it, injured in its own natural powers and subjected to the dominion of death, that is transmitted to all men, and it is in this sense that every man is born in sin.

We must not think that God deals with us unfairly because we come into this world with less than would have been the case had our first parents not sinned. For the gifts that were lost were not due to us in any way. We have no right to them as human beings. Yet, while their loss does not essentially change human nature, the loss of them has caused deep "wounds" in human nature, body and soul, as we shall see.

Consequences of the Fall

1) Loss of Sanctifying Grace

With one act of disobedience prompted by pride, our first parents not only lost the divine gift of grace by which God shared with them His own divine life, constituting them in a state of *friendship with God* as His adopted children; but they fell into a state of *aversion from God*, and came, in a sense, under the dominion of Satan. Man is either in the state of grace, or in the state of sin; there is no middle ground. *"He that is not with me, is against Me"* (Mt. 12:30). One is turned to God through grace, or from God through sin (actual or original). Lost also was the abiding presence of the three Divine Persons who dwell in the soul in the state of grace; and the gates of heaven were closed to mankind.

2) Loss of Integrity

The order intended by the Creator was that man's lower nature be subject to his higher nature, and that his higher nature be subject to God. And as long as man's higher nature was subject to God, his lower nature was totally subject to reason and will. But with the rebellion of Adam's mind and will against God, there began at once the rebellion of the flesh against the spirit. St. Thomas Aquinas explains this:

> In man's primitive state, as long as his mind was subject to God, the lower powers of his soul would be subject to his rational mind, and his body to his soul. But inasmuch as through sin man's mind withdrew from subjection to God, the result was that neither were his lower powers wholly subject to reason, whence there followed so great a rebellion of the carnal appetite against reason; nor was the body wholly subject to the soul.[4]

With the loss of this gift, man's bodily appetites and passions demanded one thing, and his reason another; and his will was no longer always strong enough to master the situation. Thus it was that St. Paul complained, *"I see another law in my members, warring against the law of my mind and making me a prisoner to the law of sin that is in my members"* (Rom. 7:23).

St. John speaks of a threefold concupiscence that became man's lot as a consequence of the loss of the gift of integrity (Jn. 2:16).

a) Concupiscence of the Flesh: a disordered desire and hunger for the pleasures and satisfactions of the body (especially lust and gluttony), and the revolt of the body against the necessary restraints and mortification in these matters.

b) Concupiscence of the Eyes: a disordered desire for worldly goods and riches, and the tendency to become overly attached to them, so that instead of possessing them, we can easily be possessed by them. *"No one,"* said Our Lord, *"can serve two masters"* (Mt. 6:24), that is, God and worldly goods. Either we *master them* (that is, own, use and share them with detachment), or they *master us*, and cause us to neglect the rights of God and neighbor. St. Paul wrote of this to Timothy:

They (those seeking riches) are letting themselves be captured by foolish and harmful desires which drag man down to ruin and destruction. The love of money is the root of all evil. Some men in their passion for it have strayed from the faith, and have involved themselves in many troubles (1 Tim. 6:9-10).

c) Pride of Life: the disordered desire for one's own glory and exaltation apart from God. It is a disordered desire for freedom and independence that leads to disobedience to the order established by God, and to rebellion against lawful authority. Pride brought about the downfall of the fallen angels and Adam, and we have inherited that same tendency. This "wound" of our nature makes it difficult for us, not only to obey, but also to accept correction, humiliation, failure, and so forth. We are put into this world to give glory to God by fulfilling His will; but pride causes us to seek our own glory, by seeking our will in opposition to His. Just as the satisfactions of the body and worldly goods can become our master, so can the satisfactions of the ego, so that one pays homage to himself rather than to God, claiming for himself the credit for all the good he accomplishes.

With the loss of this inner harmony between man's bodily appetites and his intellect and will, there followed not only the *weakening of the will*, but also an *obscuring of the judgment*; for our judgments are slanted by our desires, so that we are given to much wishful thinking. And with this loss of control by our higher nature, we inherit an *inclination to sin*, that is, an inclination in varying degrees to pride, avarice, lust, anger, gluttony, envy and sloth.

3) Loss of Bodily Immortality

God had warned our first parents: *"From that tree you shall not eat; the moment you eat from it you are surely doomed to die"* (Gen. 2:16). Yet, eat from it they did; and so St. Paul wrote, *"By one man sin entered into the world and with sin death; and thus death comes to all men"* (Rom. 5:12).

Even though death is natural to man, it comes as a punishment for sin, for by Adam's sin the special gift preserving him from death was forfeited. Natural as death is, it is also the penalty for rebellion. As St. Thomas Aquinas states, *"Death is natural on account of the condition of matter, but it is penal on account of the loss of the divine gift which has the power to preserve from death."*[5]

4) Loss of Impassibility

Having lost the gift of immunity from suffering, the life of Adam and Eve and their descendants would henceforth be strewn with wearisome toil and suffering. Daily toil that had been man's pleasure, now became a laborious task. On the woman God imposed the pains of childbirth, and subjection to her husband (Gen. 3:16); and on the man He imposed the task of laboriously tilling the soil, and of earning his bread by the sweat of his brow. Henceforth, suffering in many forms would be an inescapable part of human existence.

Dogma of Faith

While our everyday experience tells us of *"the law in the members warring against the law of the mind"* of which St. Paul speaks (Rom. 7:23), we rely mainly on the teaching of our faith for certainty in these matters. The doctrine of original sin has been defined by the Councils of Mileve (416), Carthage (418), Orange (529), Trent (1445), and First Vatican (1870).

Modern philosophy rejects the idea of original sin, as have all who through the centuries have sought the goal of human living by natural powers alone. Fifteen centuries ago St. Augustine wrote against the errors of Pelagius, an English monk who taught that original sin was not passed on to Adam's descendants, and that the baptism of children is held not for the remission of sin, but as a sign of their acceptance into the Church. This error, condemned by the Church, is far from dead today, and has found its way into some of our present-day explanations of the liturgy.

Pope John Paul II pointed out in a general audience that modern man, not enlightened by faith, *"cannot admit the idea of a hereditary sin, connected with the decision of a progenitor and not with that of the person concerned."* However, he went on to say that *"the Church's teaching on original sin can be extremely valuable also for modern man who, having rejected the data of faith in this matter, can no longer understand the mysterious and distressing aspects of evil which he daily experiences; and he ends up by wavering between a hasty and unjustified optimism and a radical pessimism bereft of hope"* (Sept. 24, 1986).

Chapter Notes

1. St. Thomas Aquinas, *Summa Theologiae,* II-II, q. 163, a. 1
2. *Ibid.,* q. 163, a. 2
3. *Ibid.*
4. *Ibid.,* q. 164, a. 1.
5. *Ibid.*

Chapter 2

Conscience, Our Guide
Part 1: Its Difficulties

Following the Second Vatican Council there were not a few Catholics who looked upon what they call the "spirit of the Council" as a source of a newly discovered freedom, a reliance on conscience alone in determining one's moral obligations. If there were a conflict between the official teaching of the Church and one's own thinking, one would be told, *"Let your conscience be your guide."*

In answer to this, Pope John Paul II declared in a general audience:

> It is not sufficient to say to man: *"Always follow your conscience."* It is necessary to add immediately and always: *"Ask yourself if your conscience is telling you the truth or something false, and seek untiringly to know the truth."* If we were not to make this necessary clarification, man would risk to find in his conscience a force which is destructive of his true humanity, rather than that holy place where God reveals to him his true good (Aug. 17, 1983).

This being so, it might be helpful to discuss this matter of conscience, some of its problems, and the sources upon which we must rely if we are to have a true conscience, one that truly reflects the Divine Will.

What is Our Conscience?

When God created man, He not only endowed him with *freedom of will,* that is, with the power to choose freely among various alternatives in seeking a given goal; He also endowed him with an *intellect* that can know universal truths, and can make practical judgments which apply those truths to particular cases. Or, as this is sometimes expressed, man's intellect is endowed with:

a) a speculative power – which knows in general that something is right or wrong, true or false; for example, lying is wrong, murder is wrong, stealing is wrong, helping one in need is good, and so forth.

b) a practical power – of making a practical judgment applying this or that universal truth to a particular case in such a way that it admonishes one in the depths of the heart. For example: this particular action is wrong, avoid it; that particular action is good, do it. This practical judgment is what we call conscience.

God gave to man this built-in guide for his actions, a guide that is meant to direct him toward good and turn him away from evil, in such a way that man is responsible for his actions.

Not an Infallible Guide

This built-in guide, however, is not something that always automatically points in the right direction, as does the needle of a compass. That is to say, this built-in guide can be in error. It can fail to reflect the eternal truth that exists in the mind of God, the highest and ultimate norm of all morality.

While God's truth never changes, man's conscience is not only changeable, but is also affected by many things that can either lessen or increase its power of discerning truth. In other words, our conscience is part of us, and it changes as we change for better or for worse. Like other natural and God-given faculties or powers, it must be properly trained if it is to function properly.

We hear much about the importance of following one's conscience, but how little we hear about the importance of forming one's conscience. Yet, as it is formed, so it functions.

Our mind doesn't *make* truth, it merely *knows* it. So also, our conscience doesn't *create* obligations, it merely *discerns* them, or fails to discern them. Moral obligations have their source in the Creator.

Conscience Needs Training

We have a faculty of speech given by God. This can be trained so that we can speak well or speak poorly, articulate well or poorly. It is subject to development, to being trained, to being formed.

We have the faculty to appreciate the beautiful in various forms of art, music, and so forth. But it must be trained if it is to serve us well in this respect.

In a similar way, conscience is a God-given faculty or power of determining what is right or wrong in a given situation. Even though it has been implanted in man by the Creator, it needs education if it is to function as intended by the Creator, if one is to have a true conscience.

The Sensitivity of Conscience

An English theologian, Fr. Bede Jarrett, O.P., points out that the more one grows in grace and the love of God, the more clearly and truly will conscience perceive between right and wrong; the more sensitive and delicate an instrument will conscience become in pointing out the little things that God would have us do or not do. On the other hand, the more one offends God, going against conscience, the duller becomes its perception, first in regard to little things, and gradually in regard to greater things.[1]

Consequently, if a person habitually disregards the urge of conscience in some small matter, after a time, conscience no longer urges in this matter, at least not as much as before; it no longer rebukes him for doing the wrong thing, at least not as much as before. It is precisely in this way that a *lax conscience* is formed.

So there is no room for complacency, simply because we have no qualms of conscience in doing this or that which the law of God or the law of the Church forbids. That is, we cannot always conclude that this or that is right merely because conscience does not rebuke us; for this power of judging rightly can be dulled, can lose its sensitivity, can even be quieted altogether through habitual disregard of its dictates.

The Second Vatican Council bears this out in *The Constitution on the Church in the Modern World:*

> Conscience frequently errs from invincible ignorance without losing its dignity. The same cannot be said for a man who cares little for truth and goodness, or of a conscience which by degrees grows practically sightless as a result of habitual sin.[2]

Divine Wisdom has revealed this same truth through the writer of the Psalms: *"Sin speaks to the sinner in the depth of his heart. There is no fear of God before his eyes. He so flatters himself in his mind that he knows not his guilt. In his mouth are mischief and deceit; all wisdom is gone"* (Ps. 36).

Commenting on this lack of sensitivity of conscience, Fr. Jarrett wrote:

> It is not enough for me to say that my conscience lets me do this or that since the further point can properly be put: Has my conscience any right to do it? Certainly it is possible to have a false conscience, and it is possible that this falseness may be my own fault entirely. The question, then, is not so simple as it sounds, for conscience is not the external voice of God whispering to me, but is really just the voice of my whole being.[3]

It must be noted that a *sensitive* conscience must not be confused with a *scrupulous* conscience. The first is a *true* conscience, the second a *false* conscience. The first lives *in peace,* for such is the fruit of growth in charity, while the latter lives *in fear,* seeing sin where it does not exist.

The Seared Conscience

To explain the sensitivity of conscience, spiritual writers use the example of the fingertips. The sensitivity of the fingertips can be highly trained and developed, as in the case of the blind reading braille, or of the violinist. Yet, if those fingertips are burned, where the burn exists, the skin is hardened and much of the sensitivity is lost.

Sin has a similar effect on conscience. In fact St. Paul refers to the *"seared conscience"* of the sinner (1 Tim. 4:2).

What formerly would have upset one considerably, now has little or no effect at all. The individual might tell himself the difference is that he has grown up, has matured, has broadened his vision.

It is true, one's view can change, can mature, so that certain things are viewed differently; but if the change is because of a disregard of conscience, it is the opposite of maturing, of growing up in Christ.

Fr. Jarrett refers to this changeableness of conscience:

> Conscience is always changing, always fluid, so that we do things today that our conscience is silent about, whereas tomorrow it may furiously upbraid us for even thinking about them. I have, then, obviously to train my conscience, for of itself, except in the very simplest things, it will not necessarily act aright. There are souls, indeed, that are naturally Christian, but how few, and these not on every point.[4]

Wishful Thinking

If, as we have seen, habitual sin dulls the sensitivity of conscience, one of the underlying problems we are contending with in this matter is one of the effects of original sin. We are told that because of the fall of our first parents, our *will* has been weakened, and our *intellect* clouded. What this clouding of the intellect amounts to is this: our ability to judge objectively has been affected, so that our judgments are colored and slanted by our desires, our dislikes, our attachments.

St. Thomas Aquinas refers to this when he points out that we easily *believe* to be true what we *wish* to be true.[5] St. Augustine refers to the same when he declares that one will never find an atheist, except that he finds one who wishes that God did not exist.

St. Catherine of Siena, another Doctor of the Church, describes at length in her *Dialogue* how sensuality clouds the light of reason, and thus distorts the guidance of conscience.

> You know that every evil is grounded in selfish love of oneself. This love is a cloud that blots out the light of reason.... If sensual affection wants to love sensual things, the eye of the understanding is moved in that direction. It takes for its

object only passing things with selfish love, contempt for virtue, and love of vice, drawing from these pride and impatience. And so memory is filled only with what affection holds out to it.

This love so dazzles the eye that it neither discerns nor sees anything but the glitter of these things. Such is their glitter that understanding sees and affection loves them all as if their brightness came from goodness and loveliness. Were it not for this glitter, people would never sin, for the soul by her very nature cannot desire anything but good. But vice is disguised as something good for her, and so the soul sins. Her eyes, though, cannot tell the difference because of her blindness, and she does not know the truth. So she wanders about searching for what is good and lovely where it is not to be found.[6]

We see, then, why it is so easy to rationalize and justify doing what we want to do, or not doing what we do not want to do. As the axiom has it: *"The wish is the father of the thought."* What we want colors how we judge. It should be the other way around. The light of right judgment should determine what we choose. St. Thomas Aquinas explains how this deception comes about. *"Inordinate self-love is the source of all sin, and darkens the intellect; for when will and sensuality are ill disposed (i.e., when they tend to **pride** and **sensuality**), everything that is in conformity with these inclinations appears as good."*[7]

Arnold Lunn, noted English writer, once stated: *"We don't distinguish between those who are biased, and those who are not; but between those who realize they are, and those who do not."* So, too, we don't distinguish between those who are given to wishful thinking and those who are not; but between those who realize they are, and those who do not. Since conscience is simply a practical judgment of the intellect, it is not exempt from this self-deception. And as St. Thomas pointed out, the more we are dominated by pride or sensuality, the more we are given to this self-deception.[8]

Conscience Becomes What We Make It

We must keep in mind that we are the product of our own free actions. We ourselves (aided by divine grace, or hurt by our lack of cooperation with it) determine what we become. If some of our characteristics have been inherited, by and large, the countless actions of our own free choice go into molding us into what we are. And since conscience is part of what we are, this is true of conscience as well.

That is to say, your conscience is what you have made it. As you are, so is your conscience. And as such, it will serve you well, or serve you poorly.

If this built-in guide is not properly trained, it will lead us astray; and as Pope John Paul II stated, it can be *"a force which is destructive of our true humanity, rather than that holy place where God reveals to us our true good."* On another occasion the Holy Father cautioned: *"When conscience is weakened, the sense of God is obscured, and as a result, the sense of sin is lost"* (Jan. 1985).

These considerations of conscience might seem to present a very pessimistic view of the built-in guide that God has given us, but we are merely looking at the difficulties of conscience when left to itself alone, and the problems it faces when little or no care is given to its proper formation or education; and too, they help us to understand the warning of the Holy Father quoted above. *"It is not sufficient to say to man: 'Always follow your conscience.' It is necessary to add immediately and always: 'Ask yourself if your conscience is telling you the truth, or something false, and seek untiringly to know the truth."*[9]

In the next chapter, we will take up what must be involved in *"seeking untiringly to know the truth,"* that is to say, what we must do to have a true conscience, one that reflects the will of God.

Chapter Notes

1. Bede Jarrett, O.P., *Meditations for Layfolk*, pp. 208 *ff*
2. Vatican Council II, *The Constitution on the Church in the Modern World*, n. 16
3. Bede Jarrett, O.P., *Meditations for Layfolk*, pp. 208 *ff*
4. *Ibid.*
5. St. Thomas Aquinas, *Summa Theologiae* II-II, q. 1, a. 62, 3, ad 2
6. St. Catherine of Siena, *Dialogue,* Ch. 51
7. St. Thomas Aquinas, *Summa Theologiae,* I-II, q. 77, a. 4; Garrigou-Lagrange, *Three Ways,* p. 41
8. St. Thomas Aquinas, *Summa Theologiae* II-II, q. 162, a. 3, ad 2
9. General Audience, Aug. 17, 1983

Chapter 3

Conscience, Our Guide
Part 2: Its Formation

Conscience is sometimes referred to as the "voice of God." If that is so, then how can it be wrong? This must be understood correctly. When one has a *true conscience,* then, yes, it is the expression of truth as it exists in the mind of God; but one can have a *false conscience,* which is but an expression of his own selfishness, his pride, his greed, his lust. ... And as the Irish bishops pointed out in their document on *Conscience and Morality,* I can easily mistake the latter for the voice of the Spirit.

> It is not always a simple matter to recognize the authentic voice of the Spirit in our heart as it points out the right and reasonable path. For it is often obscured by other voices, the voices of our own bias or prejudice, or our self-interest or passion. To distinguish it from these competing voices can at times be extremely difficult.[1]

In a word, if I am filled with the *spirit of Christ,* the voice of Christ will come through in my conscience; if I am filled with the *spirit of the world,* the voice of the world will be heard in my conscience; and the spirit of the world has little respect for authority. As I am, so my conscience is.

The Law of God Written in the Heart

Conscience is also referred to as the law of God written in the heart.

Every human person will be judged by this law of God written in his heart, that is, by the natural moral law rooted in human reason by the Creator. In addition to this, the Jewish people will be judged by the Mosaic law, and Christians will be judged by the teachings of Christ recorded in the Scriptures and handed down by the Church He founded (cf Rom. 2:12-15).

As the Irish bishops pointed out:

> God has indeed inscribed the moral law in the heart of every man, but this does not mean that it is a simple matter for the individual to know it clearly and with certainty, especially in its more detailed application. For this he requires the help of an external guide. The very diversity of moral opinion we see around us, even in matters of fundamental importance, is enough to show what a great need there is for such a guide.[2]

Conscience and Freedom

In regard to the New Law that Christ gave, He said to His followers: *"If you live according to my teaching, you will be my disciples, and you will know the truth, and the truth will make you free"* (Jn. 8:31). In our present context, that means: If you live according to Christ's teaching, you will know the truth (that is, you will have a *right conscience*), and you will be free, free from error and from enslavement to worldly pleasures. And conversely, if you reject Christ's teaching, with its restraints, you will not know the truth (that is, yours will be a *false conscience*), and you will not be free, but enslaved by the very pleasures and satisfactions that are sought without restraint. The truth that Christ taught *"makes us free"* (Jn. 8:32); not free to do what we wish, but free from that kind of enslavement.

Moral freedom, then, which has to do with rights, does not give us the right to do what we *want* to do, but the right to do what we *ought* to do, the right to choose among various means to do what God allows.

Applying this to conscience, one should ask himself not merely *does* my conscience allow this, but *ought* my conscience to allow it, in the light of God's revelation handed down by the Church.

Conscience Alone is Not Sufficient

For many today who do not accept the teaching of the Church, freedom is the right to do whatever one wants, as long as the civil law allows it (for example, abortion). Yet both the natural law and the divine law forbid the taking of innocent life.

Every single one of the countless persons in our country who are claiming they have the "right to choose" in regard to abortion, has (or had) the *"law of God written in the heart"* (Rom. 2:15). What has happened to it? This brings out so clearly how conscience can be clouded, and altogether silenced, when again and again it is not heeded.

The more we examine this question, the more we see that *conscience alone* is not a sufficient guide in moral decisions. There are needed external sources of guidance, and these God has provided. He has not only given His revelation recorded in the Scriptures, but has founded His Church, and promised to it the guidance of the Holy Spirit to insure the true interpretation of that message. Note the following official statements of the Church in that regard:

> In the formation of their conscience, the Christian faithful ought carefully to attend to the sacred and certain doctrines of the Church. The Church is, by the will of Christ, the teacher of truth. It is her duty to give utterance to, and authoritatively to teach, that truth which is Christ Himself, and also to declare and confirm by her authority those principles of the moral order which have their origin in human nature itself.[3]
>
> The conscience of the faithful . . . must be subject to the magisterium of the Church, whose duty it is to explain the whole moral law authoritatively, in order that it may rightly and correctly express the objective moral order.[4]
>
> The more a correct conscience holds sway, the more persons and groups turn aside from blind choice and strive to be guided by objective norms of morality.[5]

The Role of the Holy Spirit

We are concerned here with the formation of a "Catholic" conscience, that is, one that reflects God's truth, as revealed by Him and transmitted by His Church.

It should be apparent to all that merely having the official teaching of the Church is not enough, for there are not a few within the Church who "pick and choose" what they will accept among its official teachings, with the result that there are conflicting views both on moral and doctrinal issues.

This makes it clear that there is needed not only the *exterior guide* established by Christ (the Church), but the *interior gift* of "catholic and divine faith," enabling one to accept all the Church teaches as divinely revealed, whether by its ordinary or extraordinary magisterium.[6]

In a word, there is needed in addition to our natural powers of reason, the interior assistance of the Holy Spirit to open one's mind and heart to the truth as transmitted by the Church under the guidance of the same Divine Spirit. This is clearly stated by the Irish Conference of Bishops:

> Because of the difficulty conscience often experiences in discerning the truth, Christ is at hand to teach and guide it. This He does on the one hand, by an *outward word* ... first written down in Scripture, and now proclaimed and applied by the teaching Church. On the other hand, again by the guidance of the Spirit, Christ acts on the mind and heart of the individual to help him discern what is good and right.... Each (of these) supports and complements the other. The outward word makes it possible for the *inward voice* of the Spirit to be heard more clearly. On the other hand, the interior activity of the Spirit prepares the way for the voice which comes from the outside, so that it receives a more attentive hearing and a more ready and generous response.[7]

As one, with the assistance of the Holy Spirit, grows in grace and in the practice of the Christian life, his conscience is less distorted by wishful thinking, and more and more he wishes only what God wishes, cost what it may. That is, as one grows in *God's love,* he also grows in the knowledge of *God's truth.* The Holy Spirit is responsible for this, who, in the measure that grace grows, comes with His gifts to guide one along right paths. *"I will give you understanding, and I will instruct you in the way in which you should go"* (Ps. 32: 8). *"If any man will love Me, My Father will love him, and I will love him, and will manifest Myself to him"* (Jn. 14:21).

The Need of Discipline

Looked at from another angle, one's conscience attains a truer insight into what God wants, a clearer insight into what is right and what is wrong, in the measure that (with the help of God's grace) he attains a certain emancipation from the selfish tendencies of our fallen nature. That emancipation is the "freedom" Our Lord spoke of, and the light of a true conscience is the *"truth that makes one free"* (Jn. 8:32).

Yet that emancipation does not come without much prayer, frequent and fruitful reception of the sacraments, and a prolonged struggle against the various forms of selfishness and egoism that are deep within us, and that hinder us from making the sacrifices that the Christian life demands.

If the law of God is *"written in the heart of man"* (Deut. 30:14), so also subtle egoism is deeply rooted in the heart of man. Hence the inevitable struggle, a struggle in which the victory will be ours only with the help of divine grace.

> Man achieves his (full) dignity, when, emancipating himself from all captivity to passion, he pursues his goal in a spontaneous choice of what is good. . . . Since man's freedom has been damaged by sin, only by the help of God's grace can he bring this relationship with God into full flower.[8]

Beware of Presumption

It would be sheer presumption to imagine that the Holy Spirit is going to give us special interior lights, if we neglect these ordinary means of grace. There is no such thing as the formation of a Christian conscience apart from training in true Christian living.

It would likewise be presumption to imagine that the Holy Spirit is going to give us special interior insights if we ignore the clear exterior guide He has provided through the Church.

> For a believer, the teaching of the magisterium. . . cannot be just one element among others in the formation of conscience.

It is the definitive cornerstone upon which the whole edifice of conscience judgment must be built.

What must be kept in mind is that we are in the dimension of faith. And we should be encouraged and hopeful, because we can count on the continued assistance of the Holy Spirit in a manner which pure reason could never give.

If the ultimate practical judgment to do this or avoid that does not take into account the teaching of the Church, an account based not only on reason but on the faith dimension, he is deceiving himself in pretending that he is acting as a true Catholic must.[9]

From the above we can see that for the true "Catholic conscience" these two things are indispensable:

1) The action of the Holy Spirit — without which there can be no dimension of supernatural faith in the judgment of conscience.

2) Obedience to the Church — without which, except for invincible ignorance, there will be no action of the Holy Spirit.

> The religious submission of will and of mind must be shown in a special way to the authentic teaching authority of the Roman Pontiff, even when he is not speaking *ex cathedra*. That is, it must be shown in such a way that his supreme magisterium is acknowledged with reverence, the judgments made by him are sincerely adhered to, according to his manifest mind and will.[10]

The more one accepts the external guide that Christ has given (the official teaching of His Church), the more the Holy Spirit opens the mind and heart to His divine influence. *"It would be unthinkable,"* wrote the Canadian bishops in the document quoted above, *"that the Spirit, speaking in the heart of the redeemed Christian, would be in opposition to Himself teaching in the authority established by Jesus."*[11]

Summing Up

The attaining of a true conscience for the Catholic requires, then, in addition to heeding the teaching of the Church, prayer, the proper use of the sacraments, and a struggle against our selfishness in our effort to keep God's commandments and to fulfill the duties of our state in life.

If we are faithful to these means to the best of our ability, even though at times the path is obscure, even though at times we fail through human frailty, we can take it for granted that our conscience is serving us rightly. On the other hand, the more one is careless about these means, with little concern about what the Church teaches, the less will his conscience serve him rightly, and the more it will allow careless living.

In the last analysis, as we said in the beginning, we will have a right conscience in the measure of our spiritual growth. That is true, because as one grows in grace, there is a progressive growth in detachment, a liberation from those attachments that color and slant our judgments. And the more this becomes a reality, the more the words of the Holy Spirit are fulfilled. *"I will give you understanding, and I will instruct you in the way in which you should go"* (Ps. 32:8).

Chapter Notes

1. *Conscience and Morality,* A Doctrinal Statement of the Irish Episcopal Conference, n. 13
2. *Ibid.*, n. 3
3. Vatican Council II, *Decree on Religious Freedom,* n. 14
4. *General Catechetical Directory*, ordered by Pope Paul VI
5. Vatican Council II, *The Church Today,* n. 16
6. Vatican Council I, Sess. 3, Ch. 3; *Code of Canon Law*, n. 750
7. *Conscience and Morality,* n. 15
8. Vatican Council II, *The Church Today,* n. 17
9. Canadian Bishops, *Formation of Conscience*, n. 38, 40
10. Vatican Council II, *The Church*, n. 25
11. Canadian Bishops, *Formation of Conscience*, n. 46

Chapter 4

The Human Soul

Those who have studied the old Baltimore Catechism will remember the definition of man as a creature composed of body and soul and made in the image and likeness of God. Man, then, is composed of a *material* element (the body) and a *spiritual* element (the soul), not as two independent elements that happen to be joined together, but as two incomplete elements that need each other to form a complete whole, namely, the human person. As the new Catholic Catechism explains, *"Spirit and matter, in man, are not two natures united, but rather their union forms a single nature."*[1] While the soul after death can exist apart from the body, there is an incompleteness in its condition apart from the body until it will be reunited with the body at the end of the world. Our salvation, then, will be fully realized only with the resurrection of the body, when the whole man will enjoy the beatitude of the life to come.

In the account of creation in the book of Genesis, reference is made to both of these essential elements in man. The biblical account expresses this reality in symbolic language when it affirms that *"the Lord God formed man of the dust of the ground, and breathed into his nostrils the breath of life, and man became a living being."*[2] The human soul, though unseen, is just as real as the body. It is unfortunate, however, that man is often much more aware of and concerned about the care of his body and its needs than of the soul, even though the welfare of the soul is by far the more important. It is the condition of the soul at the end of our life on earth that determines our eternal lot, not that of the body.

Both philosophy and theology contribute to our knowledge of the soul. While theology relies on God's word as it comes to us through revelation, philosophy can tell us much about the soul from the light of natural reason.

Made to God's Image and Likeness

God is a pure spirit of infinite knowledge and power. He is the source of all that is good and beautiful and true. Infinitely happy and at peace within Himself, in His boundless love and goodness He willed to bring into being creatures capable of sharing His own eternal beatitude. After creating the physical universe and *"all kinds of living creatures: cattle, creeping things, and wild animals of all kinds . . . God said: 'Let us make man in our image, after our likeness'"* (Gen. 1:24, 26). In what sense are we made to God's image and likeness?

If we consider this question from what we know from psychology, we have no difficulty in seeing the likeness to consist in man's spiritual nature, his intellect and will which separate him from the rest of animal creation. As the Catholic Catechism explains, *"The soul refers to the innermost aspect of man, that which is of greatest value in him, that by which he is most especially in God's image."*[3] The whole science of psychology, however, was entirely unknown to the writer of Genesis, who did not have our concept of the rational soul and its spiritual faculties. For that reason, Scripture scholars tell us that the image of God found in man, in the mind of the author of Genesis, was man's dominion over creation, making him like God who has absolute dominion over all. That is, man is given a share in God's lordship, yet subject to God's supreme rule.

> Let us make man in our own image, after our likeness. Let them have dominion over the fish of the sea, the birds of the air, and the cattle, over all the wild animals and all the creatures that crawl on the ground (Gen. 1:26). God created everything for man, but man in turn was created to serve and love God and to offer all creation back to him.[4]

It is being created in God's image, making us capable of sharing in God's own life through divine grace, that constitutes the unique dignity of the human person.

Being in the image of God the human individual possesses the dignity of a person, who is not just something, but someone. He is capable of self-knowledge, of self-possession and of freely giving himself and entering into communion with other persons. And he is called by grace to a covenant with his Creator, to offer him a response of faith and love that no other creature can give in his stead.[5]

The Soul — The Source of Life

The common classification of living things in this world is: plant, animal and man; and this classification is made according to the special kinds of activity that each of these grades of life is capable of. Each of these categories has a principle of life (or soul) which is the source of the activity proper to that category. For example, *plant* life is capable of nutrition, growth and reproduction. *Animal* life is capable of all the activities of plant life, plus the activity of sensation and local motion. *Human* life (the rational animal) is capable of all the activities of the brute animal plus the power of reasoning, of conceiving abstract ideas, and of free will. For example, a dog can recognize one individual as friendly, and another as mean; but the human mind can conceive and understand the abstract concepts of friendliness and meanness.

Thus, there is a vast difference between the principle of life (the soul) in man, and that in plants and brute animals. For the soul of man is a spiritual being, created immediately by God at the moment of conception, which can exist independent of matter, living on after the dissolution of the body; whereas, the principle of life in plants and brute animals is material, entirely dependent on matter, and ceases to exist at the death of the plant or animal. Moreover, the human soul, a spiritual being, is capable of being perfected and elevated to a higher order of being, a sharing in the very life of God through sanctifying grace. *"Of all visible creatures only man is able to know and love his Creator. . . . He alone is called to share, by knowledge and love, in God's own life. It was for this end that he was created, and this is the fundamental reason for his dignity."*[6]

The human soul, therefore, is the ultimate interior principle by which man lives, and is the indispensable source from which all his human operations flow, namely: *(of the body)* nutrition, growth, reproduction and local motion; *(of the soul)* the spiritual activities by which we know and understand truth, reason to new truths, and make judgments as to what is right and wrong. In all these functions of the *intellect* we mirror the all-wise and all-knowing God. The other spiritual power of the soul is that of the *will,* by which we deliberately and freely choose to act or not to act, in which we mirror the infinite freedom that God possesses.

The Soul and Its Faculties

When we speak of the soul as the source of life and all of man's activities, we mean the soul and its faculties or powers. For, in itself, the soul is not immediately operative.[7] That is, the soul is the source of life for the body, but not its spiritual activities of thinking and choosing. For this it needs the spiritual faculties or powers of operation, intellect and will, which flow from the essence of the soul.[8]

When we consider the faculties of the soul we can see why God made us in His image and likeness. God is Life (Jn. 14:6), and it is by reason of the spiritual soul of man that he is capable of sharing in the life of God through grace. God is Love (1 Jn. 4:8), and it is by means of the *will* that man is capable of loving God and sharing in God's love. God is Truth (Jn. 14:6), and it is by means of the *intellect* that man is capable of knowing God and sharing in God's knowledge. In other words, since God is a pure spirit, only a spiritual being could share in the life and love and truth that pertain to God's very essence.

When we speak of sharing in God's life and love and truth, we are referring to a soul in the state of grace. By reason of this divine gift of grace there is in man a *supernatural organism* made up of grace and the infused virtues and gifts of the Holy Spirit, parallel to and perfecting the *natural organism* made up of the soul and its faculties of intellect and will. Just as the soul is not immediately operative, but needs the powers of intellect and will to think and choose, so grace (which divinizes the soul) is not immediately operative, but needs the infused powers (infused virtues and gifts) to perfect and elevate the intellect and will. The following refers to this parallel:

> Grace, which is the formal principle of supernatural life, is rooted in the very essence of the soul in a static manner. The virtues and gifts which are the dynamic elements of the supernatural organism, reside in the human faculties or powers precisely to elevate them to the supernatural order. Sanctifying grace is the formal principle of our supernatural organism, just as the soul is the formal principle of our natural organism.[9]

The Soul Created by God

Not only did God, at the beginning of time, create the heavens and earth and all living creatures, but the work of creation still continues and will continue until the end of time. For each time that human conception takes place, God creates another human soul and infuses it into the minute fertilized element that is capable of developing to full maturity. So the soul does not exist before the body as do angels, one of whom is assigned as guardian of the new human person, but comes into being at the very instant of conception. But what about the first man? According to the scriptural account our first parents came into being not through human conception but through the direct action of God. Did God accomplish this at one time, or in stages? That is, was there evolution of the body? Whether God formed the body of the first man in one act, or by an unfolding process (under the special guidance of God) so that the soul was created and infused into the body at a later stage of formation, the Church has not made a formal statement on the matter. What the Church has emphatically stated is that the human soul of every human being is created by God constituting a human person.

Scripture scholars do not understand the *"days of creation"* in the same sense that we understand the word *day*. Whether the forming of the body of the first man was done in a short period of time or over a long period of development, is not important as far as our faith is concerned. As Pope Pius XII declared in his encyclical *Humani Generis*:

> The teaching authority of the Church does not forbid that, in conformity with the present state of human sciences and sacred theology, research and discussions on the part of men experienced in both fields, take place with regard to the doctrine of evolution, insofar as it inquires into the origin of the human body as coming from pre-existent and living matter, for Catholic faith obliges us to hold that souls are immediately created by God.[10]

In other words, the Church is more concerned about *what* God did in this matter, than *how* He did it.

The Spirituality of the Soul

A spirit is a being without a body, that has an intellect and free will. A pure spirit is one that has no dependence on matter either for its existence or any of its activities. God is uncreated pure spirit; the angels are created pure spirits. The human soul is a spirit which, while not dependent on the body for its existence, is dependent on the body (during life in this world) for its operation. While it exists apart from the body after the death of the body, it retains a natural affinity for the body to which it will be reunited at the end of the world.

Since the soul is spiritual with no material parts, it has no size, no shape, no weight, nothing that could be observed by the senses. It cannot be measured, nor can it be divided. While the soul, in itself, is not in space, it can operate in space, in the sense that it is the spiritual source of life that vitalizes every part of the human body. It is in this sense that the soul is where it operates.

Because the soul is spiritual, it is *immortal*. Not only can the body be destroyed, but of its very nature it is destined for dissolution. But the soul has no material elements that can decompose or be destroyed. It comes into being by the creative hand of God, and only that same divine power can cause it to cease to exist. God implanted in the human soul a longing for happiness which will be perfectly fulfilled only in the life to come.

Body-Soul Relationship

While the soul is independent of the body in its existence, it operates in and through the body. When God created the first man and woman, there was perfect harmony within the whole being of both of them. All of man's *lower nature* (appetites, inclinations and passions of the body) was perfectly subject to his *higher nature* (intellect and will), and man's higher nature was perfectly subject to the plan and will of God.

But as we know, that harmony was gravely marred. When our first parents rebelled against the plan and will of the Creator, the source of that harmony was lost, causing a rebellion within man. As a result of that revolt against God, our first parents lost sanctifying grace by which the soul was elevated and perfected to share in the very nature of God; their *intellect* (which was obscured) and their *will* (which was weakened) were no longer in control of the appetites, inclinations and passions of the body. Man's life on earth became a warfare (Job 7:1), the flesh rebelling against the spirit (Gal. 5:17), and his higher nature more inclined to seek his own will rather than God's (Rom. 7:19).

The whole of the Christian life is a struggle to restore the order and harmony that was lost by the fall of our first parents. But this will be realized only in the measure that there is restored the subjection of our bodily appetites and inclinations to our intellect and will, and the subjection of these latter to God. This, however, is possible only with frequent prayer for the help of God's grace, and true penance and discipline of our self-seeking tendencies.

The Soul — Temple of God

God created us in His own likeness, not only that He might share with us His own divine life through grace, but that the three Divine Persons might come to dwell in the depths of the soul. What a great mystery this is. The Creator of the entire universe delights to dwell in every soul in the state of grace. Yet, we can become so immersed in the externals of life that we are completely oblivious of the Divine Persons, hidden but truly present, in our inmost being. The Lord waits for us to be attentive to His presence: to breathe a prayer of adoration, to express a word of thanks, to seek pardon for some failing, to ask help to overcome some weakness. He awaits our attention to speak to us; but how often we are so impatient to give our attention to other matters, that His voice is drowned out by the clamor of superficial and passing demands. *"Do you not know that you are temples of God, and the Spirit of God dwells in you?"* (1 Cor. 3:16)

Chapter Notes

1. *Catechism of the Catholic Church*, 365
2. Gen. 2:7; *CCC* 362
3. *CCC* 363
4. *CCC* 353
5. *CCC* 357
6. *CCC* 356
7. St. Thomas Aquinas, *Summa Theologiae,* I, q. 77, a. 1
8. *Ibid.,* a. 6
9. Antonio Royo, O.P. and Jordan Aumann, O.P., *Theology of the Christian Life*
10. Pope Pius XII, *Humani Generis*, n. 36

Chapter 5

Our Free Will
A Wonderful Gift
A Frightening Responsibility

God created us to His own likeness and image, in order that He might share with us His own divine life and beatitude. In order to make us capable of sharing in His divine life, He fashioned us with an *intellect* capable of sharing His infinite truth, and a *will* capable of sharing in His infinite love by the surrender of our will to His.

He not only gave us a will capable of loving Him, but a will that is *free* to love Him or not love Him, that is free to choose God as our ultimate good, or something other than God. He not only wanted to share with us His own happiness, but He wanted us *to merit* that beatitude; and no act is meritorious that is not free. He would give us all the help necessary to merit that eternal reward, but we would have to freely prefer His will to our own whenever there is a conflict between the two.

Human freedom includes two things: on the part of the *mind,* there is a judgment that one thing is preferable to another; on the part of the *will,* there is a choice by which this judgment is accepted and acted upon. The will is such that, of its nature, it always tends to the good in much the same way as a falling stone always tends to fall downward. If that is so, how can we explain how we can so easily choose what is evil? The answer to that lies in the difference between *real* good and *apparent* good. The will seeks what is good or what appears to be good. The appetites and passions of the body can be so intense that the judgment of the intellect can be gravely obscured, so that the will chooses not the *true good* which the light of reason proposes, but the *apparent good* which the appetites of the body are seeking, and which could be against the law of God. In such cases, says St. Thomas Aquinas, *"the judgment of reason often follows the passions of the sensitive appetites, and consequently the will's movement follows it also, since it has a natural inclination to follow the judgment of reason."*[1]

The Will — The Key Faculty In Man

The human will is the key faculty in man. As the will is, so man is, good or evil. To the extent that the *intellect* is perfected, we have a better-informed person; but to the extent that the *will* is perfected, we have a better person. The will is the faculty ultimately responsible (under God) for our salvation or our damnation.

We are *saved* or *damned* according to what we love; and this is the work of the will. It is customary to speak of the heart as the seat of human affections, but in reality it is the will that chooses, rejects, loves, becomes attached, and so forth. If we love *God* to the end by our choices in keeping with His will, we shall ultimately possess God and eternal beatitude. If, at the end of our life, we love *self* in preference to God, choosing our will in preference to His in something gravely commanded or prohibited, we shall ultimately experience total separation from God, which is the essence of damnation. That is to say, we shall get what we choose. *"God made man from the beginning and left him in the hand of his own counsel. . . . Before man is life and death, good and evil, that which he shall choose shall be given him"* (Sir. 15:14, 18).

It should be clear, then, that the will is in the driver's seat, is the master of all the other faculties and members of the human body. Yet the will's reign is not an easy one; the subjects it controls—our sense faculties—are always ready for rebellion. As Fr. Walter Farrell, O.P. points out, the sense appetites are neither a *"den of iniquity,"* even though they occasion many a downfall, nor are they a *"holy of holies,"* even though they may be the instrument of much mortification.[2] By means of them one can rise to great heights, or can sink to great depths, but only because of the decisions of the will, which alone receives the blame or the praise. Our will had no part in our creation, in our becoming man; but as to what sort of man we become, it will be decisive.

The Need of God's Grace

Speaking of the freedom of will, the Second Vatican Council declared that man will achieve his human dignity when, emancipating himself from the captivity of passion, he freely chooses a goal that is good (that is, in keeping with God's will), and procures apt means to that end. It then continues:

> Since man's *freedom* has been damaged by sin, only by the help of God's grace can he bring such a relationship with God into full flower. Before the judgment seat of God man must render an account of his own life, whether he has done good or evil.[3]

This statement of the Council regarding man's freedom could be stated in another way: Since man's will has been damaged by sin, only by the help of God's grace can he bring about the due subjection of his will to God's; only by the help of God's grace can his will become the master of his lower nature.

It is clear from the above that man must strive to make his lower nature submissive to his will, and his will submissive to God; but that battle will never be won by his natural powers alone. In spite of the emphasis placed on the need for mortification, the detachment of the heart (the will) from created goods is primarily a work of divine grace. It is effected primarily by God rather than by man. As St. Thomas Aquinas states, *"Man's will can only be subject to God when God draws man's will to Himself."*[4] Yet God demands a definite cooperation on our part before He liberates the heart from the strong hold that worldly goods and pleasures exercise over it.

With each increase of grace and charity one is able to love God with a greater intensity, that is, with a greater willingness to sacrifice one's own will in order to fulfill the will of God. With each increase of grace, God more and more attracts the heart of man to Himself. *"No man can come to Me, except the Father who sent Me draw him"* (Jn. 12:32).

Two Notions of Freedom

Pope John Paul II pointed out in his *Apostolic Constitution on the Family* that there is in the world a struggle between two freedoms that are in mutual conflict, because it is based on a conflict between two loves which are in mutual conflict, as expressed by St. Augustine: *love of God* to the point of disregarding self, and *love of self* to the point of disregarding God.

1) Love of God, to the point of disregarding self: This brings about the freedom of which Our Lord spoke, *"If you live according to My teaching, you are truly My disciples. Then you will know the truth, and the truth will make you free"* (Jn. 8:31). *"He who loses his life for My sake will find it"* (Mt. 10:39).

The above expression of St. Augustine does not mean a disregarding of the basic necessities of life, but rather the self-denial needed to bring one's lower nature under the control of the will. Only when one is liberated from the unruly demands of our fallen nature with its inclination to evil is one truly free. This liberation is within the heart of man. It is a freedom from being dominated by the world, the flesh and the ego; a freedom from the domination of anything that would cause the will to choose other than what God wills. It is a freedom that ennobles, that builds up, that brings man to his true fulfillment as intended by the Creator.

2) Love of self, to the point of disregarding God: This kind of freedom could better be called *license,* for it is a seeking of one's own will in opposition to God's. Such persons think they are free, as they understand freedom, but in reality they become *slaves* of this or that passion, material possession, or worldly satisfaction which dominates the heart and holds them captive.

There are many references in the Scriptures to this false freedom:

> In truth I say to you, everyone who lives in sin is a slave to sin (Jn. 8:34). They promise others freedom, whereas they themselves are slaves of corruption; for surely anyone is a slave to that by which he has been overcome (2 Pet. 2:19). No man can serve two masters; for either he will hate one and love the other, or else he will stand by one and despise the other. You cannot serve both God and mammon (Mt. 6:24).

The more the love of self becomes one's master, the more he rejects God's will and the limitations it imposes. Unlike true freedom which *ennobles,* this is a freedom that *destroys* both the individual and society, for it disregards the will of the Creator and the order He imposed.

A Union of Wills

The goal of the Christian life is to grow in union with God through growth in divine grace. But here again, the will is the key faculty as regards that growth. In our life here on earth, that union is essentially a union of our will with God's, aided by the infused virtues and the gifts of the Holy Spirit. And there can be a union between an inferior being and an infinitely superior being, only by the surrender or submission of the lower to the higher. There can be a great latitude in the extent or fullness of that surrender, but the completeness of it indicates the growth in holiness. With each addition to the completeness of the surrender of man's will to God, added grace flows from the divine Font of Life to that human soul.

All forms of submission to God's will are ways of opening the soul to the Holy Spirit, who is the source of holiness in the Church. And the more one obeys God's will, the freer that surrender becomes, a freedom perfected by the Holy Spirit. As Fr. Pierre-Andre Liege, O.P. states, speaking of this action of the Holy Spirit: *"The Spirit issues no edicts, rather, He appeals to the heart; He opens men's eyes, He gives the power to fulfill His commands. His compulsion is all from within."*[5] This is a freedom whose perfection is attained, not by removing the external obstacles of the law, but by the Father drawing the heart of man to Himself through the action of the Holy Spirit. Yet the Holy Spirit respects our liberty, and will not make Himself the Master of our will unless we are disposed to surrender it to Him freely.

Although both men and angels were created with a *free will,* they are nevertheless subject to the providence of God. That freedom can be the source of great potentialities and the source of great responsibilities. Man knows that he *can* do wrong; but he also knows that he *ought* to do what is right. He knows that he can choose not to obey, to reject the Sovereign Good and choose instead created joys and satisfactions as his supreme good and last end; but he cannot choose the consequences of his choice. He can abuse his freedom; he can rebel — and every sin is a rebellion — but he cannot frustrate the plan of God's providence as to the punishment to be meted out to those who refuse to submit to God's all-wise and merciful laws.

Human freedom is real, but it is limited. It is not the right to choose between good and evil. Man has the *capacity* to choose evil, but not the *right.* Rather he has the right to choose apt means to attain an end in keeping with God's laws. It is not a freedom *from* those laws; it is a freedom *within* them. Although it may sound like a contradiction, freedom is always bound up with obedience to the law of God. Every law that is habitually obeyed increases our freedom, for it further strengthens the mastery of the will over the other powers of the soul.

For this reason, one rather reliable guide as to the kind of freedom one is seeking is one's attitude toward obedience: for the worldly person looks on obedience as standing in the way of being free, while the true Christian sees it as an indispensable condition of becoming free.

True Freedom Requires Discipline

Our will retains strong attachments to creatures, especially to the ego, to which we stubbornly cling.

OUR FREE WILL

Hence, to cooperate with the action of the Holy Spirit, it is important to strive to discipline all forms of selfishness. So many of our good resolutions do not last because they are not true resolutions at all, but mere wishes; and when they are confronted with something we really want, they come tumbling down.

In stressing the role of the Holy Spirit and grace in liberating the will from undue worldly attachments, it would be sheer presumption to imagine that God will come with His liberating grace, if we do not do what we can. That inner freedom must be fought for with perseverance, and can be won only at a considerable price. We will never in this life attain the perfect freedom that our first parents had before the fall, but the whole of our spiritual life will be a striving for that goal.

The will can be trained in the same way as the memory or the intelligence, by the actual exercise of self-discipline. One important means of training the will is to strengthen the motive, that is, to strive to retain a vivid idea of the goal to be attained. So often, the vivid sense images presented by the imagination tend to overshadow and cloud out the good which the light of reason enlightened by faith presents to the will, causing the will to choose the former.

Consistent practicing of discipline and self-control will result in the acquisition of good moral habits. One can, for example, conquer a bad temper by recalling that the frustrations, irritations and humiliations that make one angry are but aspects of the cross we are asked to carry, and are opportunities to surrender our will to the all-wise providence of God. Or one can conquer a lazy disposition by making punctuality a point of persistent voluntary control. It is such efforts as these, along with prayer, that open the soul to the strengthening and liberating action of the Holy Spirit.

We speak of strong and weak characters. A person who consistently adheres to his decision to conquer some weakness shows a strong character; and one who easily gives in to impulses and changes his decision when the going becomes difficult shows a weak character. Since, however, the key to those decisions is *the will,* it is obvious that strength of character depends on strength of the will aided by divine grace.

The expression *"strength of will,"* however, needs some clarification, for the will is a spiritual faculty and the act of the will is not subject to measurement. Too, one might be said to have a "strong will" who is stubborn and intractable in clinging to his own satisfactions. *Strength of will* in the Christian sense means *a strength in sacrificing one's own will in order that God's will be done.*

Commenting on an article of St. Thomas who is explaining St. Paul's reference to *"slaves of sin"* and *"slaves of God,"*[6] Fr. Garrigou-Lagrange, O.P. sums up well what we have tried to say:

> During our lifetime we always run the unhappy risk of throwing off our Lord's yoke, no matter how light it may be, and resisting His grace. This misfortune is the more to be feared when our will pretends to be its own master instead of abandoning itself to divine Providence; for the perfection of the will consists in placing itself in God's hands, in making use of its own proper activity only to become more dependent on Him, in being always docile to grace. Let us offer our liberty to Jesus through Mary and try never to take it back again; in this holy slavery we find deliverance and a most sure road to heaven.[7]

Chapter Notes

1. St. Thomas Aquinas, *Summa Theologiae,* I-II, q. 77, a. 1
2. Walter Farrell, O.P., *Companion to the Summa,* I, p. 317
3. Vatican Council II, *The Church Today,* n. 7
4. St. Thomas Aquinas, *Summa Theologiae,* I-II, q. 109, a. 7
5. Pierre-Andre Liege, O.P., *Consider Christian Maturity,* p. 87
6. St. Thomas Aquinas, *Summa Theologiae,* II-II, 183, 4 and Rom. 6:20-22
7. Garrigou-Lagrange, O.P., *The Love of God and Cross of Jesus,* II, p. 346

Chapter 6

This Body of Ours

We know from the basics of our Catholic faith that man is a creature composed of body and soul, and made to the image and likeness of God. During life on this earth, body and soul are so interdependent that one of them cannot function without the other. Without the soul, the body is a corpse. Without the body, the soul cannot function, for all that the soul knows on the natural level comes through the senses of the body. The body is not merely an instrument of the soul, for both were made for each other and each is incomplete without the other. Together they make a single living person.

The soul can and does operate without the body after the death of the body, and it will continue to do so until the general resurrection at the end of the world, when the body will be brought back by the power of God and reunited with the soul. However, it is the body, the living body animated by the soul, on which we will be mainly focusing our attention, examining how its actions and reactions have an impact on the activity of the soul and its spiritual growth.

The soul and its condition is more important than that of the body, since our eternal welfare will depend on the state of the soul at the moment of death; yet, the person that I am must act and operate in and through this body that is mine. This body can be an *instrument* of spiritual growth, or an *impediment* to spiritual growth, depending on whether or not it is under the control of reason enlightened by faith.

We are made to God's image by reason of the soul, a spiritual being having the powers of reason and free will, giving us the capacity of loving in a way far superior to brute animals. The soul has the capacity of being elevated by grace to a supernatural level, receiving an infused knowledge and love that is a sharing in the very life of God. However, as we will see, the growth of that supernatural life of grace, or the lack of it, will depend on the extent to which the body is the servant of the soul, and not its master.

Consequently, we will not be considering the body as the scientist would, examining its wonderful composition, nor as the physician, concerned about its health, but as the theologian, seeing the body in its relation to the Christian life.

Dependence of the Soul on the Body

Philosophers tell us that the soul, when it comes from God, is like a clean slate, with no impressions whatever, no knowledge of any kind. Little by little, however, it begins to receive impressions through the five senses of the body. In the beginning its knowledge is purely on the sense level. After some maturing of the body, from these sense impressions the soul can abstract ideas. Gradually, the growing person begins to know in a way proper to man. Since the soul is so dependent on the body in its attainment of knowledge, it will be helpful to understand how the body and its reactions can have a decided influence on the choice of the will, and therefore, on Christian behavior.

It is a fact of experience that the more the bodily appetites and desires are indulged and gratified, the less the soul is disposed for spiritual endeavor. Body and soul are meant to work in harmony, but that harmony will be the fruit only of a well-disciplined life. Before the fall of our first parents that harmony existed. Man enjoyed a perfect balance of his powers and faculties, the body being a perfect partner and docile instrument of the soul. But after the fall, the balance of man's nature was upset. Whereas before the fall, the appetites and inclinations of the body were perfectly subject to the dictates of reason and the command of the will, after the fall, man's lower nature rebelled against the limitations set by reason, and demanded and often attained satisfactions contrary to the law of God. In that historic fall, in addition to the loss of grace, our human nature lost a precious gift resulting in the conflict we all experience within us in our efforts to live the Christian life. Of this conflict St. Paul testifies: *"The flesh lusts against the spirit, and the spirit against the flesh; for these are opposed to each other, so that you do not do what you would"* (Gal. 5:7).

In this present life, the body must be properly cared for and properly nourished in order that it be an aid to the soul in its activity. However, it also must be restrained when it becomes a hindrance to that activity. Not infrequently, proper care of the body will require denying the body what it seeks. As long as the soul is the master and the body is the servant (as God and nature intend), a man will lead a peaceful and fruitful life. All too often today, however, the body is the master and the soul the servant, with the result that man is neither at peace within himself, nor with his neighbor, nor with his God. In other words, the body is meant to be an *instrument* of spiritual growth, and it will be for the true Christian; but it can be an *impediment* to that growth in the measure that a worldly spirit rules one's life.

Like Two Different Persons

We, at times, can act and think like two different persons. In our moments of right thinking we can clearly see that something should be done or not done. It might be a matter of overeating, or watching too much television or the wrong kind of programs, or keeping the wrong company, or abusing alcohol or drugs, and so forth. However, when one is exposed to the actual situation, the actual temptation, his thinking changes considerably. The satisfaction not only seems legitimate, but in a sense needful at the moment. And the greater the attraction to this particular satisfaction, the easier it is to justify it. St. Thomas Aquinas explains why this is so. *"Inordinate self-love is the source of all sin and darkens the intellect; for when the will and sensibility are ill-disposed (i.e., when they tend to pride and sensuality) everything that is in conformity with these inclinations appears as good."*[1]

This explains how the clear knowledge and conviction that we have at other times can be completely overshadowed by the sense impression or emotion that overwhelms us when the object or temptation is present and we are confronted with the decision to do or not to do, to indulge or not to indulge. This conflict between what a true conscience says, and what the body wants (that is, the blinding influence of our bodily emotions on our judgment) is one of the consequences of original sin. It has, as we have pointed out, robbed us of the balance between body and soul, that is, of the docile submission of our bodily appetites and their demands to our intellect and will, obscuring the light of reason as to true good, and weakening the will as to the choosing of it. St. Paul complained of this inner conflict: *"I am delighted with the law of God according to the inner man, but I see another law in my members, warring against the law of my mind and making me a prisoner to the law of sin that is in my members"* (Rom. 7:22). That is why so often the appetites of the body rule the day, instead of the light of reason enlightened by faith.

One might justify his conduct as follows: *"My soul, not my body, rules my life, because I follow my conscience; and my conscience allows me to indulge in this or that satisfaction."* Conscience is a true guide only when its dictates are in line with God's revealed word as handed down by the Church. In the measure that one's conscience puts up little objection when inordinate desires and appetites of the body are satisfied, in that measure conscience is distorted, and is leading one astray.

How the Passions Affect Our Judgment

Because man is composed of body and soul, he has two sets of appetites:

1) The Sense Appetites, the movements of which can cause emotional changes in the body (called passions) which are usually listed as the following: love or hatred, desire or aversion, joy or sorrow, hope or despair, fear or courage, and anger.

2) The Rational Appetite (the will), which seeks the good apprehended by the light of reason. But, as we have seen, because of original sin the appetites of the body are not docile servants of the soul, but often rebel against the limitations which reason enlightened by faith imposes as the norm of action. Thus, the conflict between the two sets of appetites. Yet, it is up to the will to control the whole man.

However, as we have seen, St. Thomas Aquinas points out that the movement of the passions (for example, anger, envy, hatred, lust) can be so intense that it can gravely obscure the light of reason, or even suppress it altogether.[2] In such cases, the will chooses not the *true good* which the light of reason proposes, but the *apparent good* which the bodily appetites are demanding, and which could be against the law of God.

The basic reason why this happens is the unity of the soul's powers. All the powers of the soul — those that are purely spiritual (intellect and will), and those that operate in and through the body (for example, sense appetites) — are all rooted in one and the same source. And all energy is weakened when it is divided. This is especially true of the powers of the soul. In the operations of the soul, a certain attention is requisite, so that if one's attention is closely fixed on one thing, less attention is given to another. In this way, when the movement of the body's appetites is intensified with regard to any passion whatever, the light of reason is obscured and the freedom of the will is lessened or altogether impeded.

This is because the appetites of the body clamor loudly for attention, since they are directed at visible, pleasurable and attractive things that appeal to the senses, and can be had at once. In support of this, the imagination, an internal sense rooted in the body, keeps before the mind images of the pleasurable things the body desires. In contrast with this, the objectives of the higher faculties of the soul — such as growth in virtue and salvation — although more important, are less obvious and more distant as regards attainment, and consequently are easily obscured. Because of this, those who experience strong emotional reactions, says St. Thomas, *"do not easily turn their imagination away from the object of their emotion, the result being that the judgment of reason often follows the passions of the sensitive appetite, and consequently the will's movement follows it also, since it has a natural inclination always to follow the judgment of reason."*[3]

Now, the obvious question that comes to mind is this: If reason can be gravely obscured, or even entirely suppressed under the influence of passion, is one morally responsible for actions performed under the influence of passion?

The Morality of the Passions

There are, deep in human nature, strong desires for satisfactions of the body, such as the satisfactions of food, of drink, of rest, of sexual activity, and so forth. These desires have been planted in human nature by the Creator, and are necessary for the welfare of the individual and of the human race. It would be wrong, therefore, to think of these innate desires or inclinations as evil, just because they often lead man to sin by seeking their satisfaction excessively, or when not lawful. The disorders or unbalance between body and soul are man's doing, not God's. Our first parents started it all, and we can enlarge on that disorder by repeated failures which increase the difficulty by forming habits in regard to those satisfactions.

The loss of the harmony or balance between body and soul, of which we have been speaking, is called *concupiscence*, or an *inclination to evil*. Concupiscence is not something sinful, as some of the founders of

Protestantism claimed. Rather, as the Council of Trent pointed out, it is a *tendency to sin*, which *"has no power to injure those who do not consent and who, by the grace of Jesus Christ, manfully resist."* The human nature of Christ had the same emotional reactions as we have, but not the concupiscence. He was angry when He drove the money changers from the temple. He was saddened unto tears at the death of Lazarus.

In themselves, the passions are neither morally good nor evil, because, in general, they are independent of reason and will, and are the movements of the sense appetites. Yet, as St. Augustine comments, they are *"evil if our love is evil; good if our love is good."*

That an act be morally good or evil, both of the main powers of the soul (the intellect's judgment of reason and the free exercise of the will) must be involved. That is, the action must be performed *knowingly* and *willingly*. Yet, as we have seen, passion tends to obscure the power of reason and can even eliminate it entirely, so that the responsibility and guilt can be diminished. So we ask again, does this mean that actions performed under the influence of passion always lessen the guilt or sinfulness of the action? To answer that, theologians make a distinction between passion which *comes before* the act of the will, and passion which *follows* it:

Antecedent passion: When the flare-up of passion occurs before the act of the will, moral guilt or responsibility is diminished. For example:

— One flares up suddenly in a rage of anger and loses self-control, and utters cutting and degrading things of another, something he would not have done otherwise.

— One strives to repel strong and persistent temptation regarding sins of the flesh, to which he eventually succumbs. In such cases as these, moral responsibility is lessened in the measure that reason is obscured. However, we do not want to convey the idea that one can simply let the passion of anger or lust, etc., take over so that his guilt will be lessened.

We have an obligation to flee temptation insofar as we can. Not to do so would be presumptuous, would invite disaster; and any passion that followed would be indirectly voluntary and therefore would not lessen one's responsibility.

Consequent passion: When the emotional reaction *follows* the act of the will, so that it is either directly or indirectly voluntary, the moral responsibility and guilt are not lessened. For example: One sets out to *"get"* a hated enemy, or one sets up a date with impure motives in mind. In such cases, regardless of how much passion might obscure reason, one's actions are at least indirectly voluntary, and responsibility and guilt are not lessened.

We have touched on just a few of the problems that all of us have to contend with in striving to live our Christian vocation. The Christian life, in a sense, is a striving to restore the order lost by our first parents, that is, to bring our body with its unruly tendencies to be a faithful servant of the soul, and to bring the soul to be a faithful and obedient servant of God. That, of course, implies a lifelong struggle against the selfish tendencies of our fallen nature, and the constant assistance of divine grace sought through persevering prayer and faithful reception of the sacraments. This counter-attack is dealt with in some detail in Chapter 10, *Freeing the Heart.*

Chapter Notes

1. Garrigou-Lagrange, *The Three Ways,* p. 41, note
2. St. Thomas Aquinas, *Summa Theologiae,* I-II, q. 77, a. 2; II-II, q. 55, a. 8, ad 1
3. *Ibid.*

Chapter 7

Why Are We Tempted?

Every time we pray the *"Our Father"* we ask, *"Lead us not into temptation."* That seems to be a prayer that is never answered, for all of us encounter temptation most of the days of our life. What is the meaning of that petition? What are we really asking? Why did Our Lord insist that it be included in our prayer to our heavenly Father? These questions we will briefly examine.

I am sure that every person reading these reflections can say with St. Paul: *"I cannot understand my own behavior ... for though the will to do good is in me, the performance is not, with the result that instead of doing the good things I want to do, I carry out the sinful things I do not want"* (Rom. 7:15-19). From these words it is clear that temptations assail saints as well as sinners, and they will do so until the hour of one's death. Too, we read in the book of Sirach: *"Son, when you come to the service of God, stand in justice and in fear, and prepare your soul for temptation"* (Sir. 2:1).

Apparent Contradictions

Temptation would seem to be something *harmful* if Jesus asks that we pray not to be led into it; yet, on the other hand, it would seem to be something *profitable,* if we consider the words of St. James: *"Blessed is the man who endures temptation; for when he has been tried, he will receive the crown of life which God has promised to those who love him"* (Jas. 1:12).

Another apparent contradiction is found in Scripture as regards the cause of temptation, for St. James says: *"Let no man say when he is tempted, that he is tempted by God; for God is no tempter to evil, he himself tempts no one"* (Jas. 1:13). Yet in the book of Genesis we read that *"God tempted Abraham"* by asking him to sacrifice his son, Isaac (Gen. 22:1-12).

The opposition expressed in the above two paragraphs is only apparent, not real, for theologians distinguish two kinds of temptation – those of *solicitation* (an inducement to sin), and those of *probation* (a testing of virtue). God is never the author of the first kind, but He is frequently the source of the second.

Temptations of Probation

The word *temptation* comes from the Latin word *tentare* (to test, to try, to prove). We certainly don't expect to be free from temptation of this sort, for God is continually using persons and situations to test our patience, our purity, our humility, our faith, our trust in Him, our love of Him. Without this kind of temptation there would be little growth in virtue, which is the one thing that God wants. Most of the basic virtues are not exercised in any notable way until they are put to the test.

Even temptations by the Evil One — who knows our weaknesses so well and how to exploit them, and who wishes only our eternal damnation — God allows at times to test our virtue and bring about spiritual growth by our resisting of these allurements to sin.

In the service of God souls are tested and tried, in order that the quality of their love of God and their devotion to Him may become known, and that they may be given opportunities of winning for themselves and others additional treasures of grace. Thus temptations reveal whether our love of God is real and sincere or shallow and weak. They are the acid test of the spiritual life. They are not needed that God might be enlightened, but we ourselves, who can so easily be deceived as to our spiritual growth.

In a sense, any form of the cross, such as sickness, loss of fortune, poverty, enmities, false accusations, persecutions, and so forth, can be called temptations willed by

God, temptations of probation. It was in this sense that Tobias said, *"Because you were acceptable to God, it was necessary that temptation should prove you"* (Tob. 13:3).

It should be clear, then, that the real evil is not temptation, but sin. So, in the Lord's Prayer, we are not so much asking to be delivered from temptations as to be strengthened in them, to be delivered from the evil of falling into sin, the evil of failing to cooperate with the graces that accompany every temptation. St. Paul referred to this when he wrote: *"God is faithful and will not permit you to be tempted beyond your strength, but with the temptation will also give you a way out that you may be able to bear it"* (1 Cor. 10:13). He infallibly grants all the graces necessary for victory, provided that one asks for them with humble and fervent prayer, and does all in his power to refuse consent to the wrong suggested.

We should not, however, be overconfident and flirt with temptation, so to speak. If we do, we will often be outwitted by the devil, who is so much more intelligent and clever than we, and fall a prey to his snare.

Temptations of Solicitation

Temptations of solicitation, which, as we saw, are an incitement to sin, can never be attributed to God. They are permitted by Him for the testing of our virtue, and for the promotion of our greater glory in heaven. The sources from which such temptations spring might be listed as: 1) the devil, 2) the wounds of our nature caused by original sin, and 3) the world about us. We will consider them briefly.

The Devil

St. Paul wrote to the Ephesians: *"Our wrestling is not against flesh and blood, but against principalities and powers, against the rulers of the world of this darkness, against the spirits of wickedness in high places"* (Eph. 6:12). And St. Peter compares the devil to *"a roaring lion, who goes about seeking someone to devour"* (1 Pet. 5:8).

Yet, because of the godless materialism of our present age, many scoff at belief in the devil as a myth. This very disbelief gives Satan an immense advantage in his warfare on souls, making those who disbelieve an easy prey to his attacks. Some unbelievers are so deceived that they actually further his cause among men.

Satan, as we know, is a fallen angel. Before his fall he held one of the highest ranks in the angelic creation. As an angel he was endowed with powers and gifts of intellect that far exceed those of men. Those gifts were not lost in his fall because they were proper to his angelic nature. He lost only the supernatural gifts of grace, and the right to glory in heaven, as was lost by our first parents after their fall. This applies to the countless numbers of angels who fell with him, all of whom have an intense hatred for God who deprived them of the glory of heaven and condemned them to hell. In addition they have an intense malice and envy toward us, who are destined to enjoy the glory that they lost. For this reason they will do all in their power to bring about our downfall.

By reason of his angelic powers, the devil can work on our senses, especially on the imagination. He cannot *directly* cause the will to consent to sin; but *indirectly* he can put much pressure on the will, by causing images in the imagination that can be the source of severe enticement to sin. For this reason, one should realize that just because one is plagued at times with hateful or impure temptations, it does not necessarily follow that these proceed from within one's inner self, that they are an indication that one's heart is filled with hatred or lust.

On the contrary, the fact that one is severely tempted could be precisely because he is striving to lead a virtuous life. As we read in the book of Revelation, after the dragon (the devil) was foiled in his attempt to destroy the offspring of the woman, he *"was enraged with the woman and went away to make war on the rest of her children, that is, all who obey God's commandments and bear witness for Jesus"* (Rev. 12:7).

WHY ARE WE TEMPTED?

Because of the devil's superhuman powers, however, God limits the extent to which he can tempt humans. As St. John Chrysostom wrote, *"The devil does not tempt man as long as he would like, but as long as God allows; for although he allows him to tempt for a short time, he orders him off on account of our weakness."*[1]

Too, as St. Paul warns, the devil *"disguises himself as an angel of light"* in order to deceive us (2 Cor. 11:14). This deception and the importance of not flirting with temptation are brought out forcefully in the words of the Mother of God, who appeared to a religious of the Sacred Heart in France in 1921.

> "My daughter," she said, "I will give you a lesson of very great importance: the devil is like a mad dog, but he is chained, that is to say, his liberty is curtailed. He can, therefore, only seize and devour his prey if they venture too near him, and that is why his usual tactics are to make himself appear as a lamb. The soul does not realize this, and draws nearer and nearer, only to discover his malice when in his clutches. When he seems far away, do not relax your vigilance, child; his footsteps are padded and silent, that he may take you unawares."[2]

Other Sources of Temptation

St. Thomas Aquinas asks whether all sins are due to the temptation of the devil, and answers that while he is not the *direct* cause of all temptation, he is the *indirect* cause of all temptations, insofar as *"it was he who instigated the first man to sin (original sin), from whose sin resulted the proneness to sin in the whole human race."*[3]

From that original sin there resulted four wounds in human nature, two of which affect the spiritual faculties of the soul, and two the sense faculties of the body. Following is a brief description of those wounds as explained by St. Thomas.[4]

The Wounds of Fallen Human Nature

1) The *intellect* was obscured, so that the acquisition of truth has become more difficult. Whereas before the

fall *prudence* reigned, there was inherited the wound of *ignorance*. Because of this we are given to much wishful thinking. Our judgments are slanted, colored by our desires, so that we easily justify doing, or not doing, what we want. St. Thomas refers to this when he points out that we easily *believe* to be true what we *wish* to be true.[5]

2) The *will* was weakened as to the choosing of good, resulting in a proneness to evil. Whereas before the fall *justice* reigned, there was inherited the wound of *malice*. Because of this we often do not have the strength to do what our reason tells us is right, as St. Paul testified (Rom. 7:19). Too, because of this wound, the will is inclined to such disorders as pride, ambition, envy, and so forth.

3) The *sense faculty (irascible)* that responds to emergencies to resist an impending danger, or to overcome difficulties in the struggle for good, was weakened. Whereas before the fall *fortitude* reigned, there was inherited the wound of *weakness*. Because of this wound we often do not persevere in doing good or avoiding evil because of the sacrifice required, or for fear of opposition, danger, or suffering.

4) The *sense appetites* that crave what is pleasant and shun what is unpleasant were so affected that only with much difficulty are they subordinated to the dictates of reason. Whereas before the fall *temperance* reigned, there was inherited the wound of *concupiscence*. Because of this wound, man is inclined to an inordinate love of sensual pleasure (gluttony and lust), that is, pleasure sought for its own sake, apart from its divinely intended purpose.

In addition to the *"concupiscence of the flesh,"* referred to just above, St. John mentions the *"concupiscence of the eyes"* (1 Jn. 2:16), which is the vice of greed or avarice, a disordered love for material wealth and possessions irrespective of the means employed to acquire them, or merely to satisfy one's ambition or pride.

Because of the manifold wounds of our fallen nature, it should be obvious that many temptations have their source from within our own weakened self. As St. James testifies: *"Everyone is tempted by being drawn away and enticed by his own passions"* (Jas. 1:14).

The World

In addition to those temptations that come from the devil and from our own weakened nature, there are those that come from the world around us, that is, from the spirit of the world (worldliness) that permeates the culture in which we live. It comes from those who leave God out of their lives; those who ignore God's unchanging standards of right and wrong, and replace them with standards that are more agreeable to our ease-seeking and pleasure-loving human nature. From this we can see that because of the enmity that must of necessity exist between the *spirit of the world* and the *spirit of Christ* (Jas. 4:4), for the sincere Christian, the world about him will be a frequent source of temptation.

We must never forget the basic truth that what we seek we tend to become. The more we seek Christ, the more through grace we become like Him. The more we seek the world, the more we become imbued with its spirit.

The Overall Picture

Considering the many kinds of temptation that surround us and our inherent weakness in confronting them, and the power and cleverness of the devil in exploiting our weaknesses, this would present a very discouraging picture if we were not assured by God's revelation that sufficient grace to conquer will invariably accompany every temptation.

All this is part of God's providence, that we may be convinced of two basic truths: our own need and helplessness without grace, and the sufficiency of that grace, if through our efforts and prayers we do what we can, relying on God's grace for the light to see our way, and the strength to make the sacrifices needed to keep His commandments.

In a sense, the whole spiritual life is a struggle to restore the order lost through original sin, to restore — with the help of divine grace — the reign of the moral virtues of prudence, justice, fortitude and temperance, the purpose of which is to remove the obstacles to union with God through the three theological virtues of faith, hope and charity.[6]

Due to the many enticements of the world and our unruly inclinations, a battle must be fought within the heart of each individual seeking to follow Christ. *"The life of man on earth is a warfare"* (Job 7:1).

Doing What We Can

There is an axiom of theology that goes like this: *To him who does what he can, God will not deny grace.* Doing what we can would include such things as:

1) Trusting and persevering prayer, especially in times of temptation. Spiritual writers encourage prayer to the Mother of God, the Mediatrix of all grace who crushed the serpent's head with her virginal heel; and to one's guardian angel, who has as one of his principal duties to defend us from the assaults of the devil.

2) The avoiding of unnecessary occasions of sin, that is, persons, places, or things that easily lead to sin. It would be sheer presumption to expect the help of grace if one deliberately and unnecessarily exposed himself to a dangerous occasion of sin.

3) Frequent and fervent reception of the sacraments. Neglect of these, for those who can receive them, would be equivalent to concluding that one has little need of grace.

4) An occasional mortification or self-denial in satisfactions that are lawful, to strengthen us to resist those that are unlawful.

One who understands the wounds of human nature and the wiles of Satan will not be unduly anxious about all this, because of his confidence in the efficacy of grace; nor will he fret anxiously because of occasional falls through human frailty, because of his trust in God's mercy. As Fr. Gabriel of St. Mary Magdalene points out:

> The distinguishing mark of fervent souls, even of saints, is less their lack of faults, than their promptness in rising after each fall. The annoyance felt by so many when they see themselves continually falling is not so much the fruit of humility, but of pride.[7]

Perhaps now we can appreciate better the words of St. James: *"Blessed is the man who endures temptation; for when he has been tried, he will receive the crown of life which God has promised to those who love Him"* (Jas. 1:12).

Chapter Notes

1. St. John Chrysostom, *Commentary on St. Matthew*
2. *The Way of Divine Love,* p. 99
3. St. Thomas Aquinas, *Summa Theologiae,* I, q. 114, a. 3
4. *Ibid.,* I-II, q. 85, a. 3
5. *Ibid.,* II-II, q. 162, a. 3, ad 2
6. The moral and theological virtues will be treated in detail in Vol. II, *To Know Him, The Way, The Truth and The Life*
7. Fr. Gabriel of St. Mary Magdalene, *Divine Intimacy,* n. 295, I

PART TWO
The Christian Life

Chapter 8

The Call to Holiness

In the Sermon on the Mount Our Lord told His listeners, *"You are to be perfect as your heavenly Father is perfect"* (Mt. 5:48). He was not speaking to the small group of His apostles and disciples, but to the multitude who followed Him. The call to sanctity, then, is not reserved for a select few.

In more recent times Pope Pius XI was speaking to the modern world in his encyclical on St. Francis de Sales when he said:

> We cannot accept the belief that this command of Christ (to be holy) concerns only a select and privileged group of souls, and that all others may consider themselves pleasing to Him if they have attained a lower degree of holiness. Quite the contrary is true. . . . The law of holiness embraces all men and admits of no exceptions.

The Attainment of Holiness — A Command

From the above it is clear that the call to sanctity (holiness) is not just an invitation. It is a command, as Our Lord clearly stated: *"You shall love the Lord your God with your whole heart, your whole soul, your whole mind, and with all your strength. . . . This is the first and greatest commandment"* (Mk. 12:30). So it is not just a counsel. Each of us will have a debt to pay when we leave this world in the measure that we fall short of that perfect love, for no one can enter heaven until purified of all forms of self-love that stand in the way of loving God with one's whole being.

It is much to our spiritual loss when one has to undergo that purification in purgatory where one gains no merit for all that it costs him, instead of striving to bring about that purification here and now where one gains merit and grows spiritually in the process. Our divine Savior who calls us to sanctity, has merited for each of us all the graces needed to attain it; but one who has reached the age of reason must be submissive to God's will to receive them.

Sanctity, the Normal Development of Grace

Each of us, at baptism, received the seeds of sanctity. A seed, as we know from experience, when planted in the ground in proper conditions, grows and eventually produces fruit. This general idea is true both in the order of nature and the order of grace. The seeds of sanctity are, firstly, *sanctifying grace* through which we share in the very life and nature of God. Out of this grace there flow the *seven infused virtues* (infused powers), namely, the *three theological virtues* (faith, hope and charity), and the *four moral virtues* (prudence, justice, fortitude and temperance). The *theological virtues* unite us with God (have God as their object), while the *moral virtues* remove the obstacles to that union.

In addition to the seven infused virtues, there come with sanctifying grace the *seven gifts of the Holy Spirit*. Each of the seven infused virtues is perfected by one of the seven gifts of the Holy Spirit. The gifts become more active as one makes progress in the spiritual life. When this happens, the Holy Spirit becomes more active in directing the life of the individual soul.[1]

The Garden of the Soul

The above-mentioned sanctifying grace, virtues and gifts constitute a supernatural organism, the seeds of which, as we said, are received at baptism, and which are capable, with the help of actual graces and our cooperation, of attaining sanctity. If planted in the proper surroundings and conditions, these supernatural seeds will grow and produce fruit, namely, the fruit of good works that merit an increase of grace. If they do not grow and bear fruit, it will not be the fault of the seed, but because of the lack of our cooperation or the lack of proper surroundings.

It is well known that if seeds are planted in the garden, they require water, sunshine, fertilizer and weeding. So also, those supernatural seeds (grace, virtues and gifts) which remain dormant until the use of reason, will gradually grow and produce the fruit of good works, if they are *watered* with fervent prayer, if they are *fertilized* by the fruitful reception of the sacraments, and if the garden of our soul is *weeded* by mortification and self-denial, and *warmed* by the sunshine of works of mercy and the fulfillment of our God-given duties. Because of our weaknesses and selfish inclinations due to original sin and the temptations of the devil, there must be constant vigilance on our part to cultivate the garden of the soul.

What we are saying, then, is that holiness (sanctity) is simply the normal development of the divine life infused into the soul at baptism. The garden of the soul with the help of grace is capable of producing the most beautiful flowers that do not fade or wither, but keep growing more beautiful, flowers we can offer to God through His Blessed Mother. But this beautiful garden doesn't just happen; it requires diligent cultivation, a lifelong process.

Christian Perfection (Holiness) is Perfect Charity

Theology teaches us that the perfection of the Christian life consists essentially in the perfection of charity, that is, in perfect love of God and neighbor. Of the three theological virtues that unite us to God, *"the greatest of these is charity"* (1 Cor. 13:13). It is the greatest for several reasons:

1) There can be no supernatural life without it. Every mortal sin (a refusal to return God's love) destroys it.

2) Charity will last forever. In heaven, faith gives way to vision, hope gives way to possession, but charity remains and comes to full bloom; and the extent of that

love as one leaves this world determines the degree of sharing Christ's glory for all eternity.

3) It is the sole source of merit, that is, of good works that merit an increase of grace, and it must animate all other virtues to make their acts meritorious.

This, then, is the perfection to which we are called, the holiness to which we have been commanded — to love God *"with our whole heart, our whole soul, our whole mind, our whole strength, and our neighbor as ourself"* (Mk. 12:30).

Holiness and God's Will

Since God is infinite Love, infinite Truth, infinite Goodness, the more closely we are united with Him the more we share in the love and truth and goodness that He is. And, as we saw, the key virtue in uniting us with God is charity (infused love of God), which essentially involves a union of our will with God's, a surrender of our will to His. It is the will that loves, that surrenders, that says, *"Your will, Father, not mine be done"* (Lk. 22:42).

Yet, because of our many selfish inclinations, deep attachments and blind spots due to original sin, we find that surrender, that *"Yes, Father,"* will at times be difficult and painful. The *self-seeking* of our fallen nature is directly opposed to the *self-giving* of charity, a conflict which is at the very heart of the struggle of the Christian life. For this reason, progress in charity presupposes that we are actively cultivating the garden of the soul by the exercise of important moral virtues (such as obedience, patience, humility, chastity), which keep in check the obstacles to grace. While moral theology lists the moral virtues under the general categories of *prudence, justice, fortitude* and *temperance,* all other virtues that regulate our moral life come under the umbrella of those four general virtues.

There is an axiom in theology according to which God gives grace in the measure that we do not place obstacles in the way. Yet, even in the removing or restraining of those obstacles, God plays a greater part than we, but we must do what we can through the exercise of the moral virtues and prayer. It is like lifting the shade to allow the sunlight to come in. We don't cause the light, we merely remove the obstacle that prevents the light from entering.

We treat of this in more detail in Chapter 10, dealing with freeing the heart from attachments. In spite of what is said about the need of mortification, the detachment of the heart of man from created goods is primarily the work of divine grace. It is effected primarily by God rather than by man. As St. Thomas states, *"Man's will can be subject to God only when God draws man's will to Himself."*[2] Yet God demands a definite cooperation on our part in the way of mortification and sacrifice before He accomplishes this work of liberating the heart from the strong hold that worldly goods and pleasures exercise over it.

Too, we must remember that the supernatural virtue of charity is *God's love*, not ours. It is a gift He shares with us, perfecting and healing the weaknesses of the will, so that when we love someone, moved by supernatural charity, it is really God loving in us, God living His divine life in and through us. *"I live now, not I, but it is Christ living in me"* (Gal. 2:20). We must cooperate in those good acts, but as we will see in dealing with actual grace,[3] we are only the *secondary cause* of the good acts we perform. God, through the medium of actual grace, is their *primary cause.*

Holiness Does Not Require Extraordinary Achievements

Since holiness is something that God accomplishes in us by His grace, and something He does in the measure that we surrender our will to His, how can we always be sure of what His will is for us? There are various ways we can know this:

a) It is His will that we fulfill His commandments, for their fulfillment is a requisite of loving Him. *"If you love me, keep my commandments"* (Jn. 14:15).

b) It is His will that we accept and put into practice His word revealed in the Scriptures and handed down by the Church; that is, whatever the Church teaches in doctrine and morals.

c) It is His will that we accept the little crosses that come our way each day, for example, little frustrations, irritations, disappointments, slights and inconveniences. God uses these little trials: 1) to test our patience, our unselfishness, and our trust; 2) for our purification, for they have a healing effect if seen and accepted as allowed by God for our good. *"The Almighty's chastening do not reject. For He wounds, but He binds up; He smites, but His hand gives healing"* (Job 5:18); 3) to give the opportunity of meriting an increase of grace.

We are not implying that we should not defend ourselves or others against some unjust action, or remind another of something that is out of line, or take obvious natural means to remedy some problem or ailment. We refer to the ups and downs of each day that God foresees, allows, and can bring good out of, if we see and accept the will of God in ruling our life, if we see and accept the divine Physician applying the remedy fitted precisely to our need.

d) It is God's will that we fulfill the duties of our state in life, and do so with great fidelity. It is interesting to note that Pope Benedict XV decreed the following, in giving guidelines to the Sacred Congregation of Rites as to the norm of holiness required that one be eligible for beatification: *"Sanctity properly consists in the conformity to God's will, expressed in a constant and exact fulfillment of the duties of our state in life."*

Sanctity, therefore, does not consist in doing extraordinary things, but is essentially reduced to the fulfillment of our duties to God and neighbor by reason of our state in life. Consequently, it is something possible for all of us. For this reason each person should strive to see the expression of God's will in the daily duties toward God and neighbor that fall to him by reason of his calling in life.

Before a person can be beatified, it must be proven that the person whose sanctity is being considered practiced the Christian virtues to a heroic degree. This indicates that the Church considers the faithful fulfillment, day in and day out, of one's duties by reason of his state in life as *heroic*, as Pope Pius XI pointed out: *"It takes uncommon virtue to fulfill with exactitude, that is, without carelessness, negligence or indolence, but with attention, piety and spiritual fervor, the whole combination of ordinary duties which make up our daily life."*

In keeping with our statement that great achievements are not necessary for holiness, St. Teresa of Avila comments:

> The highest perfection consists not in interior favors, or in great raptures or in visions, or in the spirit of prophecy, but in bringing our wills so closely in conformity with the will of God that, as soon as we realize He wills something, we desire it for ourselves with all our might, and take the bitter with the sweet.[4]

This untiring fidelity will not always be easy. However, we should not be discouraged by our failures, but begin again each day, fully confident that our efforts will bear fruit, even though much of that fruit is not seen, and will contribute to the building up of the body of Christ.

But as we said in the beginning, this presupposes that we are faithful in cultivating the garden of the soul: that we *water* it with frequent prayer; that we *fertilize* it with fervent reception of the sacraments; that we *weed* it by mortification and self-denial; that we expose it to the *warm sunshine* of works of mercy and the faithful fulfillment of our daily duties.

Chapter Notes

1. A detailed explanation of sanctifying and actual grace, along with the infused virtues and gifts will be found in *To Know Him, The Way, The Truth and The Life,* Vol. II, ch. 20-34.
2. St. Thomas Aquinas, *Summa Theologiae,* I-II, q. 109, a. 7
3. *To Know Him,* Vol. II, ch. 21
4. St. Theresa of Avila, *Foundations,* 5

Chapter 9

Loving is Self-Giving

Continuing the theme of the previous chapter that the perfection of the Christian life consists in the perfection of charity,[1] that virtue which enables us to *"love God above all things, and our neighbor as ourself "* (Deut. 6:5; Mt. 22:37), St. Thomas Aquinas asks whether it is possible in this life to have a perfect love of God. In answering this question, he distinguishes three kinds of perfect love.[2]

1) The infinite love of the Divine Persons. God alone can love Himself (His infinite goodness, beauty and truth) to the full extent that He is lovable. No creature is capable of infinite love.

2) Perfect love of the blessed in Heaven, who always love God to the fullest extent of their capacity. There one's mind and heart are always actually and completely occupied with God. We, in this life, are not capable of this love, for we have our ups and downs as to the intensity and extent of our love.

3) Perfect love of God in this life implies not only avoiding what is contrary to charity, that is, grave sin, but, says St. Thomas, a striving *"to remove whatever hinders the mind's affections from tending wholly to God."*[2] This implies a striving to avoid all deliberate failures against God and neighbor. Yet, it does not exclude sins of human frailty; for no one in this life without a special privilege from God (as the Blessed Virgin Mary enjoyed) can avoid all sins of human frailty. For this reason their presence should not be a source of discouragement, if one is striving to avoid them. As St. James tells us: *"In many things we all offend"* (Jas. 3:2).

Since the above speaks of loving God in terms that are rather abstract, we will look at this perfection to which we are all called, more from the angle of how this love will manifest itself. We will see that love manifests itself in *giving,* and especially in the *giving of oneself,* and this, whether we look at it from the part of God, or from the part of man.

Loving is Giving

1) On God's Part: In His infinite love, God wishes to share with us His own divine life, that is, His truth, His love, His beatitude. For this reason He gave us our very existence, creating our soul to His own likeness and image. He gave us not only the gift of divine grace, but came to dwell personally in the soul sanctified by grace. And when man in his pride and independence rejected God, He gave His only-begotten Son to redeem us, and His Son in turn gave His life on our behalf. Too, He gave us the Eucharist, the sacrament and sacrifice of His own Body and Blood. As St. Augustine exclaimed: *"He who is infinitely rich had no more to give."* And St. Paul had to remind the Corinthians: *"What have you that you have not received as a gift from God?"* (1 Cor. 4:7)

This list of God's gifts could be endless, but this should suffice to help one see that *God loving* is *God giving*, a giving of His very self.

2) On Our Part: With us too, loving will be manifested by giving. But what can we give God that He does not already have? All that we have that is good we have received from Him. Loving God is giving God His way, a surrendering of our will to His, a saying "yes" to God, no matter what He asks or allows. To surrender *one's will* is to surrender oneself, for the will is the key faculty that controls all one's deliberate actions.

"If you love Me," said Our Savior, *"keep My commandments"* (Jn. 14:15). But keeping His commandments and fulfilling our God-given duties require much giving on our part, a giving of our time, of our efforts accompanied by stress and fatigue, a giving up of some of our comforts and satisfactions; in short, a giving of ourself, which is loving in the deepest sense. God has given us much, that we might have much to give back to Him, whether by

sharing with others in need, or by accepting His will in the setbacks of life. However, because we are often slow and sluggish in surrendering to His will, God at times takes the initiative, taking back some of His gifts, hoping that we will consent to His action, hoping that our attitude will be that of Job: *"The Lord has given, and the Lord has taken away; blessed be the name of the Lord"* (Job 1:21).

How difficult it is at times to let go, to accept what God asks or allows. It might be the loss of health, the loss of a friend, the loss of a prized possession, or of a position of security.

If at times this surrender to God's will, this giving God His way, is difficult and painful, it was for Christ too. *"Let this chalice pass from Me, nevertheless not My will but Yours be done"* (Lk. 22:42). The measure of one's love is the extent that he or she is willing to give at a cost. *"Greater love than this no one has, that one lay down his life for his friend"* (Jn. 15:13).

Perfect Loving is Total Giving

As we saw above, Our Lord declared that we must love God *"with all our heart, with all our mind, and all our strength."* And this was given not as a *counsel,* but as *"the greatest and first commandment"* (Mt. 22:37-39). This means, in the language we are using, total giving, at least a striving to give or surrender all that He asks. And because this is a commandment, each of us will have a debt to pay at the end of our life in the measure that we fall short of that total giving.

How accurate is the expression of Fr. Bede Jarrett, O.P.: *"The art of perfect living is the art of perfect giving."* It is important to see our Christian life and its demands, not simply as giving up things, but as giving them to God.

If one person deeply loves another, one of the most instinctive things is to want to give to that other, to give oneself, to spend oneself for that other, to give some precious thing. And the more costly the giving, the more satisfaction and joy it brings to the one who gives. As we read in the exhortation often read before the marriage ceremony:

> Whatever sacrifices you may be required to make ... always make them generously. There will be problems which might be difficult, but genuine love can make them easy, and perfect love can make them a joy. And when love is perfect, the sacrifice is complete.

We should try to see our constant submission to God in that light. We will never be impoverished through our giving to God, or to our neighbor for His sake, for He will always outgive us many times over. *"For the Lord makes recompense, and will give you seven times as much"* (Sir. 35:10). *"God refuses to force our will. He takes what we give Him, but does not give Himself wholly until He sees that we are giving ourselves wholly to Him."* [3]

Love Has Many Facets

We have been looking at loving God in terms of self-giving, but this must be seen in our relationships with our neighbor as well, for *"as long as you did it for one of these, the least of My brethren, you did it for Me"* (Mt. 25:40).

Since we have identified loving at its deepest level as *giving of self*, it might be helpful to consider a few of the qualities or characteristics that self-giving should have. Christian love has many facets, as St. Paul explains in his first epistle to the Corinthians (Ch. 13), but we will consider a few of its most obvious characteristics. This self-giving should be:

1) Generous

Some years ago, when Cardinal Michael Browne was Master General of the Dominican Order, he made a visitation of the novitiate house in California. When speaking to the community, he made a few remarks on the requisites of a religious vocation. He pointed out that of all the positive qualities a superior should look for in a prospective candidate, none was more important than what he called a *"generosity of spirit,"* that is, a willingness and a readiness to give of oneself, a readiness for sacrifice, a readiness to serve.

Fr. Browne was a highly intellectual man, serving for years in the position of Master of the Sacred Palace, the Pope's personal theologian. As Master General he held the highest position in an Order that places much emphasis on intellectual development. Yet in speaking on the foremost quality to look for in new members, it was not a keen intellect, or special talent, but a generous spirit. Not that beginners are expected to be heroic, but where there is that unselfish willingness to sacrifice, there is the potential for heroism, for true spiritual growth.

True Christian living in the world, as well as in religious houses, demands a generous giving of self in the fulfillment of God's commandments, of the duties of one's state in life, and in the service of others in need. This kind of giving of oneself, day in and day out, is heroic giving, which when done for God, is what the Church understands by sanctity. No matter what the cost, no matter how much we are called to give of ourselves in following Christ, He will not only outgive us, but will do so for all eternity. *"He who sows sparingly will reap sparingly; and he who sows bountifully will reap bountifully"* (2 Cor. 9:6).

2) Cheerful

Here we refer mainly to the testimony of the Scriptures. St. Paul, who suffered very many trials, encourages us to be cheerful givers. *"Let everyone give . . . not grudgingly or from compulsion, for God loves a cheerful giver"* (2 Cor. 9:7). *"I rejoice now in the sufferings I bear for your sake, and what is lacking in the sufferings of Christ I fill up in my flesh for His body, which is the Church"* (Col. 1:24). *"Gladly therefore will I glory in my infirmities, that the strength of Christ may dwell in me. . . . I will most gladly spend myself and be spent for your soul"* (2 Cor. 12:9, 15; also 7:4). *"In every gift show a cheerful countenance, and sanctify your tithes with joy"* (Sir. 35:10).

If at times one is unable to manage an exterior smile when things go roughly, he should at least try to manage one interiorly for God in willing surrender. All this must be seen in the light of faith, because we are talking about the cross that each Christian is asked to bear. Otherwise it becomes a *"stumbling block,"* as it did for the Jews of old (1 Cor. 1:23).

3) Unselfish

Our giving to God, or our doing things for Him and for our neighbor for His sake, should be unselfish, that is, without seeking something in return; or as St. Catherine of Siena expressed it, it should not be mercenary. The more one can give of himself without seeking something in return on the human level, the more pure is the love expressed in that giving, and the greater the return on the divine level.

Because of original sin, however, we are egocentric, concerned mainly with self, and with *receiving*. With the help of divine grace, we must strive to become deocentric, concerned about God and neighbor, and with *giving*. Thus while love as the world sees it is *self-seeking,* true Christian love is *self-sacrificing*. Our Lord was speaking in this light when He said, *"It is more blessed to give than to receive"* (Acts 20:35).

More often perhaps than is realized, people perform good acts, or do something for others, in large part because they want something in return; if not some material return, at least the gratitude of the other. The proof of this is that at times they will stop performing some work of mercy because the recipient of this assistance isn't grateful. So much were they seeking the gratitude of the recipient, that the work of mercy was terminated because that return was not forthcoming. They were more concerned about *receiving* than with *giving*.

How seldom is there pure unselfish love that seeks nothing in return. It is not possible to love God or neighbor with true Christian charity without receiving a supernatural reward from God; but we can and should be ready to love both God and neighbor without expecting some temporal or tangible recompense. St. Paul refers to this when he says, *"Charity seeks not her own"* (1 Cor. 13:5). The same is beautifully expressed in the *Dialogue* of St. Catherine of Siena, where the Lord revealed to the saint: *"I have placed you in the midst of your fellow men, that you may do to them what you cannot do to me, that is, that you may love your neighbor of free grace, without expecting any return from him, and what you do to him I count as done to me."*

Practical Reflections:

1) The inner life of the divine Persons of the Trinity is one of *infinite self-giving*. The Father, in the contemplation of His divine essence, communicates the totality of His being and perfection to His only-begotten Son; and in their mutual exchange of Love, the Father and the Son communicate the totality of their being and perfection to the Holy Spirit, who is the Love of the Father and the Son, the infinite self-giving of the Father and the Son.

This is the Holy Spirit whom the Father and the Son have sent to dwell in our souls, to share with us their divine life, that is, that capacity of giving ourselves to God and neighbor for His sake. We begin to see a deeper meaning of Our Lord's words: *"Be perfect, as your Heavenly Father is perfect"* (Mt. 5:48).

2) Just as our love and our knowledge of the truth in this life is but a faint image of the perfect love and the fullness of knowledge we will enjoy in the life to come, so also, the joy of true self-giving in this life is but a faint image of what it will be in the life to come. For in heaven our beatitude for all eternity will consist in beholding and sharing in the infinite self-giving of the divine Persons, in that eternal communication of infinite love and truth and goodness that is God.

3) When we say that our self-giving should include our neighbor, and that it should be generous, we do not mean that we should give ourself to the service of others or to apostolic works, to the neglect of the prayer side of our life. Very often, getting in our prayers, and giving them

due time and attention, requires a greater sacrifice, a greater giving of self, than the accomplishment of some feverish apostolic labors.

Chapter Notes

1. St. Thomas Aquinas, *Summa Theologiae,* II-II, q. 184, a. 2
2. *Ibid.,* q. 184, a. 2
3. St. Teresa, *The Way,* Ch. 12

Chapter 10
Freeing the Heart

Many years ago I saw a film of a safari in the jungles of Africa that showed an interesting and unique way of capturing monkeys. The trap used to catch them was a coconut. A hole was cut in the coconut and the liquid drained out, the hole being just large enough for the monkey to insert its small hand. The coconut was anchored with a chain and inside the cavity of the coconut was placed grain attractive to the monkey.

On discovering the grain within the coconut, the monkeys would reach in to take a handful, but with a clenched fist full of grain they could not withdraw the hand from the coconut. The monkeys were thus held fast and easily captured.

Monkeys are considered to have a certain degree of animal intelligence, but it seems that in this case it was not displayed. If only they would have *let go* of the grain, they would have remained free.

I mention this episode because we are much like those monkeys in certain respects; for we too are held captive because we are unwilling to "let go" of certain things to which we cling, things which enslave the heart and hold us captive, robbing us of our inner freedom.

As we have frequently explained, when we speak of the *heart* loving, we speak symbolically, for it is the *will* that chooses, that loves. Consequently we will be using these two terms interchangeably, as did Our Lord Himself, for while the second is more technically correct, the first is the more common mode of speaking.

Two Concepts of Freedom

Freedom as the world usually understands it is a *freedom from without*. It is a freedom from external sources interfering with one's doing what he has a right to do, living his life in keeping with his natural rights.

In contrast with this, the freedom that Christ spoke of, and which He promised to those who accept and live His message is a *freedom from within,* a liberation of the heart of man, a freedom from being dominated by the world, the flesh, or the ego. The true follower of Christ strives not to be subservient to any of these masters, in order the more freely to love and serve the divine Master *"with his whole heart, his whole soul, his whole mind, and with all his strength"* (Mk. 12:29). One is free in this Christian sense, in the measure that his heart is liberated from domination by anything that makes him choose other than what God wishes.

This notion of freedom is intimately bound up with the notion of man's fallen nature, his inclination to pride, to avarice, to lust, to gluttony, and so forth. It is from the domination by any of these that one must be liberated to be truly free. How much we are like the foolish monkey, unwilling to "let go" of what is robbing us of our freedom.

Attachments are Unavoidable

God has so created the heart of man that it must love. It will of necessity cling to something. For this reason attachments are unavoidable. Man will choose and cling to the right thing or the wrong thing as regards his eternal salvation. Or again, he may choose and become attached to things that are good, but in the wrong way, that is, becoming too attached to them. He must choose between *created (temporal) good* which he knows by his natural faculties, and *uncreated (eternal) good* which is God, whom he knows by the light of faith, and is enabled to seek by the infused virtue of charity or love of God.

St. Thomas Aquinas was speaking of these two categories of good (created and uncreated) when he said that man is placed between the *things of this world* and the *things of God,* so that the more he cleaves to the one, the more he withdraws from the other. Consequently, to love God with one's *"whole heart,"* one's heart must be totally free from domination by any created goods. He must be able to use and enjoy them in such a way that they in no way become an obstacle to loving and serving God.

Our Lord was speaking of these two goods when He said that no man can serve two masters, God and mammon. He can *love* both God and mammon, but he cannot *serve* both, that is, become a slave of both, for *"either he will hate one and love the other, or he will stand by one, and despise the other"* (Mt. 6:24).

Liberation of the Heart from These Attachments

Since in the Christian life man is aided by *natural acquired virtues* (good habits), and by *supernatural infused virtues* (theological and moral virtues infused by God with sanctifying grace), both of these play an essential part in freeing the heart of man from domination by things of this world. Progress in the *acquired* virtues requires mortification and self-discipline, while progress in the *infused* virtues comes with growth in grace, which presupposes fidelity to prayer and other means of grace. We will consider them separately, but in practice they overlap, for the second must vivify and make fruitful the first; and the first is presupposed for progress in the second.

1) The Need of Mortification

While the Church in recent years has lessened considerably the former laws of fasting and abstinence, some type of mortification is necessary as a consequence of the fallen nature that we inherit, a nature in which the lower powers are in revolt against the higher so that *"the flesh lusts against the spirit"* (Gal. 5:17). If these lower powers are not to gain the upper hand, making it impossible for us to love God with our *"whole heart,"* we must take some means of reestablishing the order lost by original sin. Restoring that order means subjecting the lower powers to the higher (intellect and will), and subjecting these higher powers to God.

What is more, these inherited weaknesses of our nature are further complicated by our own personal sins. The self-indulgence involved in these sins increases the rebellion of the lower powers that original sin initiated; for the more we indulge our natural appetites and desires, the stronger and more insistent they become in demanding satisfaction. In addition to this, repeated sins leave behind bad habits against which we must take action.

Because of all this, it is not enough to merely aim at avoiding what is forbidden; we must at times deny ourselves the satisfaction of certain *lawful* pleasures, if we are to have the strength to say *"no"* to those that are *unlawful*. The snares that most of us have to guard against are things that are lawful in themselves, but which are so attractive that it is difficult to seek them in moderation. This can be true regarding food, alcoholic beverages, TV and other types of recreation.

It is not our purpose here to suggest ways of voluntary mortification or self-denial, but merely to stress its importance. Each person should know the area of his or her own weaknesses, and should take action accordingly.

Because, however, we are so sluggish and hesitant to undertake voluntary mortification, and because we are so blind as to our underlying attachments, the Lord Himself takes the initiative and chooses penances for us. And this brings up a broader and very important aspect of mortification.

2) God Takes the Initiative

Spiritual writers seem to be in agreement that, important as are the penances and mortifications that we choose for ourselves, the best and safest penances are those which God chooses; that is to say, the trials which God in His providence lets come our way from outside sources over which we have no control. Each day provides us with a variety of opportunities for mortification that we cannot escape. We can use them profitably, or we can squander them, depending on whether or not we recognize the hand of God behind them and accept them with patience and resignation to His will. They can be profitable both as regards reparation for the punishment due to our past sins, and as a means of undermining the attachments that enslave the heart.

God knows far better than we both our weaknesses and our areas of strength. He knows where mortification is needed most; and for every trial He allows to come our way, He offers the grace to profit by it. He uses both people and situations to test our patience, our unselfishness, our humility, our love of Him, our trust in Him, and so forth. He knows our hidden attachments better than we, and often He lets others touch us on some sensitive area, to make us aware of those underlying attachments that are obstacles to our complete surrender to Him. Thus He gives us an opportunity to discipline those attachments by accepting the upsetting incident in a spirit of resignation to His will.

The stronger our reaction against one of these daily crosses, the deeper the underlying attachment that caused it, and the more God will apply this kind of therapy if He sees the person in question will profit by it. The upsetting incident might be some frustration, or irritation, or inconvenience, or discomfort, or delay. Since these are part of God's providence, they are divinely chosen for each of us, perfectly suited to our needs. Not only does the heavenly Father provide *"what we shall eat, what we shall drink, or what we shall put on"* (Mt. 6:31), but also the trials and crosses that are necessary for our purification and growth in grace.

The person, however, who rarely practices mortification on his own initiative, will rarely profit by these unsought trials and crosses of daily life. Not seeing the hand of God behind them, he will often react with impatience, or discouragement, or murmuring against his lot, seeing them simply as annoyances he must put up with.

On the other hand, those who do practice mortification on their own initiative must be careful not to become like the Pharisee in the Gospel: *"I thank God that I am not like the rest of men. I fast twice a week, I pay tithes on all that I possess"* (Lk.18:12). Penances that are occasioned by the daily trials and crosses of life tend to make us humble rather than to make us proud.

Recall that Our Lady at Fatima pleaded for prayer and penance for sinners, revealing that many souls go to hell because there is no one to make sacrifices for them. We don't have to look around for means of penance and mortification; opportunities for them are built into our daily life if we can but see and use them.

3) The Role of Divine Grace

In spite of all that we have said about the need of mortification, the detachment of the heart of man from created goods is primarily the work of divine grace. It is effected primarily by *God* rather than by *man*. As St. Thomas states, *"Man's will can only be subject to God when God draws man's will to Himself."*[1] Yet, God demands a definite cooperation on our part in the way of mortification and sacrifice, before He accomplishes this work of liberating the heart from the strong hold that worldly goods and pleasures exercise over it. Let us see briefly how growth in grace accomplishes this liberation.

With each increase of grace, there is a corresponding growth in charity, or love of God. This gift of charity is a share in the very love with which God loves Himself and all that He has made to His own likeness and image. With each increase of grace charity becomes more deeply rooted in the will, enabling one to love God with a greater willingness to sacrifice self in order to fulfill His will. And as charity grows, God more and more attracts the heart of man to Himself. *"No man can come to Me, unless the Father who sent Me draws him"* (Jn. 6:44).

Thus, grace transforms the heart of man, not doing violence to it, but perfecting it, drawing it strongly and gently to its Creator, giving it a greater desire and strength to do His will. As St. Theresa of Lisieux expressed it, the more God wishes to give of Himself, the more does He cause Himself to be desired.[2]

This is basically what happens in the detachment of man's heart from creatures: as grace grows, God gradually draws the heart of man to Himself, giving it a greater capacity and desire to do what God wishes, and to reject what is contrary to His wishes, a greater capacity of saying "no"to the attraction of creatures. As St. Augustine expressed it, *"As charity increases greed decreases; when charity is perfect, greed ceases to exist."*

4) God's Way of Dealing with Us

While detachment is principally the work of God's grace, that grace will not be forthcoming without our cooperation, that is, without an active role on our part in disciplining our unruly tendencies, without our submission to God's purifying trials, without fervent and persevering *prayer,* and without a generous striving to make the *sacrifices* needed to keep His commandments and to fulfill the duties of our state in life.

Since detachment flows from growth in grace, it might seem to follow that, with progress, the doing of God's will becomes easier and easier. The fact is that the very opposite is often the case; for as God increases His gifts, He asks more of those who receive them. This will be seen more clearly if we give a brief picture of God's way of dealing with the soul in its struggle for spiritual progress.

In the spiritual life all persons at times run into periods when prayer and the practice of the virtues becomes more difficult; when they not only experience dryness and interior obscurity, but things which were formerly pleasant and easy become burdensome and a drudgery. This can be traced to one of two causes, or a combination of both:

a) Lukewarmness of life: This lessens the fervor of charity, causes one's interior life to dry up, and paves the way for indifference, half-hearted efforts, neglect of prayer, and so forth.

b) God's purifying trials: There is a normal period in the life of everyone making progress in the spiritual life in which he or she will experience these difficulties, this helplessness and distaste for prayer and even for the practice of virtue.

This need not be the result of lukewarmness, but can be God's doing. If one earnestly desires to make progress and is sincerely trying in the way of prayer and effort, futile though these may seem, such persons need not fear that their problems spring from lukewarmness or tepidity.

It seems that God allows every person intent on spiritual progress to pass through such periods, sometimes for a comparatively short time, sometimes for many years, depending on how quickly one is humbled thereby. Man tends to depend too much on himself until he is convinced of his weakness; and he usually has to be convinced of this the hard way. This is one of God's ways of bringing one to that conviction.

Keep in mind, however, that in the battles one must wage with his faults and weaknesses and in bearing patiently with the crosses of life, perfect success in these matters is not as important as the persevering and generous struggle they give rise to. It is possible to continue to grow in grace even though we never seem to conquer certain weaknesses, provided we earnestly desire and sincerely try to do so. God often leaves us with certain weaknesses, in spite of our prayers and efforts, in order to further humble us, and that we might continue the fervent prayers and the generous struggle they occasion.

Letting Go

To return to our thought in the beginning, the monkeys lost their freedom because they would not "let go." Every type of mortification, which is necessary for true freedom, requires a letting go of something to which we are strongly attached. In fact the whole of the Christian life requires a certain letting go of the *things of this world,* that we might possess more fully the *things of God.* Loving God requires a letting go of our own will in order to fulfill His. Knowing God through faith requires a letting go of *our own opinions,* in order to possess *His truth* made known through the Church.

These are all different ways of letting go of the *creature,* in order to more fully be made one with the *Creator.* In many ways we are afraid to let go, clinging to the creature, like the soul described by the poet Francis Thompson, fleeing God, the Hound of Heaven. *"I was sore adread, lest having Him, I must have naught beside,"* not realizing that possessing Him, loving Him with one's whole being, would fill every yearning and desire of the human heart.

Chapter Notes

1. St. Thomas Aquinas, *Summa Theologiae,* I-II, q. 109, a. 7
2. St. Theresa of Lisieux, *Autobiography*

Chapter 11

"Yes, Father"

Our Blessed Lord has given us the command, *"Be perfect, as your heavenly Father is perfect"* (Mt. 5:48). Obviously we can never attain the infinite perfection, the infinite sanctity and holiness that is God's; but, with the help of God's grace, each person can attain the degree of sanctity in keeping with the graces and gifts received. God has His plan for each of us and He has given each of us all the graces and opportunities, all the qualifications and capacities needed to fulfill what He calls us to accomplish. Yet *His plan* will be fulfilled in us only in the measure that *His will* is fulfilled in us, that is, only in the measure that we can bring our will to surrender to His. Only in that measure will we attain the perfection, the sanctity, to which we are called.

Because, however, of the damage that original sin has done to our nature with the obscuring of our judgment, the weakening of our will and our inclination to evil, the accomplishment of God's will in all circumstances is impossible for us without God's help. Add to that the ability of the Evil One to distract us from our divine goal by holding up before us the enticements of the world, and we can see that *"becoming perfect, as our heavenly Father is perfect"* (Mt. 5:48) will be an uphill battle and a lifelong struggle.

God's Will is Our Sanctification

St. Paul wrote to the Thessalonians, *"This is the will of God, your sanctification"* (1 Thess. 4:3). These words of St. Paul are true not only in the sense that God wishes or intends our sanctification, but also in the sense that our sanctification will come about only in the measure that His will is fulfilled in us. Our sanctification will be obtained only in the measure that we humbly and faithfully fulfill His commandments and the God-given duties of our state in life, and accept freely — with a *"Yes, Father"* — the crosses and hardships, the setbacks, disappointments and sorrows that He allows to come our way.

The divine grace that was infused into our soul at baptism by the Holy Spirit has made us adopted children of the Father. We are His children in a very real sense, sharing in His own divine life. In a very real sense He is our Father, who loves us with an infinite love, who understands our needs and weaknesses, and who is an infinitely wise and loving provider looking after the needs of His children. Some may seem to think that God is not a loving Father, that He has not provided for the needs of all, when they see the hunger and starvation of so many, the wars and displacement of peoples, and so forth. Yet God provides sufficiently for the needs of mankind, but the greed and hatred of some are responsible for the want and suffering of others. And God cannot prevent this without taking away man's free will, that is, his ability to choose between good and evil; and this God will not do.

When we read some books on the spiritual life with the long lists of exercises and mortifications, it can be discouraging to the fainthearted, and cause one to focus more attention on self than on God. Yet our Blessed Lord said: *"But one thing is necessary"* (Lk. 10:42). *"He who does the will of My Father in heaven shall enter the kingdom of heaven"* (Mt. 7:21). The road to sanctity, then, is not complicated, even though at times not easy.

If the work of sanctification were so complicated, our Blessed Lord would not have demanded it in such clear terms: *"Be perfect, as your Father in heaven is perfect"* (Mt. 5:48). All have been called to holiness whether they receive ten talents, or five, or one; therefore the way must be simple enough for all to attain, not by themselves, but by the aid of divine grace, and of God's guiding and purifying hand.

The expression *"Yes, Father"* is not just a prayerful formula. It expresses the basis of the spiritual life. It is the heart of our prayer. It keeps us ever mindful of God's guiding and healing hand in our lives, both as to joys and pleasures, or sufferings and sorrows. It is the royal highway of carrying the cross behind Jesus. However, following Him in this manner requires a constant alertness to the hand of God guiding all the events of our life. At times He even uses our mistakes and the opposition of others to bring out the exercise of the Christian virtues, to afford us the opportunity of making reparation, and to undermine the attachments that stand in the way of our surrender to Him.

Pope Benedict XV decreed, in giving the guidelines to the Sacred Congregation of Rites as to the norm of holiness required that one be eligible for beatification: *"Sanctity properly consists in the conformity to God's will, expressed in a constant and exact fulfillment of the duties of our state in life."*

Sanctity, therefore, does not consist in doing extraordinary things, but is essentially reduced to the fulfillment of our duties toward God and neighbor by reason of our state in life. Consequently, it is something possible for all of us. For this reason, one should strive to see the expression of God's will in each of his duties. Each task will then be seen as an opportunity of offering a *"Yes, Father"* to a God of infinite love and mercy, thereby loving Him in return. Persevering faithfully in the fulfillment of one's duties, not merely when they come easily and with satisfaction, but when tired, or sad, or disappointed, calls for uncommon generosity of spirit. *"It takes uncommon virtue,"* said Pope Pius XI, *"to fulfill with exactitude, that is, without carelessness, negligence or indolence, but with attention, piety and spiritual fervor, the whole combination of ordinary duties which make up our daily life."*

This constant fidelity to our God-given duties does not come easily, as we all know from experience. Yet one should not be discouraged at failures, but see each day as a new beginning to start again, knowing that God can make fruitful our efforts and desires.

The Divine Physician

Various persons may visit a medical doctor for help, each having a different problem or illness. For each he will prescribe a special remedy to get at the root of the illnesses. Whether we know it or not, each of us has spiritual illnesses, weaknesses and attachments, that tend in some measure to enslave our will, making it difficult for us to surrender our will to God's.

Our Heavenly Father, the divine Physician, knows our weaknesses and attachments that interfere with our total surrender to Him. And in His loving concern for us, He not only offers strengthening and healing graces, but He also uses human instruments as part of the healing process. For example, he lets people touch the sensitive areas of our ego with incidents that upset, irritate or frustrate, and so forth. He does this not only to make us aware of hidden attachments that often make us respond impatiently, angrily or uncharitably, but in hope that we will see His hand allowing it and surrender to His action. Because of the wounds of our fallen nature referred to above, that surrender will not be without pain. Yet each time we can manage to do so with a "Yes, Father," His action chips away ever so slightly at that attachment, and our action has both a meritorious and a satisfactory value. That is, it not only merits an increase of grace, but in some measure also pays the debt of temporal punishment due to sin.

There are certain basic weaknesses and faults in our makeup that we will never overcome by ourselves alone. We need God's help, not only to overcome them, but even to be clearly aware of them. But God will not do it alone. He demands our cooperation, our surrender to His action. He supplies the opportunities that test our patience, our charity, our humility, our trust. But those opportunities will be lost if we fail to recognize His hand in them and respond in our heart with a "Yes, Father."

We all need to undertake a certain amount of mortification *of our own initiative* in overcoming our weaknesses; but those opportunities for mortification which God provides, where *He takes the initiative,* are far more important and efficacious in getting at the root of our spiritual problems and healing the wounds of our fallen nature, if only we see His hand and submit to His action. With every cross He sends, there is an accompanying grace to help us to bear it.

What we have been saying does not mean that we should not defend ourselves or others against some unjust action, or remind another of something that is out of line. It refers more to those cases where emotion takes over and blinds us to the hand of God providing an opportunity for self-discipline, and our hurt pride causes us to respond in an uncharitable, impatient or angry manner.

One with deep faith sees the providence of God in all that is beyond his power to control, and trusts that God can bring good out of every situation. He follows that straight and narrow way where God is his guide, his provider, his physician. It is a road that he could never find of himself, nor would he of himself choose, for it is rough going in places. Yet the more he gives God a free hand in guiding him, the richer will be his inheritance when he arrives at that final destination.

God's Way Makes Us More Human

In surrendering oneself to the guidance of God, we need never give up anything of our normal or natural self. God's action will never stunt our human nature, for sanctity *completes,* not *lessens,* our humanity. There is a most intimate connection between nature and grace. Grace builds on nature and perfects it. The human person will attain the perfection of his humanity only in the measure of his growth in holiness, for only with the help of divine grace can we hope to rid ourselves of all our faults. When we speak of the perfection of our humanity, we are not referring to bodily or physical well-being, but to the subjection of our lower nature to the higher, so that one more perfectly fulfills the purpose for which he was created.

We will get rid of our faults and weaknesses, not so much by the negative process of suppression (though a certain self-denial is essential), but more through the positive effort to exercise the virtues in which we are weak, and through surrender to God's touch — His pruning hand, which is always accompanied by His healing grace.

If there is this spiritual alertness to see and accept the demands of God's will, it will bring into action all of the theological and moral virtues. And the law of charity can never be perfectly fulfilled without them. It will bring about, too, a greater activity of the gifts of the Holy Spirit received at baptism.

A Marvelous Exchange

In the liturgy for the feast of Mary, the Mother of God, January 1, reference is made to the *"marvelous exchange"* brought about by the incarnation of the Son of God. In that mystery God took on our *human nature* in order to share with us His *divine nature.* A similar marvelous exchange takes place at Mass. We offer the gift of *ourselves* at the Offertory in our promise or resolve to surrender to His will, and He gives *Himself* in Holy Communion, not merely coming bodily under the species of bread and wine, but by giving us an increase of His divine life through grace.

Yet, that same marvelous exchange also takes place every time we say "Yes, Father," renouncing our will in favor of His, especially when it is not easy. What happens when we renounce our will in order to embrace God's? We give up what *we want* (some temporal satisfaction), in favor of what *God wants* to give (some gift of grace) which is of infinitely greater value. Every time this happens, God gives us something *eternal* in exchange for something only *temporary,* something *divine* in exchange for something merely *human.* Each day will bring frequent occasions of surrendering to His will, in sacrifices needed to keep His commandments, in the fulfillment of our God-given duties, or in the acceptance of the crosses He sends our way, in order to receive His gifts, in order to return His love.

We should pray for a strong faith that helps us to recognize the little crosses of each day, to recognize the hand of God behind the ups and downs, the trials and disappointments, the little irritations and frustrations. We cannot *accept* what we don't *see*; and if we do not see God's hand behind these little trials which He allows for our spiritual growth, our nature will shrink back or rebel against them. In doing so, we will have rejected opportunities for that *marvelous exchange.*

Our Blessed Lord expressed this in another way: *"He that shall lose his life for my sake, shall find it"* (Mt. 16:25). He says in effect, one that will give up his own will — in spite of the hardship, inconvenience and sacrifice, in order to conform it to Mine — will allow Me to live My divine life more fully in him. Such a one will attain a fulfillment that having his own way could never bring.

None of us knows what lies ahead, but God does. His will, springing from infinite love and wisdom, has prepared a path for us. Every detail of our life is seen in the divine mind. One should pray for the grace to embrace with courage and readiness all that God wishes and permits, confident that in His will we shall find our peace and sanctification.

The will of God is *"the beginning and the end of all things"* (Apoc. 1:8). It is the source of every good both on earth and in heaven. And yet how many reject it in favor of their own personal wants. How often one chooses the creature in preference to the Creator.

Transformation in Christ

According to an axiom in theology, God gives grace in the measure that we do not place obstacles in the way, in the measure that we do not reject His advances, His pruning hand. Each time we surrender to His action, that *"marvelous exchange"* of which we spoke takes place.

In the measure that one habitually strives to conform his will to God's, with the growth of grace that it brings, the soul is gradually transformed into the likeness of Christ. As Fr. F.D. Joret, O.P. states, grace is *"a crucifying thing, inasmuch as it is an inflowing of the very grace which Jesus received in its fullness and which led Him to the cross."*[1] Our human nature recoils from the Cross, but as it is perfected by grace one more readily embraces it, to share in Christ's redeeming action for souls.

That transformation, however, will be slow and at times painful. Christ suffered much in His surrender to the will of His Father; and at times, because of our attachments, our surrender to the will of the Father will not be easy. Yet the grace to do so will be given if we ask for it and try to give God His way. This is part of the process whereby God purifies the soul from the attachments that stand in the way of our surrender to His will. Each "Yes, Father" furthers that process. With each increase of grace there is growth in that love which makes *"His yoke easy, and His burden light"* (Mt. 11:30). If we do all we can to do what Christ did, to submit ourselves entirely to the will of the Father, the Father will do the rest.

St. Teresa of Avila stressed much the general theme of these reflections:

> The sole concern of him who has but entered into the way of prayer . . . must be to strive courageously to conform his will to that of God. . . . Herein lies, whole and entire, the highest perfection to which we can attain. The more perfect the accord is, the more do we receive from the Lord and the greater is our progress.[2]

> The highest perfection consists not in interior favors, or in great raptures, or in visions, or in the spirit of prophecy, but in the bringing of our wills so closely into conformity with the will of God, that as soon as we realize He wills anything, we desire it with all our might, and take the bitter with the sweet.[3]

Chapter Notes

1. Fr. F.D. Joret, O.P., *Dominican Life*, p. 268
2. St. Theresa of Avila, *Interior Castle,* 2nd Mansion
3. St. Theresa of Avila, *Foundations* 5

Chapter 12

Two Kinds of Self-Love

Whenever we hear the expression *"self-love,"* it usually conveys the concept of selfishness. If one would make the remark, *"He certainly loves himself,"* that is usually not meant as a compliment, but rather refers to one who has an exaggerated idea of his own excellence or one who is solely concerned about his own welfare with little concern for others.

Yet, love of self, if rightly understood, is something that is not only good, but commanded by God: *"You shall love the Lord your God with your whole heart, with your whole soul, with all your mind. This is the greatest and first commandment. The second is like it: You shall love your neighbor as yourself"* (Mt. 22:37).

When our first parents were created by God, they had the kind of perfect love described above by Our Savior. That is, they had the capacity for that perfect love of God, self and neighbor; and there was nothing inherent in their human nature that interfered with the exercise of that perfect love. But among the gifts that God had given them was a free will. They had to freely choose God's will, God's plan for their life. And before admitting them to the eternal beatitude for which He had created them, God put them to the test. Theirs was not an absolute freedom, for God placed a limitation to their dominion over all that He had created. In their failure to pass that test, they rebelled against the limitation God had placed on their freedom, and they not only lost divine grace and the capacity to love with a supernatural love, but their intellect was obscured, their will weakened, and they were left with an *inclination to selfishness*, a tendency to seek their own will rather than God's.

So we have the *rightly ordered love of self* which God commanded, and the *inordinate love of self* to which we are all inclined by reason of our wounded human nature. The whole of the Christian life is a struggle to overcome the latter in order to attain the former.

True Self-Love

The rightly ordered love of self that Christ commanded is a love of self whereby man wills and seeks his own true good, both spiritual and temporal. It is a love guided by right reason and the truths of divine faith. It is the love of charity. The good that the Christian wills for himself is primarily God Himself, with whom we are united in the measure of our surrender to His will, and the eternal beatitude with Him in the life to come. And, secondarily, true self-love has for its object the sanctification and salvation of one's own soul and that of his neighbor. From this it is clear that man loves himself in the true Christian sense in the measure that he avoids sin and exercises the Christian virtues, making good use of the sacraments that God provided for his spiritual needs. It is obvious, then, that true love of self demands discipline and self-denial in regard to our unruly self-seeking tendencies. Fr. Alfonso d'Amato, O.P. brings this out in speaking of the commandment of love:

> In practice, to love ourselves means above all to combat our natural egoism which tends to impoverish our nature, to shrink it, to hinder its expansion towards our brothers and its fulfillment in God. True love of self should push us to work indefatigably to be fully ourselves, to realize the perfection which is the fullness of our being, as God views it from eternity. Now the chief obstacle to this true love of self is a false love, egoism, which makes us lose sight of the model, the ideal to be attained, lowers our aspirations and makes our existence miserable.[1]

True Christian love of self also causes men to seek such temporal goods as are required for the well-being of the body: suitable food and clothing, shelter, lawful pleasures, and so forth. But these are sought not as an end in themselves, but insofar as needed for the attainment of the soul's sanctification and salvation.

There is an order, however, which must be observed in our love of self. God created us as humans made of body and soul. Of the two, the soul is the more important, for our eternal destiny depends on the condition of our soul, not of our body, at the end of earthly life. It is the soul that loves or hates, that chooses God or rejects Him. Where a conflict arises between what the soul sees as good and what the body seeks, true love of self will choose the former. True Christian love of the body is marked by the desire to use its members in the service of God, in direct opposition to the worldly worship of the body so common today.

True Love of Self and Love of Neighbor Inseparable

Since Christian love of self is the love of charity, we cannot love ourselves truly without loving God and our neighbor for His sake. We love ourselves when we love our neighbor, for we are members of the same body. As St. Paul explains, *"If one member suffers anything, all members suffer with it; and if one member glories, all members rejoice with it"* (1 Cor. 12:26). Too, we truly love ourselves when we love our neighbor, for in doing so we merit an increase in grace. The more we are concerned about the needs of others, the more God comes to our aid. Finally, loving our neighbor is a true way of loving ourselves, for by directing our focus away from ourselves it enriches our personality, as Fr. d'Amato points out:

> If we think of ourselves too much, our personality is impoverished, impeded; the extent of our horizons is diminished. The human spirit is a powerful force for expansion and man fulfills himself only if he leaves the narrow circle of his "I". Not only does our personality not suffer, but it is strengthened when it gives itself to others. The best way to affirm our own personality and enrich it is to work and sacrifice ourselves for others, to profit from every occasion (even to seek occasions) to make ourselves useful to others. It is only in giving ourselves to others that we attain perfection of self. The more one gives, the more one has. It is only in leaving

our egoism, in giving ourselves generously to God and to our brothers for His sake, that we are truly ourselves and that our personality develops to the fullest. This is the meaning of the commandment, "Love thyself."[2]

False Self-Love

In contrast with true Christian love of self there is *inordinate self-love,* in which one is guided by one's own likes and dislikes instead of by right reason and the will of God. Such self-love often causes one to seek the gratification of one's sense appetites and the pleasures of the body in a way contrary to the good of the soul and to the law of God. Inordinate self-love will at times manifest itself in a spirit of rebellion against lawful authority, or in extreme pride in one's good qualities, achievements or possessions, as if one were the sole source of those goods or good deeds. Such a one is oblivious of the warning of St. Paul, *"What have you that you have not received and if you have received it, why do you boast as if you had not received it?"* (1 Cor. 4:7)

False self-love may also cause an excessive desire for honors and for the praise and esteem of others, as well as an excessive sensitivity to criticism of any kind. From all this we can see that inordinate self-love is not concerned about one's own true good, nor that of one's neighbor, but rather is destructive of that good, and that of the neighbor. In fact, St. Thomas Aquinas explains that inordinate self-love is the root cause of every sin:

> Every sinful act proceeds from inordinate desire for some temporal good. Now the fact that anyone desires a temporal good inordinately, is due to the fact that he loves himself inordinately; for to wish some good to someone is to love him. Therefore it is evident that inordinate self-love is the cause of every sin.[3]

The egoism of which the Angelic Doctor speaks is the basic source of every form of turning away from God. From inordinate self-love proceed what St. John calls the three concupiscences of the flesh, the eyes and the pride of life (1 Jn. 2:16); and from these three concupiscences are derived the seven capital sins, the root sources of all other sins.[4] In other words, every sin whatever is a form of inordinate self-love.

Love or Hate

As we have seen, to *love* someone (self or others) is to wish him true good, both spiritual and temporal. In contrast with this, to *hate* someone is to wish him evil, whether spiritual or temporal. In light of this, the sinner can be said to hate himself, as the Scriptures testify: *"He who loves iniquity hates his own soul"* (Ps. 10:6) and *"Those who do evil are enemies of their own soul"* (Tob. 12:10). It is in this sense that we understand the words of our Blessed Savior, *"He that loves* (inordinately) *his own life in this world shall lose it; and he that hates his life in this world* (i.e., hates his unruly tendencies and disciplines them) *keeps it safe unto eternal life"* (Jn. 12:25).

The two self-loves of which we have been speaking are diametrically opposed to each other. One is *self-giving, self-sacrificing;* the other is *self-seeking.* One builds up; the other is self-destructive in the light of eternity. One turns to God; the other turns away from God. St. Augustine expresses this paradox in his usual terse way, *"The one loves God to the point of disregarding self; the other loves self to the point of disregarding God."*

Our Blessed Lord was referring to these conflicting loves when He said, *"No man can serve two masters: for either he will hate the one and love the other; or else he will stand by the one and despise the other. You cannot serve both God and mammon"* (Mt. 6:24).

Today's Confused World

Because of the secular culture of today's society, many are growing up with their minds and hearts turned away from God. The educational system of our country and the media champion a concept of freedom that contradicts certain basic moral teachings of the Catholic Church. Even among many who call themselves Christian, their guiding light is reason alone, not reason enlightened by faith.

The concept of love we see portrayed day in and day out in the movies, on television and in the press portrays as normal and acceptable pre-marital sex, the use of contraceptives, divorce and remarriage, and so forth. It is concerned only about the goods and pleasures of the body, with complete disregard of the soul. Those who promote this concept of love are clearly against any particular religion imposing its views, while in reality they are championing the religion of secular humanism.

Let us take the case of a young unmarried man who seeks the affection of a young lady. He aggressively, by his words and actions, expresses how much he loves her, all of which ends in fornication. What he calls *love* is in reality *lust*. If he truly loved his friend, he would be concerned about her true good (spiritual and temporal), and would be willing to sacrifice in order to attain it. But the fact is that he not only was not concerned about her true good, but rather robbed her of her most precious possession, the state of grace. In a word, in the language of the Scriptures, he hates her. His intense love was not for her, but for himself. He seeks her company not for her own good, but for the pleasure he derives from that relationship. That kind of love (lust) will never stand the test of the trials of married life. It is because so many relationships are based on that kind of love that many of them end in divorce.

Or take the case of a young couple who engage in pre-marital sex, and do so with mutual agreement. They are mutually self-seeking, mutually unwilling to make the sacrifices that God demands to call down His blessings on their relationship. Those who without qualms of conscience engage in pre-marital sex will very likely have few qualms of conscience about adulterous relationships during married life.

Love Your Neighbor as Yourself

How are we to understand those words, *"as yourself"*? Theologians make the distinction between the *love of esteem,* which proceeds from our judgment as to the objective good or value of the object loved, and the *love of intensity,* which is a subjective experience or feeling with regard to the object loved. We should have the same *"love of esteem"* for our neighbor as for ourselves, in the sense that we desire his spiritual good and eternal salvation as we desire our own; but we will not, as a rule, have the same subjective feelings as to his gains or losses as we have for our own.

Some may be disturbed that they do not feel a greater love for God. The virtue of charity enables one to love God above all things with the *love of esteem*, but not necessarily with the *love of intensity*. God has commanded us to *have* love for Him above all things, not to *feel* that love. And the test as to whether or not we have it, is whether we would prefer Him above everything else, whether we would be willing to give up whatever might come between us and our love of God.

Every individual should think of his own salvation, his own pursuit of the truly good, as his first responsibility; for if he does not have right love of self, a love that flows from a grateful love of God, he is unable to love his neighbor rightly. So in this sense we must love God above all things, and after love of God comes love of self, not a self-centered love, but a God-centered love, a love like that of Christ that is self-sacrificing, self-giving, that is more concerned with serving than being served. In the measure that we have that kind of love of self, we will love others as Christ loves us. And as our Blessed Lord has told us, what we do to them, we do to Him. In that roundabout way we return His love.

Consequently, in the commandment to love our neighbor *as ourselves,* the "as" does not signify *equality,* but *likeness,* that is, to love others as ourselves inasmuch as we have the same end. Just as we should love ourselves in God, so we should love them in God.[5] As we wish good for ourselves, so we wish good for them, for we are both God's children sharing His divine life.

Christian love of self, then, is a concern about what contributes to one's spiritual growth, and a zeal to discipline those self-seeking tendencies that stand in the way. *Self-centered love,* on the other hand, is but another name for egoism, which inclines one to self-seeking and self-exaltation in countless ways, leaving one an easy prey to the dragons of pride and sensuality.

We would do well to entrust ourselves to the Mother of Jesus, who, in her fullness of grace, had the most perfect love of self, because hers was the most perfect surrender to the will of God. She knew so well that God wills only what is best for us, and she sought only the fulfillment of His will, cost what it may.

Mother of God, teach us that perfect love of self which makes us aware of our self-seeking tendencies, and of our need of God's grace to support our efforts in countering them. Help us to see that we cannot love ourselves as we should in isolation, but must (at least through prayer) be concerned about the welfare of those around us in need. They too are your children. Pray for us now and at the hour of our death.

Chapter Notes

1. Fr. Alfonso d'Amato, O.P., "The One Commandment," *Cross & Crown,* Dec. 1952.
2. *Ibid.*
3. St. Thomas Aquinas, *Summa Theologiae,* I-II, q. 77, a. 4
4. St. Thomas Aquinas, *Summa Theologiae,* Cf. I-II, q. 77, a. 5
5. Cf. d'Amato, *ibid.*

Chapter 13

The Love of Forgiveness

All of us are sinners, and therefore all of us need pardon from God; but our divine Savior has made it clear that an essential condition for receiving pardon from God is that we pardon one another. *"If you forgive men their offenses, your heavenly Father will also forgive you your offenses. But if you do not forgive men, neither will your Father forgive you your offenses"* (Mt. 6:14). Our Blessed Lord explained this in detail in His parable of the servant who was forgiven a large debt by his master, but would not himself forgive a small debt of a fellow servant. Thereupon the master demanded that the first servant pay his debt in full (Mt. 18:23).

Our own condition is similar to the first servant referred to above. Time and again God has forgiven us when we asked His pardon with humble and sincere contrition, thereby pardoning an infinite debt, for sin is an injustice against a person of infinite dignity who has a strict right to our obedience. And yet, at times we are unwilling or reluctant to forgive another. While we can atone for an injury or injustice to our neighbor, we can never, by ourselves alone, atone for the least offense against God, unless He assists us by His grace to do so.

One who is unwilling to forgive another who has offended him, should be fearful of praying the *Our Father,* for in that prayer we ask God to forgive us *"as we forgive those who trespass against us."* That means, if we do not forgive another, we are asking God not to forgive us; and that is exactly what He will do.

We are not suggesting that some should not pray the *Our Father,* but rather that those who find forgiving difficult should let that prayer be a plea that God will enable them to forgive others, so that He in turn will pardon them.

True Love is Forgiving

Our Blessed Lord, being a divine Person, is infinite Love, is Love Itself (1 Jn. 4:8). Dying on the cross, He begged forgiveness for the very ones who were putting Him to death. He forgave them from His heart, and begged His Father to forgive them. And He was begging pardon for our sins as well, for He was making satisfaction for the sins of all mankind.

We should strive to forgive others, then, not merely for the selfish motive that we ourselves might be forgiven, but also because forgiving is a form of loving. As the renowned Carmelite theologian, Fr. Gabriel of St. Mary Magdalen, wrote:

> Indeed one of the greatest opportunities for the practice of charity is offered us by those who by their evil conduct give us so many occasions of forgiving them, for returning good for evil and for suffering injustice for the love of God. Moreover, we should consider that, while cockle cannot be changed into wheat, it is always possible for the wicked to be converted and become good.[1]

The Mass Continues Christ's Forgiveness

We all know that the most central and essential part of the Mass is the Consecration, when Christ makes present His sacrifice, changing bread and wine into His own Body and Blood, and offering these divine gifts with His merits to the Father. Notice the words of Our Savior, which the priest repeats at the consecration of the Precious Blood: *"This is the cup of My Blood, the Blood of the new and everlasting covenant. It will be shed for you and for all — so that sins may be forgiven. Do this in memory of Me."* Not only is Christ asking that we continue offering this sacrifice. He is asking that we continue this work of pardon.

Christ suffered and died precisely to gain pardon for our sins, and to share with us the capacity of pardon. His redeeming death gave to forgiveness (done out of charity) a special efficacy in gaining grace and help from

God. For this reason, we unite ourselves to Christ and His Passion in a very special way when we forgive another out of the motive of charity. This is so central and so basic in the Christian life because it is an intimate participation in the principal thing that Christ became man to do. It should be clear, then, that as long as we have an unforgiving frame of mind and heart, our prayers and offerings will not be acceptable to God. *"If you bring your gift to the altar and there recall that your brother has anything against you, leave your gift at the altar, go first and be reconciled with your brother, and then come and offer your gift"* (Mt. 5:23).

During the sacrifice of the Mass Our Savior invites us to unite ourselves with Him who was the victim of an injustice infinitely greater than any injustice we will ever suffer, and who asked forgiveness for all who were responsible for His death. How, then, can we be united with Him in the renewal of His sacrifice, if we ourselves have an unforgiving heart toward someone who has offended us?

The Power of Forgiveness

In the prayer at the beginning of the Mass on the 26th Sunday of ordinary time, we read these words: *"Father, you show your almighty power in your mercy and forgiveness."* We are accustomed to think of God's power in terms of creating out of nothing, curing the sick, raising the dead to life, and so forth. But here the Church refers to His *mercy and forgiveness* as a manifestation of His power. We can understand this, however, when we remember, as we said above, that forgiving is a form of loving. It requires great *spiritual strength* to forgive from the heart. An unwillingness to forgive, or an inability to forgive, is spiritual weakness. One who loves God *"with his whole heart, his whole soul, his whole mind, and with his whole strength,"* as God has commanded us (Mk. 12:30), will have the power and strength to forgive.

We cannot imitate God's power to create, raise the dead, and so forth, but we can and are called to imitate

His power to forgive. In fact, we have the opportunity of exercising this form of charity more often than any of the other works of mercy. For example:

— to *give alms* we need money; but we don't need money to forgive.

— to *instruct the ignorant* we must have certain knowledge and training, but not to forgive.

— to *give food to the hungry* we must have food to give, but not to forgive.

— to *give clothes to the needy,* we must have clothes to share, but not to forgive.

— to *give shelter to those who need it* we must have a place to offer, but not to forgive.

So, certain types of charity are limited to the situation in which one finds himself; but we should never be limited in our capacity to love our neighbor by the love of forgiveness, in our capacity to give witness of God's love, by pardoning another.

Forgiveness, then, is one type of alms that we can always give. It is a type of charity that can be exercised at any time, by anyone, be he rich or poor, young or old, sick or in good health. If we can't manage this type of alms, then our poverty is much greater than being without money, or food, or clothing, or shelter.

The Obstacle of Pride

At times a person can be dominated by a grudge which he holds against another, or a deep resentment, or even hatred and a desire for revenge. In all these cases, what is lacking is the charity and humility that disposes one to pardon.

It has been said, and with much truth, that *"to offend is human, to pardon is divine."* Without the aid of divine grace strengthening us in the virtues of charity and humility, it is often very difficult, if not impossible, for our proud and selfish nature to forgive.

This we know to be a fact, and it should make us reflect: the more we grow in the love of charity and humility, the more we are inclined to forgive; but the more that self-love, pride and egoism dominate us, the more difficult it is for us to pardon and to ask pardon, and the more inclined we are to hold grudges and deep resentments.

This is true, for when we are offended, both our emotional and intellectual being is affected. While the intellect may know the need of forgiving, the will finds it difficult because of hurt feelings that do not easily or quickly go away. And the Evil One, who does not want us to forgive, does what he can to make it more difficult. If we cannot forget, it is more difficult to forgive; and the devil can make it harder for us to forget. Just as he can bring an image to the imagination that will tempt one to impurity, so he can bring an image that will remind one of a past painful offense. And if one is not on his guard, this can give rise to resentment and bitterness that would influence his decisions and actions.

A good way to handle such situations is by prayer, praying for the one who caused the offense. The hurt feelings may not quickly disappear; but if one can bring himself to pray for the one who offended him, deep in his heart he is well disposed toward that person. He is loving in a true Christian sense, even though on the surface the feelings haven't completely quieted down. In this way one can reap spiritual gain through such temptation instead of loss. Isn't that why God allows temptations?

Confused Notions of Forgiveness

A person can at times confuse *pardon* with *softness* in regard to sin, crime, and so forth. God is not asking us to overlook the injustice of robbers, murderers, those who exploit the poor, those who sell drugs. He asks us to *hate sin,* but *love the sinner.* Yet the love of forgiveness does not mean that we overlook the injustice done. It does not mean that it should not be corrected. Our Blessed Lord was severe in driving the money changers out of the temple. He was severe in condemning the Pharisees. Yet, He died for them. The Scriptures testify that the love of forgiveness does not mean that wrongs are not punished: *"For them you were a God who forgives; yet you punished all their offenses"* (Ps. 99:8). *"For whom the Lord loves, He disciplines; and He scourges every son whom He receives. . . . God deals with you as sons; for what son is there whom the father does not discipline"* (Heb. 12:6, 7).

Too, many worldly-minded persons see forgiveness as a weakness, as not having the courage to stand up for one's rights. If we follow the philosophy of the Western movies, not to fight back when one is insulted or offended, not to defend one's *"honor"* as they call it, is to be a coward.

Yet, in a deeper sense, to retaliate, to fight back when one is offended, is often a weakness. It is to lack the strength to control one's pride. It is to fail to be strong enough to forgive.

The Extent of Forgiveness

On one occasion Peter asked our Blessed Lord how often he must forgive another who offends him. Must he pardon him as many as seven times? Jesus answered him, *"Not seven times, but seventy times seven times"* (Mt.18:22); that is, countless times if the offender is sincere in asking pardon, wanting and trying to avoid offense. Peter thought his charity was quite commendable in being willing to pardon seven times, which was four more than was required by the Jewish teachers, who based the duty of forgiving three times on the sacred books (Amos 1:3; Job 33:29).

Did not Our Lord say to His apostles the night before He died, *"Love one another as I have loved you"* (Jn. 15:12), which can mean *"Forgive one another as I have forgiven you;"* and has He not forgiven each of us countless times? And not only that, but He forgives us a debt far greater than that which our neighbor owes us; for when our neighbor offends us, he offends a weak person who himself offends often, while God pardons a debt against Himself, a being of infinite majesty and power and goodness. The best way we can thank God for forgiving us is to forgive, for His sake, those of His children who have offended us

The Fruit of Forgiveness

The effect of pardon can be more extensive than we might imagine. Any true conversion of life must come from within, from a conversion of heart aided by God's grace, and not merely imposed from without. The love of forgiveness can help win those graces.

When we give alms, or clothing, or food, or lodging, we are helping another *exteriorly*. When we forgive another from the heart, as Christ asks, we are touching him *interiorly*, in his heart, where any true conversion or amendment of life must originate.

As regards our own conversion of life, the more we forgive the offenses of others, the more God is going to pardon us our faults, and give us the graces and help needed to overcome them.

And as to the faults of others and their conversion of life, if one can bring himself, not only to forgive the offense of another, but to offer to God the pain and suffering for the person who caused it, he will be doing exactly what Christ did on Calvary. Such a love of forgiveness will draw down graces both on the one who forgives and the one who is forgiven. This seems to be what Fr. Gabriel of St. Mary Magdalen means when he says, in connection with forgiveness, that *"while cockle cannot be changed into wheat, it is always possible for the wicked to be converted and become good."* [2]

St. Paul is talking in the same vein when he tells us not to render evil for evil, not to take revenge. On the contrary, he says, quoting the book of Proverbs: *"If your enemy is hungry, give him food; if he is thirsty, give him drink; for by doing so you will heap coals of fire upon his head"* (Rom. 12:16-20; Prov. 25:21). Saints Augustine and Jerome understand these words to mean that generosity toward an enemy will inflict upon him healing pains of remorse and repentance for his past conduct, and thus effect his conversion. This implies, of course, that these *exterior* forms of charity are accompanied by an *interior* love of forgiveness. In this, one would be fulfilling what St. Paul recommends: *"Be not overcome by evil, but overcome evil with good"* (Rom. 12:21).

Chapter Notes

1. *Divine Intimacy,* 70, 2
2. *Ibid.*

Chapter 14
Blessed are the Meek

Our Blessed Lord began the Sermon on the Mount with eight short maxims which summarize, or contain in embryo, the gospel message He came to live and teach. We refer to the eight beatitudes, the message of which is in great contrast to the wisdom of the world. While salvation is promised to those who live by them, the perfect fulfillment of what they promise is not in this world, but in the next. Yet, in the measure that their demands are met, they bring, even in this world, the peace of Christ in the midst of life's tribulations.

Three of these beatitudes constitute the subject matter of this and the following two chapters. The present chapter examines the beatitude, *"Blessed are the meek, for they shall possess the earth"* (Mt. 5:4). This requires an examination of the virtue of meekness, a virtue that is little understood and little esteemed in a world that glorifies power and might, where often *might is right.*

The Virtue of Meekness

Meekness is a virtue which moderates the passion of anger according to the dictates of reason, and calms the desire for revenge.[1] It restrains one from wanting to inflict injury for injury. It enables one, relying on the Father's will, to remain tranquil in the face of wrongs done him.[2] St. Paul stressed the need of this virtue in his letter to the Thessalonians: *"See that none of you repays evil for evil, but always seeks to do good to one another and to all"* (1 Thess. 5:15).

Because of the inclinations of our fallen nature we are usually inclined to avenge every offense, and to resist every adversary. Such is the spirit of the world, but not the spirit of Christ. In time of adversity meekness inclines not to revenge, but to gentleness and patience, to pardon personal insults; and in trials allowed by God's providence, to patience and resignation. It helps us to endure difficulties that we encounter in those of different tastes and dispositions. It is an indispensable aid to charity in bearing wrongs patiently, and avoiding bitterness when misunderstood or undervalued. It saves one from answering back quickly with wounding words that afterwards one wishes had never been said. In a word, it enables one to endure affronts and injuries in a spirit of mildness dictated by reason enlightened by faith. In all such situations it drives the thought and inclination to revenge out of one's mind and heart, thereby removing a key obstacle to the work of the Holy Spirit in the soul. *"Do nothing to sadden the Holy Spirit with whom you were sealed against the day of redemption. Get rid of all bitterness, all passion and anger, harsh words, slander, and malice of every kind"* (Eph. 4:30).

"Blessed are the meek," said our Blessed Lord, *"for they shall possess the earth."* The earth that is promised to the meek is not tracts of land or the earth's riches, but the riches of Christ's inheritance. In the Old Testament God promised land (the Promised Land) to the Israelites as a reward for their obedience, but that was only a type or figure of the greater promise made by Christ in the New Law. As we have pointed out, the perfect fulfillment of that promise is in heaven; but Christ promised to provide even in this life the basic temporal necessities to those who *"seek first the kingdom of God and His justice"* (Mt. 6:33).

When we say that meekness moderates the passion of anger according to the dictates of reason, it is because the passion of anger, in itself, is neither good nor evil. It can be either. There is such a thing as a just and righteous anger. We have examples of this when Christ drove the money changers out of the temple (Mt. 21:12), and when He looked upon the pharisees with anger because of their hardness of heart as He cured the man with the withered hand on the Sabbath (Mk. 3:5). Again,

Moses was filled with righteous anger when he broke the tablets of the Law as he came upon the Israelites worshiping the golden calf (Ex. 32:19).

Consequently, while anger when aroused in fallen nature is most often blameworthy, we see that it can be praiseworthy and just, when meekness directs it according to the dictates of justice and charity. We are speaking of just anger that tries to destroy sin, without wishing to destroy the sinner. *"Be angry and sin not"* (Eph. 4:26; Ps. 4:5). Even in just anger, however, one must be careful not to sin by excess. St. Bernard reminds us that there are two extremes one must avoid in this matter: *"It is a sin not to be angry when one should be angry; but to be angry more than is necessary is equally sinful."* Fr. Walter Farrell, O.P. speaks in similar language: *"There are times when our failure to be angry is a weakness, when we hold back the punishment because our love is not strong enough to be just."*[3]

False Concepts of Meekness

It would be a grave misconception of meekness to confuse it with timidity or cowardice. The modern world may look upon meekness as a weakness, as one afraid to stand up for his rights, as one unwilling to fight back in the face of insult or offense. Yet, on the contrary, as Fr. W. Farrell, O.P. explains, *"The meek man is a conqueror; for he has subdued the wildest passion of man, the passion that strikes most suddenly and most devastatingly. This is not the task of the timid person, but rather of a fearless rider of a wild steed he has subdued."*[4]

In contrast to this, our modern movies at times hold up as hero the macho who in his unbridled anger inflicts untold damage and destruction to seek revenge, and who deals with his victims with unbelievable brutality. If such a one might display physical strength, it is a pitiful display of spiritual weakness. For such a one is often a slave of the demands of the ego, and uses the passion of anger to his own selfish ends.

Meekness, then, is rooted in spiritual strength, for it requires great spiritual strength to keep the emotion of anger under control; and the very practice of that virtue calls for frequent acts of such strength. Understood properly, the meek are those who are truly strong in the Christian sense, strong with the strength that brings about conquests the fruits of which are eternal. Yet, as we saw in the case of a righteous anger, the meek person will fight back with controlled anger, when his rights or the rights of others are abused. However, since it is so easy to be mistaken in judging the just motive of anger, and since anger easily gets out of control when the ego is hurt, one must be vigilant lest a sudden movement of anger would carry one beyond the limits of justice and charity. In this regard, Fr. Jordan Aumann, O.P. warns: *"In case of doubt it is better to incline to the side of meekness than to the danger of excessive rigor."* [5]

The Meekness of Christ

When our Blessed Lord calls our attention to His own meekness, He singles out another virtue which is its immediate foundation, and without which one will never control the passion of anger. *"Learn of Me,"* He said, *"for I am meek and humble of heart"* (Mt. 11:29). Neither of these two virtues is popular in our secular society, but both are essential for the follower of Christ. Just as meekness calms the passion of anger, so humility restrains the inclination to pride. And as Fr. Gabriel of St. Mary Magdalen, O.C.D., points out, *"It takes only a small amount of pride, of self-love, of attachment to our way of seeing and doing things, to make us unable to stand opposition."* [6]

In our Blessed Lord, then, we see both the expression of just anger, and the suppression of the passion of anger when falsely accused and roughly treated during the Passion. Both of these are the fruit of the virtue of meekness. He who is Lord and Master of all mankind and Creator of the entire universe, remained meek and humble of heart when being treated with sheer contempt by His own creatures. In this, Christ the Redeemer made reparation for our pride, and Christ the Teacher pointed out the way to the Father.

The Passion of Anger

We will better understand the work of the virtue of meekness if we see a bit in detail the violent passion it keeps in control. Anger is the spontaneous reaction to some injury, opposition, frustration, restraint or coercion, insult, etc., actual or imaginary, that inclines one to respond in kind. It is an emotion implanted in man by nature and intended to be governed by the dictates of reason. Since anger is a passion, the first impulse of it is independent of reason or will, and therefore, as we have seen, is neither good nor evil. It becomes sinful insofar as it influences or interferes with the judgment of reason, or if it is out of proportion to the injury that provoked it, or when it seeks means of revenge that are contrary to reason. Anger is listed among the capital sins, because it is the mother of many offenses against charity and justice. The more violent the anger, the more passion becomes man's master, rather than reason enlightened by faith.

One with deep faith in God knows that everything that happens to us, no matter how painful, is permitted by God for our sanctification. Yet, when anger flares up, this thought vanishes and one sees only the person against whom the anger is directed and against whom one is inclined to react. *"Man is master of his actions,"* says St. Thomas, *"through the judgment of reason,"*[7] and anger interferes with that judgment, and can completely wipe it out. The stronger the passion, the more blindly one acts.

Even when the degree of anger is not extreme, the calmness of judgment is lost, and one no longer sees God's will, the image of God in his neighbor, and the fact that what he does to another he does to Christ. One loses control of his actions in the measure that his decisions are dominated by pride and self-love, for these vices frequently give rise to resentment and anger, preventing one from seeing things in their true light, from making unbiased judgments and wise decisions, and from refraining from words and actions that offend against courtesy and kindness.

It might be helpful to see how the passion of anger affects the whole person, body and soul, not only clouding the mind, but bringing about rapid physical changes that mobilize the body's forces for aggression. The *New Catholic Encyclopedia* describes the bodily effects of anger as follows:

> As a passion or emotion, anger is psychosomatic. The visible physiological changes involved in the passion of anger are increased pulse, trembling, flushed face, knit eyebrows, tensed facial muscles, dilated and flashing eyes, and sometimes impaired speech. Internal changes are increased output of adrenaline, thus causing increased circulation, heartbeat, and blood pressure, which results in increased sugar in the blood and makes energy available faster to the brain and muscles; increased respiration and perspiration, change in skin temperature, and slowing down of the stomach, gall bladder, kidney and liver functions. The physiological changes accompanying anger are proportionate to the greater or lesser violence of the angry reaction.[8]

We have given in detail these effects of anger to show how greatly and how quickly this emotion affects the entire body as well as the powers of the soul, and how important it is to check the initial stirrings of this emotion.

Remedies for Anger

One who by natural temperament is more prone to anger must especially be on guard. Prayer is an indispensable means to grow in the virtue of meekness which controls the emotion of anger. Ask God for the grace to see His providential hand behind the disturbing and upsetting circumstances, allowing this situation, this inconvenience, this humiliation, this setback, this disturbance to test our humility, our patience, our unselfishness, our faith and trust in His providence. We squander many difficult situations that could be sources of grace and growth. We must never lose sight of the fact that the divine Physician heals as He wounds if we are submissive to His healing hand (Heb. 12:5, 6; Rev. 3:19).

Looking at anger from a purely natural point of view, some would encourage various types of physical exercise, various physical discharges of energy, such as playing sports, rail splitting, or physical workouts, which frequently assist in the dissipation of pent-up rage. These might bring some temporary relief, but they do not get at the causes of anger. As long as any trace of pride and self-love remain in us, we will encounter situations in which resentment and anger cause us to lose some of our control and self-mastery. For as St. Thomas says, *"Meekness makes a man master of himself."*[9] Without the interior control that meekness brings of impulses of animosity, or antipathy, or indignation, and so forth, we will never face calmly the trials of daily life.

We have made little progress in the virtue of meekness if when unexpected trials, contradictions, injuries or offenses come along, our peace of heart vanishes. The meekness of which we speak comes from a habitual frame of mind that sees the merciful and purifying hand of God in all the trials of life, and from a concern to calm the first feelings of anger or resentment lest they blind one to God's purpose.

By our own efforts alone, however, even aided by grace and the infused virtues, we will never completely eradicate all traces of pride and selfish tendencies. But to those who do what they can, the Holy Spirit comes with an added gift, the gift of piety, which erases the last traces of ill-feeling toward others, and softens the hardness of heart that stands in the way of His action in the soul. True Christian meekness, then, requires concern and effort to discipline all forms of pride and self-love that give rise to resentment and anger, to calm the first feelings of anger when they arise, and to seek with fervent and persevering prayer the indispensable help of the infused virtues and gifts.

The help we ask from the Holy Spirit is expressed in the sequence of the Mass for Pentecost: *"Come, Holy Spirit, bend the stubborn mind, warm the chilled heart, guide the steps that go astray."*

Importance of Meekness

From all that has been said there should be little need to stress the importance of this virtue. If our Blessed Lord summarized the whole of the Old Law and the New Law in the two great commandments of charity, love of God and neighbor, meekness is one of the main custodians of that love. This is because it controls anger, which in so many ways causes one to offend God and neighbor. How often do we find people who are angry with God because of the trials which His merciful providence allows for the good of their soul, or because their prayers seem not to be heard.

Too, meekness keeps one from usurping God's rights, restraining the inclination to seek revenge. *"Revenge is mine, I will repay, says the Lord"* (Rom. 12:19).

If one would win others to the acceptance of goodness and truth, of God's view of things, it will not be by force or by sheer authority which can be counter-productive and arouse opposition, but rather by meekness and patience along with prayer, after the example of Our Savior who is *"meek and humble of heart"* (Mt. 11:29).

Meekness is especially important for progress in prayer, for one agitated with feelings of anger and resentment cannot sincerely apply himself to recollection and conversation with God, nor be open to the inspirations of the Holy Spirit.

Each of the Christian virtues relies on the help of other virtues for its perfect fulfillment. This is true of meekness. We have seen how meekness cannot get along without *humility* which keeps pride in check, for the main source of anger is hurt pride and frustrated self-will. Too, meekness leans heavily on the virtue of *fortitude* in its passive aspect of bearing wrongs patiently. And it needs the *gift of piety* that brings a filial reverence of the Father in heaven, and an awareness of His permissive will in all things.

Pray to the Mother of Jesus who, like her Son, was *"meek and humble of heart."* In her fullness of grace she was more like Him than any other, for more than all the angels and saints she shared in His divine life. How truly, at the foot of the cross, she bore wrongs patiently, offering to the Father her Son and herself for the same redemptive purpose as Jesus. Obtain for me, Blessed Mother, the grace to be more like your Son, *"meek and humble of heart."*

Chapter Notes

1. St. Thomas Aquinas, *Summa Theologiae,* II-II, q. 157, a. 1 & 2
2. *Ibid.,* I-II, q. 69, a. 3
3. Fr. Walter Farrell, O.P., *Companion to the Summa,* III, p. 457
4. *Ibid.,* p. 456
5. Jordan Aumann, O.P., *Spiritual Theology,* p. 301
6. Fr. Gabriel of St. Mary Magdalen, O.C.D., *Divine Intimacy*
7. St. Thomas Aquinas, *Summa Theologiae,* II-II, q. 158, a 2, ad 3
8. M. W. Hollenbach, *New Catholic Encyclopedia*
9. St. Thomas Aquinas, *Summa Theologiae,* II-II, q. 157, a. 4

Chapter 15

Blessed are the Merciful

St. Thomas Aquinas lists three effects which flow from the virtue of charity, namely, joy, peace and mercy.[1] We are concerned here only with the third effect. Charity is a unitive force, uniting us with both God and neighbor. With regard to God, it inclines us to surrender our will to His; and with regard to our neighbor, it makes us rejoice over the good of our neighbor and sorrow over the evil that befalls him, because true charity causes us to consider his good or bad fortune as our own.

Mercy, then, is charity's response to the suffering of others. It is compassion for the misery or suffering of another which stirs us to do what we can to alleviate that misery. It is not pure sentimentality, or merely the distress one experiences at the sight of suffering, which might bring forth many tears but does not incline one to do something to relieve that sorrow or misery.

The merciful person is saddened by any kind of human wretchedness, physical or moral, for he sees the afflicted ones as brothers or sisters in Christ, and beseeches His mercy on their behalf, at least by prayer if other means are not possible or feasible. It might be the wretchedness or suffering of poverty, sickness, business failure, loss of a friend, the moral misery of habitual sin, or other such misfortunes.

God's Merciful Plan

The whole story of our redemption is a story of God's merciful love, of His special goodness toward sinners. In His infinite love, God created man in His own likeness and image, making him capable of sharing in that love and truth which is a sharing in the very life of God. But when the first man and woman rebelled against the restrictions in God's plan for them, causing them to lose the divine life of grace and the possibility of entering heaven, the eternal Father, in His merciful love, revealed that He would send His only-begotten Son to rescue them from the pitiful state into which they had fallen.

Thus, the Son of God became man in order to share in the misery of the human lot and to rescue man from it. *"It was right,"* says St. Paul, *"that He should in all things be made like his brethren, that He might become a merciful and faithful high priest to expiate the sins of the people"* (Heb. 2:17). Jesus, being the image of the Father, by His words and actions, and especially by His Passion and death, makes visible the mercy of the Father.

Conditions of God's Mercy

1) Repentance and conversion: The greatest sin imaginable is not too great to be forgiven, if the sinner is truly repentant. Thus we see the limitless mercy of God toward sinners, all of whom He wills to be saved. *"I desire not the death of the wicked, but that the wicked turn from his way and live"* (Ez. 33:11). Even to the worst of sinners God gives sufficient grace to repent and amend their ways. *"If your sins be as scarlet, they shall be made white as wool"* (Is. 1:18).

While hardened sinners are never denied the grace of conversion, they can and at times do resist God's invitations and inspirations, clinging to their own will and ideas. Speaking of this resistance to God's merciful love, Pope John Paul II commented:

> The only thing that can limit its effect in human beings is the lack of good will, that is, of repentance and conversion; or in positive terms, a persistent, stubborn rejection of grace and truth, especially by refusing the testimony of the cross and resurrection of Christ.[2]

One refuses the testimony of the cross who closes his mind and heart to the redeeming power and love of Christ's Passion and death. One must believe that Christ's sacrifice is infinite in its redeeming and healing power, more than sufficient to enable the sinner to make the sacrifice of letting go of his sinful ways.

> To believe in the Crucified Son . . . means believing that love exists in the world and is stronger than any evil in which an individual person or race or the world is ensnared. To believe in such love as this is to believe in mercy, for mercy is a necessary component for love. It is even another name for love as well as the specific way in which love is revealed and exercised against the real evil in the world that tempts and besieges human beings and works its way into their hearts.[3]

2) Works of mercy: While both the Old and New Testaments reveal the limitless dimensions of God's mercy, the New Testament goes beyond the Old in its emphasis on mercy as a divine characteristic which men must share. If they are to be the recipients of mercy, they must practice mercy. There are as many ways of exercising works of mercy as there are human needs. However, tradition has arranged the most common works of mercy into two series of seven as follows: *corporal works of mercy*: to feed the hungry, to give drink to the thirsty, to clothe the naked, to give shelter to those who need it, to visit the sick, to minister to prisoners, and to bury the dead; and *spiritual works of mercy*: to admonish the sinner, to instruct the ignorant, to counsel the doubtful, to comfort the sorrowful, to bear wrongs patiently, to forgive all injuries, and to pray for the living and the dead.

Our Blessed Lord, after explaining various ways in which merciful love responds to offenses and enemies, declares how we must be merciful to our fellow humans if we expect to receive divine mercy:

> Do not judge, and you shall not be judged; do not condemn, and you shall not be condemned. Forgive and you shall be forgiven; give, and it shall be given to you, good measure, pressed down, shaken together, running over, shall they pour into your lap. For the measure you measure with will be measured back to you (Lk. 6:37, 38).

Our Savior laid down the same condition for mercy in the prayer He taught us: *"Forgive us our trespasses, as we forgive those who trespass against us."* (Mt. 6:12). Those few words which we repeat often can bring us a more lenient or a more severe judgment according as we are willing or not willing to forgive others. *"Judgment is without mercy to him who has not shown mercy"* (Jas. 2:13). So it is not God who puts limits on His mercy, but rather we ourselves.

Mercy Involves Sacrifice

Christ gave the ultimate expression of merciful love in His sacrifice on Calvary, and He asks that we return His love through sacrifices of merciful love toward our neighbor in need. Each passing day, with our minor faults and self-centered decisions, we add to our need of mercy. It is true, as St. Peter says, that *"charity covers a multitude of sins"* (1 Pet. 4:8), but that is only because of the merciful sacrifice of Christ which gives our merciful deeds their redeeming quality.

The more we need God's mercy, therefore, the more we should practice the spiritual and corporal works of mercy. It is a most efficacious way of attracting the merciful Heart of Our Savior to our needs, for *"as long as you did it for one of these, the least of my brethren, you did it for me"* (Mt. 25:40). Although we all need God's mercy, we do not sense that need as we do the needs of the body. We do not feel the soul's needs as we feel the hunger of the body. And for that reason we can easily forget Christ's warning as to the importance of showing mercy if we are to receive mercy, and can be unforgiving in regard to another's offenses, and unmindful in regard to his needs. Selfishness in all its forms is an obstacle to mercy, for it is directly opposed to charity which is essentially self-giving, self-sacrificing. That is why St. Leo the Great speaks of the *"sacrificial offerings"* of works of mercy, and sees them as a fruitful remote preparation for our union with Christ in the Eucharistic sacrifice of the Mass. Any act of mercy of whatever kind pleases God, for He sees it as a reflection of His own merciful love.

Only at the end of the world will love conquer all of the innermost sources of evil in all the elect, and bring forth the reign of justice and charity. For the basis of this final victory, says Pope John Paul II, *"is the cross and death of Christ.... In our state and in the course of human history, love must be shown explicitly in the form of mercy and exercised in that form."*[4]

Mercy Enriches

While one motivated by true charity does not perform good deeds in order to enrich himself, the fact is that he cannot perform charitable deeds without enriching himself. And so it is with works of mercy. The one who gives often benefits more than the one who receives. Give to the poor and you receive from Christ. The benefit you bestow is of the natural and temporal order, whereas the benefit you receive is supernatural and eternal. And God always outgives us a hundredfold. St. Leo the Great speaks beautifully of merciful love, referring especially to almsgiving.

> No act of devotion on the part of the faithful gives God more pleasure than that which is lavished on the poor. Where He finds charity with its loving concern, there He recognizes the reflection of His own fatherly care.... In these acts of giving do not fear the lack of means. A generous spirit is itself great wealth. There can be no shortage of material for generosity when it is Christ who feeds and Christ who is fed. In all this activity there is present the hand of Him who multiplies the bread by breaking it, and increases it by giving it away. The giver of alms should be free of anxiety and full of joy. His gain will be greatest when he keeps back least for himself.[5]

St. Basil the Great speaks in a similar vein:

> When you give to the poor you are bearing fruit which you will gather in for yourself, since the reward for good works goes to those who perform them. Give to the hungry man, and what you give becomes yours, and indeed it returns to you with interest.[6]

When we have nothing to share with others in a material way, there is always the spiritual gift of prayer and sacrifice, which can be offered to God for the needs of others. When one learns to give of himself in this way, he is never without the means of giving.

How much some are willing to spend on temporal satisfactions and enjoyments that bring no eternal reward. They are industrious about investing their wealth in ways that bring a material reward, but have little concern about investing some of it with the needy, where it increases the one kind of wealth they can take with them to the life beyond.

Divine Mercy and the World's Misery

Since God is infinitely merciful, and since mercy seeks to eliminate the misery of another, why does God allow such misery to exist in the world? That is a question many ask. It even makes some doubt God's concern for us, His providence over all that He has created. How do we reconcile the providence of God, and so much misery in the world? Why does He leave so many in their misery, their sickness, their dire poverty?

God is concerned primarily about our eternal welfare. Not that He is not concerned about our welfare in this world, but as St. Paul declares, *"I reckon that the sufferings of the present time are not worthy to be compared to the glory to come that will be revealed in us"* (Rom. 8:18). In His infinite wisdom God can bring good out of evil. He can use the sufferings of this world to cancel the debt of sin, the punishment of which would be far greater in the life to come. Too, He can use the misery of some to bring out the mercy of others. If there were no suffering in the world, there would be no mercy, for the object of mercy is the misery of others.

But the bottom line is that suffering in this world is the result of sin. Sin entered into the world with the rebellion of our first parents, and its effects are continually compounded by sins of avarice, hatred, lust, pride, jealousy, and other such sins, the roots of which we all have. God cannot remove sin from the world without taking away man's free will, which He will not do. If man abuses his freedom, he must take the consequences. The unfortunate thing is that many suffer because of the abuses of others.

Only in the light of faith can we understand that the *spiritual misery* of sin is a far greater evil than the *physical misery* of poverty, sickness, and so forth. Because of this the eternal Father's merciful love led Him to send His only-begotten Son into the world to remove the greatest evil for the whole of mankind, the loss of friendship with God and the exclusion from heaven. Thus our divine Redeemer by His life, Passion and death won the graces to restore man to His friendship, reopened to mankind the gates of heaven, and established the Church as the channel through which the graces won by His Passion would be dispensed to mankind. He did not remove suffering from human life. On the contrary, He declared that only by carrying one's cross (which implies suffering) can one be His disciple. Pope John Paul II speaks of this paradox of divine mercy in his encyclical already referred to:

> The true and proper meaning of mercy is not simply that one gazes, however penetratingly and compassionately, on moral or physical or material evil. No, what is special about true mercy is that it discerns, fosters and elicits good from all forms of evil in the world and in human beings. Thus understood, mercy is the central teaching of Christ's messianic message and the power that explains His work.

Seeing Christ in His Members

The true practice of mercy requires a deep faith that makes the mystery of the Mystical Body of Christ a vivid reality, enabling one to seek Christ in those in need, ever aware that *"as long as you did it for one of these, the least of my brethren, you did it for me"* (Mt. 25:40).

Since goodness begets goodness, the more one ponders prayerfully that mystery and God's merciful love toward sinful mankind, the more he begins to see the various forms of human wretchedness as wounds in the Mystical Body of Christ, for example, the poor, the sick, the sinner, the abandoned, and the more he is inspired to reach out, whether by prayer or action, a helping hand.

It seems that no one in our present-day world had a truer understanding of the virtue of mercy, and no one practiced it more heroically than Mother Teresa of Calcutta, as her words testify:

> The shut-in, the unwanted, the unloved, the alcoholics, the dying destitutes, the abandoned and the lonely, the outcasts and the untouchables, the leprosy sufferers, all those who are burdens to human society, all who have lost hope and faith in life . . . (all of these) look to us for comfort. If we turn our back on them, we turn it on Christ. . . . I appeal to everyone to give your hands to serve Christ in the poor, and your hearts to love Him in them.

Mother Teresa bore with joy the hardships involved in caring for the unfortunate and unwanted, and could say with St. Paul, *"I rejoice now in the sufferings I bear for your sake; and what is lacking in the sufferings of Christ I fill up in my flesh for His Body, which is the Church"* (Col. 1:24).

"Blessed are the merciful, they shall obtain mercy" (Mt. 5:7).

Chapter Notes

1. St. Thomas Aquinas, *Summa Theologiae,* II-II, q. 28
2. *Rich in Mercy,* n. 13
3. *Ibid.,* n. 7
4. *Ibid.,* n. 8
5. St. Leo the Great, Homily, *Roman Breviary*
6. St. Basil the Great, *ibid.*

Chapter 16
Blessed are the Clean of Heart

The sixth of the eight beatitudes that our Savior gave in the Sermon on the Mount is: *"Blessed are the clean of heart, for they shall see God"* (Mt. 5:8). We will examine this brief maxim to see in what sense, and why, it is true.

Clean of Heart

When the Scriptures refer to the *heart,* it is not the physical organ that is meant, but rather the source and seat of the dispositions of soul in the very depths of one's being, the source of one's choices and commitments, whether good or evil. In keeping with this broader meaning of the word, theologians point out that the *purity of heart* referred to in this beatitude is the fruit of a twofold purification: a purification of the *will,* or the affective side of our nature (of undue attachments to persons, places, things, etc.) in which disorderly attachments are rejected, and which is effected by the exercise of the moral virtues and the gifts of the Holy Spirit that perfect them; and a purification of the *mind,* by which all errors against faith are rejected, and which is effected by the gifts of understanding and knowledge.

This cleanness of heart presupposes that God is present in our *mind* as the object of our *faith,* and present in the *will* as the object of *hope* and *charity*. That is to say, our minds must be enlivened by a *living faith,* made vital by the state of grace and charity, for only as such can faith help us to see God and be called the beginning of eternal life in us. Too, the assent of the mind to what God has revealed would not be meritorious, if that assent did not come from the command of the will motivated by the virtue of charity, the supernatural love of God. Thus, charity gives supernatural life to faith, as the soul gives natural life to the body.[1]

They Shall See God

The declaration that the clean of heart shall see God does not mean that such persons will experience visions of some sort. It refers rather to seeing God with the eyes of the mind, and an awareness of His presence in daily life. God is *Love*, and the many expressions of His will in the events of daily life (even trials) are expressions of His love at work. The *pure of heart* recognize that love (that is, they see God) and surrender their will to His. God is *Truth*, and His word contained in the Scriptures and handed down by the Church is an expression of His truth. The *pure of heart* recognize that truth (that is, they see God) and humbly submit their judgment to the truth of faith. Thus St. Thomas does not hesitate to say that in this very life *"when the eye of the mind is purified by the gift of the Spirit one can, so to speak, see God."*[2] Since we are speaking of seeing the love and truth that is God, as *seeing God,* it will be helpful to see the various grades of our knowledge of God.

1) The natural power of understanding

Man can arrive at a knowledge of God's existence and attributes as known by the natural light of reason, and this apart from supernatural revelation.

2) The supernatural light of faith

Faith is a special gift of God bestowed at baptism that becomes operative at the age of reason, and disposes and enables one to believe all that God has revealed for our salvation on the infallible authority of Him who revealed it. It is a divine light elevating and perfecting the intellect, bringing knowledge and conviction of the supernatural order, an entirely different order of being than that known by the senses. While it brings knowledge of supreme truths, it does not bring an understanding of them, nor, of itself, does it add to the goodness of man. As we have seen, only faith vitalized by charity and expressed in action is meritorious before God. *"It was ignorance of this fundamental philosophical truth,"* comments Fr. Walter Farrell, O.P., *"that was the root of the exaggerated optimism of Luther and the reformers relative to faith."*[3]

3) The Gift of Understanding

Since faith enables the mind to assent to the truths of revelation, not because one understands them but because God revealed them, it needs the *gift of understanding* which brings a deeper insight into the things of God, a fuller understanding of the mysteries accepted by faith. This gift of the Holy Spirit lifts us above our natural mode of knowing (which depends on the light of reason) and enables the intellect, as by a divine instinct, to grasp the deeper meaning of revealed truths. It involves a supernatural mode of knowing in which the mind understands divine truths more by intuition than by the natural powers of reasoning. In every article of faith there is always something which is mysterious or hidden, some obscurity due to the weakness of the human mind. While the gift of understanding does not remove the veil of obscurity, it gives, even in this life, a certain foretaste of the divine manifestations of the life to come.

The pages of Sacred Scripture are full of instruction, but a fuller and deeper grasp of the divine message they contain requires the gift of understanding. For that reason those pages do not reveal their secrets to one who is out of tune with God, that is, one not possessing the divine life of grace.

This gift does not enable one to see God as He is in Himself; that is reserved for heaven. Rather it helps one to see, as St. Thomas explains, what God is not;[4] and as one knows God more perfectly in this life, he better understands that God exceeds everything that the human mind can imagine.

This gift of understanding purifies the mind of errors that can result from too worldly or too self-centered judgments, giving one a true understanding of God's laws and commandments and counsels. This gift is not reserved for a select few far advanced in the way of sanctity. It is possessed by every soul in the state of grace, and is needful for the normal living of the Christian life. Yet it is not possessed in the same degree by all, just as the growth of sanctifying grace in the soul is not

4) The Gift of Knowledge

While the *gift of understanding* enables one to penetrate the revealed truths of our faith, bringing a deeper understanding of them through the special enlightenment of the Holy Spirit, the *gift of knowledge* is a special enlightenment in rightly judging created things in relation to the purpose for which God created them. It enables one to judge the true worth of creatures as coming from God, and intended for His glory. In a word, it enables one, by a divine instinct, to have a correct estimation of the present life in relation to eternal life. Under the impulse of this gift, the Holy Spirit gives intuitive insights as to the emptiness and vanity of the allurements of this world, the temporariness and uncertainty of earthly things, and their powerlessness to bring true and lasting happiness. If these insights take hold of the mind and heart, and one (aided by grace) determines to rely on the guidance of the Holy Spirit, he is freed from the attractions of the world, free to follow God's plan for his life with a detachment of heart. *"If you abide in my word . . . you shall know the truth, and the truth shall make you free"* (Jn. 8:31).

The world then ceases to be an obstacle to seeing God and becomes an aid, a constant reminder of the God who made it. The starry heaven, the mountains, the landscape, the sunset, become mirrors of God's beauty and wisdom. In nature such a one is constantly seeing *"God's footsteps,"* as spiritual writers express it. When suffering, misfortune or sickness comes, it is seen to have its place in the light of Christ's redeeming Passion.

The detachment, or purity of heart, that this gift helps to effect is a gradual process; but it is utterly impossible without the insights and urgings of the Holy Spirit, and our cooperation with His gifts.

The gift of knowledge guides one with certitude concerning what we must believe or not believe.[5] One in whom this gift is intensively operative without even having studied theology, instinctively senses that some practice, or devotion, or teaching, or counsel is or is not in accord with the true faith. The fact that many true mystics were simple uneducated persons bears this out. Our Lord referred to it in the Gospel: *"Father, Lord of heaven and earth, to you I offer praise; for what you have hidden from the learned and the clever, you have revealed to the merest children"* (Mt. 11:25).

Vices That Impede Spiritual Vision

St. Thomas dedicates an entire question to two vices that are special obstacles to the gifts of understanding and knowledge. They are *lust* which causes spiritual blindness, and *gluttony* which causes dullness of the spiritual sense. Both of these are sins of the flesh. He describes these vices as follows:

> Carnal vices, namely gluttony and lust, are concerned with pleasures of the sense of touch in matters of food and sex; and these are the most impetuous of all pleasures of the body. For this reason these vices cause a man's attention to be very firmly fixed on corporeal things, so that in consequence man's operation in regard to intelligible things is weakened, more however, by lust than by gluttony, inasmuch as sexual pleasures are more vehement than those of the table. Wherefore lust gives rise to blindness of the mind, which excludes almost entirely the knowledge of spiritual things, while dullness of these senses arises from gluttony, which makes a man weak in regard to the same intelligible things.... Dullness of sense in connection with understanding denotes a certain weakness of the mind as to the consideration of spiritual things; while blindness of the mind implies a complete privation of the knowledge of such things. Both are opposed to the gift of understanding, whereby a man knows spiritual goods by apprehending them, and has a subtle penetration of their inmost nature.[6]

A certain spiritual blindness is characteristic of those referred to as lukewarm souls. Every person in the state of grace possesses the gifts of understanding and knowledge, but those gifts can be activated only by the Holy Spirit. And the lukewarm are so captivated by the things of the world, and their inner attention and affections focused so strongly on them, that the insights and inspirations of the Holy Spirit are hardly noticed or are ignored. They never arrive at a clear awareness of God's presence in the world, in their neighbor, in the crosses and trials of life. A spirit of prayer is foreign to them.

However, sins of the flesh are not the only ones that impair spiritual vision. The deepest rooted and most subtle of the weaknesses of our fallen nature is pride, and it is that weakness that so often becomes an obstacle to the action of the Holy Spirit and the divine light He brings to perfect the gift of faith. For that reason, another basic requisite for that purity of heart that enables one to see God is humility. We call to mind again St. Thomas's reminder that *"humility removes pride, whereby a man refuses to submit himself to the truth of faith."*[7] The divine truth that is God is expressed in His revealed word and handed down by the Church. If one is so attached to his own judgments that he refuses to accept the official teaching of the Church, he places an obstacle to the enlightening and liberating action of the Holy Spirit. It is the Holy Spirit who safeguards the deposit of faith in the Church down through the centuries, and it is that same divine Person who creates a *clean heart* in those open to His action (Ps. 51:10).

There are many degrees of *cleanness of heart* corresponding to the different degrees of growth in grace and holiness. This is true because God gives his graces and gifts in the measure that we do not place obstacles in the way, in the measure that we are *clean of heart.*

Ordinarily in the natural process of knowing, no thinking is possible without our mind relying on internal images formed from things perceived by the external senses from which our ideas are abstracted. However, when the Holy Spirit acts through the gifts of understanding and knowledge, those internal images are not needed, for then one is enlightened by divine instinct rather than by the natural aid of reason. This brings an immediate and deeper understanding of the divine truths, a certitude in judging what is to be believed or not believed, and a greater awareness of God in His creation.

It is this action of the Holy Spirit through the gifts in more advanced stages of *cleanness of heart* that is referred to as *infused contemplation*.

God has given us a free will, and demands our cooperation in His work in our sanctification and salvation. But He is the principal cause of the growth of grace in the soul. We are only secondary causes, our work being to remove the obstacles that interfere with His work, to trust in His guidance, and to give Him a free hand to deal with us as He will. This might seem like a simple solution, but it demands a painful discipline of our fallen and self-seeking nature. A crucifixion has to precede the resurrection. Neither of these is possible without the aid of the Holy Spirit. We would do well to make our own the words of the Psalmist: *"A clean heart create for me, O God, and a steadfast spirit renew within me. Cast me not out from your presence, and your Holy Spirit take not from me"* (Ps. 51:12).

Chapter Notes

1. *Cf. Summa Theologiae,* II-II, q. 4, a. 3
2. St. Thomas Aquinas, *Summa Theologiae,* I-II, q. 69, a. 2, ad 3
3. Fr. Walter Farrell, O.P., *Companion to the Summa,* III, q. 16
4. St. Thomas Aquinas, *Summa Theologiae,* II-II, q. 8, a. 7
5. *Cf. Summa Theologiae,* II-II, q. 9, a. 2, ad 1
6. *Ibid.,* q. 15, a. 2, 3
7. *Ibid.,* q. 161, a. 5

Chapter 17

Redemptive Suffering

It was not in the plan of God that suffering and death be a part of human existence. That they became the lot of the human race was not God's doing, but man's. God made man in His own likeness and image, desiring to share with him His own infinite happiness and goodness. He endowed man with special gifts that made him immune from all suffering and free of the necessity of undergoing death. These gifts, however, were not essential to human nature and could be lost.

God endowed man with free will, in order that man would have to freely choose God above all things before entering into the beatitude of heaven. But, as we know, it was man's free will that upset what God had planned, for our first parents rebelled against the restriction placed on their freedom, wishing to decide for themselves what they could do or not do. As a result, they not only were not admitted into heaven, but they lost for themselves and their descendants those gifts that made them immune from suffering and death.

The Need of Redemption

Because of his sin Adam was utterly displeasing to God, and because of the loss of grace he was unable to do anything that would win God's favor. God could have left mankind in that helpless state of eternal separation from Himself, or He could simply have pardoned man, restoring all the gifts he had lost. But God would accept neither of those solutions.

In His mercy He sent His only-begotten Son to become a member of the human race to offer, on behalf of mankind, the infinite reparation that divine justice demanded. The divine Word took on a human body and soul in order that He could suffer to pay the penalty that a just God demanded in expiation for the sins of the world. Because He was *man*, He could pay the debt on the part of the human race; and because He was *God*, the reparation He offered was infinite.

Why the Passion?

Christ could have offered sufficient reparation without the Passion, for His every deliberate act was one of infinite love, sufficient to redeem the whole of mankind. But the Father willed the way of the Passion, the way of suffering. St. Thomas Aquinas explains why:[1]

1) The Passion made God's love for us so much more manifest, Jesus having suffered so much on our behalf. *"You have been bought at a great price"* (1 Cor. 6:20). *"Greater love than this no man has"* (Jn. 15:13). By His Passion man is stirred to love God in return, and in this love of God lies man's perfection.

2) It helps man to realize the enormous evil of sin, when God would go to such length to make reparation for it.

3) It helps us to see more clearly the *justice* of God, who willed the death of His own Son to repair for sin; and the *mercy* of God in the way He applies to sinners the merits of Christ's sufferings.

4) It gives such a wonderful example of *humility* and *obedience,* those indispensable virtues in loving God. Through *pride* and *disobedience* Adam refused God the love and homage due Him. Through *humility* and *obedience* Christ offered His Father the love and submission due Him.

5) It shows clearly the immense love of Jesus for His Father, whom He obeyed *"even to the death of the cross"* (Phil. 2:8). When Christ went forth to the Passion, He told the apostles that He did so *"that the world may know that I love the Father"* (Jn. 14:31).

6) The Passion of Christ was especially valuable in teaching the necessity of suffering if fallen man (having the use of reason) is to attain his eternal salvation.

Additional scriptural passages clearly testify to the need of the Passion in fulfillment of the divine plan: *"The Son of man must be lifted up, that whosoever believes in Him may not perish, but have everlasting life"* (Jn. 3:14). *"Shall I not drink the cup that the Father has given Me?"* (Jn. 18:11) *"Ought not Christ to have suffered these things, and so enter into His glory?"* (Lk. 24:26) To His disciples before the Ascension: *"Recall those words I spoke to you when I was still with you; everything written about Me in the law of Moses and the prophets and the psalms had to be fulfilled. . . . Thus it is written that the Messiah must suffer and rise again from the dead"* (Lk. 24:44, 46).

Our Sharing in the Redemption

By the sufferings in His human nature during the Passion by which mankind was redeemed, Christ gave to all suffering experienced in the members of His Mystical Body *a redeeming power* when accepted and offered up in union with His Passion. As Pope John Paul II wrote: *"In bringing about the Redemption through suffering, Christ raised human suffering to the level of the Redemption. Thus each man, in his sufferings, can also become a sharer in the redemptive suffering of Christ."*²

Speaking on one occasion to a group of infirm persons suffering from various illnesses and handicaps, Pope John Paul II recalled the great mercy of Christ in the many times He miraculously cured the lame, the blind, the deaf, the leprous; and how, to save the newlyweds embarrassment, He miraculously changed water into wine. But, he said, there is here an even greater miracle, a greater mercy when *He gives to human suffering a supernatural value.* All the miracles mentioned were changes on the purely natural level; that is, the gift given in each miracle was some benefit of the natural order. But when He transforms human suffering, giving it a supernatural value, a supernatural power, that is a far greater gift, a far greater miracle. But it is a gift so little appreciated, for it is known only in the light of faith; and the faith of many is weak. How many opportunities for spiritual growth and for helping others are wasted in complaining about the crosses of life.

Filling Up What is Lacking

St. Paul was so filled with the idea of the redemptive power of suffering that he exclaimed, *"I find joy in the sufferings I endure for you. In my own flesh I fill up what is lacking in the sufferings of Christ for the sake of His Body, the Church"* (Col. 1:24).

Those words of St. Paul are a puzzle to some, for they seem to imply that something is lacking in the Passion of Christ. St. Paul is speaking here of the Mystical Body of Christ, made up of Christ, *the Head,* and all souls in the state of grace who are *the members* of His Body. It is in the members of His Body that something is lacking. Shortly before He died Christ exclaimed: *"It is consummated!"* He says in effect: *"All is accomplished that I came to do. By My painful obedience to the Father I offered infinite reparation for the sins of mankind and merited the restoration of grace for the whole human race."* There is no grace that comes to any human that was not merited by Him. He had no need of any other in redeeming the human race. But Jesus willed that *the mystery of His Passion continue on in us,* so that we may be associated with Him in the work of redemption. Jesus could have accomplished this alone, but *He willed to need us* in order to apply the infinite merits of His Passion to souls. Pope Pius XII spoke of this in his encyclical on the Mystical Body:

> In carrying out the work of redemption Christ wishes to be helped by the members of His Body. This is not because He is indigent or weak, but rather because He so willed it for the greater glory of His spotless Spouse. Dying on the cross, He left to the Church the immense treasury of the Redemption. Towards this she (the Church) contributed nothing. But when those graces come to be distributed, not only does He share this task of sanctification with His Church, but He wants it, in a way, to be due to her action. What a deep mystery ... that the salvation of many depends on the *prayers* and

voluntary penances which the members of the Mystical Body offer for that intention, and on the assistance of pastors of souls and of the faithful, especially fathers and mothers of families, which they must offer to our divine Savior as though they were His associates.

Think of it. By accepting willingly and without complaint the little inconveniences, irritations, frustrations, delays, and setbacks which God in His providence allows to come our way, we can pay in part the debt that we, or others, have incurred by our sins. Because God is *just,* He demands that the debt of suffering be paid, but because He is *merciful,* He allows one person to *"fill up what is lacking"* in another member of the Mystical Body which is the Church. As St. Thomas Aquinas says, *"By the cooperation of Christ's satisfaction, much lighter penalty suffices than one that is proportionate to the sin."*[3]

Embrace the Cross

The cross was the instrument chosen by God for the redemption of mankind. That is why Our Savior refers to the hardships and fatigue and trials of daily life as the *"cross"* that we must embrace if we are to be His disciples. Accepting them in union with the Passion of Christ gives them a redeeming power, a redeeming value, a share in the fruits of His Passion. The *"cross"* can include everything that goes against the grain, and that can be an endless list. To mention a few examples: physical pain, mental anguish, disappointments, depression, humiliations, delays, sickness, poverty, setbacks in business, loneliness, being misunderstood or falsely accused, being rejected, hardships and fatigue of daily routine, sadness at the death of a family member or friend, the difficult sacrifices in fulfilling God's commandments and the duties of our state in life. All these entail suffering, and are part of the penalty of our fallen nature inherited from our first parents.

We naturally try to eliminate all forms of suffering from our life, but insofar as they are beyond our power to control, they are part of God's providence.

God foresees them, allows them, and can bring good out of them if we trust in Him. Suffering in some form or other is the lot of every human, saint as well as sinner. But since our attitude toward them can make them profitable or unprofitable and even increase our misery, it is important to see them in the light of the Gospel, in the light of God's providence. That is because suffering can get one down, or it can bring one closer to God. It can make one resentful and bitter, even blaming God for his lot, or it can make one more conscious of God's providence at work. It can make one turn in on himself in self-pity, or it can help one to open out upon the world in apostolic and redemptive action.

That suffering is not something good in itself, is clear from the great number of Christian institutions (hospitals, sanitariums, etc.) established to alleviate human suffering. While the ills, hardships and setbacks of life can be instrumental in spiritual growth, in themselves they are something evil. Christians are not forbidden to seek the comforts of life, or to enjoy lawful amusements, or to seek remedies from pain. The Church does not glorify suffering for its own sake; but one does glorify God by the loving acceptance of suffering when the fulfillment of His will entails it.

Testimony of the Pope

We have already mentioned the frequent comments of Pope John Paul II on the salvific value of suffering when addressing the sick and disabled. He wrote at length on that topic in his Apostolic Letter *Salvifici Doloris,* in which he remarked:

> Christ does not speak in the abstract.... He says: "Follow Me! Come! Take part through your suffering in this work of saving the world, a salvation achieved through My suffering ... through My Cross...." Without the vision of faith one has a sense of the uselessness of suffering. This feeling not only consumes the person interiorly, but makes him feel a burden to others ... and useless to himself. The discovery of the salvific meaning of suffering in union with Christ transforms this depressing feeling. Faith in sharing the suffering

of Christ brings with it the interior certainty that the suffering person completes what is lacking in Christ's afflictions; the certainty that in the spiritual dimension of the work of redemption *he is serving*, like Christ, *the salvation of his brothers and sisters.* Therefore he is carrying out an irreplaceable service.

Mary's Role

In the divine plan, Mary was destined to share in a unique way in the redemptive mission of her Son, and therefore in His suffering. She received an early confirmation of this at the words of Simeon that a sword of sorrow would pierce her heart (Lk. 2:35). On Calvary Mary's suffering, beside the suffering of Jesus, reached an intensity which can hardly be imagined from a human point of view, but which was supernaturally fruitful for the redemption of the world. As the application of the fruits of the redemption will continue until the end of the world, so will the unique role of Mary in the distribution of those graces. Pope John Paul II speaks of this in relation to the Immaculate Heart of the Mother of God:

> The Divine Redeemer wishes to penetrate the soul of every sufferer through the heart of His holy Mother, the first and most exalted of all the redeemed. As though by a continuation of that motherhood which by the power of the Holy Spirit had given Him life, the dying Christ conferred upon the ever Virgin Mary a new kind of motherhood, spiritual and universal, towards all human beings, so that every individual, during the pilgrimage of faith, might remain together with her, closely united to Him unto the Cross, and so that every form of suffering, given fresh life by the power of the Cross, should become no longer the weakness of man but the power of the Cross.[4]

Not My Will...

In spite of Jesus' willing acceptance of the Passion and His insistence that His followers must embrace the crosses of life, His human nature shrank from pain just as ours does. We see that in the Garden of Gethsemane; yet He willingly accepted it when commanded by His heavenly Father. *"I seek not my own will, but the will of*

Him who sent Me" (Jn. 5:30). The same should be the goal of His followers. Those sincerely seeking to grow closer to Christ know that it must be by way of the cross. Each day brings many little opportunities to submit willingly to various kinds of self-giving that go against the grain. Like Christ, we too can pray in certain painful situations, *"Let this chalice pass from me,"* as long as we are willing to add, *"nevertheless, not my will but Yours be done"* (Lk. 22:42).

Chapter Notes

1. St. Thomas Aquinas, *Summa Theologiae,* III, q. 46, a. 3; III, q. 48, a. 1, ad 2
2. Pope John Paul II, *Salvifici Doloris*
3. *Ibid.,* q. 49, a. 3, ad 2
4. *Ibid.*

Chapter 18

Reparation for Sin

When the Mother of God appeared in Fatima to three small children with a plea for prayer and penance, part of her message included the following warning: *"Pray, pray very much. Make sacrifices for sinners, for many souls go to hell because there is no one to offer prayers and sacrifices for them."*

What Our Lady is asking for in this plea is reparation on behalf of sinners. She is asking that we do for them what her Son did for us. Our Blessed Lord took upon His shoulders the burden of our sins, and paid the price for them. We are not able to shoulder the whole burden, pay the whole price for the sins of others; but what little we can do, when placed in the hands of the Blessed Mother of us all, can accomplish much toward lessening their debt of punishment, and opening their hearts to the healing and strengthening grace of God.

It is true that these souls have rejected the graces and inspirations offered them by God, but Our Lady implies that many of them can be saved by the prayers and sacrifices of others, if among her children some are generous enough to put themselves out for this purpose.

In recent times many have contributed generously to help victims of famine in various parts of the world; but that was to save them from *death of the body.* The *death of the soul,* a far greater tragedy, is caused by the deliberate grave violation of God's law. If that rejection persists until the end of one's earthly existence, it is eternal death. So we can see the anguish of the Mother of God at the loss of her children, for whom her Son gave His life.

Filling Up What is Wanting

What Our Lady is asking for in the plea expressed above, is simply that we do what St. Paul did time and again, namely, to *"fill up what is wanting in the sufferings of Christ,"* that is, in those members of Christ's Body who have turned away from Him, and who will not turn back to Him unless other members of His Body win that grace for them by their prayers and sacrifices.

Those who remain unmoved by such a plea from our Blessed Mother, seem to say along with Cain, *"Am I my brother's keeper?"* (Gen. 4:9) Keep in mind that the teaching of Our Savior on love of neighbor is a *commandment,* not merely a *counsel.* Our neighbor is not just the person who lives next door, but someone in need; and Our Lady called our attention to many souls in dire need, in danger of eternal punishment, souls who are our brothers and sisters in Christ.

There is but one virtue of charity by which we love God and neighbor, and we love both with the same intensity of that virtue. That means if our concern for others in need is feeble, so is our love of God. And remember Our Lord's warning that *"the measure you measure with will be measured back to you"* (Lk. 6:38). From that, it follows that the more we help those in need, especially dying sinners, the more we will be sustained by the grace of God in that crucial moment. And finally, the Lord reminds us, *"What you do for the least of my brethren, you do it for Me"* (Mt. 25:40).

Need we more incentive, then, to heed the pleas of Our Lady for souls in danger of eternal loss? What can I do? I can pray for them. But what kind of sacrifices can I make for them? The angel who appeared to the three children at Fatima prior to the coming of Our Lady answered that question: *"Make everything you do a sacrifice, and offer it to God as an act of reparation for the sins by which He is offended, and in supplication for the conversion of sinners."*

The decree on the Church in the Second Vatican Council also pointed out how the ordinary routine of each day affords many opportunities for "spiritual sacrifices" which give glory to God and contribute to the salvation of souls.

The laity, dedicated to Christ and anointed by the Holy Spirit, are marvelously called and equipped to produce in themselves ever more abundant fruits of the Spirit. For all their works, prayers, apostolic endeavors, their ordinary married and family life, their daily labor, their mental and physical relaxation, if carried out in the Spirit, and even the hardships of life, if borne patiently — all of these become *spiritual sacrifices* acceptable to God through Jesus Christ.[1]

And recall, too, how David prayed after he had sinned, *"My sacrifice, O God, is a contrite spirit; a heart contrite and humbled, O God, you will not spurn"* (Ps. 51). Every person in the state of grace is frequently performing such acts as obedience to lawful authority, fulfillment of duty, and endurance of the crosses of life, all of which, if done with a *humble and contrite spirit,* are as a sacrifice before God; for they involve the humble submission of our will to God's, something the sinner refuses. They have, therefore, a reparatory value.

One can have a general intention of placing in the hands of Our Lady the fruits of all such acts as regards atonement, and in this way make much of his day a continuous *"filling up what is wanting in the Body of Christ"* (Col. 1:24).

Breaking Through the Barrier

If we can think of the straw that breaks the camel's back, we can also think of the prayer or sacrifice that breaks the sinner's resistance to God's grace, causing him to open up to the merciful Heart of the Redeemer.

If a dying sinner can be brought to make a sincere act of perfect contrition for his sins, regardless of how great or how many, God will restore grace to that soul, and change the debt of eternal punishment to one of temporal punishment, that could be satisfied in this life or in purgatory.

If, under God, we could be responsible for, or notably contribute to the salvation of just one soul, winning for that person the grace of true contrition by our prayers and sacrifices, saving it from eternal damnation, how grateful that soul would be to us for all eternity. And yet, it could be that one who is generous in his concern for souls in need, as we have explained, could be responsible for, or contribute to, the salvation of thousands of souls in the course of a lifetime.

Do we bear the trials, the frustrations, the hardships of each day, grudgingly or wholeheartedly? No one welcomes suffering as such. Our nature shrinks from it. But if seen in the light of God's providence and of the cross that Our Lord said His disciples must carry, and if borne with patience, it not only pays in part the debt of temporal punishment due to sin, but helps to mellow our rebellious and proud tendencies and form us in the image of Christ.

As Fr. F. D. Joret, O.P. states, grace is *"a crucifying thing, inasmuch as it is an inflowing of the very grace which Jesus received in its fullness and which led Him to the Cross."*[2] Our human nature recoils from the cross, but as it is perfected by grace, one more and more embraces it, to share in Christ's redeeming action for souls.

Sharing Christ's Work of Redemption

Speaking of the redeeming sacrifice of Christ, St. Thomas Aquinas wrote:

> He properly atones for an offense who offers something which the offended one loves equally, or even more than he detested the offense. But by suffering out of love and obedience, Christ gave more to God than was required to compensate for the offense of the whole human race.[3]

However, just because Christ offered to the Father sufficient satisfaction to atone for the sins of the whole human race and merited sufficient grace to enable every member of the human race to enter heaven, that does not mean that we are all automatically saved. Regarding this, St. Thomas wrote:

> Christ's passion is a *universal cause for the forgiveness of sin,* yet it *needs to be applied to each individual soul* for the cleansing of his personal sins . . . that is, He has provided for our redemption so that each of us *could be delivered* from

our sins and restored to grace, just as if a doctor were to prepare a medicine by which all sickness could be cured in the future.[4]

To share in the graces Christ merited for us, or to win for others a share in them, we must use the means of grace that He has established: the sacraments, prayer, keeping the commandments, bearing the crosses of life, voluntary penance, and so forth.

Strictly speaking, Christ needed no one, not even His Mother, in the gaining of those graces, nor in their distribution. But in His merciful plan, He chose to associate others with him in this great mystery of salvation. He allows us to share not only in the fruits of the Redemption, but in the very work of redemption itself. He depends on those who know and love Him to win needed graces for those who do not know or love Him.

Meriting and Atoning for Others

Every good act performed in the state of grace is in some measure meritorious. Yet unless it is an act of the full intensity of which we are capable, it does not bring about an immediate increase of grace.

To use a distinction employed by theologians, no one can merit *condignly* the beginning of the life of grace either for himself or for another, that is, with a *strict right* to that reward. Only Christ, *"the author of salvation"* (Heb. 2:10), can do that. Yet man can merit *congruously* the state of grace for others, that is, with a merit based on *fittingness,* the fittingness that God would hear the request of a friend. It may take, however, many good acts, many sacrifices, many rosaries, many years. And we can obtain grace for others by our prayers, relying on the mercy of God and on His promise, *"Ask and it shall be given to you"* (Mt. 7:7).

We can also help others by our good acts as regards the *satisfactory* value of them, that is, as regards paying the debt of punishment incurred by sin. That an act have satisfactory or atonement value, the state of grace presupposed, it must have two conditions:

1) It must involve some degree of difficulty, hardship, pain (physical or mental), some degree of suffering, for it goes to pay the debt of punishment. The reason for that is this: Since the sinner chooses *his own will* and rejects *God's will,* seeking some personal satisfaction in preference to due reverence and subjection to God, seeking the creature in preference to the Creator, the *pleasure* sought wrongly must be repaired by *pain.* St. Thomas explains this as follows:

> That a guilty person (a sinner) be brought back within the order of justice, it is necessary that the will *suffer privation in what he desires;* this is done by its being punished whether by being made to *forego the good things it would wish to have,* or by the *infliction of the evil things which it shrinks from enduring.*[5]

2) The difficult act or incident must be *borne patiently.* Again St. Thomas:

> If the scourges which are inflicted by God on account of sin, become in some way an act of the sufferer they acquire a satisfactory character. Now they become an act of the sufferer insofar as he accepts them for the cleansing of his sins, by taking advantage of them *patiently.* If, however, he refuses to submit to them patiently, they do not become his personal act in any way, and are not of a satisfactory character.[6]

Two Consoling Thoughts

There are two things to remember with regard to reparation for sin, for which we should be eternally grateful:

1) Because Christ has offered infinite satisfaction for the sins of mankind, a lighter punishment is required of us than otherwise would be necessary. St. Thomas speaks of this:

> It is necessary that those who sin after baptism be likened unto Christ suffering by some form of punishment or suffering which they endure in their own person; yet, by the cooperation of Christ's satisfaction, much lighter penalty suffices than one that is proportional to the sin.[7]

To give an example: It is as if we owed a debt of one hundred dollars, and not having the wherewithal to pay it, Our Savior paid ninety-nine dollars of it, but required that we pay the remaining one dollar. The disproportion is even greater than this example, considering the infinite malice of grave sin, and the infinite dignity of the Person offended, even in venial sin.

2) When one makes atonement for another, less punishment is required than if the sinner himself paid the debt. Again St. Thomas:

> As regards the payment of the debt (of temporal punishment), one man can satisfy for another, provided he be in the state of charity (grace), so that his works may avail for satisfaction. Nor is it necessary that he who satisfies for another should undergo greater punishment than the principal would have to undergo . . . because punishment derives its power of satisfaction chiefly from charity whereby a man bears it. And since greater charity is evidenced by a man satisfying for another than for himself, less punishment is required of him who satisfies for another, than of the principal. . . . Nor is it necessary that the one for whom the satisfaction is made be unable to make satisfaction himself, for even if he were able, he would be released of his debt when the other satisfies in his stead.[8]

Eucharistic Reparation

Bishop Venancio, the former administrator of the diocese in which Our Lady appeared, when asked to summarize the Fatima message, answered: *"Fatima is reparation, reparation, reparation, and especially Eucharistic reparation."* He added that this includes such things as visits to the Blessed Sacrament, holy hours and vigils, but especially the Holy Sacrifice of the Mass. This is true, for there our prayer, our sacrifices, are offered up in union with the prayers and sacrifice of Jesus.

Too, St. Thomas points out that since we are one with Christ, as members of His Body, all that He endured on the cross is ours to offer to the Father as if we ourselves had undergone that penalty.[9] Therefore, when we cannot attend Mass, a most efficacious prayer of reparation is the one taught to the three children at Fatima by the Angel, in which we offer *spiritually* to the Father the same offering (the Body and Blood of Christ) which the priest offers *sacramentally* at Mass:

Most Holy Trinity, Father, Son and Holy Spirit, I adore You profoundly. I offer You the most precious Body, Blood, Soul and Divinity of Jesus Christ present in all the tabernacles of the world, in reparation for the outrages, sacrileges and indifference by which He is offended. By the infinite merits of the Sacred Heart of Jesus and the Immaculate Heart of Mary, I beg of You the conversion of poor sinners.

Chapter Notes

1. *Lumen Gentium,* 34
2. Fr. F. D. Joret, O.P., *Dominican Life,* p. 268
3. St. Thomas Aquinas, *Summa Theologiae,* III, q. 48, a. 2
4. *Ibid.,* q. 49, a. 1, ad 3 & 4
5. St. Thomas Aquinas, *Opuscula* 3, c. 7, Ed. Rom.
6. St. Thomas Aquinas, *Suplementum,* 15, 2.
7. *Ibid.,* a. 3, ad 2
8. *Supp.* 13, 2
9. *Ibid.,* q. 48, a. 2, ad 1; & q. 69, a. 2

Chapter 19

What Has Become of Sin?

With the loss or the weakening of the gift of faith there is a gradual loss of the sense of God, and an increasing attempt to lead one's life and attain one's goals without God. And with the loss of this sense of God, there is a corresponding loss of the sense of sin, which is an offense against God.

"But," it might be asked, "doesn't one's conscience point out what is right and what is wrong?" Our conscience is precisely one of the casualties of the loss of faith, for when we are no longer guided by the light of faith which is the wisdom of God, we gradually come to accept the wisdom of the world. As Pope John Paul II pointed out in his Apostolic Exhortation *Reconciliation and Penance,* to which we are much indebted in this chapter, *"When conscience is weakened, the **sense of God** is also obscured, and as a result, with the loss of this decisive point of reference, the **sense of sin** is lost."*

With our already weakened will, our obscured judgment and inclination to evil due to original sin, and the fact that these guiding powers are further obscured and weakened by personal sin, it is not difficult to see how the Evil One, who is far more intelligent and clever than we, can gradually bring us more and more under his influence.

Objectively, the law of God seems to be disregarded on a universal scale as never before in human history; and the "sense of sin" seems to be noticeably absent in so many of those who disregard His laws. Even of those who have the gift of faith, a considerable percentage seem to have little consciousness of sin, if we are to judge from the neglect of the sacrament of penance or reconciliation.

In line with this, Cardinal Joseph Ratzinger wrote recently:

> Sin has become almost everywhere today one of those subjects that is not spoken about. Religious education of whatever kind does its best to evade it. Theater films use the word ironically or in order to entertain. Sociology and psychology attempt to unmask it as an illusion or a complex. Even the law is trying to get by more and more without a concept of guilt. It prefers to make use of sociological language, which turns the concepts of good and evil into statistics, and in its place distinguishes between normative and non-normative behavior.[1]

What Has Brought This About?

When we consider the worldly atmosphere in which we live, we can understand the uphill struggle it is to maintain, with the help of God's grace, a sense of God, a true conscience, and an awareness of sin. Referring to the present-day loss of the sense of sin, our Holy Father lists the following causes:

1) The secularism of our culture: Secularism is a system of ideas and behavior which advocates a way of life totally without God. The secular humanism which permeates much of the culture of our times has no place for God, for the supernatural, for an after-life, and is caught up with the quest for worldly gain, power and pleasure. What is recognized as sin is reduced mainly to what offends man.

In addition to those who do not believe in the existence of God, there are many who do not deny His existence, but in practice eliminate Him from their daily lives as if He did not exist. With the disappearance of an awareness of the *fatherhood of God*, there is lost an awareness of the *brotherhood of man*, with the consequent lack of awareness and concern about injustices against one's neighbor. *"It is vain,"* said the Holy Father, *"to hope that there will take root a sense of sin against men and human values, if there is not a sense of sin against God — namely the true sense of sin."*[2]

2) Errors in human sciences: Another reason for the lessening of the sense of sin in today's society, the

Holy Father points out, are *"errors made in evaluating certain findings in the human sciences."* On the basis of certain affirmations of psychology, he said, *"Concern to avoid creating feelings of guilt or placing limits on freedom leads to a refusal ever to admit of any shortcoming."*[3]

Again, through an undue extension of the criteria of sociology, all failings are blamed upon society and social structure, and the individual is declared innocent of them. Too, the Holy Father pointed out, a *"certain cultural anthropology so emphasizes the undeniable environmental and historical conditioning and influences which act on man, that it reduces his responsibility to the point of not acknowledging his ability to perform truly human acts, and therefore his ability to sin."*[4]

3) Moral relativism: The sense of sin will decline in any system of ethics which makes moral norms depend on personal judgment of the situation at hand, and not on unchanging external norms. This moral relativism, said the Holy Father, *"may take the form of an ethical system which relativizes the moral norm, denying its absolute and unconditional value, and as a consequence denying that there can be intrinsically illicit acts, independent of the circumstances in which they are performed by the subject. Herein lies a real overthrowing and downfall of moral values."* An effect of this relativism, the Holy Father pointed out, is *"such a diminution of the notion of sin as almost to reach the point of saying that sin does exist, but no one knows who commits it."*[5]

Social Sin

In the strict sense, sin is a *personal act,* a free and deliberate act on the part of an individual, and not of a group or community. The individual may be influenced by various external factors that might lessen to some extent his freedom and therefore his responsibility, but the Holy Father points out:

> The human person is free. The truth cannot be disregarded in order to place the blame for individuals' sins on external

factors such as structures, systems, or other people. . . . There is nothing so personal and untransferable in each individual as merit for virtue and responsibility for sin.[6]

Yet, at the same time, we can speak of "social sin" in the sense that practically every sin has social consequences, not only in relation to *human society* in which we live, but also and especially in relation to the *supernatural society* of which we are members, the Mystical Body of Christ. Every act of virtue helps to build up the Body of Christ, and every sin is in some way detrimental to it. Speaking of this, the Holy Father said:

> By virtue of a human solidarity which is as mysterious and intangible as it is real and concrete, each individual's sin in some way affects others. . . . There is no sin, not even the most intimate and secret one, the most strictly individual one, that exclusively concerns the person committing it. . . . With greater or lesser harm, every sin has repercussions on the entire ecclesial body and the whole human family. In this sense every sin can be considered a social sin.[7]

Yet, the Holy Father points out that while all should be conscious of the social consequences of their acts, the concept of "social sin" is sometimes applied today in a way that distorts the truth and leads to a watering down of personal sin, with the recognition only of social guilt and responsibility.

> According to this usage, he said, which can readily be seen to derive from non-Christian ideologies and systems . . . practically every sin is a social sin, in the sense that blame for it is to be placed not so much on the moral conscience of the individual, but rather on some vague entity or anonymous collectivity, such as the situation, the system, society, structures or institutions.[8]

When the Church condemns "social sins," she is condemning the *personal sins* of those who cause or support the evil situation or exploit it.

The Bishops' Report

The Pastoral Research Committee of the National Catholic Council of Bishops made a study of why the use of the sacrament of penance has so declined. The results of their study indicated that the most important factors for the disuse of the sacrament are: 1) a less dominant sense of sin; 2) a lack of clarity about the true nature of sin; 3) confusion about what is morally right or wrong; and 4) disagreement with the Church's moral teaching. We will dwell a bit on the second above-mentioned factor.

The Nature of Sin

We are all familiar with the traditional definition of sin that goes back to St. Augustine, as any thought or desire, word, deed or omission contrary to the law of God. We are familiar, too, with the distinction between *mortal* (grave) and *venial* sin; yet as the Bishops' report indicates, there is often confusion as to what they are in practice. We can define or describe sin in various ways, but it will still remain for us a mystery until we can know without obscurity the God whom we offend. No matter how we define it, our definition or description will convey little to us as to its horrible reality. We will look first at mortal sin, especially as seen in its consequences.

1) Mortal Sin: Pope John Paul, speaking of grave sin, describes it in these words:

> We call *mortal sin* the act by which man *freely and consciously* rejects God, His law, the covenant of love that God offers, preferring to turn in on himself or some created and finite reality, something contrary to the divine will. . . . This can occur . . . in every disobedience to God's commandments in *grave matter* (emphasis ours).

We can see in the Pope's description the three conditions traditionally listed for mortal sin: 1) it is a rejection of God's will, God's law, in some grave matter; 2) it must be known to be grave; 3) there must be full consent of the will to this known grave evil. While the exercise of the virtue of charity *unites us* with God by conforming our will with His, grave sin *separates* us from God by opposing His will. For this reason grave sin is the greatest evil that can befall man here and now. It is called *mortal* because by it man incurs spiritual death. One thereby voluntarily separates himself from God, losing the divine life of grace and the store of merit that he had acquired up to that moment. He is rendered incapable of gaining merit for any good work until he returns to God through true repentance. As the branch cannot live if separated from the vine, so the soul is spiritually dead as long as it is separated from God (Jn. 15:5).

A little reflection, by way of contrast, will give some idea of how great is the misfortune of mortal sin. One who is in the *state of grace* is a child of God, a sharer in His divine nature, a temple of the Holy Spirit, an heir of heaven, a living member of the Mystical Body of Christ, sharing in the redeeming merits of Christ the Head, and capable of further growth. Yet, one in the *state of mortal sin,* by deliberately turning away from God, has forfeited all the above blessings, seeking some passing satisfaction forbidden by God, some "forbidden fruit." God is thereby rejected and the Evil One is enthroned in His place until the sinner repents and turns back to God. *"He who is not with Me is against Me"* (Mt. 12:30). As some of the saints have testified, if one could see the hideous state of a soul turned from God in mortal sin, it would horrify him beyond what words can express.

Our Blessed Lord made it clear that we cannot serve two masters; yet in mortal sin man tries to do just that. St. John, in his first epistle, lists our main stumbling blocks in this regard under three general categories: *"the lust of the flesh, the lust of the eyes, and the pride of life"* (2:16). As to the first of these, the carnal man turns from God to the satisfactions of the body. As to the second, the avaricious man turns from God to material gain. As to the third, the proud man, turning from God, turns in on himself, seeking unduly his own exaltation, refusing to subject himself to God. The first two of these are in pursuit of a false happiness, seeking to serve two masters. The third, seeking his own excellence apart from God, and seeing God's word as a limitation of his freedom and self-exaltation, can even end up making no pretense of serving two masters, but saying in effect with the Evil One, *"I will not serve."*

Mortal sin, then, is the preference of some passing forbidden satisfaction (for example, bodily pleasure, worldly wealth, glory, power) to the infinite Good who is God. It is the gravest injustice, because God the Creator has the strictest right to the obedience of His creatures. It is especially an offense against God's love, a deliberate refusal to return the love of One who loved us first with an infinite love. It is an abuse of our God-given freedom, given so that we might merit an eternal reward by freely submitting to God's commandments.

2) Venial Sin: Listed above were the three conditions needed to make a sin mortal. If any one is lacking, the sin is venial. It can be seen, then, that there is an extremely wide latitude as to the gravity of venial sin. Yet, unlike mortal sin, venial sin does not cause the loss of the divine life of grace, nor does it lessen the degree of charity in the soul. It does, however, lessen the fervor of charity, which makes the will less inclined to the exercise of that virtue. If such failings are frequent and fully deliberate, they give rise to habits and undue attachments to worldly satisfactions that make the exercise of virtue more difficult. While both mortal and venial sin share the common name of sin, there is an infinite distance between them, for the first involves a certain infinite evil, being a deliberate grave offense against a Person of infinite majesty and glory and power and love. For this reason, venial sins, no matter how numerous, can never equal a mortal sin. Yet, repeated deliberate venial sins can and do dispose to mortal sin. When one frequently yields to selfish impulses, they can, in time of stronger temptation, draw one into grave sin.

It is customary to speak of venial sin as a *light* sin as opposed to *grave*. It would be a grave error, however, to understand this in the sense that it is something of little importance, something that one need not be disturbed about. Venial sins, such as most of us commit daily (little failures of impatience, subtle forms of selfishness, of pride, of uncharity), are failures to accept the will of Him who loves us with an infinite love. One who deeply loves another strives to avoid even the little things that offend or displease that person. How much more should that be our attitude toward our divine Savior. As St. Teresa of Avila asks, *"Can anything be small if it offends God?"*

Theologians describe as "lukewarm" one who strives to avoid grave sins, but is little concerned about the little failures of each day. Spiritual writers compare such a one to a man who retains his strength but is partially bound, or to a lamp that cannot give full light because the lampshade is covered with carbon and dust.

It is important to distinguish between: a) venial sins of *human frailty*, failures for which we ask God's pardon and are trying to overcome, but which, because of human weaknesses, seem to continue with a certain regularity; and b) venial sins that are *fully deliberate*, that is, failures of which we are fully conscious, but which we are doing little or nothing to overcome. The former can be found in a soul making progress, for God can bring good out of them, if they occasion true contrition and a renewed effort to overcome them. The latter, on the other hand, indicate the "lukewarm," and gradually lessen the sense of God and the sense of sin of which we have been speaking.

Sin and Divine Friendship

Sanctifying grace and charity in the soul establish a friendship between the indwelling divine Persons and the individual soul. As grace grows, that friendship deepens, with a growing willingness to sacrifice, on the part of man, that God's will be done. This growth is accompanied by a growing desire to avoid even the little things that displease Him.

Sin should be seen in the light of that friendship. Fully deliberate venial sin stifles its growth; mortal sin destroys it completely. One will never arrive at a deep sense of sin if there is not a growing awareness of God's immense love for us. *"You are my friends if you do the things I command you"* (Jn. 15:14).

Chapter Notes

1. Cardinal Joseph Ratzinger, *In the Beginning*, p. 78.
2. Pope John Paul II, Apostolic Exhortation: *Reconciliation and Penance,* Part II, Ch. 1: The Mystery of Sin
3. *Ibid.*
4. *Ibid.*
5. *Ibid.*
6. *Ibid.*
7. *Ibid.*
8. *Ibid.*

Chapter 20

Cafeteria Catholics

Most of us, at one time or another, have enjoyed a meal in a cafeteria. Customers pass down the line of a great variety of foods, picking this or that according to their taste, and passing up other things they do not want. You might say it is a "pick and choose" kind of eating house.

It seems that some Catholics look upon their Church in the same way, that is, as regards the doctrines of the Catholic Church. They are sometimes referred to as "cafeteria Catholics." They feel they can "pick and choose" among the various doctrines and laws of the Church, some of which they accept, others which they feel they are not obliged to obey. More and more today there are those who call themselves Catholic, who feel they can, and must, decide for themselves which of the teachings of the Church they will accept, and which they will not. How many, for example, do not accept the clear teaching of the Church in regard to such basic things as birth control, premarital sex, divorce and remarriage, and so forth. They look upon these teachings not as laws, but at best, as ideals that they may not be able to live up to. Many things have changed in the Church, they say, since the Second Vatican Council.

Yet, Pope Benedict XVI, when he was the Prefect of the Sacred Congregation for the Doctrine of the Faith, stated clearly and emphatically in the book, *The Cardinal Ratzinger Report,* that it is absolutely incorrect to refer to *Pre-Vatican Council II* and *Post-Vatican Council II,* as if there were changes in the Church's position in matters of faith and morals. The only changes have been in disciplinary matters, for example in the liturgy of the Mass, which now is in the vernacular, with the priest facing the congregation, and so forth.

CAFETERIA CATHOLICS

As regards the "picking and choosing" of what teachings of the Church one will follow or not follow, Pope John Paul II stated in his talk to the Bishops in Los Angeles in 1987:

> It is sometimes reported that a large number of Catholics today do not adhere to the teaching of the Catholic Church on a number of questions, notably sexual and conjugal morality, divorce and remarriage. Some are reported as not accepting the clear position on abortion. It has to be noted that there is a tendency on the part of some Catholics to be selective in their adherence to the Church's moral teaching. It is sometimes claimed that dissent from the magisterium is totally compatible with being a "good Catholic," and poses no obstacle to the reception of the sacraments. This is a grave error that challenges the teaching of the Bishops in the United States and elsewhere.

If we can believe the polls, we are experiencing in the Church at the present time (1993) a considerable amount of dissent from the teaching of the Church. However, if we would call this dissent what it really is, it is a crisis of one's Catholic faith. We will examine that virtue to see what it demands of us, and how we can lose it, if we reject the light and guidance given us by the Church.

The Gift of Faith

The First Vatican Council, which ended in 1870, defined the gift of faith as follows:

> Faith is a supernatural virtue whereby, under the inspiration and assistance of grace, we believe those things revealed by God to be true, not because the intrinsic evidence of those things has been perceived by the natural light of reason, but because of the authority of God Himself revealing, who can neither deceive nor be deceived.

The above definition explains *why* we believe when we are motivated by the virtue of faith. The Second Vatican Council continues explaining *what* we must believe when motivated by supernatural faith.

> All those things are to be believed, on divine and Catholic faith, which are contained in the written and unwritten word

of God, and which are proposed by the Church as divinely revealed, whether this is accomplished through her *solemn pronouncements* (*ex cathedra* definitions), or through her *ordinary and universal teaching power.*[1]

We notice that the Vatican Council does not make any distinctions, in relation to the virtue of faith, between the solemn pronouncements and the ordinary universal teaching power of the Church, that is, between her *solemn magisterium* and *ordinary magisterium*; nor does it refer to one as *infallible* and the other as *non-infallible.*

The First Dissenters

Today's dissenters from God's revealed truth as handed down by the Church are similar to some of the first disciples of Jesus who refused to accept His veiled words regarding the Eucharist long before the Last Supper (Jn. 6:28-59). *"This is a hard saying,"* they said. *"Who can accept it?"* Jesus was aware that they were murmuring in protest at what He had said. Yet, He made no attempt to soften or modify his words. He was testing their faith in Him. *"Does it shake your faith?"* He said to them. *"The words I spoke to you are spirit and life. Yet there are some among you who do not believe. ... No one can come to Me unless he is enabled to do so by my Father"* (Jn. 6:62,64).

St. John tells us that from that time on those disciples broke away and would not remain in His company any longer. Faith is a gift of God, and only those who have received it can accept His word in its entirety when put to the test. Our Lord had given them plenty of evidence of His divine power by His miracles. They should have accepted His words, even though they did not comprehend what He was saying. When they rejected it, it was because they were relying on the light of *reason alone*, and not on *reason enlightened by faith*. It was too much for them.

But note the language referring to those who believe: *"No one can come to me."* One *"comes"* to Him, not by approaching Him physically, but by believing in His word, believing even when it is hard to believe, for He is *Truth* (Jn. 14:6).

Today's Dissenters

There are some in the Church today who are similar to those who walked away and would follow Christ no longer. Included in that category are some who come to Mass, receive our Blessed Lord in Holy Communion, but who do not accept this or that teaching of the Church. Yet, they look upon themselves as followers of Christ, as His disciples.

To come to Jesus, to accept Him in the deepest sense, it is not enough to receive Him sacramentally, for one can receive Him in Holy Communion and not accept His word in its entirety. We must accept not just *most* of what the Church teaches as divinely revealed, but *all* of it.

Let us suppose I tell someone about five incidents that happened to me on a trip (all of which are true), and this person says to me, *"I believe the first four, but I can't believe the fifth."* The fact that he will not believe one of the incidents related in spite of my word as to its truth, means he no longer believes I always tell the truth. My credibility (for him) is shattered.

We have a parallel to this in regard to the Church. Christ still speaks through His Church when it makes official pronouncements in faith and morals for all the faithful, declaring something to be divinely revealed. If an adult Catholic rejects just one of those official teachings, that is saying in effect: The Church cannot always be relied on to teach the true interpretation of God's revelation. What happens, in that case, to the gift of divine faith? It is no longer one's guiding light. St. Thomas Aquinas spoke of this centuries ago: *"If, of those things taught by the Church (as divinely revealed), one holds what he chooses to hold, and rejects what he chooses to reject, he no longer adheres to the teaching of the Church as an infallible guide, but to his own will."* Such a one may accept other teachings of the

Church, but he does so not out of divine faith, but *"only by a kind of opinion in accordance with his own will."*[2]

Pope Leo XIII, who relied much on St. Thomas, expressed the same idea in his *Encyclical on the Unity of the Church:*

> If it be certain that something be revealed by God, and this is not believed, then nothing whatever is believed by divine faith. ... He who dissents even in one point from divinely revealed truths absolutely rejects all faith, since he thereby refuses to honor God as the supreme truth.

There are some today, not only among the laity, but even among the clergy, who cry out like the first disciples: *"This is a hard doctrine. Who can accept it?"* When some of His first disciples said that, our Savior did not soften His words in order to keep them from walking away. He let them go away, because they had failed the test, failed to accept a difficult teaching on His word.

Today also, the Church does not change its teaching to fit the mentality of the times. It cannot do so, because it is based on the revealed word of God.[3] As Pope Paul VI revealed in an address in January 1972:

> The teaching Church does not invent her doctrines; she is a witness, a custodian, an interpreter, a transmitter. As regards the truths of Christian marriage, she can be called conservative, uncompromising. To those who would urge her to make her faith easier, more in keeping with the tastes of the changing mentality of the times, she answers with the apostles, we cannot (Acts 4:20).

Since adult Catholics have an obligation to form their conscience under the guidance of the teaching authority of the Church, they are responsible for the weakening of their faith when they look to other sources for guidance. The Irish Bishops spoke of those "other sources" in a statement on *Conscience and Morality*:

> In practice, those who dissent from authoritative Church teaching very often give as their reason for doing so, not so much their own personal insights, as the authority of dis-

senting theologians. This, however, is to misunderstand the role of theologians in the Church, for their authority does not, and cannot outweigh the authority of the Pope in declaring the faith of the Church.

Theologians and the Magisterium

Without doubt, the Church does rely on theologians in the expression of doctrine. Nevertheless, it is up to the teaching authority which Christ gave to His Church, authority centered in the Roman Pontiff and the Bishops in union with him, to accept or reject their explanations or conclusions.

St. Thomas Aquinas, by his writings, has contributed to the expression of Catholic doctrine more than any other theologian in the history of the Church. Pope John XXII said of him at his canonization, *"He has illuminated the Church more than all the other Doctors."* Centuries later, Pope Pius X wrote of St. Thomas, *"Since the death of the holy Doctor there has never been a council of the Church at which he was not present by his doctrine and influence."* And yet this great saint, whose humility was as great as his learning, once wrote that should there be a dispute between the teaching authority of the Church and a private theologian, *"we must abide rather by the Pope's judgment than by the opinion of any of the theologians, however well versed he may be in the divine Scriptures."* [4]

Where Some Have Gone Astray

The great wave of dissent in the Church after the Second Vatican Council seems to have been given its greatest impetus with the rejection on the part of some priests and theologians of the encyclical of Pope Paul VI, *Humane Vitae,* on the regulation of birth, in 1968. The main argument those dissenters offer to justify their action is this: The encyclical of Pope Paul VI was not an *ex cathedra* decree; therefore, they say, it is not infallible. Hence it could be reversed, and therefore one is not bound by this teaching.

This reasoning completely ignores the following declaration of the Second Vatican Council:

> In matters of faith and morals...religious submission of will and mind must be shown in a special way to the authentic teaching authority of the Roman Pontiff, even when he is not speaking *ex cathedra*. That is, it must be shown in such a way that his supreme magisterium is acknowledged with reverence, the judgments made by him sincerely adhered to, according to his manifest mind and will. His mind and will in the matter may be known chiefly either from the character of the documents, from his frequent repetition of the same doctrine, or from his manner of speaking.[5]

Too, the above reasoning of the dissenters was flatly rejected by the U.S. Bishop's Committee on Doctrine when they issued a critical statement on the two-volume work entitled *Catholicism* by Fr. Richard McBrien, who at the time was head of the Department of Theology at Notre Dame University. Their statement goes to the heart of the issue of dissent in the Church when it stresses the following:

> In addition to those doctrines which have been taught by the Magisterium of the Church in the *extraordinary* way of infallible definitions, the *ordinary* teaching of the Pope and the Bishops in union with him preserves many revealed truths which have never been solemnly defined, but which, nevertheless, are infallibly true and definable. These are truths which cannot be rejected or neglected without injury to the integrity of the Catholic faith, because they are either *explicitly* contained in Holy Scripture, or, although only *implicit* in Sacred Scripture, they have been taught universally and continually, are professed in the liturgy, and are believed and witnessed by the faithful as divinely revealed.

There are apparently many in the Catholic Church today who outwardly live and worship as Catholics, but who do not accept in its entirety the Catholic faith. That faith is no longer the guiding light of their life. They seek the *sacraments* of the Church, but are unwilling to accept some of the *teachings* of the Church. They want the gifts God gives through the Church, but not the sacrifices He asks through the Church.

CAFETERIA CATHOLICS

They foolishly think they do not need the guidance and protection of the chief Shepherd that Christ has provided for His flock. Yet just as the sheep that wanders off and gets separated from the fold becomes an easy prey to wild animals that would kill and devour it, so Catholics who wander aside from the protective guidance of the Roman Pontiff, the chief Shepherd whom Christ has provided, become easy prey to the deceptions and wiles of the devil. Such a one may be clever about worldly things, but his vision has become clouded (without the light of faith) as to his own innate weakness, and as to the wisdom of seeking God's will rather than his own.

Whether or not the rejection of this or that teaching of the Church as divinely revealed causes total loss of faith, only God knows. Only a grave sin of disbelief can cause this, and only God knows when all the conditions are present. But those who deliberately reject something taught by the Church as divinely revealed, even if taught only by the ordinary magisterium, are walking dangerously close to the edge of the precipice.

The Christian life has always demanded many sacrifices of the true follower of Christ. That is a major part of the cross that His followers are asked to carry. And now the time has come when greater and greater sacrifices are going to be required in order to be a true and practicing Catholic, when more and more, what we stand for, what we believe, is going to be challenged and ridiculed. It will take a strong faith, a firm hope and a courageous love to encounter all this and not accept the wisdom of the world. Without these divine helps, that cross will become a *stumbling block,* and will be rejected as *foolishness* (1 Cor. 1:23-25). Strengthen our faith, Lord, to accept and live *all* that You have revealed and made known through Your Church. *"Blessed are they who have not seen, and yet have believed"* (Jn. 20:29).

Chapter Notes

1. Encyclicals, decrees of Sacred Congregations, etc.
2. St. Thomas Aquinas, *Summa Theologiae,* II-II, q. 5, a. 3
3. Vatican Council II, *Gaudium et Spes,* n. 50
4. *Quodlibetum* IX, Q. 8, *Quaest. Quodlibetales*
5. *Lumen Gentium,* n. 25

Chapter 21

Worldliness

At the very beginning of our Christian life, when the waters of baptism washed away the stain of original sin, we (personally or through our parents and godparents) renounced Satan and all his works and pomps, that is, all worldliness and false maxims of this world which would lead us to love pleasure, riches, honors and power more than Christ. It is not that these things are evil, but that, because of the weakness of human nature, they easily enslave the heart of man so that he seeks them in a way or to a degree that causes him to disregard the laws of God. By our baptism, then, we have not renounced the world as such, for all that God has created is good (Gen. 1:31). It is the misuse or abuse of what God has created that we renounce, for the world and its attractions can draw us away from the love and service of God and neighbor. It is in this sense that St. John wrote, *"The whole world is in the power of the evil one"* (1 Jn. 5:19).

The ultimate warfare in this world that has gone on since the fall of our first parents and will continue until the end of time, is the warfare between our divine Savior and Satan. It is a spiritual battle for the souls of men. The ultimate defeat of Satan is already assured through the Passion of Christ, yet in the divine plan, the devil and his angels are allowed to tempt souls through their own human weaknesses and the enticements of this world; for it is the will of the Creator that our love for Him be tested and proven in order to attain the eternal beatitude for which we were created.

The danger lies in that the world offers so many attractions that seem to promise happiness. Though many of those attractions are not in themselves sinful, they can captivate the heart to such an extent that one becomes negligent and forgetful of his duties to God. Then too, many of the world's attractions are clearly sinful, yet the prince of this world, the *"father of lies"* (Jn. 8:44), deceives so many into believing that they are not only justifiable, but beneficial to mankind.

So many of the sources that form public opinion (the daily press, television, movies, books, magazines), deceived by the Evil One, are presenting, under the guise of good, practices that are forbidden by the divine and natural law: artificial contraception, abortion, euthanasia, physician-assisted suicide, premarital sex. The more one is captivated by the spirit of the world, the more one is open to this deception of the *"father of lies,"* and tends to look upon the Church as old-fashioned and failing to keep up with modern progress. How many are misled by all this, failing to see that the arguments put forth are simply an appeal to the baser appetites and passions of man. The guidance of reason enlightened by faith is pushed into the background.

Because of all this, there is need to be on our guard as to what the world puts forth as lawful and normal. What we used to refer to as needed "discipline" in certain areas, is now at times looked upon as self-repression and unnatural. Natural instincts, we are told, should not be repressed lest this give rise to disturbances of one's psyche. In line with this, many restrictions are placed on the correction and discipline of children, even though the Scriptures warn again and again of the ill effects where such discipline is lacking (Prov. 13:24; 22:14,15).

Pilgrims on the Way

For the most part, what draws many away from following Christ, or what makes them lax in doing so, are not the pleasures or practices that are clearly against the law of God; but attractions innocent in themselves when used in moderation, but which have the power to bring one to prefer them to the demands of religion and the benefits of the sacraments. We are told to be *in the world, but not of the world,* that is, not captivated by its spirit. We are to use the goods of this world and its enjoyments for the purpose that God intended, as *means* in the attainment of our final end, and not to allow them to become the *end* of all our striving. As St. Leo the Great warns, we must be careful not to become like the man who set out on a journey, but became so attracted by the many enticements along the way, that he forgot where he was going. The Scriptures admonish us to keep in mind that we are but pilgrims on the way to our fatherland (1 Pet. 2:11), and that here we have *"no permanent city"* (Heb. 13:14).

So we are on a journey for the few short years of our earthly life, the destination of which is eternal beatitude with God in the life beyond. This journey can be a happy one in the enjoyment of the lawful pleasures of life if they are sought in moderation, and in keeping with God's word handed down by the Church. But because of the weaknesses of our fallen nature, that moderation will not be observed without applying discipline to our weaknesses and self-denial to our appetites. And the necessary self-denial will be lacking if we do not seek the help of God's grace through prayer and the sacraments, and reflect often on the final goal of our existence.

A pilgrim traveler carries along what he needs, but does not like to be burdened with things not needed for the journey, or that would impede its fulfillment. And since life is but a journey, it is important that one not become burdened with unnecessary possessions and attachments to the extent that he frequently loses sight of his eternal goal. To safeguard against this, he must achieve a healthy detachment toward the goods and goals of this world, so that they *serve* and not *hinder* his progress.

The detachment of which we speak does not imply giving up everything, nor does it mean a lack of interest in worldly projects. It means that one is free from undue attachment to the world's goods, giving one the capacity to enjoy the satisfactions the world offers that are in keeping with the divine plan, and to refrain from those that are not.

The human soul, by its very nature, yearns for happiness; and man, in his obscured spiritual vision and his innate self-seeking tendencies, can easily be deceived into thinking it can be found among the pleasures of the world. Yet, the happiness offered by the world is only a temporary enjoyment of some passing satisfaction, that invariably loses its attraction and ends in delusion. It was meant to be so by God, who made man for Himself, that we might turn to Him who alone can satisfy all the cravings of the human heart.

Sources of Worldliness

Among the effects of original sin, in addition to the loss of sanctifying grace, is that man's bodily appetites and passions are no longer under the perfect control of his intellect and will, and this opens the door to conflict in three weakened areas of human nature referred to by St. John.

> Do not love the world, nor the things that are in the world. If anyone loves the world, the love of the Father is not in him; because all that is in the world, is the *concupiscence of the flesh*, the *concupiscence of the eyes,* and the *pride of life,* which is not from the Father, but from the world (1 Jn. 2:15, 16).

Insofar as one is affected by this threefold concupiscence, he is imbued with the spirit of the world (worldliness), which rebels against the guidance of reason enlightened by faith. The spirit of the world and the spirit of Christ are irreconcilable; the more one is influenced by one of them, the less he is by the other.

As we have already pointed out, the prince of this world and his countless army of fallen angels are engaged in a struggle to win souls redeemed by Christ. The waging of this battle for souls has been entrusted by Christ to His Mother, who, by the power of Christ, will crush the serpent's head (Gen. 3:15). The point we are stressing is that the more one is influenced by the spirit of the world, to that extent such a one is veering away from Christ, and is gradually succumbing to the enticements of the Evil One whose wish is our eternal damnation. *"No man can serve two masters; for he will either hate the one and love the other, or he will stand by one and despise the other. You cannot serve both God and mammon"* (Mt. 6:24). We will examine briefly these three weaknesses of our wounded human nature.

1) Concupiscence of the Flesh is the inordinate desire for the pleasures of the body (especially lust and gluttony), and the revolt of the body against the necessary restraints and mortification in these matters.

St. Thomas defines concupiscence as the appetite for pleasure, which is something good when its fulfillment is sought and enjoyed in keeping with the intentions of the Creator. As the author of nature, God has endowed certain actions with pleasure that are necessary for the preservation of the *individual* (nutrition), and for the preservation of the *species* (generation). As a result of original sin, however, the appetite for pleasure in these matters, because of its intensity and because of the lack of full control by reason, often makes demands that go beyond the limits placed by reason enlightened by faith. It is for this reason that St. Paul speaks of the combat between the flesh and the spirit. *"I am delighted with the law of God according to the inner man, but I see another law in my members warring against the law of my mind, and making me a prisoner of the law that is in my members"* (Rom. 7:21-23). For this reason Christian mortification has always recommended that one deprive himself at times of certain lawful pleasures, not because they are in any way wrong, but to strengthen the will to refrain from pleasures that are not lawful, and to make reparation for the many times and ways that this concupiscence has led one to seek pleasures that are contrary to the guidance of reason enlightened by faith.

Lack of control in this particular weakness not only distances one from God, but also causes one to lose the taste for divine things, as St. Paul explains: *"The sensual man does not perceive the things that are of the Spirit of*

God" (1 Cor. 2:14). And as St. Thomas points out, *lust* causes spiritual blindness, and *gluttony* causes dullness of the spiritual sense.[1]

2) Concupiscence of the Eyes is another name for avarice or greed. It is an inordinate desire for or attachment to, the goods and riches of this world, so that instead of possessing them, one can be possessed by them. Either we *master them,* that is, use and share them with detachment, or they *master us,* that is, our attachment to them causes us to disregard the rights of God and neighbor. St. Paul wrote of this to Timothy:

> They *(those seeking riches)* are letting themselves be captured by foolish and harmful desires which drag men down to ruin and destruction. The love of money is the root of all evil. Some men in their passion for it have strayed from the faith, and have involved themselves in many troubles (1 Tim. 6:9-10).

However, just as the appetites of the body for pleasure are not obstacles to salvation when sought and enjoyed in keeping with the intention of the Creator, so neither is the world as such. Many Christians living in the world, some with considerable possessions, live truly saintly lives. Fathers of families must work to secure the goods of this world and their increase as needed for the well-being of their families. Yet, because of the particular weakness of human nature of which we are speaking, attachment to the goods of this world can become a formidable obstacle to spiritual growth. Today's society has in many respects created a culture without God; and without the inspiration and motivation that come from God's grace, the selfish inclinations of our human nature tend to take over, and cause one to seek this world's goods not as a *means* to an end, but as an *end* in itself, so that they become the prime concern of one's existence, leaving one with little concern about the rights of God and the needs of others. How often does it happen that the more one acquires, the more he desires, and the laws of God do not stand in the way. And this, even though as a rule, the more one has, the greater his anxiety about guarding it and his fear of losing it. To such a one, wealth may bring prestige and renown, but it does not bring peace of mind and true happiness.

The Christian spirit of detachment from the goods of this world is inseparable from trust in the providence of God, who is the ultimate source of all the goods of this world, and who provides for the needs of those who trust in Him. Our Lord, in the Sermon on the Mount, chides those who are lacking in this trust. *"Do not be anxious, asking: 'What shall we eat?' or 'What shall we drink?' or 'What are we to wear?'. . . for your heavenly Father knows you need all these things. But seek first the kingdom of God and his justice, and all these things will be given you besides"* (Mt. 6:31-34).

And for those not wanting in the goods of this world, but in the detachment from them, St. Basil, Doctor of the Church, has this admonition. *"If you acknowledge your possessions as coming from God, is He unjust because He apportions them unequally? Why do you receive more and another less, unless it be that you have the merit of stewardship?"* But none has expressed the need of trust combined with sharing more beautifully than St. Leo the Great.

> No act of devotion on the part of the faithful gives God more pleasure than that which is lavished on the poor. Where He finds charity with its loving concern, there He recognizes a reflection of His own fatherly care. In these acts of giving do not fear the lack of means. A generous spirit is itself a great wealth. There can be no shortage of material for generosity when it is Christ who feeds and Christ who is fed. In all this activity there is present the hand of Him who multiplies the bread by breaking it, and increases it by giving it away.[2]

3) The Pride of Life is an inordinate desire for one's own glory and exaltation apart from God, a desire for freedom and independence that leads to disobedience to the order established by God, and to rebellion against what interferes with one having his own way. This was the sin of the angels and of our first parents. All who share their fallen nature have inherited that same rebellious tendency. This wound of our nature makes it difficult for us to obey, to admit mistakes, to accept correction, humiliation, failure and so forth.

Of the three sources of worldliness that we have considered, pride is the most subtle, the most deeply rooted, the most damaging, and the most difficult to eradicate. For that reason the proud man is more difficult to convert than the sensual man, or one attached to the goods of this world. It is the greatest of all obstacles to grace, and causes souls to seek their own will rather than God's, their own glory rather than God's, their own version of truth rather than God's. Is there any wonder why St. Gregory the Great calls it *"the queen and mother of all vices?"* Is there any wonder why St. Peter warns that *"God resists the proud, but gives grace to the humble"*? (1 Pet. 5:5)

* * * * * * * * * * * * *

One temptation in reading about the three main sources of worldliness is that we might begin to visualize someone we know who is especially worldly in one or other of those areas. But the fact is that all of us have all three of those weaknesses in varying degrees, and the warfare of the Christian life is the struggle to overcome them. One may make progress against those weaknesses and keep them under control, but the underlying concupiscence will always remain part of our fallen nature. And if one begins to let up on his vigilance, not cooperating with graces received, those weaknesses, no matter how much progress one has made, will again make themselves felt. God has His own way of keeping us aware of our basic human frailty and of our need of His grace.

The more we make progress against this threefold concupiscence of our fallen nature, the clearer becomes our spiritual vision, and the less our will is impeded in choosing the path that Christ marked out for us. That is why St. Paul admonishes: *"Be not conformed to the world, but be transformed in the newness of your mind, that you may discern what is the good and acceptable and perfect will of God"* (Rom. 12:2).

Chapter Notes

1. St. Thomas Aquinas, *Summa Theologiae,* II-II, q. 15, a. 3
2. St. Leo the Great, *Roman Breviary*

Chapter 22

Is Lent Dead?

On the front cover of *Time* magazine, April 8, 1966, there appeared in large bold type three words: *"Is God Dead?"* The question referred, among other things, to the apparent lack of any impact that religion seemed to have on the lives of so many people today.

Has the season of Lent made any difference in your mode of living? With all the mitigation of the Lenten mortifications in recent years and the apparent lack of impact on the lives of so many Catholics, one might be tempted to ask: *"Is Lent Dead?"*

Many of us can remember the time when Lent was truly a time set aside for mortification: when we tried to cut down on the sweets, the smokes, the drinks, the movies, and so forth. And before the advent of television, giving up the movies was, for some, no small sacrifice. Has this former concept of mortification and penance become outdated?

It is not Lent with its mortification that is outdated or dead, it is man's sense of the need of it that has been deadened. The constant bombardment of a materialistic and worldly viewpoint through TV, the movies, the newspapers and magazines, the schools (in which any reference to religious teaching is prohibited), has done much to confuse and obscure the minds of Catholics, so that the moral conscience of many has been clouded. As Pope John Paul II declared in his *Apostolic Exhortation on Penance and Reconciliation*, *"When the conscience has been weakened the sense of God is also obscured, and as a result . . . the sense of sin is lost."*[1] And where there is lost the abiding conviction that we are sinners, there is lost the sense of the need of mortification. Let us examine briefly how this subtle deadening of our sense of sin and of the need of mortification can come about.

The Spirit of the World

St. John wrote in his first epistle (2:15), *"Love not the world, nor the things which are in the world. If any man love the world, the charity of the Father is not in him."* What is this *"world"* which we are forbidden to love?

The first book of the Bible tells us that the world and all the goods it contains are God's creatures, and that everything God made is good. So the fault lies not in *the world,* but in *man,* who because of his wounded nature easily becomes overly attached to the world's goods and pleasures, and seeks them excessively. The world need not be an obstacle to sanctity. Many saints lived in it, came in contact with its allurements, but through a life of prayer and self-discipline, remained detached from its attractions. They lived *in the world,* but were not *of the world*. They were not contaminated by *the spirit of the world,* because they were so filled with *the spirit of Christ*. These two things are mutually exclusive of each other, so that the more one grows in the heart of man, the more the other is excluded.

Each of us, as the result of the three-fold concupiscence of our fallen nature (avarice, lust, pride), has deeply rooted in our being the seeds of worldliness. In the measure that these seeds and inclinations grow and dominate us, in that measure they block the growth of grace; while on the contrary, as grace grows, this deep inclination to seek excessively the world's pleasures is gradually diminished.

We must be aware of the battle that is necessary to insure this growth. As we have already stated, as one comes under the influence of the "world" with its false maxims and attractions, his spiritual perception tends to be dulled. If there is not a constant struggle to live our life according to the spirit of Christ, it is being shaped by an environment that is hostile to Christ. Living in a materialistic culture, and constantly being bombarded with its ideas, unless there is a conscious effort to seek the guiding norms of the Gospel, we slowly and imperceptibly tend to accept the world's evaluation of things.

The Need of Self-Discipline

That the world contains many attractions that are in themselves sinful (if deliberately sought), few will deny. But these are not the main snares that most of us have to guard against. For many persons, the main stumbling blocks are things which are *in themselves lawful,* hence so easy to justify, but which are so attractive and satisfying that it is difficult to seek them in moderation.

A few examples will clarify what we mean: There is nothing wrong with enjoying food, but how easy it is to overeat. It is not wrong to drink an alcoholic beverage, but how many get themselves in trouble because of the lack of moderation. It is not wrong to watch television (it can be very educational and wholesomely entertaining), but because of the general content of a good portion of its programs, and because of its accessibility and of its ability to captivate the mind and monopolize our time, it can pose some real problems. It is not wrong to play cards, even with a little money on the table; but how easy it is to get involved over one's head. There is nothing wrong with wanting nice clothes, or enjoying nice things of various sorts; but how easy it is to be extravagant with the resources that God has entrusted to our care, and unmindful of others in want, and so forth. As St. Paul warns, there are many things that are lawful, but which are not expedient (1 Cor. 10:22).

We Can't Serve Both God and Mammon

It should be clear, then, that a good portion of the excesses for which people will have to answer to God involve things that are *good in themselves,* but which, through lack of self-discipline and moderation, were sought excessively. The more satisfying a good thing is, the more difficult it is to use or seek it with moderation; and therefore the greater the need of occasional self-denial.

As we know from our own experience, our mind cannot fully attend to two things at the same time. In the measure that our attention is absorbed by one thing, to that extent it is incapable of giving full attention to something else. In a similar way, *our heart* cannot fully cling to two diverse things at the same time. In the measure that man's heart is held captive by *created goods* (lawful though they may be), in that measure he is incapable of serving and giving his heart to the *Creator of those goods,* that is, of *"loving God with our whole heart, our whole soul, our whole mind,"* as we have been commanded to do (Mt. 22:37). We cannot serve both God and mammon (Mt. 6:24).

As the English Benedictine, Dom Hubert Van Zeller, puts it, *"It isn't strictly the extent to which a man is in water that causes drowning; it is the extent to which water is in him."* So, it is not how much a person is surrounded by the distractions and allurements of the world that causes his downfall, but how much these dominate his heart.

The Full Meaning of Penance

The notion that many persons have of penance is quite superficial, extending merely to acts of self-denial. These are part of Christian penance, but the true notion of that virtue must go deeper than that.

Pope John Paul II, in his *Apostolic Exhortation on Reconciliation and Penance,* pointed out that the concept of penance is complex, for it involves an inner change of heart, and an exterior *"changing of one's life in harmony with the change of heart."* [2]

The *interior aspect* has to do with sorrow for sin, and with a firm resolve to amend one's life and offer satisfaction for the sins committed; the *exterior aspect* has to do with the self-denial, good works, and sacrifices made in correcting one's faults and in expiation for them, and is seen as a necessary means of overcoming the selfish tendencies that lead us to sin. The need of this exterior discipline is clear if we recall the weakness of human nature due to original sin, for *"the flesh lusts against the spirit, and the spirit against the flesh; the two are directly opposed"* (Gal. 5:17). As Pope John Paul II explained:

> Doing penance is something authentic and effective only if it is translated into deeds and acts of penance. In this sense penance means, in the Christian theological and spiritual vocabulary, asceticism, that is to say, the concrete daily effort of a person, supported by grace, to lose his or her own life for Christ as the only means of gaining it (Mt. 16:25) . . . an effort to overcome in oneself what is of the flesh in order that what is spiritual may prevail; a continual effort to rise from the things of here below to the things where Christ is (Col. 3:1). Penance is therefore a conversion that passes from the heart to deeds and then to the Christian's whole life.³

This is in accord with the notion of penance the Mother of God asked of the three young children at Fatima. As Sr. Lucia explained, the penance Our Lady asked includes not only individual personal sacrifices and self-denial, but also and especially the sacrifices and effort involved in keeping God's commandments, and in fulfilling the God-given duties of one's state in life.

Pope John XXIII and Penance

After Pope John XXIII issued his Apostolic Constitution *Paenitentiam Agere,* officially proclaiming the Second Ecumenical Vatican Council, he urged the faithful to make a worthy spiritual preparation for that great event by means of *"prayer . . . and voluntary mortification."*⁴

Pope John stressed both the interior and the exterior aspects of penance mentioned above. Speaking of *interior repentance,* he said:

> Our first need is for internal repentance; the detestation of sin, and the determination to make amends for it. This is the repentance shown by those who make a good Confession, take part in the Eucharistic Sacrifice and receive Holy Communion. The faithful should be specially encouraged to do this . . . for external acts of penance are quite obviously useless unless accompanied by a clear conscience and the detestation of sin.⁵

As to *outward acts of penance,* the Holy Father continued:

> But the faithful must also be encouraged to do outward acts of penance, both to keep their bodies under the strict control

of reason and faith, and to make amends for their own and other people's sins. St. Paul was caught up to the third heaven — he reached the summit of holiness — and yet he had no hesitation in saying of himself: *"I chastise my body and bring it into subjection."*[6]

External penance includes particularly the acceptance from God in a spirit of resignation and trust all of life's sorrows and hardships, and of everything that involves inconvenience and annoyance in the conscientious performance of the obligations of our daily life and work and the practice of Christian virtue.[7]

But besides bearing in a Christian spirit the inescapable annoyances and sufferings of this life, the faithful ought also to take the initiative in doing voluntary acts of penance and offering them to God.[8]

The Conflict Within Man

There is within every Christian, then, a battle between two opposing forces for the domination of his heart. Within him are the *roots of worldliness*, rooted in his fallen nature, which make him inclined to accept the *maxims of the world,* which unduly exalt pleasure, comfort, riches, independence, renown, power, and so forth, and to fix his heart on them to the neglect of God and the detriment of his soul. There is also in him the *grace of Christ,* which brings with it at least a minimum of knowledge and acceptance of the *maxims of Christ* in direct opposition to those of the world. Unfortunately, man possesses these divine gifts imperfectly, and understands them obscurely. The grace of baptism, which brings a sharing in the life of Christ, does not suppress the roots of worldliness, yet it does give the power to struggle against them. Hence the conflict within us between the *spirit of the world* and the *spirit of Christ.*

We all know how difficult is victory in this battle; yet there is room for perfect confidence that the grace of Christ will win out, if we but do what we can, namely: 1) bring self-discipline to bear on the obvious points of weakness, and 2) make frequent and fervent use of the means of grace, especially prayer, the sacraments, and works of mercy. These means of grace are as indispensable as the self-discipline, for triumph over worldliness and the weaknesses of the flesh will never be accomplished without them. It will be accomplished in the measure that we grow in grace, for in that measure we will share in the strength and triumph of Him who said: *"Take courage, I have overcome the world"* (Jn. 16:33).

Chapter Notes

1. John Paul II, Apostolic Exhortation *On Penance and Reconciliation,* n. 4
2. *Ibid.*
3. *Ibid.*
4. Pope John XXIII, Apostolic Constitution *Paenitentiam Agere,* n. 2
5. *Ibid.* n. 28
6. *Ibid.* n. 29
7. *Ibid.* n. 30
8. *Ibid.* n. 31

Chapter 23

The Vice of Sloth

Because of the fall of our first parents, we come into this world with an inclination to evil, that is, with certain basic tendencies that incline us away from the goal for which we were created — union and friendship with God. The new *Catholic Catechism* lists these inclinations as follows: pride, avarice, envy, wrath, lust, gluttony and sloth.[1]

These inclinations are not sins in themselves, but they give rise to sins when one acts knowingly and willingly under their influence; and one will act under their influence unless disciplined by the practice of the Christian virtues with the aid of divine grace. Those seven inclinations are commonly referred to as capital sins, not because they are the greatest of sins, but because they can and do give rise to many other kinds of sin. For example, the inclination to pride can be the root source and cause of one breaking every one of the ten commandments.

Every sin is an action against some particular virtue, the purpose of which is to direct our actions Godward in accordance with the light of reason enlightened by faith. Among the capital sins there is one, spiritual sloth, also called acedia, which is directly opposed to the love of God and the joy that results from generosity in His service.

How Sloth Opposes Charity

Charity is an infused virtue by which we love God above all things for His own sake, and our neighbors as ourselves because they are His children and members of His Mystical Body. It is a virtue which establishes a friendship between God and ourselves. *"You are My friends if you do the things I command you"* (Jn. 15:14). As a rule, one delights in the presence of a friend, and that should be especially true of one whose love for another is motivated by charity, for one of the effects of charity is joy.[2] However, friendship with God has its obligations, and those obligations can in time come to be seen as burdens, as joy-killers rather than sources of joy, and can give rise to a sadness that stands in the way of fulfilling those obligations. *"This peculiar sadness,"* comments Fr. F. Cunningham, O.P. *"which leads to a neglect of the spiritual duties that flow from sharing in God's friendship is called sloth . . . a kind of spiritual paralysis that leads to the neglect of our duties."*[3] To examine this problem more deeply, it will be useful to look a bit more in detail at the kind of joy that is proper to charity, and the kind of sadness that is proper to sloth.

The Joy of Charity

The saints are singled out for their great love of God, because perfect charity is the essence of Christian perfection; and that love fills their heart with great joy. It is the joy of knowing and experiencing how much they are loved by their divine Friend whose goodness is beyond their capacity to comprehend. It is the joy of being appreciative of the priceless gifts He has bestowed on them, namely: a share in His own divine life through sanctifying grace, bringing the indwelling of the divine Trinity in the soul; a share in His love and truth through the infused virtues and gifts of the Holy Spirit; a knowledge of the divine beatitude to which they are called, and the sacramental helps given to them to attain that end.

Where there is charity, there is joy. And where that joy is found, the divine life of love is lived more intensely. Joy, therefore, is both an effect of charity and an aid in its exercise, whether that charity be exercised by the scrubbing lady or by one in authority, whether it involves failures or successes.

This joy, however, has nothing to do with the feelings. It is rooted not in the body, but in the will, and is

THE VICE OF SLOTH 187

compatible even with suffering, as St. Paul declared: *"I rejoice in the sufferings I bear for your sake; and what is lacking in the suffering of Christ I fill up in my flesh for His Body, which is the Church"* (Col. 1:24).

It is not something experienced only by those who have received the gift of mystical prayer, but by all who strive to be faithful to their divine Friend. It is not blotted out by the sorrow of the loss of a friend, or by setbacks beyond one's power to control, for the will of God is seen and accepted. The more one is aware of God's love and wisdom and concern for us in the midst of trials, misfortunes and sickness, the more he will be buoyed up and maintain a joyous trust and surrender to his divine Friend. The joy of charity is not insensitive to sorrow and suffering; it is accompanied by a deep confidence and loving trust that God can use every situation for our good and the good of others.

However, if one allows this knowledge and awareness to be overshadowed or blotted out by worldly concerns and occupations so that he becomes unmindful of God's indwelling presence and of the priceless gifts he has received, he is gradually deprived of that underlying joy that gives all Christian life its flavor. If his whole attention is fixed on the sorrows, the misery and misfortunes of life, he has not only blocked off the source of Christian joy, but is preparing the way for an actual distaste for divine things that will tempt him to choose what is not compatible with friendship with God.

The human heart must have joy, and if it is not forthcoming from one's friendship with God, one will begin to look for it elsewhere to fill that need. As Aristotle, the pagan philosopher, declared: *"No one can long remain in sadness without any joy."* [4] And when spiritual joys are absent because of one's own negligence, he will not delay in seeking pleasures of a worldly nature. This condition is accompanied by a gradual disdain for the things of God because of the effort and sacrifices they require. Such a one is drawn more and more to the attractions of the flesh, and less and less to the joys of the spirit. In place of those joys that flowed from the love of God and the use of the means of grace, there has developed a spiritual boredom that has brought an actual distaste for spiritual things that formerly brought joy. This condition into which one has drifted is called *spiritual sloth*.

The Oppressive Sadness of Sloth

Sloth, as understood in theology, is a sadness or dejection of the will about the divine good one possesses, and arises from a lack of esteem for that good, and for one's last end and the means to attain it. It occasions an aversion or repugnance in the will to the output of energy — whether physical or intellectual — in the service of God, and a tendency to negligence, arising from a lack of desire for and joy in the divine good. To clarify more precisely what sloth is, and the sadness it occasions, it will be helpful to see what it is not.

The sadness of sloth is not the same as spiritual dryness, which, in divine trials, is accompanied by true contrition for one's sins with a fear of offending God, fidelity to prayer, a desire for spiritual progress, and a generous fidelity to service of God. This is vastly different from the depressing sadness of sloth, the result of negligence, which brings a distaste for spiritual things.

Sadness, depression and melancholy that are due to physical or nervous causes, and are not deliberately embraced by the will, do not come under the definition of sloth.

Sloth differs from bodily weariness, which is not a moral deficiency but a natural occurrence. However, that weariness disposes one to the passion of sadness, and this in turn may tempt the will to sloth when it concerns duties owed to God.

Whereas true devotion brings a promptness of the will in the service of God, spiritual sloth weighs down and oppresses the soul, bringing a voluntary distaste for spiritual things, which become joyless burdens because of the abnegation and effort they demand, leading one to perform spiritual duties negligently, to shorten them, or eventually to omit them under vain pretexts. In spite of Our Lord's words that *"My yoke is easy, and My burden light"* (Mt. 11:30), the slothful person finds them unbearable, and closes his eyes to the light.

Sloth is not to be confused with inactivity, for at times inactivity is necessary, either because our nerves demand it, or because charity demands it. A certain amount of distraction and amusement is often necessary, but one has to be on guard lest what is meant to be a medicinal *means* becomes an *end* in itself to the detriment of other more important ends.

Sloth is not mere laziness. It is not the drag that is felt getting up in the morning, nor the slowness with which one operates in getting a job done. It is rather a perverted sorrow that moves one to neglect things of the spirit, and holds him back from the one important thing in life that will lead him to life's goal.

The Capital Sin of Sloth

St. Thomas defines a capital sin *as "one which easily leads to other sins."*[5] The sin of sloth causes one to shun many things because of the sorrow or unpleasantness involved, and to seek many unlawful things as a means of escape from his depressing state; and because of this it begets many other sins. Thus sloth involves both a *fleeing from God,* and a *pursuit of the world,* for as St. Thomas explains, *"Those who find no joy in spiritual pleasures, have recourse to pleasures of the body."*[6] In light of this we will see some of the sins begotten of sloth as explained by the Angelic Doctor.

1) **A fleeing from God:** The divine goods which the slothful man shuns are both an *end* and a *means*. To forsake the divine good as *one's final end* leads to the sin of despair. It is hoped that sloth will seldom go to this extreme, but when it does, it is the sin of sloth that begets it. To forsake the divine good as a *means to that end* can give rise to: a) timidity or faintheartedness when it concerns the evangelical counsels, making one fearful of making a

commitment; and b) apathy or indifference with regard to the commandments of God. This can give rise to an actual detestation of spiritual things.

2) **The pursuit of the world:** This pursuit of objects of pleasure gives rise to a wandering after unlawful things, which may express itself in: a) *an uneasiness of mind,* when the mind is desirous of rushing after various things without rhyme or reason. Such a one is lured by the idea that the grass is greener elsewhere, and can experience a tendency to wander after unlawful things, that is, persons or places that a true conscience would tell him he should avoid; and b) *curiosity,* when one's mind is curious about what does not concern him, even about things that can open the door to countless temptations. It was St. Augustine who said, and no doubt he was speaking from personal experience, that many a grave sin against chastity has its first beginning in curiosity. The devil understands this far better than we do, and how well he makes use of it through the modern media. *"Where your treasure is, there your heart also will be"* (Mt. 6:21).

Remedies for Sloth

Sloth slows down spiritual progress, and can even bring it to a standstill, and when it does, one's heart and attention are focused earthward. The reason is because one is saddened by the vigilance, effort and self-surrender that the Christian life entails. How is this inertia overcome?

Sloth especially weakens three key virtues, and the vigor of the spiritual life will be restored in the measure that those three virtues are strengthened:

1) **The vigor of faith** will be renewed if one focuses his vision on the heavenly beatitude that God has prepared for those who remain in His friendship. He should strive to be more conscious of God's merciful love for us, and of the priceless gifts He has bestowed on us, for which we will have to give an account. *"The more we think of*

spiritual goods," says St. Thomas, *"the more pleasing they become to us . . . and from this sloth is diminished."*[7] Fr. Garrigou-Lagrange, O.P. states that *"to recover the spirit of faith, enthusiasm and generosity in the love of God, we must daily courageously impose little sacrifices on ourself in those matters in which we are weakest . . . The first steps are costly, but after a bit the task becomes easier . . . even when sensible joy is lacking."*[8]

One fruitful way of focusing our mind and heart on spiritual things is by the daily recitation of the rosary.

2) Fortitude in the face of sadness and unpleasantness will be forthcoming when one overcomes the fear of embracing God's will, and is constant in keeping his resolutions. One must actively continue to seek God even in the face of desolation, even when God seems distant, and not be discouraged by failure. There is no walk in life so continuously joyous that it is completely free of periods of depression. But it is one thing to feel depressed, and quite another thing to give way to that feeling and allow it to dominate one's attitude and conduct. Our Lord Himself on the cross was not spared that desolation: *"My God, My God, why have You forsaken Me?"* (Mt. 27:46) So He will be most understanding of our needs in times of sadness and depression.

3) The activity of charity must be restored, for this is the chief virtue that has been weakened by sloth, bringing an aversion for spiritual things, and causing one to turn away from God and inward toward self. One weighed down by sloth, therefore, must counter his selfish tendencies and strive to be more conscious of the needs of others seen as his brothers and sisters in Christ, and more self-giving through works of mercy. Yet, no one can restore the activity of the infused virtues by himself. He can never rise above his weaknesses unless God (through grace) gives him the inclination and strength to do so; and for those graces he should beg God ardently, trustingly and perseveringly.

The overcoming of the seven vices we spoke of in the beginning, is like making a clearing in a dense tropical jungle. One works hard to clear an area for cultivation, but as soon as he stops working, the jungle slowly tends to take over again. So it is with the innate weaknesses of our fallen nature. It takes persistent effort and prayer to keep them in check. It takes a faith that never loses sight of the final goal in life, and that sees that the Christian life is but a returning of God's merciful love. It takes a love and fortitude that does not shrink back from the sacrifices to be made, that does not lose heart because of the hardship to be endured and the sorrows to be encountered.

It may be that this root vice does not reach extreme levels in most Christians, but it affects all of us to some extent, and to the extent that it does, it stifles the growth of grace, for it counters the key virtue of charity. It is important to at least be aware of this subtle tendency in our nature, and to take means to keep it in check.

Chapter Notes

1. *CCC,* #1866
2. Cf. St. Thomas Aquinas, *Summa Theologiae,* II-II, q. 28
3. Fr. F. Cunningham, O.P., *The Christian Life,* p. 424
4. Aristotle*, Ethics*, VIII, 5
5. St. Thomas Aquinas, *Summa Theologiae,* II-II,. q. 35, a. 4
6. *Ibid.,* a. 4, ad 2
7. *Ibid.,* a.1, ad 4
8. Fr. Garrigou-Lagrange, O.P., *The Love of God and the Cross of Jesus,* p. 396

Chapter 24

The Slaughter of the Innocent

Speaking to His apostles, Our Lord said: *"I am the Way, the Truth, and the Life"* (Jn. 14:6). There is no *way* to the Father, except through Christ. There is no *truth* except that it conforms to the infinite Truth that is God. There is no *life* that does not have God as its ultimate source. That is true from the lowest form of life to the highest angel. As regards human life, God alone is the cause of the *human soul*, the source of man's natural life, and of *divine grace*, the source of man's supernatural life.

With all the progress of modern science and technology, the world of science cannot produce even the smallest living cell. Life in the order of nature comes only from pre-existing life, each cell coming from a pre-existing cell which divides and causes growth. Science can analyze a blade of grass and tell us all the elements or chemical components that go to make it up; but if that blade of grass dies, the scientist cannot restore its life; nor can he take those chemical components, put them together and have a blade of grass. There is a life that has been lost, and no power on earth can restore it. To pass on life, there must be pre-existing life, pre-existing cells. Such is the law of nature established by the author of all life.

God, the Author of Life

With human life, however, there is needed not only pre-existing life, but also special intervention on the part of God. In the divine scheme of things, God has so ordered the laws of nature that man would cooperate with Him in bringing new human life into the world. He has given this tremendous power to man and woman, to initiate the process that will occasion God's creating another immortal human soul, made to God's image. Each time the ovum is fertilized, God brings into being another human being, another human person. As the Sacred Congregation for the Doctrine of the Faith stated in 1974 in its *Declaration on Abortion*:

> As soon as the egg is fertilized, a life begins that belongs not to the father or mother but to the new living human being who now develops on his own account. . . . Science has shown that from the very first moment this living being possesses a stable structure or genetic program; it is a human being, an individual human being with all its characteristic traits already fixed. At the moment of fertilization the marvelous course of human life begins, even if each of the great powers by which that life is exercised requires time to become properly disposed and readied for action.[1]

Abortion — An Abominable Crime

All the above makes it clear that the deliberate destruction of the human fetus at any stage of its development is the taking of human life. For this reason the Second Vatican Council declared that *"from the moment of its conception life must be guarded with the greatest care. Abortion and infanticide are abominable crimes."*[2]

Since God alone is the source of every human life, God alone has the right to take it away (Wis. 15:11). We are speaking of the natural right to life of every innocent person, including the unborn, who are especially innocent of any crime . . . and who, before God, are *persons,* regardless of what any human court might declare. As the Sacred Congregation for the Doctrine of the Faith stated: *"It is indeed amazing that there should be, on the one hand, a widespread outcry against capital punishment and against war in any form, and on the other, a growing demand for the freedom to have abortions."*[3]

The culture in which we live is deeply infected with secular humanism, a philosophy of life that has no place for God, and which dominates much of our educational system, the media, and even our government. As a result, the concept of "human rights" has become so distorted that millions in our country claim the right to kill the unborn.

The lasting solution to the rights of the unborn goes a lot deeper than victory at the polls. We will be successful in eliminating or noticeably lessening the slaughter of the unborn only when the majority of our people recognize the divine source of all human life and God's absolute right over it. If there were no human soul made to God's image, then destroying a human fetus would be of no more consequence than destroying a cat or dog.

Human life is being sacrificed because the divine source of human life is being denied. Human life becomes cheap when man thinks that he alone is its creator. The attitude is: *"What I can bring into being, I can destroy."* Ignore God's role in the great mystery of life, and chaos, destruction and misery invariably follow.

What happens when a human fetus is destroyed? The material element of the person is destroyed, but the soul (created at conception) will live on for all eternity. All the while that mangled body cries out to heaven for vengeance against those who have deprived it of the opportunity of participating more fully in the divine life for which it was created.

God's Unfailing Intervention

Even when God foresees that two persons who are misusing their procreative powers will seek the destruction of any human life that comes forth, He will still intervene and create a human soul destined to live for all eternity.

How selfish and blind can man be who would destroy another human life, just to make one's own life more convenient, as if one's convenience is more important than the human life that is destroyed. Yet this happens by the millions in our U.S.A. What a terrible reckoning must be in store for our country, if this enormous holocaust continues.

What is more, many forms of birth control do not prevent conception, but merely prevent the fertilized ovum from nesting in the uterus. In each such case a human soul is created by God. A human being begins to exist only to be destroyed shortly thereafter. How often this happens in the life of one who uses contraceptives, only God knows.

God's Providential Safeguards

Because this procreative power with which God has endowed man and woman can be so terrible in its consequences if it is misused, God has made gravely binding laws as to the use of that power in the sixth and ninth commandments. And yet, our godless society is making a mockery of God's laws, seeing this procreative power as merely an instrument of pleasure. To control the use of this power (and prevent its misuse), God, from the beginning, established the institution of marriage; and then to further strengthen parents in safeguarding and respecting that power, Christ raised marriage to the dignity of a sacrament, making the proper use of that procreative power a means of grace.

All this helps us to see the meaning and necessity of the virtue of purity. This virtue instills a reverence for that sublime power of procreation, and becomes a safeguard lest it be misused. That power, seen in the light of Christian faith, is something beautiful and awesome; but by the same token, its misuse is a terrible disruption of God's plan, terrible in its consequences.

There will be no respect for human life without a reverence for and a safeguarding of this procreative power that brings forth new life. In other words, respect for human life is inseparable from the virtue of purity. When human love is cheapened, human life itself becomes cheap. Yet, perhaps never before in human history has this power, so beautiful in God's plan, been dragged down into the mire on so wide a scale. One has but to turn on the television, or to read the page of movie advertisements to see how true this is.

A Cry for Vengeance

For those of us who are Christian and Catholic, the unborn child, whether it be healthy or deformed, whether it gives promise of a normal life or one that is not normal, is seen not only as a *human person* with a *right to life,* but as a child of God. And God is going to demand an accounting of every human soul entrusted to every human parent. As Pope Paul VI stated, speaking to the Medical Association of West Flanders:

> The Catholic Church has always regarded abortion as an abominable crime, because unqualified respect for even the very beginning of life is a logical consequence of the mysteries of creation and redemption. In our Lord Jesus Christ every human being, even one whose physical life is utterly wretched, is called to the dignity of a child of God.

Then, after speaking of the sacredness of human life, the Holy Father continued:

> They know this truth, they are well aware of it indeed who have had the misfortune, the inexorable sense of guilt, the ever-living remorse, of having deliberately ended a life. The voice of innocent blood cries out in the heart of the killer with torturing insistence, and tells that person that sophistries in the service of self-satisfaction can never bring interior peace.

In the book of Genesis we read that Cain, after killing his brother Abel, was asked by the Lord, *"Where is your brother Abel?"* Cain answered, *"I do not know. Am I my brother's keeper?"* The Lord answered: *"Your brother's blood cries out to me from the soil"* (4:9-10). The blood of millions upon millions of the unborn who were deliberately killed cries out for vengeance. And to the end of each mother's life who *"chose"* abortion, God's voice will ask in the depth of her soul what He asked Cain: *"Where is your child?"* And no preoccupation with other things will ever completely stifle that voice.

The Signs of the Times

On one occasion our Blessed Lord scolded the Israelites for not recognizing the fulfillment of the prophecies of the Old Testament. *"You hypocrite! If you can interpret the portents of the earth and sky, why can you not interpret the present times?"* (Lk. 12:54) They should have recognized Him as the Messiah. They should have recognized their day as the time of His coming.

From our knowledge of the Scriptures, are there signs at the present time that should indicate things to come? Only God knows the future, but there are situations in the Scriptures that find a striking parallel in our present day. And if the events recorded in the Scriptures are for our instruction, we can well afford to reflect on man's failure in the past, and God's dealing with him as a consequence. When the Israelites observed His laws, they enjoyed prosperity; when they notably failed, He punished them severely.

I would like to single out a few verses of Psalm 106 which have a frightening parallel to our present day. When God led the Israelites to the promised land, He commanded them not to mingle with pagans, lest they be influenced to turn to false gods. They disregarded this, intermarrying with them, adopting their practices, even worshiping their god. We read in the Psalm:

> They did not destroy the pagans, as Yahweh told them to do, but intermarrying with them adopted their practices instead. Serving the pagan idols, they found themselves trapped into sacrificing their own sons and daughters to the demons. They shed innocent blood, the blood of their sons and their daughters, whom they sacrificed to the idols of Canaan, desecrating the land with bloodshed. They defiled themselves by such actions.
>
> And the Lord grew angry with his people. . . . He gave them over into the hands of pagans, those who hated them became their masters. Their enemies oppressed them, and they are humbled under their power (Ps: 34-42, *American Catholic Bible*).

It might be fruitful to examine those lines in the light of our present day. We are not called to destroy a nation, or anyone, as they were; but as Christians we are called to be apostolic, that is, to seek to Christianize our surroundings, at least to give witness of our Christian faith. But instead of changing those around us, it is the

THE SLAUGHTER OF THE INNOCENT 199

pagan world that is changing us, or at least a sizable majority of us. We are adopting the ways, the thinking, the practices of the pagan world, at least we as a nation.

Millions of Americans (many of whom call themselves Christians) are offering sacrifice to the pagan god of pleasure, the god of science, the god of the almighty dollar, sacrificing their own sons and daughters through the "legalized" sacrifice of killing the unborn.

How well the inspired words of Psalm 94 apply to our time and our country: *"They do injustice under cover of law; they attack the life of the just, they condemn innocent blood."*

Worship of demons from the most ancient times has been associated with human sacrifice. We are not far from that today as a nation. There is little difference between the Aztec Indians of Mexico offering human sacrifice by the thousands (including their own offspring) to appease the unknown spirit, to obtain favors, and the millions of Americans who sacrifice the child of the womb, in order that this unwanted child will not interfere with the pleasure, the convenience or comfort of their life, in order not to increase the cost of living.

Those millions of parents and doctors may not be expressly and intentionally giving homage to Satan, but they certainly are delighting his satanic heart in their defiance of God who said, *"Thou shalt not kill"* (Ex. 20:13).

When the Israelites sacrificed their children to the pagan god, the Lord allowed their enemies to conquer them, to become their master. Does this pattern of the Old Testament indicate things to come? Only God knows, but the parallel is frightening.

Under Our Lady's Banner

The main enemy we must contend with is not a foreign nation, not a political power. As St. Paul expressed it, *"Our wrestling is not against flesh and blood, but against the Principalities and the Powers, against the world-rulers of this darkness, against the spiritual forces of wickedness on high"* (Eph. 6:12). Then he went on to explain the need of spiritual weapons. Our Lord, too, emphasized the importance of weapons of the spirit. On one occasion His disciples were unable to cast out a certain demon. *"This kind,"* He said, *"can be cast out only by prayer and fasting"* (Mk. 9:28). Fasting here can mean renunciation of anything man craves.

The ultimate forces of evil behind the immorality of today are such that no human power can match them if man is left to himself. But under the banner of Our Lady, who in the divine plan is to be the instrument of God's power in crushing the head of Satan, it is a different story. Place your prayers and sacrifices in her hands, who can do so much with so little. As Pope John Paul II admonished in speaking to the pro-life movement:

> Do not be discouraged by the complexity and the length of the struggle. Truth and good will triumph, even if not in the short term. . . . Since (this struggle) goes beyond human resources, do not fail to invoke the protection and help of the Blessed Virgin, Mary Most Holy.

Chapter Notes

1. Sacred Congregation for the Doctrine of the Faith, *Declaration on Abortion* (1974), n. 12, 13
2. Second Vatican Council, *Gaudium et Spes*, n. 51
3. *Ibid.,* n. 1

Chapter 25

Humanae Vitae *Reviewed*

On July 25, 1993, there was celebrated the 25th anniversary of the publication of *Humanae Vitae* by Pope Paul VI, the encyclical giving the Catholic doctrine on the regulation of birth, and condemning the use of contraceptives in that regard. There has perhaps never been a papal document that has met with as much opposition and caused as much controversy as this encyclical. It was not because the Church has taught something that was not true, but because it has taught something that was not popular, something that calls for sacrifice, something that our pleasure-seeking world flatly rejects, something that some Catholics with weak faith have not accepted.

The Basis of the Church's Teaching

Pope John Paul II, speaking to an International Congress on Moral Theology on the 20th anniversary of *Humanae Vitae*, explained: *"It is not a doctrine invented by man; it is stamped on the very nature of the human person by the Creator's hand, and confirmed by Him in revelation."* This encyclical confirms the doctrine expressed by Pope Pius XI in his encyclical *On Christian Marriage:* *"Any use whatever of Matrimony exercised in such a way that the act is deliberately frustrated in its natural purpose to generate life is an offense against the law of God and of Nature."*

Pope Paul VI explained the basis of the doctrine of *Humanae Vitae* as follows:

> That teaching, often set forth by the magisterium, is founded upon the inseparable connection, willed by God and unable to be broken by man on his own initiative, between the two meanings of the conjugal act: the unitive meaning and the procreative meaning (12).

Commenting on this teaching of Paul VI, Pope John Paul II declared in his Apostolic Constitution, *Familiaris Consortio*:

> When couples, by means of recourse to contraception, separate these two meanings that God the Creator has inscribed in the being of man and woman and in the dynamism of their sexual communion, they act as judges of the divine plan, and they manipulate and degrade human sexuality (and with it themselves and their married partner) by altering its value of total self-giving (32).

As to the Scriptural basis of this doctrine, the Lord referred to the *unitive* meaning of the conjugal act when He said in the beginning: *"A man leaves his father and mother and clings to his wife, and the two become one flesh"* (Gen. 2:24; Mt.19:5). He referred to its *procreative* meaning when He said to our first parents: *"Increase and multiply, fill the earth"* (Gen. 1:28).

Yet, we must not misunderstand the Church's teaching in this respect. As the noted moral theologian Monsignor William Smith points out, *"While the Church declares that these two dimensions of the conjugal act are inseparable, that does not mean that the two must be realized in every single instance, but rather that one must never act against them in any single instance. Why? Because this is God's design, God's plan; and we are meant to be cooperators with God's plan, not its judge."*

This doctrine, the Monsignor declared, *"comes to us from three sacred sources: the **Sacred Scriptures** revealed by God, **Sacred Tradition** guided by the Holy Spirit, and the **Magisterium** which has been endowed with the gift by Jesus Christ to teach in His Name."* Of these three sources the Second Vatican Council declared in its decree on Revelation:

> It is clear that sacred tradition, Sacred Scriptures, and the teaching authority of the Church (the Magisterium), in accord with God's most wise design, are so linked together that one cannot stand without the others, and that all together and each one in its own way under the action of the one Holy Spirit contribute effectively to the salvation of souls (n. 10).

Every situation involving human sexuality that has been rejected by the Church as immoral because contrary to God's design, involves an attempt in one way or another to separate these two fruits of married love (unitive and procreative) that God has put together. To mention a few of them: artificial insemination, *in vitro* fertilization (test tube reproduction), surrogate motherhood, sperm banks, cloning, artificial birth control, and so on.

While the following words of Christ were spoken in reference to divorce, they are equally applicable to the inseparable connection between the unitive and procreative meaning of the conjugal act: *"What God has joined together, let no man separate"* (Mt. 19:6).

Peter, the Rock

It is important to see the role of the Pope in these difficult times of dissent and crisis of faith on the part of many within the Church. Christ founded His Church on Peter: *"Upon this rock I will build my Church"* (Mt. 16:18). He entrusted His message to the apostles headed by Peter, and gave them the authority to teach and to bind: *"He who hears you, hears Me. He who rejects you rejects Me, and he who rejects Me, rejects Him who sent me"* (Lk. 10:16). *"What you shall bind on earth, shall be bound in heaven"* (Mt. 16:19).

Christ gave to His Church a twofold source of unity, a twofold guide. One is an interior guide, the *light of faith*; the other is an exterior guide, the *voice of Peter*. For Catholics, those two guides must always go together. One without the other will not stand. If the voice of Peter is rejected, the light of faith will go out. Without the light of faith, the voice of Peter will be rejected.

Conscience — Not Always a True Guide

Once one rejects this twofold source of guidance that God has given, he is no longer guided by the *light of faith,* but only by *human reason* which has been obscured by original sin. Such a one (whether he knows it or not) is given to wishful thinking, one of the weaknesses of our fallen nature. That is, we easily justify doing what we want to do, or not doing what we do not want to do. This is because our judgments are colored or slanted by our desires. And the greater our attachment to some created good, some satisfaction, the more our bodily and rational appetites tend to obscure our reason, and the more we are given to this self-deception.

That is why our conscience, which is simply a practical judgment of the intellect, is not always a reliable guide. This is the root of the problem of many in the Church today who reject this or that teaching of the Church. "I am following my conscience," they say, "which allows me to reject this teaching of the Church (for example, regarding contraception), and do what common sense tells me." What they are saying amounts to this: "My conscience allows me to reject what the *Spirit of Christ* dictates, and follow what the *spirit of the world* suggests."

Pope John Paul II, speaking on this topic in a general audience on August 17, 1983, said:

> It is not sufficient to say to man: "Always follow your conscience." It is necessary to add immediately and always: "Ask yourself if your conscience is *telling you the truth* or *something false*, and seek untiringly to know the truth." If we were not to make this necessary clarification, man would risk to find in his conscience a force which is destructive of his true humanity, rather than that holy place where God reveals to him his true good.

Once one rejects the *wisdom of Christ* handed down by the Church (that wisdom which includes the cross), he will invariably accept the *wisdom of the world*. There is no middle course, no neutral zone. *"He who is not with Me, is against Me"* (Mt. 12:30).

Once one rejects the teaching of the Church on any key issue, it is easy to reject other basic teachings of the Church. We read of those who consider themselves Catholic, and yet favor abortion, "pro-choice Catholics" as they like to call themselves. In all probability, a great percentage of these first began their rejection of Church authority by joining the ranks of those who rejected *Humanae Vitae*. Once one is no longer guided by the light of divine faith, the spirit of the world takes over.

Pope John Paul II, on the 20th anniversary of the publication of *Humanae Vitae*, commented:

> It cannot be said that the faithful have embarked on a diligent search for truth if they do not take into account what the Magisterium teaches, or if, by putting it on the same level as any other source of knowledge, one makes oneself judge; or if in doubt, one follows one's own opinion or that of theologians, preferring it to the sure teaching of the Magisterium.
>
> Closely connected with the theme of moral conscience, is that of the binding force of the moral norm of *Humanae Vitae*. By teaching that the contraceptive act is *intrinsically illicit,* Paul VI meant to teach that it does not admit exceptions. No personal or social circumstance could ever, can now, or will ever, render such an act lawful in itself. This is the constant teaching of Tradition and of the Church's Magisterium which cannot be called into question by the Catholic theologian.

The Holy Father makes it clear that the Catholic theologian cannot call this teaching into question lawfully; and where it happens, we have the blind leading the blind. *"If a blind guide leads the blind, both fall into the pit"* (Mt. 15:14).

The Garden of Eden Today

It will be helpful to consider briefly how all that we are speaking of ties in with what happened at the very beginning of the human race. In the story of Genesis, we read how Adam and Eve rebelled against God's command not to eat of the tree of the knowledge of good and evil. The devil deceived them. *"You will not die. God knows that the moment you eat of it your eyes will be opened and you will be like gods, knowing good and evil"* (Gen. 3:5).

Instead of recognizing God's authority and sovereignty, His dominion over all creation, they rebelled against the restriction He had placed on them; and we know the consequences.

The devil, who knows our human nature so well, uses the same tactics today, the same strategy that deceived our first parents. *"Reject that teaching of the Church. Those who issue these decrees are far behind the times. You know the world better than they do. They don't experience the same problems as you. Do whatever you feel is right for you."*

So suggests the Evil One. Once Adam and Eve had sinned, the kingdom of Satan was established, and they came under his dominion. Every descendent of Adam (with the sole exception of the Immaculate Mother of God) comes into this world under the dominion of Satan, and remains under his dominion until baptism. And even after baptism, the baptized Christian who falls away from the state of grace comes again under the power of Satan; and the greater his rebellion against the authority that God has established, the more he comes under Satan's power and influence and furthers his cause.

The Tree of the Knowledge of Good and Evil

How many today, in the use of their marriage, has the devil enticed to partake of that forbidden fruit of the tree of the knowledge of good and evil. God had allowed our first parents to partake of every kind of fruit in the Garden of Eden with one single exception. What precisely was God withholding from them? What was He not allowing the head of the human race by His command not to eat of the fruit of the tree of the knowledge of good and evil? A note in *The Jerusalem Bible* explains this as follows:

> It is the power of deciding for himself what is good and what is evil, and of acting accordingly, a claim of complete moral independence by which man refuses to recognize his status as a created being. This first sin was an attack on God's sovereignty, a sin of pride (Gen. 2:17).

Speaking of this verse in Genesis, Pope John Paul II says in his new encyclical on Christian morality, *Veritatis Splendor,* that *"it teaches that the power to decide what is good and what is evil does not belong to man, but to God alone. . . . Man's freedom is not unlimited. It must halt before the 'tree of the knowledge of good and evil,' for it is called to accept the moral law given by God"* (n. 35).

Yet, how many today, rejecting God's warning handed down by the Church, have partaken of that forbidden fruit! How many have claimed for themselves, as did Adam and Eve, a moral independence, refusing to acknowledge the restrictions placed on them by their Creator. How many, no longer guided by the light of faith but following their own selfish inclinations, have convinced themselves that they know better than the Church. How many are gradually coming more and more under the influence of the Evil One, following his suggestions rather than the voice of Christ speaking through His Church. *"He who hears you, hears Me; He who rejects you, rejects Me"* (Lk. 10:16).

Pro-Choice Catholics

Those who reject the teaching of the Church put forth in *Humanae Vitae* condemning the use of contraceptives join the ranks of *pro-choice* Catholics. "But," some will object, "that term 'pro-choice' refers to *abortion*." That is precisely the point; it does apply to abortion. And the expression fits perfectly those who use contraceptives, for many forms of contraception are abortifacient; that is, they cause abortions. Janet E. Smith, who has published two books upholding the doctrine of *Humanae Vitae*, explains this point:

> There is much evidence to show that not all contraceptive pills work by stopping ovulation. With many forms of the pill a woman may still be ovulating and thus may be conceiving. If she conceives when on the pill, she will most likely self-abort. Since the contraceptive has made the uterine wall hostile to a fertilized egg, the new young life, does not implant and dies an early death. The IUD, it is believed, nearly always works this way. Thus, IUDs and some forms of the pill not only contribute to abortion, they in fact cause abortions; they are abortifacients. Is it not clear, then, that contraception is a leading cause of abortions?[1]

Only God knows how many human lives have been conceived and then snuffed out by those who use contraceptives. It is all so minute and so hidden, but it is the destruction of innocent human life. *"Let them remember,"* warns Pope Pius XI in his encyclical *On Christian Marriage,* *"that God is the Judge and Avenger of innocent blood which cries out from earth to heaven."*

Independently, however, of the fact that abortion often follows the use of contraceptives, the deliberate use of artificial means to frustrate what God and nature intend is intrinsically wrong, and can never be justified. Such a one claims the right to negate God's plan, to interfere with the natural process established by the Creator.

O Mother of God, Mother of the Church, Mother of all mankind, obtain for your children the grace to recognize the rights of God, the plan of God, a plan that requires sacrifice, a plan that involves the carrying of a cross in the footsteps of your divine Son. Obtain for them the grace to see the Church's prohibition of contraceptives and the sacrifices it requires in the light of the cross, and the love to embrace it, that they may experience that interior peace that all the satisfactions and pleasures of the world can never bring.

Chapter Notes

1. Janet E. Smith, *Why Humanae Vitae Was Right*, p. 523

Chapter 26

The Fruits of Secularism

> *The following is, in part, a digest of a Pastoral Letter entitled "Statement on Secularism" issued by the American Bishops in 1950. Its message is even more important today when the fruits of secularism are far more advanced than they were over half a century ago.*

The word *secularism* is taken from the Latin word *saecularis,* meaning "worldly" or "earthly," as opposed to such terms as "religious" or "supernatural." In general, it is a system of thought that limits itself to human existence here and now in exclusion of man's relation to God here and hereafter. In short, it is the practical exclusion of God from human thinking and living.

We can speak of the secularism of those who deny the existence of God, as do the adherents of secular humanism, who look upon religion and any divine influence on the world and man as pure superstition; and there are not a few of these in positions of influence in our national life.

We can also speak of practical secularism as the way of life of those who, while not denying the existence of God or His influence on the world, in practice live their lives without recognizing that this is God's world. Such people may speak of God, may even go to church, but they fail to bring an awareness of their responsibility to God into daily living. They believe in a hereafter, but live with little thought of it in their daily decisions. This practical exclusion of God from daily living has done more than anything else to undermine our Christian heritage, which integrates the various aspects of human life and renders to God the things that are God's.

Secularism's Impact on the Individual

Secularism blinds the individual as to his responsibility to God. All the rights and freedoms of man derive originally from the fact that he is a human person, created by God after His own likeness and image, and *"endowed by his Creator with certain inalienable rights."*[1] Only from an awareness of himself as God's creature made to His image, and of his responsibility to God, does there grow in man a sense of sin. As one grows insensitive to God's image in every man, there is eroded in him the basic ground for mutual respect; and without a sense of accountability to God for his thoughts and actions, he lacks the foundation for stable moral virtues.

Since secularism does away with accountability to God, it leaves man with no sense of personal guilt before God. His only concern is man-made laws, and with the inclination to evil and selfishness of fallen human nature, self-interest will be his main incentive in observing them. Social justice becomes merely a political matter, as a consequence of which we have become a nation with much injustice in religious and racial matters, in education, in housing, in labor, and so forth. In public life, expediency and propriety become norms of human behavior.

Commenting on the need of a sense of responsibility to God in his Apostolic Exhortation *Reconciliation and Penance* in 1984, Pope John Paul II declared:

> This secularism cannot but undermine the sense of sin. At the very most, sin will be reduced to what offends man. But it is precisely here that we are faced with a bitter experience . . . that man can build a world without God but this world will end by turning against him.

In contrast with all this, the true Christian sees himself not only as a creature of God, but as a child of God, with holiness as his vocation and with concern about the welfare of his soul. *"What does it profit a man to gain the whole world, and suffer the loss of his soul?"* (Mk. 8:36)

While it is true that there has been a growth in Church affiliation, this has been offset by a weakening of the faith of many because of the growing influence of secularism, with a consequent lessening of the impact of Christian values in our national life. The moral regeneration which is necessary for the building of a better world must begin by bringing the individual back to a vivid recognition of his responsibility to his Creator.

Secularism's Impact on the Family

Secularism has robbed the family of its binding force with tragic consequences. Even pagan nations and peoples saw something sacred in marriage and the family. The Scriptures speak of it so sublimely that it is likened to the union between Christ and His Church. Yet secularism has robbed marriage of its sacred character by removing from it any responsibility to God. It is considered more and more a purely civil contract, not a spiritual bond between two persons under God. In place of the will of God and the good of society, secularism lets the nature and permanence of marriage rest on the will of husband and wife and man-made laws.

Our secularized society has legalized practices which violate the laws of nature and the laws of God, robbing human procreation of its sublime dignity. Self-sacrifice gives way to self-indulgence. The pursuit of pleasure replaces the pursuit of holiness.

In taking God out of family life, marriage is as a house built on sand with no solid foundation. When the storms of strife come, given the inborn weakness of our fallen nature which needs to be fortified by divine grace, the house collapses, as we see in the ever-growing number of divorces.

Our daily news media are constantly bringing our attention to the growing problem of juvenile delinquency. Yet our secularized society seems unaware that it is reaping the fruits of its own decisions. In taking God out of family life it has weakened and undermined the most basic and fundamental educational institution for the molding of character, focusing attention only on worldly goals. There is the constant cry that more money is needed for such things as expanded educational and recreational facilities, and for more law enforcement personnel to cope with the growing crime rate; but no thought is given to healing the malady caused by removing God and His teaching from daily life. As the American bishops in the pastoral letter we are reviewing declared: *"In vain shall we spend public monies in vast amounts for educational and recreational purposes, if we do not give more thought to the divinely ordained stability of the family and the sanctity of the home."*

It was the Creator who established the human family and gave it its basic constitution, and when that basic structure is tampered with, the fabric of society is gravely affected. With responsibility to God removed from the concern of parents, artificial family planning as a means of contraception has blurred the nature and purpose of sex, and the permanence of marriage intended by God has been rejected.

Secularism's Impact on Education

It is especially in the field of education that secularism has had the greatest effect in dechristianizing our society. A century and a half ago our government, in view of the different religious beliefs of students attending public schools, adopted a policy of banning formal teaching of religion from the curriculum of those schools. Yet the original intent of that policy was not to minimize the importance of religion in the training of youth. As time went on, however, secularists have managed to exclude God almost completely from public education.

Experience has proved that omission is as effective as a formal statement. When something is omitted from public education, the implication is that it is not essential to the end or purpose of education. What is implied is: either God has no place in education, or it is strictly a matter of private concern. In either case, the omission of any reference to God gives rise to a tendency to give

THE FRUITS OF SECULARISM

religion a low priority in private life, or worse, to engender young people with no sense of their responsibility to God.

In this, it breaks with the historic tradition of our founding fathers. Parents who are willing to sacrifice to maintain schools where children are trained in their religious beliefs along with their basic education, are acting in keeping with the spirit of the founders of our country. As the first president of our country declared in his farewell address: *"Of all the dispositions and habits which lead to political prosperity, religion and morality are indispensable supports. . . . Reason and experience both forbid us to expect that national morality can prevail in exclusion of religious principles."*

When an educational institution strives to teach moral values divorced from religion, it is forced to base them solely on social convention. The result is that morality becomes simply a matter of public opinion or majority vote, which is precisely the situation we have today — deciding by the legislature, or by the courts, or by public ballot such matters as contraception, abortion, euthanasia, divorce. With the legalizing of the deliberate killing of the unborn, our nation, which prides itself on its scientific and technological progress, has, in its separation of morality from religion, attained a barbarous level undreamed of a half-century ago.

Those who wish to make secularized public education obligatory for all criticize non-public education as divisive. But all differences are not divisive, just as our different political parties are not divisive in a detrimental way, but rather are an expression of the fundamental freedom guaranteed by our Bill of Rights. The differences that are harmful are those which divide people in such matters as good citizenship, patriotism, and concern for the common good. But private schools in which religion is rightly taught stress the importance of patriotism and loyalty to civic duties based on love of God, of neighbor and country. Such education is *unifying,* not divisive.

In recent years the evidence of the failure of purely secular education in many respects has not only caused many to prefer private schools in which religion is taught, but has given rise to home-schooling where the overall curriculum is blended with the teaching of religion in such a way that not only are children taught the basics of education, but also *"to render to Caesar the things that are Caesar's, and to God the things that are God's"* (Mt. 22:21).

The Need of Evangelization

Pope John Paul II, speaking on the vocation of the laity in the Church in 1989, spoke of the ever-growing religious indifference among many of the baptized as evidence of the inroads of secularism. This *"phenomenon of de-christianization,"* he said, *"strikes long-standing Christian people, and continually calls for evangelization."*

The Holy Father is speaking here, not of the evangelization of non-Christians, but of the *re-evangelization* of Christians whose faith has been weakened and whose love has been cooled. He was more explicit about this need in his encyclical *Veritatis Splendor:*

> This separation (of morality from religion) represents one of the most acute concerns of the Church amid today's growing secularism, wherein many . . . people think and live as if God did not exist. It is urgent to rediscover and to set forth once more the *authentic reality of the Christian faith,* which is not simply a set of propositions to be accepted with intellectual assent. Rather, *faith is a lived awareness of Christ, a living remembrance of His commandments, a truth to be lived out.* A word . . . is not truly accepted . . . until it is put into action. Faith is a decision involving one's whole existence. It is an encounter, a dialogue, a communion of love and of life between the believer and Jesus Christ, the Way, the Truth, and the Life. It entails an act of entrusting abandonment to Christ which enables us to live as He lived, in profound love of God and of our brothers and sisters (n. 88).

This *"authentic reality of the Christian faith"* is the fire that Christ came to enkindle in the hearts of men.

THE FRUITS OF SECULARISM

"I have come to cast fire upon the earth, and how I wish that it were already enkindled" (Lk. 12:49). That fire was ignited and burned brightly in the minds and hearts of the apostles, and that is why they were so instrumental in the spread of the faith. A fire gives forth both *light* and *heat,* and both are needed for evangelization. Both are needed for a *"living faith,"* one that *enlightens the mind* with the Truth handed down by the Church, and proclaimed by the successor of Peter, and *inflames the heart* with the Love that urges one to make the sacrifices required to love God above all things, and to love one's neighbor as oneself.

While our Blessed Lord became incarnate *"to cast fire upon the earth,"* notice that He did not deeply touch the hearts of his followers until He had given His life for them. That fire was ignited on Calvary. Only after that did the Holy Spirit come with those enlightening and strengthening graces, those purifying and healing graces, that transformed the apostles into the instruments of grace they became.

We, too, will not deeply influence the lives of others until we have borne the cross and undergone trials with patience in union with our divine Savior. Pope John Paul II reminded the Catholic laity of this in San Francisco in 1987:

> You are in the forefront of the struggle to protect the authentic Christian values from the onslaught of secularization. Your great contribution to evangelization of your own society is made through your lives. Christ's message must live in you — in the way you live, and in the way you refuse to live. At the same time, because your nation plays a role in the world far beyond its borders, you must be conscious of the impact of your Christian lives on others. Your lives must spread the fragrance of Christ's Gospel throughout the world.

Yet the dechristianization of our society is so widespread and deeply-rooted, that only special help from heaven can turn this trend around. However, divine providence requires that we do what we can. Although it is grace that turns hearts back to God, the Lord wants us to use the human means at our disposal. St. Thomas

Aquinas teaches that it would be tempting God if we omit to do what we can and expect everything to be done by Him.[2]

As to the disregard for God in our society, if every follower of Christ truly lived his or her faith, a veritable deluge of graces from heaven would flood this world. Only when the fire that Christ came to enkindle has been ignited in the minds and hearts of enough Christians will the tide of secularism begin to be reversed.

Our Blessed Lord so yearns for the return of those who have gone astray that He will mercifully pardon them, if only there is a sincere desire to return and a humble acknowledgment of guilt, and if sufficient prayers and sacrifices are offered to make up for what is wanting on the part of other members of the Mystical Body. So widespread is the crisis of faith that there is needed as never before on a world-wide scale sincere apostles (among the laity, religious and clergy) who will become the leaven, the salt, and the light of the world. Pray that God will raise up leaders in whose hearts that enlightening and strengthening fire burns brightly, to lead and inspire others to follow.

In those petitions do not fail to call on Mary, the Mother of God and of us all, who, in her own hidden way, far excelled all other humans in the one goal that counts — that of perfect love of God and neighbor. In her, the fire of love and light burned immeasurably more brightly than in all others. In her was her Son's wish most perfectly fulfilled. *"I have come to cast fire upon the earth, and how I wish that it were already enkindled"* (Lk. 12:49).

Chapter Notes

1. Declaration of Independence
2. St. Thomas Aquinas, *Summa Theologiae*, II-II, 53, 1, ad 1

Chapter 27
Our Adversary, The Devil

On November 15, 1972, Pope Paul VI began his general audience with these words: *"What are the Church's greatest needs at the present time? Don't be surprised at our answer, and don't write it off as simplistic or even superstitious: one of the Church's greatest needs is to be defended against the evil we call the devil."*

The Kingdom of Satan

In the book of Genesis we read that when God created the various things that He brought into being (for example, the light, the waters and dry land, the vegetation), after each one the Scripture says, *"He saw that it was good."* And after creating man to His own image, and giving him dominion over all that He had made, the text concludes: *"God looked on everything He had made, and He found it very good"* (Gen. 1:31).

This being so, how do we explain the existence of so much evil in the world, so much suffering, so much moral evil especially? Did something go wrong that God did not count on?

God made man to His own image, that is, with intelligence and free will, so that he was free to accept or reject the will of the Creator. We know that our first parents rejected it, and, since in them the whole human race was on trial, as a result of their sin our will is weakened, our judgment obscured and we are left with an inclination to evil. They rejected God's will, not because their will was weak, or their judgment obscured, or because they were inclined to evil as we are — but solely because of the deception of Satan, who himself had rejected God and was condemned eternally. And what is more, in bringing Adam and Eve to fall in this special trial, the devil gained a certain dominion over them and their descendants. With that fall, the kingdom of Satan was established on earth.

The Kingdom of God

The reason why Christ became man was precisely to deliver us from this *domination of Satan,* to conquer him and his kingdom, and to establish on earth the *Kingdom of God.* Even though Christ, by His Passion and death, has conquered Satan, and the ultimate destruction of his kingdom is certain, the Evil One is still allowed to roam about the world with a certain freedom to tempt souls. And though he lost the battle in his encounter with Christ, he has not lost any of his superhuman powers, his intelligence far superior to that of man, his cleverness, his hatred and envy of man, and his desire for our eternal damnation. As St. Peter warns in his epistle: *"Your adversary the devil prowls around like a roaring lion, seeking someone to devour. Resist him, firm in your faith, realizing that the brotherhood of believers is undergoing the same suffering throughout the world"* (5:8).

The Fall of the Angels

The Scriptures tell us quite a bit about the fall of man, but very little about the fall of Satan and the other angels who rebelled with him. St. Peter tells us that they sinned and were cast into hell (2 Pet. 2:4), but the Scriptures reveal nothing about the nature of their fall. However, some of the Fathers of the Church believe that some angels rebelled when they were given to know that they would have to pay homage to a *divine Person* (Jesus), who would assume a human nature inferior to theirs; or perhaps that they would have to pay homage to *a human person* (Mary), who by grace, would be raised above them as their Queen.

It must be especially humiliating to Satan that one who is inferior to the angels as to their natural powers has been raised so far above them and has become more powerful than they, through her sharing in the power of God.

The Arch-Enemy of Christ

Satan is the arch-enemy of Christ, confirmed in hatred of Him, his whole being dedicated to preventing His work of redemption. And just as there are countless numbers of fallen angels, Satan's collaborators in this war against Christ, so too, unfortunately, he has been able to deceive great numbers of human beings so that they are actually working for his cause.

We read in the Scriptures how Satan tempted Christ Himself in the desert; and we know how completely he was defeated in that encounter. However, if he sought to deceive Christ in *His physical body* and was humiliated by his defeat, you can be sure he will seek to tempt and deceive members of *His Mystical Body,* the Church. And if he did not hesitate to tempt the very Head of that Mystical Body, a divine person, he will certainly seek to tempt and deceive those in high positions in the Church, those in positions of influence over others, whether bishops, priests, sisters, theologians, educators, artists, that through them he might deceive and win over others.

Sister Lucia, the oldest of the three children who received the message of Our Lady at Fatima, wrote in a 1957 letter to Fr. Fuentes, then the postulator of the beatification of Jacinta and Francisco:

> The Most Holy Virgin has told me that the devil is about to engage in a decisive battle against the Virgin . . . and as the devil knows what most offends God, and what will make him gain the most souls in the shortest possible time, he does everything to win consecrated souls from God, for in this manner he will succeed in leaving the souls of the faithful defenseless, and so he will lay hold of them more easily.[1]

We know, however, that in spite of the divisions within the Church, Christ has promised that *"the gates of hell will never prevail against it"* (Mt. 16:18). Yet, from the beginning the Evil One has sought to deceive and win over those in positions of influence. Of the original twelve apostles, St. Luke tells us that he entered into the heart of Judas (22:3).

The Smoke of Satan

On June 29, 1972, Pope Paul warned that especially since the Second Vatican Council the devil has increased his attacks on the Church:

> We thought that after the Council there would be a day of sunshine for the history of the Church, and instead we found storms. How did this happen? We will confide this thought to you.... There was an adverse power, the devil, whom the Gospel calls the mysterious enemy of man, something preternatural — which comes to suffocate the fruits of the ecumenical Council.
>
> One could say that *from some fissure the smoke of Satan* entered into the temple of God. There is doubt, there is uncertainty, there is the problematical, disquiet, dissatisfaction.... there is confrontation.

The Holy Father refers to "fissures" (like cracks in the wall) through which the devil gains entrance, gains control over certain members of the Church, members who were freed from the dominion of Satan through baptism, but later fell back under his dominion due to the weakness of human nature and his clever deception.

In the parable of the wheat and the cockle (Mt. 13:24), a man went out to his field and sowed good grain; but while he slept an enemy came and sowed in the same field cockle — a harmful weed. When the stalks of wheat grew up and produced grain, the cockle came too. The owner of the field commented: *"An enemy has done this."*

That same enemy is today sowing weeds and cockle of error among the good grain of solid doctrine in the Church. And how does he do this? Again Pope Paul gives the answer:

> The devil undermines man's moral equilibrium with his sophistry. He is the malign, clever seducer who knows how

to make his way into us through the senses, the imagination, the libido (lust), through utopian logic . . . so that he can bring about in us deviations that are all the more harmful because they seem to conform to our physical and mental makeup, or to our profound instinctive aspirations.

Not that every sin is due to the devil's influence; but *"it is true,"* the Pope continued, *"that those who do not keep watch over themselves with a certain moral vigor are exposed to the influence of the 'mystery of iniquity' cited by St. Paul"* (2 Thess. 2:7). And without divine help they are no match for his intelligence and cleverness.

Although the devil cannot *directly* influence man's mind or will, he can and does *indirectly* affect those faculties by means of the external senses and the imagination, the sensibility, and the memory, as the Holy Father points out. He can awaken sense-images and cause us to have feelings that affect our thinking, and incline our will to accept what satisfies us.

Speaking of how the devil works through the imagination and the sensibility to achieve this deception, St. Thomas Aquinas states:

> It happens, through the rousing of a passion, that what is put before the imagination is judged as being something to be pursued, because, to him who is held by the passion, whatever the passion inclines him to, seems good. In this way the devil induces man inwardly to sin.[2]

The Tactics of Satan

The devil is too clever to show his hand, disguising himself as an *"angel of light"* (2 Cor. 11:14). He will suggest some veiled evil under the guise of something good, something part good and part evil, something part true and part false. He might, for example, encourage a little easing up on our efforts, a little less prayer, a little more indulgence in this or that, until the weakness and inclinations of our fallen nature do the rest.

It is sometimes said that one of the devil's cleverest victories is to convince man that he, the devil, does not exist. And how often do we hear today, even among Christians, of some who seek to reduce the existence of the angels to mere folklore. This is playing right into his hands.

There is a strange anomaly in this regard that is difficult to understand, except for the deception and cleverness of the devil. While on the one hand we find many intellectuals who will question or deny the existence of spiritual beings (and therefore of devils), we find on the other hand, a decided increase in recent times in the cult of Satanism. We can be sure Satan is active in fostering both evils.

The tactics of Satan over the centuries have not changed, because human nature has not changed. As mentioned above, St. Paul refers to the work of Satan as the *"mystery of iniquity,"* or as it is sometimes translated, *"the mystery of lawlessness,"* the devil being the *"Lawless One."* When we look around the world today and see the great amount of lawlessness, the great increase of every form of lustful immorality, of violence, of terrorism, of abortion, we can see the signs of Satan's influence on all sides. Truly, this is his hour.

The Devil's Subtle Suggestions

Let us consider briefly the subtle tactics of Satan, and see ways in which he manipulates many who do not realize they are being manipulated.

— Because of his great intelligence, he can suggest subtle different interpretations of the Scriptures, and of theology, that distort revealed truth.

— He will seek to persuade one to be broad-minded in moral matters, his object being a gradual weakening of one's moral fiber and a further deepening of man's tendency to wishful thinking.

— Knowing from experience how powerless he is against the humble and the obedient, he seeks to encourage a spirit of independence and of rebellion against lawful authority.

— Knowing how the Holy Spirit guides the Church in the way of truth, this *"father of lies"* (Jn. 8:44) seeks to bring us to doubt the teaching of the Church and to call into question its dogmas and moral teaching.

— Knowing the power of prayer to obtain grace, he seeks to instill in us the idea of self-sufficiency, that we don't need prayer, that we can manage our own life.

In countless ways the devil can deceive us with half-truths, as Pope Paul says, *"undermining man's moral equilibrium with his sophistry."* In some mysterious way he can bring suggestions before us that are so appealing to our pleasure-seeking, glory-seeking and freedom-seeking nature. These are a few examples:

— I need to be free of those telling me what to do, in order to attain my real fulfillment.

— If I suppress my sensual impulses and urges, I may do harm to my natural development.

— I am a mature person. I can read whatever I wish, or watch whatever kind of TV program or movies I wish. It doesn't affect me at all.

— If I always say no to others in regard to sex, or drugs, or alcohol, I will never be accepted by others. I will never have any friends.

— I don't need confession. I haven't any grave sins. And besides, if I stay away more, there will be less danger of routine confessions.

— My prayers don't seem to be answered, so what is the use of praying?

— My conscience is the only guide I need. As long as I am at peace with my conscience, I need not worry — even if some of my acts and decisions are not always in line with the teachings of the Church.

And so on without end, is the cleverness of the Evil One in exploiting our weaknesses, our likes and dislikes.

Call Upon Mary

All this may seem to present a rather pessimistic view of life, especially when we recall man's weakness and the devil's strength, our ignorance and his astuteness. In answer to this St. Thomas Aquinas reminds us that if there are countless fallen angels seeking to snare us, there is an even greater number of angels working for our salvation.

> So that the contest should not be unequal, men get some compensation, first, through the help of God's grace, and second, through the guardianship of the Angels. Thus Elisha said to his servant: "Do not be afraid, for there are more on our side than on theirs."[3]

In God's creation everything has a purpose. Even the fallen angels with their malicious deceitfulness can be used by God as instruments of testing man. Where there is no test, there is no growth. And in every temptation, sufficient grace is offered to withstand it (1 Cor. 10:13).

In the divine plan, Mary, the Mother of the Redeemer, is destined, through the power of her divine Son to crush the head of the serpent. Queen of heaven and earth, she can call upon the heavenly host to protect us from the wiles and snares of the enemy. This presupposes, of course, that we do what we can to avoid occasions of sin, and bring discipline to bear on our weaknesses, and rely faithfully on prayer and the sacraments, the chief sources of grace.

As Our Savior warned the apostles in the Garden of Gethsemani: *"Watch and pray that you enter not into temptation"* (Mt. 26:41). Prayer and vigilance are essential if we are not to be deceived and led astray by the tempter of souls, the *"father of lies"*. Pray, too, for those in positions of influence in the Church, for, as we saw, they are particular objects of the devil's attacks, as are all who keep God's commandments (Apoc. 12:17).

Whether it be moments of temptation, of doubt, or of conflict; whether the problems be ours, or those of another, heed with confidence the advice of St. Bernard: *"Look to the Star, call upon Mary!"*

Chapter Notes

1. Br. Michael of the Holy Trinity, *Third Secret of Fatima,* p. 25
2. St. Thomas Aquinas, *Summa Theologiae,* I-II, 80, 2
3. St. Thomas Aquinas, *Summa Theologiae,* I-II, 114, 1, ad 2

Chapter 28

Envy and Jealousy — Enemies of Charity

While the words *envy* and *jealousy* are frequently used interchangeably in ordinary conversation, theologians make a distinction between the two. Both envy and jealousy cause a selfish sadness at someone else's good fortune. Both of them spring from the feeling or conviction that one's stature, or image, or prestige is diminished by what someone else enjoys. *Envy*, which is a more general term, is sadness or displeasure at the temporal or spiritual good of another, because it is believed that in consequence our own excellence or image is lessened. Unlike the humble St. John the Baptist who said of Jesus, *"He must increase, but I must decrease,"* the envious person is saddened by the *increase* of another, seeing it to occasion his own *decrease*. *Jealousy*, on the other hand, implies, in addition to the above, that one has an exclusive possession of something. Jealousy is simply an acute form of envy, a more exclusive form of selfishness that wants some good to be one's exclusive possession, and is unwilling to share that possession with another. For example: the dislike of hearing another praised instead of receiving the praise oneself is *envy;* while the unhappiness or sadness resulting from some friend being with, or being attracted to another, is *jealousy*.

There is, of course, such a thing as a just and righteous jealousy, for the Scriptures speak of the jealousy of God. *"For I, the Lord your God, am a jealous God"* (Ex. 20:5). This refers to God's right to the undivided faithfulness of men and their trustful dependence. His jealousy was just, and His anger was righteous when the Israelites turned to other gods. There is also such a thing as a just and righteous jealousy on the human level, where one has a true right to the exclusive possession of another's affections, as in the case of married spouses. However, a married person would be displaying a jealousy that is not righteous, if he or she indulged in unfounded suspicion of the other partner's faithfulness, or if one denied to the other the enjoyment of normal human friendships which in no way intrude into the area of marital faithfulness.

Because there is much overlapping in the concepts of envy and jealousy, the latter being simply a particular kind of envy, we will be using both of the terms in the same general sense in much of what follows in these reflections.

Hidden Vices

The vices of envy and jealousy, like the pride from which they spring, are so deeply rooted in our fallen nature that they are hidden from the view of others, and in some measure even from ourselves. That is to say, we do not realize how much we ourselves are not entirely free from the selfish tendencies described above. We do not, in fact, always succeed in detecting the hidden motive of envy in our words and actions. The hiddenness of these vices aids their growth. Yet, if allowed to grow, they can gnaw away at one's inner self until they poison the heart, making it incapable of Christian love. Occasionally one's feelings may break out into the open and reveal what has lingered for some time beneath the surface in our mind and heart. It takes an honest and humble person to admit the presence of these vices within himself.

We are slow to admit even to ourselves that we are guilty of so mean a sin, and still less inclined to admit it to others. One test of this is: how often have we asked pardon for it in the sacrament of reconciliation? Yet, little by little there can grow such an unhappiness at another's success that it can develop into a hatred for the person preferred before us. We may feel we have worked equally hard, that we are equally well-prepared, perhaps better prepared; yet the other was chosen. It takes a truly humble and charitable person to accept such a situation without some trace of envy.

Enemy of Charity

The distinctive malice of the vices of envy and jealousy comes from the opposition it implies to the key virtue of charity. The law of love requires that we rejoice rather than be sad or distressed at the good fortune of another. As St. Paul stressed, speaking of fraternal charity, *"Rejoice with those who rejoice, weep with those who weep"* (Rom. 12:15). Yet the envious person tends to do just the opposite, to be sad at another's good fortune, and to rejoice at his failure. Such an attitude is a direct contradiction of the spirit of charity and solidarity that ought to characterize the Christian community. In both envy and jealousy, *love of neighbor* is displaced by *love of possessions,* whether the possessions be tangible (e.g., wealth), or intangible (e.g., fame, talent, virtue, friendship).

When one is jealous of the friendship of another, that is, wants it to be exclusive, the happiness of the friend counts for little or nothing unless such happiness comes through the jealous one. Such is not true love, it is pure selfishness. When a friend is happy we ought to rejoice in his happiness, no matter from what source it springs, as long, of course, as it does not spring from wrongdoing. It is clear, then, that jealousy is a sadness that springs from inordinate love of self rather than from true love of another, and it deprives one of happiness instead of giving it. Friendships, unlike the relationship of spouses, do not confer the exclusive right of possession.

What Envy is Not

Not all displeasure at another's good fortune is sinful. For example: the good received by another may be undeserved, as when an unworthy person is advanced to a position of trust and responsibility; or when the good received may create a nuisance for others, as when a neighbor boy receives a bugle for Christmas; or when

ENVY AND JEALOUSY

the good received may be harmful to the one who receives it, as when much money comes suddenly to a person who lacks the virtue to make good use of it.

The sin of envy does not consist in wishing we were as well off as someone else, nor is it the mere desire of equal success of another. That is a perfectly natural feeling. It is not the same as a competitive spirit. We might recognize someone's good points, and wish we had them, and strive to emulate them, even pass him up if we can, without envying him at all. Fr. Bede Jarrett, O.P. expressed this idea well in writing on the topic of jealousy:

> I cannot help contrasting my own poverty or want of decent livelihood with the luxury and possessions of better folk; nor again can I help wishing that this or that gift of nature or grace were mine: their charm or gracefulness or physical strength, or good looks. Again, the man who is discontented with his lot, and fired by ambition, aims at achieving a higher position for himself and his children, can hardly be called a sinner; and when I myself am so stirred by others' success as to venture into rivalry with them and attempt to oust them by fair competition from their place of supremacy, and to develop my own artistic or scientific skill which I know to be superior to theirs, am I in all these ways following after sin? Certainly not. In the case of one who attempts by fair competition to drive out a rival, he is simply putting to use the powers God gave him.[1]

In these matters trouble enters in only when the motive is wrong. If it is simply the wish to have what others have, or to compete with them fairly, there is nothing wrong with that. But if I am dominated by a secret dislike of other people enjoying what I wish to be exclusively my own, that indeed is jealousy.

Usually jealousy is found only among persons whose life and characteristics are on fairly equal terms, and generally it concerns some matter of public recognition. For example, a frailly-built fellow sitting on the sidelines might wish he had the physical build of the captain of the football team, but he is not envious of him. The fellow who would be envious of him is the unhappy fellow member of the team who feels that he should have been made captain, and that he would have been if the one best qualified had been chosen.

A Capital Sin

The sin of envy is listed among the capital sins which are customarily enumerated as follows: pride, avarice, lust, anger, gluttony, *envy* and sloth. Each of us, by reason of original sin, has inherited a tendency to each of these seven vices — usually referred to as a tendency to evil. Capital sins are so called, not because they are the worst of all sins (for sins springing from any of the above seven vices can be grave or light depending on circumstances), but because each of them is a root source of many other sins, which theologians refer to as daughters of the capital sins. For example, among the daughters of envy are resentment, bitterness and petty back-biting, tale-bearing and detraction, calumny and defamation, and other such shameful reactions. Eventually, it can lead to hatred and a desire for revenge, which can bring delight at the other's misfortune, and sorrow at his good fortune. Fr. Walter Farrell, O.P. refers to these offspring of envy as follows:

> The unlovely daughters of envy are among the most thoroughly despised sins that gnaw at the foundations of human life. They work up to the crescendo of evil which is the destruction of the mansion of a man's life: from the sly start of a furtive whisper, through detraction, then to joy in the misfortune of another and sorrow at his good fortune, and finally the climax of evil which is hate.[2]

The envious or jealous person, as we will see, is capable of going to any length, no matter how sinful, no matter how damaging, to vindicate himself. At times he will attempt to deprive another of the good name he enjoys by pointing out his faults, by minimizing any good he may do, thereby undermining his good name and reputation. By this vice, spiteful stories are spread abroad, reputations are ruined, and hatred is engendered, which often does not hesitate to take human life. As the Scriptures testify, *"Where there is jealousy and strife, there also are inconstancy and all kinds of vile behavior"* (James 3:16).

Much harm is done to religious and charitable causes because of envy and jealousy. In Church organizations, in choirs, in charitable projects, and so forth, good work is often hindered because of persons or cliques working against one another due to envy. In fact, there are more good causes, even apostolic causes, that come to naught, or are at least rendered much less fruitful because of infighting due to envy, than from all the external obstacles or challenges that confront them. How well the devil knows our weaknesses, and how cleverly by means of them he can disrupt or impede many good works.

The Grave Evil of Envy

Envy and jealousy are by their nature grievous sins, because they are directly opposed to charity, by which we are bound to love our neighbor as ourselves: to rejoice at his good fortune and happiness, and feel sad when evil and misfortune come his way. Both of these vices are among those St. Paul says exclude from the kingdom of God (Gal. 5:21). While in individual cases the moral evil of these sins may be light because they are concerned only with trivial matters, or because of inadvertence or only partial consent, they can be grave sins, indeed, as numerous examples from the Scriptures clearly show. To mention just a few:

— The downfall of the human race was the result of Satan's envy of the human race, the members of which would gain the eternal beatitude he had forfeited (Wis. 2:24).

— In the first human family, Cain, son of Adam, killed his brother Abel out of envy, because the Lord looked favorably on Abel's sacrifice but not on his own (Gen. 4:3-8).

— Joseph was sold into slavery by his brothers, who were envious of the treatment and affection given him by his father (Gen. 37:28).

— The attendants of King Darius, out of envy, had Daniel thrown into the den of lions (Dan. 6:3f).

— Miriam, sister of Moses, was struck with leprosy, because she was envious of the fact that God spoke through Moses, and not through her and Aaron (Num. 12:2,9).

— Saul, in his jealousy of David, tried to kill him (1 Sam. 18:6-11).

— The Gospel points out that Pilate perceived that envy was the underlying motive of the members of the Sanhedrin in seeking Christ's death, under the pretext of loyalty to Caesar (Mt. 27:18; Mk. 15:10). Is there any length to which envy and jealousy will not go?

Countering Envy

1) If we are honest with ourselves we have to admit that we can't help feeling jealous at times, since our feelings are not completely under control. In a similar way we can't help but feel the hurt of harsh criticism. Yet, in both cases we must be on guard to avoid an uncharitable response. It is only when jealous feelings overpower the light of reason, causing us to react in a foolish and uncharitable manner, that we succumb to this vice. It is important that we strive not to let our feelings dominate our thinking and lead us to spiteful desires and actions. To overcome such feelings we should ask God's help through prayer, for without that help our proud and selfish nature would surely react in ways not in keeping with charity; and our prayer has a healing effect in the heart when offered for the one who is the object of those uncharitable feelings. If we should suffer because someone is preferred to us, reflect that Christ was treated in the same way. Barabbas was preferred to Him by the Jewish people for whom He had done so much. We can grow spiritually by offering to the Father the pain we experience in such cases, in union with that of His Son. Becoming Christ-like must involve sharing some of the things He suffered.

2) If we would make headway against envy, we must strive to undermine the sources from which it springs. At times, one can be envious of the material wealth of another. Such a one would gain much from striving to direct his heart toward the eternal riches of heaven that, once attained, can never be lost. He must at the same time strive to detach his heart from the earthly goods that enslave his heart, riches that can easily be lost, and that he cannot take with him to the life beyond. He would do well to reflect on St. Paul's assurance that *"eye has not seen, nor ear heard, nor has it entered into the heart of man, what things God has prepared for those who love Him"* (1 Cor. 2:9). In heaven, each soul will differ in glory, according to the growth of grace at the end of his earthly life. Yet there will not be the slightest tinge of envy because another soul has a greater capacity to share in the divine life of the Blessed Trinity. Rather there will be only thanksgiving and praise and adoration of an infinitely loving Father who has given so much to all the Blessed. With perfect charity, each one will love all others as he loves himself, and will rejoice in their exaltation and glory as he does in his own.

3) Since envy is directly opposed to charity, which desires the good of one's neighbor and rejoices in his prosperity, one will find a powerful remedy against envy in striving (through prayer and effort) to practice fraternal charity. We are all members of Christ's Body, and as members of the same body the true gain of another can only redound to our good, and his loss to our loss. *"If one member suffers anything, all members suffer with it; or if one member glories, all members rejoice with it"* (1 Cor. 12:26). Too, charity requires that we *"bear one another's burdens"* (Gal. 6:2) and not add to them, as the envious person does by seeking to improve his own image by belittling another. We must learn to school ourselves to see good motives instead of bad in the conduct of others, to spend ourselves in helping others and to watch over our conversations where any trace of envy might find expression. Since God's command is that we *"love our neighbor as ourself"* (Lev. 19:18),

charity, which is the fulfillment of that command, requires that we rejoice in their merits, their virtues, their glory, their victories, as if they were our own. It should be clear, then, that in the measure that charity grows, envy will disappear.

Chapter Notes

1. Bede Jarrett, O.P., *Meditations for Layfolk*, p. 140
2. Walter Farrell, O.P., *Companion to Summa*, Vol. 3, p. 103

Chapter 29

Monica's Wayward Son

These reflections should be a source of consolation and hope to those who have a family member or someone close to them who is a source of anxiety and concern.

The prophet Jeremiah compares the man who trusts in God, come what may, to a tree planted near a stream, the roots of which reach out to the moisture below the surface. Such a tree, even in years of drought, has green leaves and bears abundant fruit (17:7).

In a similar way, the man who trusts in God is not shaken by the trials and crosses and difficult situations of life, for he has spiritual roots reaching out to God for those streams of grace that come through persevering prayer and the faithful and fruitful reception of the sacraments. His life bears fruit, not so much *in spite of* the trials and crosses of life but, in a way, precisely *because of* those trials and crosses.

There are two saints whose feasts we celebrate the 27th and 28th of August, whose lives I would like to consider briefly, since their lives bring out strikingly the point just mentioned. They are *St. Augustine*, the great doctor of the Church, and *St. Monica*, his mother, who, under God's providence, was responsible for his conversion through her many years of persevering prayer.

St. Monica

We often hear comments to the effect that if there had been no St. Monica, there would be no St. Augustine. Obviously, without the mother, the son would never have been born. But what is meant is that she, through her persevering prayers and sufferings, won for her son graces that not merely brought about his conversion, but led him to become one of the great lights of the Church.

St. Monica was born of Christian parents in the year 333. As soon as she was old enough, her parents gave her in marriage to Patricius, a pagan citizen of Tagaste in northern Africa. Patricius was a man of violent temper, yet Monica bore all trials with great patience. Her example and gentle conduct exercised such an influence over him that eventually he was converted to Christianity. He died the year after his baptism.

St. Augustine

The great cross of Monica's life, however, was not the temperament of her husband, but the conduct of her oldest son, Augustine, who was seventeen when his father died in 371. At that time he was a student in rhetoric in Carthage, where after some time he underwent an intellectual and moral crisis. He joined the Manichean sect (which held there are two supreme beings, one good, one evil) in which he remained for nine years. Monica was much distressed to learn that he had not only accepted the Manichean heresy, but was also leading a very immoral life. She prayed fervently and unceasingly for his conversion.

Eventually Augustine began to have serious doubts about the basic Manichean teachings; and in this state of confusion, at the age of 29, he decided to go to Rome to teach rhetoric. After a year in Rome, still experiencing frustration and still groping for the truth, he left Rome for Milan, where his mother joined him not long afterwards. When she found him in Milan, the preaching of St. Ambrose had already convinced him of the falsehood of the doctrines he had been following. One year later, in 387, sixteen years after the death of his father, Monica had the pleasure of seeing her son baptized by St. Ambrose. Soon after this, Augustine set out with his mother to return to Africa, but she became sick at the port where they were to embark and died there. Her work was finished. God took her to Himself.

So again we say, if there had been no St. Monica, in all probability there would be no St. Augustine.

How Some Saints are Made

Yet, there is another side to this story, another fact equally true, but one that we don't sufficiently reflect on; namely, if there had been no *wayward son,* in all probability there would be no *St. Monica.* She is revered in the Church as a saint, and is known especially for her trusting and persevering prayer. But why was she praying so fervently and so perseveringly? Because she had a wayward son.

There are many persons who are better Christians, better Catholics, because of the fact that someone close to them was a source of concern, persons who, in their concern for the wayward one, offered to God many a fervent and tearful prayer, offered to Him many times over an afflicted heart, a torn soul. As a result of such situations, it not infrequently happens that not only does the wayward one receive the graces needed to turn back to God, but the one offering those prayers grows much closer to God in the process. That affliction, caused by the loved one, was necessary to bring out a generosity of heart, to occasion many a sacrifice on the part of one whom God was using as an instrument of His love and mercy. And so it was with St. Monica. Her concern for her wayward son, Augustine, her prayers and sacrifices offered for him not only won his conversion, but brought her to the heights of sanctity.

God's Mysterious Ways

Do we ever stop to reflect that God's providence allows countless families to have someone who is a cause of worry, of anxiety, of many a heartache on the part of devout parents, but at the same time, one who occasions constant prayers on the part of those parents? God does not want failures any more than we, but He allows them, because in His infinite wisdom and love He can bring good out of evil.

God will not give any of us a cross heavier than we can carry. That truth can be stated in a positive way: He usually will give us a cross as heavy as He sees we can carry. If some people have an especially heavy cross, it is because God sees in each of them a strong soul, someone capable of being lifted higher, but needing something to draw out the best in them, as regards the oblation of self to God.

It has been said that there are so few saints because there are so few mortified souls, so few willing to share generously the redeeming cross of Christ. For that reason God has to take the initiative, sending trials to bring out the best in one, to bring out a generous response, a deeper exercise of faith and hope and love.

We sometimes hear the remark: "Why does God allow this if He loves us so much?" It is precisely because He loves us that He allows afflictions. He wants to share His gifts more than we want to receive them; but a price has to be paid for those gifts. Too, He often wants to give more than we ask for, and that is why He frequently makes us prolong the asking. He seems not to hear, not to be paying attention to our pleas. Yet, all the while He is preparing something far greater than we had ever hoped for, as in the case of St. Monica.

So a wayward son, a wayward daughter, a delinquent husband or wife, is no indication that God is not caring for us or our family. He wants the salvation of the delinquent ones infinitely more than we, but He will not force His graces upon them. He allows failures and downfalls because, as we said, He can bring good out of evil. He relies on those who love Him and trust in Him to make up for those who do not.

God often sees in souls a latent capacity, a generosity that is not being activated. Something is needed to bring out that generosity of heart, and often God uses the downfall of others dear to them to do just that. If their prayers seem to be without fruit, they should not be discouraged, but persevere in offering them, together with the heartaches involved, firmly believing that somewhere along the line, even if only at the end of the line, saving graces will be forthcoming. That is the main message that God gives us through St. Monica. If these anxious and concerned souls can only persevere in trusting prayer and the oblation of an aching heart, they themselves will have grown much closer to our Divine Savior in the process.

Filling Up What is Wanting

God needs that generosity, that unselfish love for souls. As St. Paul puts it, He needs someone to fill up what is wanting in the ailing members of His Mystical Body. *"I rejoice now in the sufferings I bear for your sake; and what is lacking in the sufferings of Christ I fill up in my flesh for His body, which is the Church"* (Col. 1:24). There is needed a circumstance where it is costly to say, "Yes, Lord, Your will be done." Often such circumstances are needed to make our prayers more fervent, our sacrifice more complete.

Yet, there is many a wayward son, or daughter, or husband or wife, who does not have some devoted member of the family praying for them, someone who really cares. For their return to God, the Mother of Our Savior calls upon her children throughout the world, seeking generous souls who will offer up their prayers and sacrifices for the conversion of sinners. And remember, she can do so much with so little.

The fruits of much of this will not be seen until the next life. The present need is to face the trials of life with trust in God, knowing that His ways are so different from ours. As Isaiah the Prophet reminds us: *"For my thoughts are not your thoughts, nor are your ways my ways, says the Lord. As high as the heavens are above the earth, so high are my ways above your ways and my thoughts above your thoughts"* (Is. 55:8).

Our permanent home, says St. Paul, is not in this life, but in the next (Heb. 13:14); and for that home, God is continually preparing us, though much of the time we are not aware of it. Even the process of growing old, with its many limitations, its humbling dependence, its aches and pains, is part of God's plan, part of the process of preparing us for the next life, part of the process of purification.

So just as without the wayward Augustine, there would probably be no St. Monica, so also, without various afflictions or trials that God in His providence allows, many a generous soul would have a less privileged place in heaven.

Many of the important Christian virtues are not exercised in any notable way until there is a difficult situation of some sort that puts them to test. For example: it takes an irritating or trying situation of some sort to bring out the virtue of *patience.* At times it takes moments of difficult decisions where, by reason alone, we cannot see the wisdom of some teaching of the Church, but believe that God is speaking through the Church, to bring out a profound exercise of our Catholic *faith.* It takes some kind of urgency, some kind of responsibility, where we cannot see our way through by ourselves alone, to bring out our *trust* in God. And it often will require a willingness to sacrifice our own will, our plans, our satisfactions in order that God's will be done, to exercise true *love* of God. And so it is with the other virtues.

We see, then, how God in His wisdom has His own way of drawing souls to Himself, allowing difficult situations, often humbling situations, which bring into play the basic Christian virtues, each of which can involve a different aspect of the cross.

A Reason for Hope

St. Paul called this kind of thinking a stumbling block for the Jews, and for the Gentiles, foolishness (1 Cor. 1:23). It can be a stumbling block for us also at times, if momentarily we see only the affliction or frustration, and not God's hand behind it. It can be foolishness for us at times, if momentarily we lose our perspective in the obscure light of faith, and see only worldly goals.

So if things get out of hand at times, if someone dear to you has strayed from the right path, reflect with faith and trust on the wayward son of St. Monica. There are situations of this kind in many families, situations which God allows, not as a punishment, but more to draw one closer to Himself. He lets the suffering one share in the pangs of His Sacred Heart, all the while being instrumental in bringing the fruits of His Passion to souls in need.

Chapter 30

The Truth Will Make You Free

In one of the Prefaces of the Mass during the season of Lent we read these words: *"This great season of grace is your gift to your family to renew us in spirit. You give us strength to purify our hearts, to control our desires, and so **to serve you in freedom.**"*

We will dwell a bit on the notion of freedom referred to above, because it has to do with a key notion in the Christian life, a notion much misunderstood by many.

Often people will quote the Scriptures to back up or justify their own efforts toward freedom and independence, and they haven't the faintest idea what freedom really means in the Scriptures, especially the New Testament.

Two Opposing Concepts of Freedom

There are two opposing concepts of freedom, one based on the *maxims of the Gospel*, and the other based on the *maxims of the world*. The first is based on divinely revealed truth, truth that makes a man free (Jn 8:32); the second ignores or rejects those truths, because they would limit or restrict doing what one wants to do. Let us examine these two opposing concepts.

a) Freedom based on the maxims of the world.

This is the only kind of freedom that many know and seek, namely, to be as independent and free as possible of whatever restricts their liberty. I am truly free, they seem to feel, only when I am completely independent of others telling me what I must do, what I must believe, how I must live my life, and so forth. They will accept, of course, certain limitations of civil law (for in this they have no choice), but all other restrictions, they feel, limit their freedom, infringe on their rights.

THE TRUTH WILL MAKE YOU FREE 243

There are certain aspects of the secular educational system of our country that encourage this frame of mind: "I must learn to make my own decisions, not allowing outside sources to impose their ideas on me as to what is right or wrong. All this is part of growing up, of becoming mature. I must make up my own mind as to *what comes first in my scale of values* — "values clarification" as they call it. In other words, I must be liberated from outside sources imposing their ideas, their concepts of morality, and so forth. Only then will the real person that I am blossom forth.

With that kind of freedom, the "real person that I am" will truly blossom forth, and the net result will not present a happy picture. With our fallen nature and its obscured judgment, its weakened will, its inclination to evil — all effects of original sin — the outcome could well be a person with little respect for parental or church authority, one resentful and rebellious against any outside source seeking to impose their system of values on him or her.

Of this notion of freedom or liberation, Pope Paul VI said:

> This word "liberation" has become an open sesame.... (Many feel) it exonerates modern man from all scruples and allows him to live according to his instincts and passions.... They have the mistaken and sometimes fatal illusion, that the best way to make life easy and happy is to free one's conduct from all authority, all prohibitions.... How far off course is the so-called "permissive morality," which frees man from absolute norms of good and evil.

b) Freedom based on the maxims of the Gospel.

The Christian notion of freedom is intimately bound up with the true concept of man's fallen nature: his weakened will, his obscured judgment, his inclination to evil, that is, his inclination to pride, to avarice, to lust, to anger, to gluttony, to envy and sloth. It is *from the domination of these that man must be liberated* — if he is to be *truly free.*

Every one of these inclinations has the power to enslave man, and they will enslave him if he gives in to them unduly. For the more we give in to any appetite or passion, the more demanding, the more domineering it becomes. It is from domination by these inclinations that man must be liberated, if he is to be truly free, liberated by the healing and strengthening effects of divine grace which will not be denied to those who are given to self-denial, to prayer, and to a striving to live the Christian life.

The Second Vatican Council speaks of the need of liberation in this sense:

> Man achieves his dignity when, emancipating himself from all captivity to passion . . . he chooses what is good . . . procuring apt means to that end. . . . Since man's freedom has been damaged by sin, only by the help of God's grace can he bring such a relationship with God into full flower.[1]

The Scriptures and False Freedom

From the above two contrasting concepts of freedom we can see there is a freedom that *ennobles,* that builds up, that brings man to his true fulfillment as intended by the Creator; and there is a freedom that *destroys* (both the individual and society), for it disregards the will of the Creator and the order He has imposed. It is a freedom that is better called license; and the Scriptures warn against confusing these two concepts. *"Live as free men, but do not use your freedom as a cloak for vice. In a word, live as servants of God"* (1 Pet. 2:16). *"My brothers, remember you have been called to live in freedom, but not a freedom that gives free rein to the flesh. Out of love, place yourself at one another's service"* (Gal. 5:13).

False Freedom Leads to Slavery

On one occasion Our Lord said to the Jews who believed in Him:

> If you live according to My teaching, you are truly My disciples . . . then you will know the truth, and the truth will make you free. They answered Him, We are the descendants of Abraham, and we have never been slaves of anyone. What

do you mean by saying "you will be free"? Jesus answered them, In truth I say to you, everyone who lives in sin is a slave to sin (Jn. 8:31-34).

It is strange how many think they are *free* (as they understand freedom), yet in reality are *slaves* to this or that passion, material possession, or worldly satisfaction which dominates the heart and holds it captive. St. Peter speaks of this in his epistle: *"They promise others freedom, whereas they themselves are slaves of corruption; for surely anyone is a slave to that by which he has been overcome"* (2:19).

We Cannot Serve Two Masters

St. Paul had a clear insight into this confusion, and asked his listeners if the fact that they had accepted Christ and were no longer bound by the Mosaic law meant that they were free to sin. *"By no means!"* he said. *"You must realize that, when you offer yourselves to someone as obedient slaves, you are the slaves of the one you obey, whether yours is the slavery to sin, which leads to death, or of obedience, which leads to justice"* (Rom. 6:16).

Just as there are *two kinds of freedom* (one based on the maxims of the Gospel, and one on the maxims of the world), so there are *two kinds of masters* that we can and will serve, corresponding to these two notions of freedom.

We will either serve God, the Creator, and become subservient to Him, or we will obey and serve the creature (mammon), that is, the world, the flesh, the ego. Our Lord told us we cannot serve both. *"No one can serve two masters"* (Mt. 6:24). But we will invariably serve one or the other; and the more we become subservient to one, the more we reject the other.

Pope John Paul II brought out this conflict in his *Apostolic Constitution on the Family*. After referring to various things that contributed to the breakdown of family life, he said:

> At the root of these negative phenomena there frequently lies a corruption of the idea and experience of freedom. ... The historical situation in which the family lives appears as an interplay of light and darkness. This shows that history is not simply a fixed progression towards what is better, but rather ... a *struggle between freedoms that are in mutual conflict;* that is, according to the well-known expression of St. Augustine, *a conflict between two loves:* the love of God to the point of disregarding self, and the love of self to the point of disregarding God.[2]

In light of this mutual conflict, and the anguish of the human heart torn between these two loves, we can see what brings one to reject this or that teaching of the Church, whether with regard to family life, marriage, human love, the sacraments, and so on. The more one becomes subservient to the pleasures, satisfactions and security of any given situation or circumstance, the more one will tend to reject any authority (in this case, the Church) that restricts or limits the enjoyment or use of them. And the more this becomes so, the more one's concept of freedom reflects that based on the maxims of the world, not those of the gospel. Such a one is seeking a freedom that destroys, not one that builds up, in the light of eternity.

The Fruits of These Two Freedoms

St. Paul refers to these two opposing notions of freedom in yet another way. He says we are dominated either by the Spirit of God, or by the flesh. *"The flesh lusts against the Spirit, and the Spirit against the flesh, for these two are opposed to each other"* (Gal. 5:17). The more one of these becomes the master, the Spirit or the flesh, the more the other is rejected. Then St. Paul proceeds to enumerate *the fruits* of these two kinds of freedom, or better, these two kinds of servitude.

1) The **worldly notion of freedom,** which glorifies and caters unduly to the flesh, seeks to be liberated from any authority that stands in the way of indulging one's attachments to the goods of this world, the pleasures of the body, and so forth.

Now the works of the flesh are manifest: lewd conduct, impurity, licentiousness, sorcery, hostilities, bickering, jealousy, outbursts of rage, selfish rivalries, dissensions, factions, envy, drunkenness, etc. I warn you . . . those who do such things will not inherit the kingdom of heaven (Gal. 5:19-21).

2) The **Christian notion of freedom** induces one, through the assistance of the Holy Spirit, to seek to overcome undue attachments to worldly goods, the pleasures of the body, and the glorification of the ego, precisely in order to be freer to seek the things of God. *"Now the fruit of the Spirit is: love, joy, peace, patient endurance, kindness, generosity, faith, mildness and chastity"* (Gal. 5:22).

Further Contrasts of These Two Freedoms

The **worldly concept of freedom** is a liberation *from without.* It says: "I don't want any outside source imposing limitations on what I want to do, or how I want to live." And when we consider: a) the condition of our fallen nature, with its weakened will, its obscured judgment, its inclination to evil; b) the materialistic culture in which we live, and the pressures and temptations with which it bombards us; and c) the cleverness of the devil to exploit both of the foregoing, one can see how destructive this kind of freedom is bound to be in the light of eternity.

The **Christian concept of freedom,** in contrast, is a liberation *from within,* a liberation within the heart of man, a freedom from being dominated by the world, the flesh, or the ego. The true follower of Christ is not subservient to any of these masters, so that he can truly love and serve God, the divine Master *"with his whole heart, his whole soul, his whole mind, and with all his strength"* (Mk. 12:29). In other words, he is free in this Christian sense, in the measure that his heart is "liberated" from domination by anything that makes him choose other than what God wishes.

While this freedom does not come without much prayer and self-denial, yet, it is in great part a work of divine grace healing, strengthening, enlightening the faculties of the soul. In this sense, *perfect freedom* is identified with *sanctity,* for God gives his graces in the measure that the soul, free from harmful attachments, is open to receive them. The more one is liberated in this sense, the more he is able to say "yes" to God, cost what it may.

One rather reliable gauge as to what kind of freedom one is seeking, is one's attitude toward *obedience*; for the worldly person looks on obedience as *standing in the way* of being free, while the true Christian (enlightened by faith) sees it as an indispensable means of becoming free.

> *"If you live according to my teaching, you are truly my disciples; then you will know the truth, and the truth will make you free"* (Jn. 8:31-32).

Chapter Notes

1. Vatican Council II, *Lumen Gentium,* 17
2. John Paul II, Vatican Council, *Apostolic Constitution on the Family,* n. 6

Chapter 31

Today's Crisis of Faith

How often in recent years have we heard the question: "What has happened in the Church since the Second Vatican Council? What has brought about the religious crisis on the part of many who were brought up in Catholic families, but no longer practice their faith? What has brought about the conflicting opinions we hear expressed in dogma and morals, opinions not always in keeping with traditional doctrine and practice?"

As Pope Paul VI stated: *"We thought that after the Council there would be a day of sunshine for the history of the Church, and instead we found storms."* The years that followed the Council have seen the rise of divisions within the Church and dissent from its teaching authority. What is the source of this turmoil, this confusion?

Not the Fruit of the Council

While the celebration of Vatican II might have been the occasion of the outbreak of these problems, it was not its cause. The causes (they are many and complex) go back many years before the Council. We will look at a few of them.

While some of the changes brought about by the Council were disturbing to "old time" Catholics, for example, in the liturgy of the Mass, those changes did express the mind of the Church. This refers, of course, to the changes that were *authorized*, not the *abuses* that followed. Yet along with these, there came gradually and almost unnoticed some changes, especially in the field of morality, that did not express the mind of the Church. New opinions of morality began to be taught and new practices accepted, which not long before were recognized as against the law of God.

There is nothing in the teachings of Vatican II that could be the source of the errors that cropped up in the years following the Council. However, when Pope John XXIII called for an *"opening of the windows of the Church in order to let in fresh air,"* that seemed to signal a certain freedom of thought in the expression of theological matters; and freedom always brings with it the possibility of being abused. As Fr. Hugh O'Connell commented:

> In the days before Vatican II, there was actually a very considerable amount of theological speculation and innovation; there were battles quite as heated as those going on today. The only difference was that such ideas were quietly presented in theological journals, and were subjected by experts to analysis and investigation, to weighing of reasons pro and con, to a more or less general acceptance or rejection by qualified theologians before they ever came to public attention.[1]

With the new climate of freedom, however, the Council, in its desire to update the expression of the Church's liturgy and practice, seemed to open the door for the appearance of new ideas, many of which were not in line with the official teaching of the Church.

The Remnants of Modernism

Around the beginning of the 20th century, Pope Pius X issued an encyclical, *Pascendi Gregis,* in which he condemned a number of errors of his day that are referred to as the heresy of Modernism. It was referred to as the *"synthesis of all heresies,"* as it affected the fields of philosophy, theology and Scriptures. It was an outgrowth of the agnosticism of his time, and belief in a form of evolution called vital immanence. It rejected, among other things, the idea of a transcendent God and the absolute unchanging norms of truth and morality. God is identified with His creation, and manifests His truth through the constant change that is going on in the universe. His revelation to man does not come from without, but from within, through personal experience. Thus, religion consists in an interior experience, an awareness of man's relationship with God.

Along with the publication of the encyclical in 1907, there was published a summary of 65 erroneous Modernist teachings rejected by the Holy See. While this helped to assure the clergy and laity of the official Church teaching, the sparks of the heresy did not entirely die out but kept smoldering, only to resurface again later in the century under what present-day theologians refer to as Neo-Modernism.

That such ideas have not disappeared is evident from a present-day educator, who, along with others of his school of thought, has had considerable influence on modern catechetics. Brother Gabriel Moran, for whom the basis of theology is not supernatural revelation but experience, wrote in his book *Catechesis of Revelation:*

> Revelation consists only in present conscious experience of people[2].... There is no revelation except in God revealing Himself in personal experience.... One must choose to structure it (the curriculum) according to the people precisely because that is where revelation is[3].... People who demand that there be a higher norm of truth than human experience are asking for an idol.[4]

Since these opinions were expressly condemned by Pope Pius X in 1907, how true are the words of G. K. Chesterton:

> Nine out of ten of what we call new ideas are simply old mistakes. The Catholic Church has for one of her chief duties that of preventing people from making those old mistakes; from making them over and over again, as people will always do if they are left to themselves.

Neo-Modernism

Msgr. Eugene Kevane, in his book, *Creed and Catechetics,* sees the well-known *Dutch Catechism* as being heavily infected with the remnants of Modernism. *"The characteristics of its Neo-Modernistic catechetical approach, its ambiguities, its omissions and its outright doctrinal errors, live on in many . . . programs of religious education, and in teaching aids which implement them."*[5]

Commenting on that Catechism, Fr. Edwin C. Garvey wrote as follows:

> The Declaration of the Papal Commission of Cardinals on the new *Dutch Catechism*, published in 1968, found it necessary to accuse this Catechism of brutal education by the omission of central truths of the Catholic faith. This commission pointed out that basic doctrines such as original sin, satisfaction and redemption by Christ, the nature of the Mass, the Real Presence, the ten commandments, the communion of saints, the angels and the devils, immortality of the soul, the nature of the Church, the role and prerogatives of Mary, were either completely neglected or were vaguely taught. Those familiar with religion textbooks presently used in America know that the same criticism can be validly made of many.... At the present time the disease of Modernism has become so pervasive and so virulent that, by comparison, as Maritain writes, the Modernism of Pius X's time was only a mild hay fever compared to the neo-modernist fever of today.[6]

It was precisely to emphasize the elements being passed over in many modern educational systems, or being incorrectly taught, that Pope Paul VI issued his *Creed of the People of God.*

The New Morality

As we have already pointed out, after the Council, there was a growing acceptance of new ideas of morality, where certain practices began to be accepted, which not long before were considered sinful. What is this "new morality," and where did it come from? Without doubt it did not come from Vatican II, nor from any branch of the teaching authority of the Church. The weakening of the faith of many Catholics by Modernism paved the way for it, but the more immediate source from which it sprang was *existentialism,* a system of thought rejected by Pope Pius XII, that is based on the premise that there is nothing that is absolute and unchangeable, that all things are in continuous evolution. Applied to human activity, it holds there are no absolute, universal moral laws.[7]

The new morality is known by various names. Sometimes it is called "existential ethics," but more often it is known as "situation ethics." It does not obligate one to rely on the Church for guidance, but allows one to rely on *conscience alone* in determining one's course of action.

Situation ethics maintains that moral decisions should no longer be based on *universal moral laws* — such as the ten commandments; that *objective moral standards* are of little value in such decisions, because moral problems are personal and unique. Thus they hold that moral decisions should be based on one's personal judgment in a given particular situation (hence "situation" ethics). They reason in this manner: since each situation is different, the individual's conscience alone must determine what is morally right for him, apart from any universal principle or law. It is a matter between the individual conscience and God. If one is sincere and conscientious, that is all that God asks. Christians must learn to take the responsibility for their own acts, instead of relying on external laws as a guide. Such, they say, is Christian maturity.

Without going into further details as to this system of ethics, it might help to a better understanding of these matters if we contrast the *traditional theology* on which the Church has relied over the centuries, and the so-called *new theology,* or *new morality* of which we have been speaking. While all who dissent from the magisterium may not do so in all of these ways, the following are some of the major areas of conflict.

1) Traditional theology stresses *God* as the center of all things; while the *new theology* makes *man* the center. Their attention is mainly on man. God is not denied, but love and service of God is reduced to love and service of neighbor. Love of neighbor becomes the first and principal commandment. Commenting on this, Pope Paul VI said that while love of neighbor is essential, and on it we will be judged, *"to give priority of place to humanitarianism leads to the danger of transforming* *theology into sociology, and of forgetting the basic hierarchy of things and their values."*[8]

2) Traditional theology stresses that *truth is eternal and changeless*, based on the changeless nature of things, and ultimately on God who is eternal and changeless Truth. The *new morality* claims that *all things are in constant evolution,* so there are no absolute norms that apply to all situations.

3) Traditional theology stresses that God gave man not only an *interior guide*, conscience, but also an *exterior guide*, the Church, which was established by Christ to safeguard and interpret divine revelation. The *new morality* stresses that *conscience alone* need be our guide in following Christ. They would not do away with the norms found in Scripture, but with any guidance of the Church in interpreting them, so that the conscience of the individual would be the absolute master of his own decisions.

This, said Pope Pius XII, is the central weakness of the new morality. It was to the Church, and not to individuals, that Christ gave His revelation; and it was to the Church that Christ promised the divine aid required for avoiding error. *"The autonomy of the individual conscience,"* said the Pope, *"cannot be reconciled with the divine plan, and can produce only poisonous fruit."*[9]

This same rejection of the Church as guide in interpreting God's revealed word is found in many who seek to apply *Liberation Theology* to the social problems of today. In line with Marxist thinking, they claim the Church is influenced by capitalistic ideology which colors its interpretation of the Gospel. The Gospel, they say, must be read from the standpoint of the poor, the oppressed. Only the poor, they believe, and those who take the side of the poor and fight for them, can understand its true meaning.

In line with this, the present writer spent eight years working with the poor in Central America, where the teachings of Liberation Theology were being applied; and the principal "liberation" that he witnessed was the liberation of those proposing these ideas from traditional theology and from the magisterium of the Church.

4) Traditional theology stresses that supernatural public revelation of God's message to mankind ended with the death of the apostles. As the *Dogmatic Constitution on Divine Revelation* in Vatican II expressed it: "*We now await no further new public revelation before the glorious manifestation of Our Lord Jesus Christ.*"

(Note: We distinguish *public revelation,* which ended with the apostles, from *private revelation*, such as Lourdes and Fatima, belief in which is not a requisite for salvation.)

The *new theology* holds that public revelation did not end with the apostles, but is still going on, something that is communicated and understood through the mode of personal experience. In this manner an "ongoing" revelation is still bringing new divine truths to mankind. Consequently they don't speak of the *development* of dogma or of moral norms, but the *evolution* of them. Thus doctrines and moral norms can change from age to age.

We can see this concept at work if we examine the instructions in faith and morals given in some of our catechetical texts. The true dogmas of our faith are slighted, if not ignored, while the students are urged to discern their feelings and experience, which means they are to draw from their own experience and feelings, whether or not they will accept this or that teaching of the Church. A common example of this in modern education methods is referred to as "values clarification."

Safeguarding the Gift of Faith

Since our Catholic faith is a divine gift enabling us to believe with conviction divine truths as proposed by the Church, we can see how the subjectivism of the false doctrines we have been considering will undermine and pave the way for the loss of that precious gift. No Catholic ever loses that gift of faith, except he deliberately rejects God's revealed word as handed down by the Church.

When a heresy has to do with the very nature of God and His relationship with His creation, it is bound to have fundamental and far-reaching effects on religion and religious beliefs. While there may be few today who publicly hold in full these erroneous religious doctrines of which we have been speaking, there are many overtones of them in some of our present-day texts; and the effects of them are seen in the thinking of many Catholics. How else could there be (if the polls are correct) a considerable percentage of Catholics who reject the Church's official teaching on contraceptives, the use of which Pope Paul VI declared is intrinsically wrong, and can never be right.

As to when one loses the gift of faith, only God knows. Externally one's life may remain much the same, still going to Mass and receiving the sacraments, but rejecting some official teaching of the Church. Such a one is no longer being guided by the divine light of faith, but only by the light of reason which is often slanted by our desires. Contrary to what the "new theology" might say, faith is not a matter of the feelings, but a humble response to and acceptance of God's revealed truth, as handed down by the Church.

The gift of faith, for those who have attained the use of reason, requires a surrender of both mind and will, which Vatican Council II refers to as *"an obedience by which man commits his whole self freely to God, offering full submission of intellect and will to God who reveals, and freely assenting to the truth revealed by Him."*[10] St. Paul refers to this as *"the obedience of faith"* (Rom 16:26).

Through the virtue of faith, the *mind of man* is brought into contact with the *mind of God,* who is infinite truth. Thus, a condition of sharing in God's truth is the humble submission of the mind, accepting His revealed word, not because one sees clearly the reasons for it, but on the authority of the infinite God revealing it, and on His promise to preserve from error the Church through which that truth is handed down.

St. Paul speaks of this submission of the mind when he says that by means of spiritual weapons *"we demolish sophistries... and all that rears its proud head against the knowledge of God... bringing every mind into captivity to the obedience of Christ"* (2. Cor. 10:4). Pope Leo XIII applies that text to those who dissent: *"They who take from Christian doctrine what they please, lean on their own judgment, not on faith . . . not 'bringing the mind into captivity to the obedience of Christ'... they more truly obey themselves than God."*

This surrender of the mind does not in any way infringe on the freedom and liberty of man. It does not degrade him, but rather perfects his knowledge of God's truth. It is a surrender, a submission, yes, but one that is *freely* given, and a surrender not to man, but to God. It is a surrender that does not *enslave,* but rather one that *frees* one from the doubts and uncertainties that would invariably arise if man were left to himself. It is a necessary condition to attain *"the truth that makes one free"* (Jn. 3:32).

Chapter Notes

1. Hugh O'Connell, *Keeping Your Balance in the Modern Church,* p. 7
2. Brother Gabriel Moran, *Catechesis of Revelation,* p. 13
3. *Ibid.,* p. 144
4. *Ibid.,* p. 45
5. Eugene Kevane, *Creed and Catechetics,* p. xvi
6. Edwin C. Garvey, *Homiletic and Pastoral Review,* "Process Theology and the Crisis in Catechetics"
7. *Humani Generis* 6
8. Pope Paul VI, Allocution, July 3, 1968
9. Pope Pius XII, Radio Address, March 23, 1952
10. Vatican Council II, *Dei Verbum,* 5

Chapter 32

Indulgences

Much of this chapter is a summary of the *Enchiridion of Indulgences* issued by the Sacred Apostolic Penitentiary in 1968 with the approval of Pope Paul VI. This *enchiridion* (or handbook) contains, in addition to the Pope's *Apostolic Constitution on Indulgences*, new norms and grants of indulgences, and a list of 70 prayers and individual works enriched with indulgences. *"All general grants of indulgences not included in this same Enchiridion,"* declares the decree of the Sacred Penitentiary, *"are hereby revoked."*

What is an Indulgence?

An indulgence is the remission before God of the *temporal punishment* due for sins for which the *guilt* has already been forgiven. This remission of punishment is granted through the intervention of the Church, which has the power, granted by Christ, of dispensing from the treasury of the superabundant satisfactions of Christ and the saints.

To understand more fully the above definition, we will have to look briefly at several things: 1) the punishment due for sin; 2) the solidarity of all men by reason of the Mystical Body of Christ; 3) the spiritual treasury of the Church; 4) the power of the keys of the kingdom established in Christ.

1) Punishment due for sin: For each and every sin that man commits, he incurs both a *guilt* before God (for it is an offense against the friendship between God and man, which it mars or destroys), and a *debt of punishment*, which Pope Paul Vl declared *"may remain to be expiated or cleansed — and, in fact, frequently does remain — even after the remission of guilt,"*[1] that is, even after sacramental confession. This is because of the imperfection of our contrition or the incompleteness of our turning away from sin.

The *punishment* due for sin can never be removed as long as the *guilt* has not yet been forgiven, that is, as long as one has not yet turned to God with sincere contrition and a firm resolve of amendment. This debt of punishment may be expiated *in this life* by the sufferings, hardships and trials of each day willingly borne, by mortification voluntarily undertaken, and above all by death; or *in the life beyond* through the purification of purgatory. It may also be expiated by *indulgences,* which can be applied to one's own soul, or the souls in purgatory.

2) The Mystical Body of Christ: Due to the unity of all the faithful in Christ, the satisfaction performed by one member can be applied to another. This transfer is possible by reason of the communion of saints, the Mystical Body of Christ. As St. Paul explained, *"Just as each of us has one body with many members . . . so too we, though many, are one body in Christ and individually members one of another"* (Rom. 12:11).

Thus, because of this great mystery, not only can the fruits of Christ's Passion be applied to His members, but the Christian faithful can help one another, as Pope Paul VI points out, by an *"exchange of spiritual goods and penitential expiation . . . carrying their crosses in expiation for their own sins and those of others, certain that they can help their brothers to obtain salvation from the Father of mercies."*[2]

3) Spiritual Treasury of the Church: This treasury of the Church is the spiritual storehouse, so to speak, containing the infinite merits and satisfaction of Christ, and the superabundant satisfaction of the Blessed Virgin and the saints. Both Christ and His Mother were without sin, so the satisfactory value of all their good deeds and acts was not needed to pay their debt, for they had none; and thus it can be applied to the debt of others. The saints too, although they sinned, offered to God far more reparation than was needed to pay the debt of their sins.

All this superabundant satisfaction, which can be applied to others, constitutes the spiritual treasury of the Church, the riches of which can be applied to pay the debt of punishment, in whole or in part, both of souls on earth, and of the souls in purgatory.

4) The Power of the Keys: The source of this power is Christ Himself: *"I will give you the keys of the kingdom of heaven; and whatever you shall bind on earth shall be bound in heaven; and whatever you shall loose on earth shall be loosed in heaven"* (Mt. 16:19).

The power of the keys includes not only the power in the sacrament of penance of removing the guilt of grave sin, and the eternal punishment due it; but also, apart from this sacrament, the jurisdiction of dispensing to souls, through indulgences, the superabundant satisfaction or expiation of Christ and the saints, thus lessening or canceling the penalty of temporal punishment for sin. When the Pope grants an indulgence for a given act or prayer, he does so by virtue of the power of "loosing," which Christ gave to His Church, drawing from her spiritual treasury, as we saw, the means by which this penalty is satisfied.

The Church, however, has no jurisdiction over the dead, and therefore she can grant an indulgence in their favor only by way of suffrage, that is, only by way of petitioning God to accept these works of satisfaction on their behalf. We can never know how much satisfaction God accepts on their behalf; for this reason, it is worthwhile to seek to gain a number of indulgences (plenary and partial) for an individual soul.

A New Norm of Measurement

One notable change in the new Decree on Indulgences is that it has done away with the former manner of designating partial indulgences by "days" and "years," for example, an indulgence of 100 days. A new norm has been established which takes into account the action itself of the faithful who performs a work to which an indulgence has been attached.

Pope Paul VI points out in his *Apostolic Constitution on Indulgences* that any good work done for God has both a *meritorious* value and a *satisfactory* value. The principal fruit is the merit, for it brings an increase of grace; the secondary effect or fruit is the remission of temporal punishment due to sin. Speaking of this, he said:

> Since . . . the remission of temporal punishment is in proportion to the degree that the charity of the one performing the act is greater, and in proportion to the degree that the act itself is performed in a more perfect way, it has been considered fitting that this remission of temporal punishment which the Christian faithful acquire through an action should serve as *the measurement* for the remission of punishment which the ecclesiastical authority bountifully adds by way of partial indulgence.[3]

The above explanation might be expressed by the following example: If a given act, because of the charity by which it was done, brought a remission of 5% of the punishment due for sin, the Church (by way of a partial indulgence) grants the remission of an additional 5% of the punishment due. In other words, when one performs a good work enriched with a partial indulgence there is granted by the power of the Church that same amount of remission of temporal punishment as already gained by the work itself. That is to say, in such a good work, the remission of the temporal punishment is doubled.

The Church has ceased to grant indulgences in terms of "days" and "years," because many of the faithful concentrated more on seeking richer grants of indulgences than on the faithful fulfillment of the duties of their state in life, which merits an increase of grace, and which St. Thomas Aquinas says *"is infinitely greater than the remission of temporal punishment."*[4]

In a word, the Church would have us devote more attention to living a truly Christian life, and to growing in the spirit of prayer and mortification in keeping with the spirit of the Gospel, than to the mere repetition of certain formulas and acts.

Three General Grants of Indulgences

In order to aid the faithful to bring their faith to bear on the actions that go to make up their daily lives, the Church has granted three general concessions in regard to the gaining of partial indulgences:

1) A partial indulgence is granted to the faithful who, in the performance of their duties, and in bearing the trials of life, raise their mind with humble confidence to God, adding — even if only mentally — some pious invocation.

This first grant is intended as an incentive to the faithful to intersperse their daily duties with brief interior invocations that help them to fulfill their labors and bear their trials in union with Christ. Note that only those acts are indulgenced by which the faithful, while performing their duties and patiently suffering the trials of life, raise their mind to God as indicated.

This shows that the work involved in our daily duties, and the trials we suffer, can profit us either little or much (both as to the increase of grace, and the remission of the debt of punishment), depending on whether we fulfill or bear them in a spirit of faith and of prayerful resignation to the will of God and a desire to help souls; or in a selfish and worldly spirit that is concerned only about worldly goals and satisfactions, with little thought of God and little concern for others.

The "pious invocation" referred to can be any ejaculatory prayer that helps one to raise the mind and heart to God, "even if only mentally." And the Holy See assures us:

> Should anyone be so zealous and fervent as to make such acts frequently in the course of the day, he would justly merit, over and above a copious increase of grace, a fuller remission of the punishment due for sin, and he would in charity be able to come to the aid of souls in purgatory so much the more generously.[5]

2) A partial indulgence is granted to the faithful who, in a spirit of faith and mercy, give of themselves or of their goods to serve their brothers in need.

This second grant is intended to serve as an incentive to the faithful to perform more frequent acts of charity and mercy, remembering the words of Christ, *"As often as you did it for one of these, the least of my brothers, you did it for me"* (Mt. 25:40).

The Decree states that not all works of charity are thus indulgenced, but only those which serve "the brothers in need." Yet this can cover a great variety of good works, such as we read in the *Decree on the Apostolate of the Laity* in the Second Vatican Council:

> Wherever there are people in need of food and drink, clothing, housing, medicine, employment, education; wherever men lack the facilities necessary for living a truly human life or are afflicted with serious distress or illness, or suffer exile or imprisonment, there Christian charity should seek them out and . . . console them with great solicitude and help them with appropriate relief. . . . Thus attention is to be paid to the image of God in which our neighbor has been created, and also to Christ the Lord to whom is really offered whatever is given to a needy person.[6]

3) A partial indulgence is granted to the faithful who, in a spirit of penance, voluntarily deprive themselves of what is PERMITTED and PLEASING to them.

This third grant is intended to encourage the faithful to mortify their appetites and bodily satisfactions, and thus bring the body under subjection in conformity with the poor and suffering Christ. As the *Apostolic Constitution* of Pope Paul points out, self-denial will be more pleasing to God when it is united to charity, for example, when what one could spend on amusements or self-indulgence is given to the poor. As Pope Leo the Great says, *"Let what we deny ourselves by fast — be the refreshment of the poor."*

This grant is offered by the Church at the present time when, with the mitigation of the law of fast and abstinence, it is more than ever imperative that penance be practiced in other ways.

To Gain an Indulgence:

The recipient of an indulgence must be *"baptized, not excommunicated, in the state of grace at least at the completion of the prescribed works, a subject of the one granting the indulgence . . . and have at least a general intention of gaining the indulgence."*[7]

To gain a PLENARY indulgence, which removes all temporal punishment due, and which can be gained only once a day, in addition to the above, the Holy See lists the following requisites: *"sacramental confession, Eucharistic Communion, prayers for the intention of the Supreme Pontiff and the absence of all attachment to venial sin."*[8]

Some theologians are of the opinion that plenary indulgences are not gained as often as some people think, because of the difficulty of being free of all attachment to venial sin. If this disposition is less than complete, or if the other prescribed conditions are not fulfilled, a partial indulgence is gained.

A single sacramental confession suffices for gaining several plenary indulgences; but Communion must be received and prayer for the intentions of the Sovereign Pontiff must be recited for the gaining of each plenary indulgence. One "Our Father" and one "Hail Mary" is sufficient in praying for the intentions of the Pope.[9]

A Few Things to Remember

1) Both partial and plenary indulgences can be applied to the souls in purgatory.

2) While the satisfactory value of any good work can be applied to another living person, indulgences cannot be gained for another living person.

3) The faithful must remember that the departed can be assisted not only by means of indulgences, but also by

other ways: prayers, penitential acts, works of mercy, almsgiving, and especially by the sacrifice of the Mass.[10]

4) While many partial indulgences have been dropped from the *Enchiridion*, the three general grants described above open up unlimited opportunities for partial indulgences, and in areas that go to the heart of the Christian life.

5) Among the various works and prayers for which one can gain a plenary indulgence, the *Enchiridion* singled out the following:

— Adoration of the Blessed Sacrament for at least half an hour

— Devout reading of Sacred Scripture for at least half an hour

— The Way of the Cross

— The rosary, when recited in a church or public oratory, in the family, or in a religious community or pious association.[11]

Chapter Notes

1. Pope Paul VI, *Apostolic Constitution on Indulgences*, n. 1
2. *Ibid.*, n. 5
3. *Ibid.*, n. 12
4. St. Thomas Aquinas, *Supp.*, 25, 2, ad 2
5. Sacred Apostolic Penitentiary (1968), *Enchiridion of Indulgences*, p. 32
6. Second Vatican Council, *Decree on the Apostolate of the Laity*, n. 8
7. *Enchiridion*, Norms on indulgences, n. 22
8. *Enchiridion*, Norms on indulgences, n. 26
9. *Enchiridion*, Norms on indulgences, n. 28, 29
10. *Enchiridion*, p. 138
11. *Enchiridion*, p. 45

PART THREE
The Church and The Sacraments

Chapter 33
Sacred Tradition

One major difference between Catholicism and Protestantism is the different way in which they view divine revelation. For most Protestant religions the only true source of divine revelation is the *Bible*, and its interpretation is left to the conscience of the individual Christian. For the Catholic Church, however, God's revelation is found not only in the *Sacred Scriptures*, the written word of God divinely inspired, but also in *Sacred Tradition,* the unwritten word of God received from Christ and handed down orally by the Apostles and their successors at His command, *"Go and make disciples of all nations . . . teaching them to observe all that I have commanded you; and behold, I am with you all days, even unto the consummation of the world"* (Mt. 28:19). In this commission, Christ established a living teaching authority for safeguarding the deposit of faith from error. The Church founded on the apostles with Peter as its head, and only that Church, has been empowered by Christ to interpret His teaching authoritatively in His name. *"On this rock (Peter) I will found my Church, and the gates of hell shall not prevail against it"* (Mt. 16:19).

What is Sacred Tradition?

The word *tradition* is taken from the Latin word *tradere,* to hand down, to pass on. In this case it refers to a handing down of God's revealed word from apostolic times to our own day. Even though a great part of divine revelation has been committed to writing and is found in the inspired books of the Scriptures, much of what Christ taught to be handed down, St. John assures us, is not found in the Scriptures (Jn. 21:25). Consequently, the Catholic Church looks upon the Scriptures and

SACRED TRADITION

Tradition, not as two separate sources of God's revelation to mankind, but as two different means of transmission of divine revelation, forming a single deposit of faith. St. Paul referred to this when he wrote to Timothy to *"hold to traditions which you have learned, whether by **word** or by our **letter**"* (2 Thes. 2:14).

Some writers refer to the written and unwritten word of God handed down by the apostles and their successors as the *passive* aspect of Tradition, and the living teaching authority (the Magisterium) established by Christ to insure that His teaching would be handed down to succeeding ages in its integrity and without error, as its *active* aspect. The many divisions of Christianity today show how important this latter aspect is.

To understand the Catholic Church's teaching in regard to sacred Tradition, we must consider several things:

a) Public revelation ceased with Christ and the apostles and evangelists who recorded His teachings;

b) Christ commissioned His apostles to preach;

c) Christ established a living teaching authority to safeguard the integrity of the gospel message, and to apply it with divine authority to succeeding ages;

d) The development of the gospel message is not new doctrine.

1) Public Revelation Ends with the Apostles

God in his goodness and wisdom revealed Himself gradually through the prophets and patriarchs of the Old Testament. But the fullness and completion of that revelation came through the incarnation of the only-begotten Son of the Father who became man to redeem us, and to bring to completion the revelation of the Godhead and the divine plan of salvation. The message that Christ brought to mankind by His preaching, His deeds, His death and resurrection (recorded by the evangelists and apostles) brings an end to *public* revelation, as opposed to *private* revelation, such as occurred in the apparitions of Our Lord and the saints to various persons throughout the Christian era. Referring to this, the Second Vatican Council declared in the dogmatic constitution on Revelation: *"The Christian dispensation, therefore, as the new and definitive covenant, will never pass away, and we now await no further new public revelation before the glorious manifestation of Our Lord Jesus Christ."* [1]

(NOTE: It is only *public* revelation that we are bound in conscience to accept by virtue of the divine gift of faith.)

2) Christ Commissioned the Apostles to Preach

Our Blessed Lord left no written record behind Him, but rather ordered His apostles to hand down His teaching *orally*. He told them to preach the Gospel to all nations. Referring to this the Second Vatican Council states:

> Christ the Lord, in whom the full revelation of the supreme God is brought to completion, commissioned the apostles to *preach* to all men that gospel which is the source of all saving truth and moral teaching, and thus imparts to them divine gifts. . . . This commission was faithfully fulfilled by the apostles who, by their oral preaching, by example, by ordinances, handed down what they had received from the lips of Christ, from living with Him, and from what He did, or what they learned through the promptings of the Holy Spirit. The commission was fulfilled too, by those apostles and apostolic men who under the inspiration of the same Holy Spirit committed the message of salvation to writing. [2]

The first Gospel was written, however, some 20 years after the death of Christ, and the last Gospel (that of John) was written at the end of the first century. That means that a whole generation of Christians knew nothing of the teaching of Christ, or the duties of the Christian life, except through the preaching of the apostles and their fellow-workers, that is to say, except through Sacred Tradition. What is more, almost 400 years elapsed before the inspired books of the New Testament were collected (by the teaching authority of the Catholic Church) into one book. And even after that, since copies of the inspired books were transcribed laboriously by hand, there were extremely few copies available. And that scarcity lasted for almost another thousand years until the coming of the printing press in the fifteenth century.

Much that Christ said and did is not recorded in the Scriptures, as St. John so clearly testifies: *"There are still many other things that Jesus did, yet if they were written in detail, I doubt there would be room enough in the entire world to hold the books to record them"* (Jn. 21:24). St. Paul, too, testifies that part of his teaching received from Christ was not included in his letters: *"The things which you have heard from me through many witnesses you must hand on to trustworthy men who will be able to teach others"* (2 Tim. 2:2; Gal. 1:12).

Consequently, while the Sacred Scriptures contain a large portion of God's revelation, some portion of it was passed on orally and eventually recorded in the writings of the Fathers of the Church, those spiritual and intellectual giants of the early centuries who further explained and developed it. The second Council of Constantinople (553) rebuked those who do not follow the *"traditions of the Fathers."* Those traditions *"hold the faith which our Lord Jesus Christ, true God, entrusted to the holy apostles, and which, after them, the holy Fathers and Doctors of the Church entrusted to their people."* While the writings of the Fathers were not inspired, they were handing down teaching that came from Christ through the apostles under the guidance of the Holy Spirit promised by Christ (Mt. 28:20).

Some practices of the Catholic Church coming down from the primitive Church are recorded only in sources other than the Scriptures. One example of this is the *Didache*, the full title of which is *The Lord's Instruction to the Gentiles through the Twelve Apostles*. That document, which dates from around the time of the Gospel of St. John, tells us of the celebration of the Eucharist on Sunday (the Lord's day) rather than on the Sabbath, and of the forgiveness of sin through confession.

The same is true of the liturgy, an important witness of Sacred Tradition, for as the Second Vatican Council testifies, *"The Church, in her teaching, life, and worship, perpetuates and hands on to all generations all that she herself is, all that she believes."*[3] Changes in the Church's liturgical customs result not only from adaptation to the times, but also from a development of doctrine that called for corresponding expression in the liturgy. Pope Pius XII referred to this in his encyclical on the Mystical Body of Christ:

> As Catholic doctrine on the Incarnate Word of God, the Eucharistic sacrament and sacrifice, and Mary the Mother of God came to be determined with greater certitude and clarity, new ritual forms were introduced through which the acts of the liturgy proceeded to reproduce this brighter light from the decrees of the teaching authority of the Church, and so to reflect this light that it might reach the hearts and minds of Christ's people more effectively.[4]

3) Christ Established a Living Teaching Authority

Our Blessed Lord not only commissioned the apostles to preach to all the world the saving message He had given them, but He empowered them to *"bind and to loose"* in His name, so that *"whatever you bind on earth will be bound in heaven, and whatever you loose on earth will be loosed in heaven"* (Mt. 16:19). Because of this, He assured them that *"he who hears you, hears Me; and he who rejects you rejects Me; and he who rejects Me rejects Him who sent Me"* (Lk. 10:16).

Immediately after commissioning the apostles to preach the Gospel to all nations, Our Savior continued: *"Behold I am with you all days, even to the end of the world"* (Mt. 28:20). By these words He assured the apostles that He would be with them, through the Holy Spirit whom He would send, so that they could hand down His teaching without error until the end of time. But since the apostles would not live that long, Christ's promise is valid for His successors, those in charge of the Church in succeeding ages. Thus, until the end of time the successors of the apostles will share the teaching authority conferred by Christ on the apostles, and the guidance of the Holy Spirit that He promised.

SACRED TRADITION

After the ascension of Christ, the apostles did in fact claim for themselves a teaching authority, sending others as they themselves had been sent by Christ, with the power to teach in Christ's name, to impose doctrine, as well as to govern the Church and to baptize.

Christ preached His message; He did not write it. In His preaching He appealed to the Scriptures, but was not satisfied merely to read them. He explained them, interpreted them. So too, in the centuries to come the Church would not merely refer to the Bible, but would explain and interpret it, applying it to the changing conditions of the times. Although the Bible is the inspired word of God, it was not meant to be our sole guide. Just as God provided mankind with the guiding light of the Scriptures, so He provided mankind, through the continued guidance of the Holy Spirit, with an official living authority to interpret those divinely inspired books. One of the main reasons for the division of Christendom into the hundreds of Christian religions we have today is the claim that the interpretation of the Scriptures is left to the individual Christian. Just as the Constitution of the United States is not left to the interpretation of each individual American, but is interpreted authoritatively by the Supreme Court, so the whole deposit of revealed truth (the Bible and Tradition) is not left to the judgment of each individual Christian, but is interpreted for us by the living authority that Christ established. *"He who hears you, hears Me"* (Lk. 10:16). The Second Vatican Council states this clearly:

> In order to keep the gospel forever whole and alive within the Church, the apostles left bishops as their successors, handing over their own teaching role to them. This *Sacred Tradition,* therefore and the *Sacred Scriptures* of both the Old and New Testament are like a mirror in which the pilgrim looks at God[5]. . . . The task of authentically interpreting the word of God, whether *written* or *handed on,* has been entrusted exclusively to the living teaching office of the Church (the magisterium) whose authority is exercised in the name of Jesus Christ.[6]

4) The Development of Doctrine

As stated above, public revelation ended with the death of John the Apostle. After him no new revelation has been added to the deposit of faith. However, that does not exclude the development of those truths contained in that revelation. As time passed on, the Church, with the guidance of the Holy Spirit, came to a greater understanding of God's revealed word. The Second Vatican Council speaks of this:

> This tradition which comes from the apostles develops in the Church with the help of the Holy Spirit. For there is a growth in the understanding of the realities and the words which have been handed down. . . . As centuries succeed one after another, the Church constantly moves forward toward the fullness of divine truth until the words of God reach their complete fulfillment in her.[7]

Development of doctrine, therefore, does not mean a changing or abandoning of a doctrine originally taught, but rather the growth of the Church's understanding of it. Revealed truths are not fixed or static concepts. Their richness is inexhaustible, so that succeeding generations have discovered new insights into God's message to mankind.

One thing that has occasioned the development of doctrine has been the attacks on the revealed truths by those not of the Catholic faith. They might deny a truth outright, or might interpret it in a way not in keeping with its true meaning as handed down by the apostles. This requires and occasions on the part of the Church a fuller expression of those truths being challenged.

Then, too, there are doctrines of our Catholic faith that were contained in divine revelation only *implicitly*. And for that reason they became obligatory dogmas only after the passing of centuries. Examples of this are the Immaculate Conception and the Assumption of the Mother of God.

From the beginning, the Church believed in the singular holiness of Mary, but it was not always clear whether or not she had contracted original sin. Some felt that the universality of Christ's redemption, and the doctrine that *"all sinned in Adam"* (Rom. 5:12), implied that Mary would need cleansing from original sin. However, with the passage of time and the reflections of saints and theologians (enlightened by the Holy Spirit), it was understood how Mary was redeemed by Christ without inheriting original sin, namely, in anticipation of Christ's merits. Since the Mystical Body of Christ is a mystery that extends beyond space and time, Mary's redemption was not curative, but preventative. Hence, only in the 19th and 20th centuries after Christ were these two doctrines, both of which are implicitly contained in divine revelation, declared dogmas of the Catholic faith. These truths had been divinely revealed from the beginning, but the explanation and understanding of them came only gradually.

The Unity of Sacred Tradition and Scripture

Since Sacred Tradition and Sacred Scripture come from one and the same divine source, there is a close connection between them, both forming one sacred deposit of the word of God. One of them is not complete without the other. As the words themselves imply, *Sacred Scripture* is the *written* word of God divinely inspired by the Holy Spirit; and *Sacred Tradition* is the divinely guided *"handing down"* of that revealed truth entrusted to the apostles, and passed on, *written* or *unwritten*. Hence the Second Vatican Council declares: *"It is not from Sacred Scripture alone that the Church draws her certainty about everything that has been revealed. Therefore, both Sacred Tradition and Sacred Scripture are to be accepted and venerated with the same sense of devotion and reverence."*[8]

And since, as we have seen, Christ established a living teaching authority to interpret in His name and hand down His revealed word, the same Vatican Council concludes:

> It is clear, therefore, that **Sacred Tradition, Sacred Scripture**, and the **teaching authority of the Church** (the magisterium), in accord with God's most wise designs, are so

linked and joined together that one cannot stand without the others, and that all together and each in its own way under the action of the Holy Spirit contribute effectively to the salvation of souls.[9]

Chapter Notes

1. *Verbum Dei*, n. 4
2. *Ibid.*, n. 7
3. *Ibid.*, n. 8
4. *Mediator Dei*, I. 52 / Pius XII, *Mystici Corporis*
5. *Ibid.*, n. 7
6. *Ibid.*, n. 10
7. *Ibid.*, n. 8
8. *Ibid.*, n. 9
9. *Ibid.*, n. 10

Chapter 34

Feed My Lambs, Feed My Sheep

God, in His infinite wisdom and providence, has provided for the needs of every living creature. This includes not only man, but the beasts of the field as well. In creating the various animals, He gave them a means of defending themselves from the attack of other animals that would seek to destroy them.

Natural Protection

For example: to some He gave great jaws and teeth and sharp claws; to others, strong horns with which to butt or gore; to others, great size and strength; to others, poisonous fangs; to others, great speed; and to others, wings with which to fly from danger.

While we could continue this list of natural means of defense, that should suffice to demonstrate what we are saying. There is one animal, however, that is quite defenseless, without these means of defense, namely, the sheep. By nature it is mild, not vicious; it does not attack. And so, to survive, sheep need a protector and guide, a shepherd, and that for various reasons: 1) to protect it from wild animals; 2) to keep it from wandering off and getting lost, for then it is particularly vulnerable to attack; and 3) to lead it to new and fertile pastures.

Christ, the Good Shepherd

When we think of all these characteristics of the sheep, we can see why our Blessed Lord used the figure of the sheepfold and the shepherd when referring to Himself in relation to His followers: *"I am the good Shepherd,"* etc. (Jn. 10:11).

Some might object to this reasoning as follows: *"Man is by no means defenseless, he can defend himself well; in fact he can kill any animal, and even other men. With all the knowledge and technology he can fall back on, he is ingenious in creating weapons that can destroy. What do you mean he is defenseless?"*

We mean that man, left to himself, is quite defenseless against the powers and snares of the devil. All the weapons and technology at his disposal do not in any way protect him from the wiles of Satan.

At the very beginning of the human race, the devil snared our first parents into disobedience and rebellion against the limitations that God had placed on them, and thereby gained a certain dominion over them and their descendents. That dominion was destroyed by the Passion and death of Christ, and each of His followers is liberated from it by the saving grace of baptism. Yet, continued light and strength coming from the divine life of grace is needed, if man is not to succumb to the snares of the Evil One.

For that reason, the divine Shepherd saw to it that at the end of His mortal life and before ascending into heaven, He would provide other shepherds to take His place, to continue the protective guidance of His sheepfold. All of the twelve apostles would be shepherds, but among them He singled out Peter, upon whom He conferred the primacy of power and jurisdiction, to secure the unity of faith within the sheepfold.

Peter, the Supreme Shepherd Under Christ

Within the year preceding His Passion and death, our Blessed Lord *promised* to found His Church on Peter:

> Blessed are you, Simon son of Jonah! No mere man has revealed this to you, but my heavenly Father. I declare to you, you are Rock (in Aramaic the name imposed on Peter was the word for rock), and on this rock I will build My Church, and the gates of hell shall not prevail against it. I will give

you the keys of the kingdom of heaven; and whatever you shall bind on earth shall be bound in heaven, and whatever you shall loose on earth shall be loosed in heaven (Mt. 16:17 ff).

After His death and resurrection, and before His ascension, Jesus *actually conferred* that power upon Peter, as the First Vatican Council teaches: *"It was upon Simon Peter alone that Jesus, after His resurrection, conferred jurisdiction over His entire fold as supreme shepherd and leader, saying: 'Feed My lambs . . . . Feed My sheep.'"*[1]

In the Old Testament the word *shepherd* is often employed for kings and rulers. In designating Peter to *"feed"* His sheep, He conferred on him the spiritual power to teach and command with His own authority.

The Roman Pontiff — The Supreme Shepherd Today

That the powers granted to Peter were handed down to his successors, and are held today by the Roman Pontiff, is clear from the declarations of both the First and Second Vatican Councils. We read in the *Decree on the Church in the Second Vatican Council*:

> This sacred synod, following the steps of the First Vatican Council, teaches and declares with it that Jesus Christ, the eternal Shepherd, established His holy Church by sending forth the apostles as He Himself had been sent by the Father. . . . In order that the episcopate might be one and undivided, He placed Peter over the other apostles, and instituted in him a permanent and visible source and foundation of unity of faith and communion.[2] The role that the Lord gave individually to Peter, the first of the apostles, is permanent, and was meant to be transmitted to his successors.[3] In virtue of his office as Vicar of Christ and shepherd of the whole Church, the Roman Pontiff has full, supreme and universal power over the whole Church, a power he can always exercise unhindered.[4]

As already indicated, this power over the whole Church is a spiritual power, that is, the right to direct its members in the way of salvation and to bind them in conscience.

Our Need of the Supreme Shepherd

Just as the sheep that wanders off and gets separated from the fold becomes an easy prey to wild animals that would kill and devour it, so the Catholic who wanders aside from the protective guidance of the Roman Pontiff, the chief shepherd whom God has provided, becomes an easy prey to the deception and wiles of Satan. Such a one may be clever about worldly things, but without the light of faith his vision becomes clouded as to his own innate weaknesses, and as to the wisdom of giving God His way. He may be strong in body, brilliant of mind, and powerful in worldly influence, but will be weak as to choosing what *God wants* in preference to what *he wants*.

A Catholic cannot have the Lord as his Shepherd, if he rejects the shepherd that the Lord Himself has provided, His vicar on earth. *"He who hears you, hears Me; and he who rejects you, rejects Me"* (Lk. 10:16).

We are not implying here that one who does not believe or accept *all* that the Roman Pontiff teaches is *"without faith,"* but one who rejects a teaching for the universal Church that the Roman Pontiff declares has been *divinely revealed.* The First Vatican Council declared in its Dogmatic Constitution:

> All those things are to be believed, on divine and Catholic faith, which are contained in the written and unwritten word of God, and which are proposed by the Church as divinely revealed, whether ... through her solemn pronouncements, or through her ordinary teaching power, such as encyclicals, decrees of the Sacred Congregations, etc.[5]

Wandering Sheep

Unfortunately, the Church is not without those who have wandered away from the protective guidance of the chief shepherd, dissenting from the official teaching of the Church even in matters that the Church has declared to be divinely revealed. Referring to this, a Doctrinal Statement of the Irish Episcopal Conference, *Conscience and Morality,* declared:

In practice, those who dissent from authoritative Church teaching very often give as their reason for doing so, not so much their own personal insights, as the authority of dissenting theologians. This, however, is to misunderstand the role of theologians in the Church, for their authority does not, and cannot, outweigh the authority of the Pope in declaring the faith of the Church.[6]

A common argument used by some dissenters against certain doctrines put forth by the Church through her ordinary teaching power — such as encyclicals — as divinely revealed, goes like this: This is not an *"ex cathedra"* definition. Therefore it is not infallible, and could be changed or reversed. Hence one is not strictly bound by this teaching.

In answer to such reasoning, the U.S. Bishops' Committee on Doctrine, in a critical evaluation of the work *Catholicism* by Fr. Richard McBrien, declared:

> In addition to those doctrines which have been taught by the Magisterium of the Church in the extraordinary way of infallible definitions, the ordinary teaching power of the Pope and the Bishops in union with him preserves many revealed truths which have never been solemnly defined, but which, nevertheless, are infallibly true and definable. These are truths which cannot be rejected or neglected without injury to the integrity of the Catholic faith, because they are either explicitly contained in Holy Scripture or, although only implicit in Sacred Scripture, they have been taught universally and continuously, are professed in the liturgy, and are believed and witnessed by the faithful as divinely revealed.

As to whether one might presume that the Church could be wrong in her universal teaching, the same document of the Bishops' Committee on Doctrine states:

> In the area of moral doctrine some have called attention to a theoretical possibility of error in some Church teaching. The Church does indeed enjoy infallibility in its ordinary and universal teaching.[7] But even when a teaching may not be infallibly proposed, it enjoys moral certainty and consequently has a normative role in the formation of Christian conscience.

St. Thomas Aquinas and the Magisterium

There is no doubt that the Magisterium, the teaching authority of the Church, relies much on the help of theologians in the expression of doctrine. Yet it is up to that teaching authority, centered in the Roman Pontiff and the Bishops in union with him, to accept or reject their explanations or conclusions.

St. Thomas Aquinas, by his writings, has contributed to the expression of Catholic doctrine perhaps more than any other theologian in the history of the Church. Of him, Pope John XXII said at his canonization: *"He has illumined the Church more than all the other Doctors."* And centuries later, Pope Pius X was to write of St. Thomas: *"Since the death of the holy Doctor there has never been a Council of the Church at which he was not present by his doctrine and influence."* And Pope Paul VI declared:

> Let teachers reverently pay heed to the voice of the Doctors of the Church, among whom St. Thomas holds the principal place; for the Angelic Doctor's force of genius is so great, his love of truth so sincere, and his wisdom in investigating, illustrating, and collecting the highest truths in a most apt bond of unity so great, that his teaching is a most efficacious instrument not only in safeguarding the foundations of the faith, but also in profitably and surely reaping the fruits of its sane progress.[8]

In light of these high praises, it would seem that if any theologian would be justified in insisting on his own interpretation of the Scriptures, it would be Thomas. Yet, as more than one Pope has pointed out, his humility was as great as his learning.

In one of his works he wrote that, should there be a dispute between the teaching authority of the Church and a private theologian, "we *must abide rather by the Pope's judgment than by the opinion of any of the theologians, however well versed he may be in the divine Scriptures.*"[9]

The Obedience of Faith

St. Paul, writing to the Romans, says that Jesus called him to be an apostle *"to bring about the obedience of faith . . . among the gentiles"* (1:5). He is referring to an obedience that is implicit in the virtue of faith, which *"is to be given to God who reveals, an obedience by which man commits his whole self freely to God, offering the full submission of intellect and will to God who reveals."* [10]

How false is the claim of those who say that this infringes on the freedom and liberty of man; that it degrades him and enslaves him to the dictates of the Church of Rome. It is true that, for the Catholic, human reason must be submissive to the guiding light of faith, a divine light that perfects and elevates reason, giving it an added dimension — an awareness of the supernatural order of being, an order of truth and reality that reason alone could never attain; but that submission is given freely, and it is to God, not to man. The Church is simply the instrument that God Himself has chosen to point out, with divine assistance, the truth of revelation. It is a surrender that does not enslave, but frees one from the uncertainties and doubts that one would invariably have, if left to himself as to how to order his life. And what is more, the true Catholic, seeing the Roman Pontiff as the chief shepherd which Christ Himself set over His Church, and the rock foundation on which He established it, has a deep faith and trust that, heeding his teaching, he is heeding and obeying the voice of Christ, the divine Shepherd, and entering into the very mystery of our Redemption.

The true exercise of obedience for the Christian is so intimately connected with the mystery of Christ's redeeming sacrifice, and with the *"building up of His Body"* which is the Church, that to the eye unaided by faith it will ever remain an enigma. The enlightened Christian realizes that not only is *God's will* manifested in the teaching of the supreme shepherd for the whole Church, but also *God's wisdom*. Only when human reason has been enlightened by the virtue of faith, and the will strengthened by the virtue of charity, will one freely choose the divine will and the divine plan in preference to his own.

Such a one freely chooses to follow the guidance of the supreme shepherd of the Church, even if at times it is a difficult path, for he knows that such compliance is closely connected with the "carrying of a cross" that is an essential requisite for being Christ's disciple. He does not question the wisdom of God's plan, for he has the assurance of Divine Wisdom that *"as the heavens are exalted above the earth, so my ways are exalted above your ways, and my thoughts above your thoughts"* (Is. 55:9). Nor is he overly anxious about the outcome of such submission, for he has the Lord's own word that he who *"seeks first the kingdom of God"* (Lk. 12:31) (Mt. 6:33) here and now, will not only not be in need in this life, but will enjoy His Kingdom in the life to come (Jn. 8:51).

Chapter Notes

1. Dogmatic Constitution, *Pastor Aeternus*, Ch. 1
2. Vatican Council II, *Decree on the Church*, n. 18
3. Vatican Council II, *Decree on the Church*, n. 20
4. Vatican Council II, *Decree on the Church*, n. 22
5. *Dei Filius*, Ch. 3 (cf. also Canon 750)
6. Irish Episcopal Conference, *Conscience and Morality*, n. 22
7. *Lumen Gentium*, 25; Canon 749
8. Pope Paul Vl, Allocution at the Pontifical Gregorian University in Rome, March 12, 1964
9. *Quodlibetum IX*, Q. 8, *Quaest. Quodlibetales*
10. Vatican Council II, *On Revelation*, n. 5

Chapter 35

The Holy Eucharist
Part I: A Sacrifice

The Holy Eucharist is both a sacrament and a sacrifice. Until recent years Catholics were familiar with the expression "the sacrifice of the Mass." Nowadays, however, that expression seems less popular. Not only is the word "sacrifice" less used in reference to the Mass, but the Mass itself is often referred to by many simply as the "liturgy."

Perhaps this is part of a misconception of some who see the Mass mainly as a meal, with less attention given to it as a sacrifice. It is a meal, indeed, and we will treat of that in the next chapter; but the Mass is preeminently a sacrifice which is the source of the fruitfulness of the sacramental meal.

The Last Supper and the Mass

The Last Supper was not just a religious meal commemorating the Jewish Passover, although it was that too. Within that meal Jesus instituted a rite of sacrifice, offering to the Father His Body that was soon to be cruelly tortured, and His Blood that would be shed on the cross in the hours that were soon to follow. Christ instituted this sacrificial rite in order that the sacrifice He was to offer the following day on Calvary could be made present again and again in a sacramental form, in such a way that the members of His Mystical Body could unite with Him in that renewal. In giving us this infinite gift to offer to the Father, His sacrifice became our sacrifice.

That sacrificial rite on the night before He died was the first Mass, and was essentially the same as the Mass of today. It was while instituting that rite that He gave Himself to His apostles to be their food and drink.

The Sacrifice of Calvary and the Mass

As we pointed out, the Eucharist is both a *sacrament* and a *sacrifice;* and these two are complementary aspects of the same mystery. They cannot be separated, for the fruitfulness of receiving the *Eucharistic meal* depends on our oneness with Christ, the Priest and Victim of the *Eucharistic sacrifice;* and the Mass can be understood as a sacrifice only in the sacramental order, as a sign that contains what it signifies. Only when the Mass is seen in this light can we see how there can be a permanent and abiding sacrifice identical in substance with the sacrifice of the cross, a sacrifice in which the crucified Christ, now in His glory, becomes present on the altar of today, offering Himself to the Father for the infinite glory of the divine Trinity and for the salvation of the world.

Christ renews this Eucharistic sacrifice through the ministry of His priests on behalf of the Church, so that *"through Him, with Him, in Him,"* she might share abundantly in the fruits of His redeeming Passion and death. Thus, the Mass occupies a central place in the life of the Church, just as the sacrifice of Calvary does in the redemption of mankind. In order to show in what sense the sacrifice of the Mass is one with the immolation of Christ on Calvary, we will examine how the two have the same Priest, the same Victim, the same oblation, and the same effects.

1) The Same Priest

During His whole life on earth Christ acted as priest in all He did. St. Paul confirms this in his epistle to the Hebrews:

> On coming into the world Jesus said: "Sacrifice and offering you did not desire, but a body you have prepared for me. Holocausts and sin-offerings (of the Old Law) you took no delight in. Then I said, 'I have come to do your will, O God.'. . . . It is in this "will" that we have been sanctified through the offering of the body of Jesus Christ once for all (10:5,10).

In one initial act of infinite love the divine Word incarnate offered His human life to the Father for the salvation of the world, both as Priest and Victim; yet it was not until Calvary that He exercised His priesthood in all its fullness.

The priest we see at the altar is only an instrument of the divine invisible Priest. The priest we see offers the sacrifice of the Mass, consecrating the sacred species, not in His own name, but in the name and person of Christ, as the words of the consecration indicate. The priest does not say, *"This is the Body of Christ,"* but *"This is My Body";* and it becomes the Body, not of the visible priest, but of Christ. He is merely an instrument of the changing, by the working of the Holy Spirit, of the substance of the bread and wine into the substance of the Body and Blood of Our Savior.[1]

Yet, he is a necessary instrument, for only by the power of priestly ordination can that change be effected, thus bringing about the sacramental presence of Christ who offers the sacrifice of the altar in union with that oblation He offers without cease in heaven. *"The interior oblation which is ever actual in the Heart of Christ,"* says Fr. M. M. Philipon, O.P., *"constitutes the very soul of the mystery of the Mass, the hidden source of its infinite value."*[2]

2) The Same Victim

In each Mass our Divine Savior, now in Heaven in glory, offers to the Father His Sacred Body so tortured at the hands of the Roman soldiers, His Precious Blood shed for the redemption of mankind, the insults and humiliations at the hands of the Jewish leaders, His obedience unto death. *"It is one and the same victim,"* says the Council of Trent, *"He who now makes the offering through the ministry of His priests, and He who then offered Himself on the Cross; the only difference is the manner of the offering"* (n. 749). This divine Victim is now offered daily in the sacrifice of the Mass, in obedience to the Lord's command: *"Do this in memory of Me"* (Lk. 22:20).

3) The Same Oblation

Even though the Priest and Victim are the same in the Eucharistic sacrifice and on Calvary, how can it be the same oblation, the same sacrifice, since there is not the shedding of blood that took place on Calvary? We must keep in mind that we are dealing with a *mysterium fidei* (mystery of faith), and that both the oblation and the immolation of the Eucharistic sacrifice take place on the sacramental level.

We are dealing with signs established by the Lord, but signs which effect what they signify. Just as the water of baptism both signifies and effects a cleansing, and the bread of the Eucharist both signifies and effects a nourishing, so the separate consecration of the bread and wine in the Mass *"both signifies and effects the sacramental separation of the Body and Blood of Christ, which constitutes the whole essence of the Eucharistic sacrifice."*[3]

In the Mass there is no new dying, no new shedding of blood. *"Christ, having risen from the dead, now dies no more"* (Rom. 6:19). Yet the crucified Christ, made present by the words of the priest, offers Himself in His glorified Body as an immolated Victim obedient unto death to repair for the disobedience of men. The separate consecration of bread and wine is not a real separation of the Body and Blood of Christ, but a sacramental separation, and therefore it contains what it signifies. *"It signifies and contains the whole reality of the sacrifice of the Cross."*[4]

The Mass then is a renewal of Calvary in the sense that it makes present that bloody sacrifice in a sacramental way. In each Mass our Divine Savior, having undergone the suffering and death of the cross, and now clothed with the merits and glory that His human nature possesses as the fruit of His sacrifice, offers Himself to the Father on our behalf. Fr. Philipon summarizes the above as follows:

> The death of Christ is "signified" by the double consecration, which ritually "separates" the Body and Blood of Christ, in imitation of the real separation that took place on Calvary. For the followers of St. Thomas Aquinas the essence of the sacrifice of the Mass consists solely in this ritualistic separa-

tion attending the consecration, which represents the offering and blood immolation of Calvary.[5]

4) The Same Effects

On Calvary, Christ made reparation for the sins of the whole world, and merited sufficient grace for the salvation of the whole of mankind. With His death on the cross, however, His time of meriting and of expiating came to an end. The action of Christ in the Eucharist does not add to the merits He gained, nor to the atonement He made, but rather applies those merits and that atonement to the members of His Mystical Body. *"Its salutary strength,"* says the Council of Trent, speaking of the Mass, *"is applied to the remission of the sins that we daily commit"* (n. 747).

In the sacrifice of the Mass, Christ offers to the Father the same adoration and thanksgiving and praise that He offers without cease in heaven. At the same time, the members of His Mystical Body on earth unite with Him in that oblation, so that, in union with the divine Priest and Victim, the Church on earth offers the same adoration and praise and thanks as the Church in heaven.

The true Christian does not pray for his own needs alone. Like the prayer of Christ, his, too, will be all-inclusive. The mind of the Church as expressed in the eucharistic prayers of the Mass is that one unite with Christ: in offering glory to the Father; in offering atonement not only for his own sins but those of the whole world, and in beseeching from heaven the grace of salvation, not only for himself and those dear to him, but for the whole of mankind. And he does this with confidence, for he knows that the Mass is a continuation of the sacrifice of Calvary, with all its infinite value for the glory of God and the salvation of souls.

The Ends of the Mass

Since the Mass makes present the sacrifice of Calvary, it fulfills the same fourfold purpose of adoration, reparation, petition and thanksgiving, having the same infinite value before God. However, our sharing in the fruits of Christ's sacrifice will depend on our interior disposition. It becomes "our sacrifice" in the measure that we are one with Christ in total self-surrender to the will of the Father. We will briefly consider these four ends of the Mass.

1) Adoration

Our Blessed Lord is the only member of the human race who can offer to the Father an adoration that is entirely adequate, for it is infinite. Even the human limitations of the visible priest do not prevent this, for the principal celebrant is Christ. One Mass, theologians tell us, gives more glory to God than do all the angels and saints in heaven, for in it there is presented to the blessed Trinity the divine Word made flesh, immolated on our behalf in obedience to the will of the Father.

In return, God showers down His blessings on those who are offering the Mass in union with His Son, and in the measure of their oneness with the Divine Victim. This indicates that routine participation could lessen the fruits of the Mass.

2) Reparation

Because we are all sinners, we have an obligation to make reparation for our offenses against God. And here, too, the reparatory value of the Mass is infinite, because Christ is again offering to the Father the infinite reparation of Calvary. The world is indeed deluged with sin, but, also, heaven is being stormed with reparation by the countless Masses celebrated throughout the world to appease the Father's wrath, and to keep back His chastising hand.

Yet, as with adoration, so, too, the reparatory value of the Mass is not applied to us in all its fullness, but rather in a limited way, according to the degree of our union with the divine Priest and Victim. In practice, this might be equivalent to the measure of our willingness to do whatever true repentance requires.

3) Petition

We are constantly in need of God's gifts, both in the order of nature and of grace. When we offer our prayers of petition to the Father through Christ, who is renewing His redeeming sacrifice, offering again the infinite merits and love and suffering of His Passion, the power of that prayer over the heart of God is great. Yet, to be truly united with Christ in the prayer of petition, our prayer must be one with His: *"Father . . . not my will, but yours be done"* (Lk. 22:42). Such prayer will be efficacious in obtaining needed graces from God, but not necessarily what we ask. And here, too, those graces will be granted in the measure that we do not place obstacles in the way, by clinging to our will, to creature satisfactions, and so forth.

4) Thanksgiving

We are so indebted to God for His benefits, both in the natural and supernatural order: for example, a sharing in His own divine life through grace, the Holy Eucharist, the indwelling of the Divine Persons, the countless times He has forgiven our offenses, the gift of Mary as our Mother. If it depended on ourselves alone, the whole of eternity would not be sufficient to pay our debt of gratitude. In the Mass, however, we can completely satisfy that debt, because in that sacrifice, Christ offers thanks to the Father in our place, adding our prayers of thanks to His. In fact, the very word *Eucharist* is a Greek word meaning "thanksgiving." There is no more perfect way of saying "thanks" to God than through the Mass; and the more grateful we are to Him, the more He continues to bestow His gifts.

The Heartbeat of the Mystical Body

As Christ continues to offer the sacrifice of the Mass through the ministry of His priests, He wishes its fruits to extend to every member of the Mystical Body in need the world over. And every soul that is open to His grace in some measure benefits by each Mass.

In the Old Testament, the Prophet Malachi foretold that from the rising of the sun to the setting, a sacrifice, a pure offering would be offered in the Lord's name (Mal.1:11). That prophecy is certainly fulfilled in the sacrifice of the cross — extended through the Mass. Every minute of every day and night, that sacrifice is being offered somewhere in the world, bringing the fruits of Christ's sacrifice on Calvary to all souls who are disposed to receive them.

As the heart continually pumps life-giving blood to all members of the human body, so each Mass is like a heartbeat sending life-giving grace of the Divine Head to all members of His Mystical Body who do not place obstacles in the way of His gifts.

St. Paul speaks of Christ in heaven always making intercession for us before the Father. *"Because He continues forever, He has an everlasting priesthood. Therefore He is able at all times to save those who come to God through Him, since He lives always to make intercession for them"* (Heb. 7:25).

The time will come, at the end of the world, when Christ will hand over His kingdom to the Father. That will be the end of the application of the fruits of His Passion, and the last of His intercession for the souls of men; for then the great mystery of the redemption will have been consummated. Then the elect, the Church triumphant, in union with Christ, will offer that oblation of adoration and praise and thanksgiving for all eternity.

Chapter Notes

1. *Eucharistic Prayer*, II & III
2. M. Philipon, O.P., *The Sacraments in the Christian Life*, p. 139
3. *Ibid.*, p. 130
4. M. J. Nicolas, O.P., *A New Look at the Eucharist*, p. 60
5. *Ibid.*, p. 144

Chapter 36

The Holy Eucharist
Part II: A Divine Banquet

In the preceding chapter we saw that the Eucharist is both a sacrament and a sacrifice, and that these two concepts cannot be separated without an incomplete notion of each of them; for they are two interrelated aspects of the same reality, the Body and Blood, Soul and Divinity of Jesus Christ.

As St. Thomas Aquinas points out, the Eucharist *"has the nature of a **sacrifice** inasmuch as it is offered up: and it has the nature of a **sacrament** inasmuch as it is received."* [1] Through the *sacrifice* of the Eucharist, the Church on earth offers fitting worship to the Blessed Trinity; through the *sacrament* of the Eucharist, the faithful receive the graces of the Incarnation and Redemption. In the divine plan, then, the mystery of the Incarnation and Redemption is extended through the centuries by means of the Eucharist, for the purpose of giving glory to the Father, and for the sanctification and salvation of souls.

It is important to see the close relationship between these two aspects of the Eucharist — *offering to God* (through sacrifice) and *receiving from God* (through Holy Communion) — for the more we are one with Christ in the offering of the *sacrifice* of His Body and Blood, the more we receive from God in the *sacrament* of His Body and Blood.

We can see, then, how much one would lose of the fruits of the Mass, if he saw it merely or mainly as a meal, with only a superficial participation in the sacrifice that Christ renews. The Mass is an action, *an exchange of gifts*, and Holy Communion is only one side of that exchange. If there is little giving of self on our part in following Christ, there will be little giving of Himself, through grace, in the reception of Holy Communion.

Speaking in 1986 of some basic differences between some Protestant Churches and the Roman Catholic Church, Rev. Msgr. Desmond Connell, Dean of the Faculty of Philosophy and Sociology in University College, Dublin, commented:

> At the source of these differences between the Churches is a difference in the interpretation of the Eucharist: the difference between the reduction of the Eucharist to a sacred meal, and the recognition of the Eucharist as a sacrificial meal in which Christ's own priestly offering is sacramentally represented and thereby made present.[2]

The Eucharistic Meal

In the preceding chapter, we looked at the Eucharist as the ritual *sacrifice* of the Body and Blood of Christ that He instituted the night before He died. Our aim in these reflections is to consider the Eucharist as the *sacrament* of His Body and Blood, the wonderful fruits enjoyed by those who receive it with the proper dispositions, and what is needful in order to have those dispositions.

1) It Nourishes and Causes Growth:

The sacrament of Holy Eucharist was instituted as food — spiritual food. *"My Flesh is real food, and My Blood is real drink"* (Jn. 6:55). That is why Jesus instituted this sacrament under the signs of bread and wine.

As in **baptism,** the outward sign (a washing with water) confers grace that cleanses the soul, so in the **Eucharist** the outward sign (bread and water) confers grace that nourishes the soul, thereby fortifying and causing spiritual growth. We see, then, the meaning of the expression that the sacraments effect what they signify, namely, that Holy Communion rightly received does for the soul what material food does for the body.

There is a notable difference in this, however; for the food that we eat is assimilated by the body, and changed

THE HOLY EUCHARIST

into our own substance, that is, into tissue, muscle, bone, etc., that make up the body. Yet when we consume the Host in Holy Communion, the Lord we receive is not transformed into us, but rather we are transformed into Him. That is, through the grace we receive, we more intimately share in His divine life, making us more Christlike, more submissive to His will, more open to His truth.

Consequently, when we receive Holy Communion, this brings about not merely a *physical union* or nearness between ourselves and Jesus in the sacred Host, which nearness is only temporary, lasting only as long as the species of bread and wine lasts, but it also brings about a deeper and enduring *spiritual union* between the soul and Jesus through divine grace.

To use an expression of theology, this sacrament produces grace in the soul *ex opere operato,* that is, by the very sacrament itself, independently of any effort on our part; and it produces grace in the measure that we do not place obstacles in the way. Our part in this is removing the obstacles — for example, pride, greed, lust, envy, sloth — which are sources of attachments or aversions that close the soul in on itself.

An example might help to understand this. When I lift up the shade to allow the sunlight to come in through the window, I do not cause the light; the sun does. I merely remove an obstacle. Yet my action is necessary to increase light in the room.

In a similar way, in the reception of Holy Communion I do not cause the increase of grace, God does; yet my action will have much to do with the amount of grace received. My remote preparation for Holy Communion will include a striving to remove the obstacles which enslave the heart and keep it from surrendering to God. It is in this sense that the sacraments give grace *ex opera operantis,* that is, according to the sincerity and generosity of heart in making the sacrifices and applying the discipline needed to bring about that detachment.

Since in this sacrament we not merely receive grace, but Him who is the very source of all grace, there is no limit to the amount of grace that one Holy Communion can bring, that is, no limit on the part of God. It is we ourselves who place the limits by our selfishness and worldly attachments that keep the heart from opening up and surrendering to the divine Person we have received.

This truth can be expressed by another example: If I walk to the edge of an immense lake to carry away water, the amount of water I bring away does not depend on the lake, but on the capacity of the container I have. So with each Communion, the amount of grace we receive doesn't depend on the Lord, who wants to give His gifts infinitely more than we want to receive them. It depends on the extent that we strive to lessen those worldly attachments which lessen the capacity of the soul to receive God's gifts. Fr. Gabriel of St. Mary Magdalen, O.C.D., speaking of the increase of grace and charity in receiving Holy Communion, states:

> This increase will be in proportion to my capacity for receiving it. If my heart is closed by selfishness and pride, if it is bound by attachments to creatures, or too much engrossed by worldly affections and affairs, it will be unable to make room for an increase of divine love, and Jesus will be, so to speak, forced to lessen the outpourings of His charity and to diminish His gifts.[3]

Yet, as we saw in chapter ten, the detachment of the heart of man from created goods is primarily the work of divine grace, yet God demands a definite cooperation on our part. So, if we continually strive to remove these attachments, Holy Communion, regularly and devoutly received, will invariably, though gradually, bring an increase of those cleansing and strengthening graces, effecting a closer union with Christ, a greater sharing in that divine life of Love and Truth that He is.

2) It Restores Our Daily Losses:

Both in the natural order and in the supernatural, there is need to repair and replenish body and soul for the losses and setbacks of various kinds.

THE HOLY EUCHARIST 297

For example, in the *natural order,* the human body is in a continual process of expending and replenishing its supply of energy. After a hard day's work, the body experiences fatigue, lack of pep. Something has been used up, burned up — as fuel in a car. This has to be restored; otherwise strength and efficiency are lessened, discomfort and irritability often increase, and resistance is lowered as regards certain sicknesses. What has been used up has to be restored by proper nourishment and rest. The body has a wonderful capacity of assimilating food, so that the fuel supply burned up by labor and activity is now replenished. After a period of rest, one is ready to go anew.

There is a certain parallel to this in the *supernatural order.* There can be a gradual growth in grace in spite of the little losses each day due to human frailty. For example, there can be moments of jealousy, greed, vanity, impatience, laziness, unhealthy curiosity, and so on. Each of these can have a detrimental effect on spiritual growth, for each of them can come under the category of venial sin.

Because of human frailty and the manifold inclinations of self-love, along with the fatigue and pressures of daily life and the enticements of the world, it is almost inevitable that, in spite of one's spiritual struggle, he will be guilty of some of these failings in his daily routine.

Yet, when in Holy Communion one receives with fervent love the Body and Blood of Christ, the divine Victim immolated for the remission of sin, that encounter can remit the guilt of those venial sins for which he has true sorrow, and even the punishment due for them, in the measure of the fervor of one's love at the time of Communion. That is why the Council of Trent stated, referring to the Eucharist, *"Its salutary strength is applied to the remission of the sins that we daily commit."*[4]

This is not to say that venial sins need not be confessed in the sacrament of reconciliation, for sacramental graces are given therein that are a further aid in overcoming those weaknesses. Too, the more one neglects sacramental confession, e.g., many months, the more insensitive he becomes to the little failings of each day and less concerned about them. Because of this, less becomes the fervor of charity, and less fruitful the reception of Holy Communion.

As Fr. M. M. Philipon, O.P. states:

> Daily Communion is a most excellent antidote to the spiritual dissipation to which we may be exposed. In performing our daily round of duties there is always the danger that God will be shoved aside and cease to be the focal point in our thoughts and desires; but if we begin our day with a fervent Communion, we shall be ready to meet the challenge. . . . Through union with Christ we can always regain the strength to free ourselves from any and all entanglements of venial sin that may be hampering our spiritual advance.[5]

This sacrament does not, however, remit mortal sin; nor should one in that state ever receive Holy Communion. One does not give food to a dead person; and one in mortal sin is spiritually dead. The reception of this sacrament in such a state not only does not cleanse and strengthen, but further aggravates one's guilt and debt of punishment before God.

3) It Diminishes Concupiscence:

The Eucharist is not only a food that nourishes and strengthens, it is a medicine that cures and heals the wounds of our fallen nature. Since Holy Communion worthily and regularly received brings an increase of grace and charity, it not only remits venial sin, as we saw; it is also a safeguard against falling into mortal sin, for it lessens the drive of concupiscence resulting from original sin. It thus allays the drive of the flesh toward evil due to disordered passions and the rebellion of the will due to pride. It helps to restore harmony in fallen nature, for it diminishes the rebellion of the flesh against the spirit. When our Blessed Lord comes to us, He who calmed the storms of the sea can give us strength to calm the storms that flare up in our lower nature. As St. Cyril of Alexandria stated: *"The chaste flesh of Jesus checks the*

THE HOLY EUCHARIST 299

insubordination of ours; by dwelling in us, Christ effectively overcomes the law of the flesh which rages in our members."

This increase of grace and charity, by increasing one's desires for the things of God, correspondingly lessens the desire for the things offensive to God, which are rooted in concupiscence. In line with this St. Augustine declares: *"The increase of charity is the decrease of passion, and the perfection of charity is the absence of passion."*

This transformation takes place not only because one becomes stronger, but also because sin begins to lose its attractiveness. One begins to recognize the emptiness of what yesterday seemed so desirable. This is a gradual process, and while our cooperation is essential, it is effected more by God's grace drawing to Himself the hearts of those who sincerely and perseveringly seek Him.

Preparation for Holy Communion

Although we all receive the same Lord in Holy Communion, His physical presence within us does not produce the same effect in each soul. As we saw, while the sacraments produce grace of themselves, this must not be misunderstood; we can place obstacles to the action of the Holy Spirit. The efficacy of this sacrament, therefore, is proportional to the dispositions of mind and heart, the fervor of faith, hope and charity with which it is received. This fervor is not so much something we feel, as it is a readiness of will for God's service, a willingness to make the sacrifices required to observe God's commandments, to fulfill works of mercy, and to bear the crosses that are part of daily life.

Fr. R. Garrigou-Lagrange, O.P. states that an important disposition of soul for fruitful Communions is *"a spirit of sacrifice";* and to that end he recommends *"at least one act of mortification a day"* in order to *"put to death our egoism, self-love and pride,"* that constitute obstacles to grace.[6]

All this should make clear what we have been stressing, namely, the close relationship between the Eucharist as a sacrament and as a sacrifice. An important remote preparation for Holy Communion is to strive to live that "spirit of sacrifice," for there will always be a certain proportion between the extent that Christ *gives Himself* to us (shares His graces with us) in Holy Communion, and our *giving ourself* to Him through surrender to His will, not merely at Mass time, but throughout the week. Fr. M. M. Philipon, O.P., stresses this in the work quoted above:

> Many Christians complain that their Communions leave them lukewarm, that they seem to derive small fruit from this sacramental contact with Christ. Could it be that they have forgotten what it is that really truly constitutes preparation for Communion? Our preparation leaves much to be desired if it consists in nothing more than the attempt to elicit, often in haste and unsuccessfully, a few simple acts of love just before we are about to approach the Communion rail. The way to find admittance into the mystery of Christ is by actual participation in His sufferings. This is the secret formula, so to speak, for living a life of love in communion with Christ: namely, to be a victim with the Victim, each morning to bring to the chalice of redemption a drop of our own blood.[7]

That *"drop of our own blood"* is the sacrifices we must make to keep God's commandments, to fulfill the duties of our state in life, to help those in need, in a word, *"to deny ourself, and take up our cross daily and follow Him"* (Lk. 9:23).

A Pledge of Future Glory

The material food we eat nourishes us for our temporary existence in this world, whereas the Eucharist nourishes us for a life that is without end. As Jesus said, *"He that eats My Flesh and drinks My Blood, has life everlasting, and I will raise him up on the last day"* (Jn. 6:55).

Commenting on this, Fr. Gabriel of St. Mary Magdalen, O.C.D., remarks: *"Notice that He said 'has life everlasting,' and not will have, because the Eucharist, by giving us an increase of grace, the seed of glory, becomes the pledge of eternal life for us, life not only for the soul but also of the body."*[8] This is beautifully expressed in an antiphon of the Divine Office for the feast of Corpus Christi written by St. Thomas Aquinas: *"O Sacred Banquet in which Christ is received, the memory of His passion renewed, the soul filled with grace, and a pledge of future glory given to us."*

Chapter Notes

1. St. Thomas Aquinas, *Summa Theologiae,* III 79, 5
2. *L'Osservatore Romano,* July 3, 1988
3. Fr. Gabriel of St. Mary Magdalen, O.C.D., *Divine Intimacy,* p. 620
4. Council of Trent, n. 747. *Cf.* St. Thomas Aquinas, *Summa Theologiae,* III, 79, a. 2 & 3
5. M. M. Philipon, O.P., *The Sacraments in the Christian Life,* p. 103
6. R. Garrigou-Lagrange, O.P., *Love of God and the Cross of Jesus*, I, p. 396
7. *The Sacraments in the Christian Life,* p. 106
8. *Love of God and the Cross of Jesus,* I, p. 611

Chapter 37

Transubstantiation

Our Blessed Lord celebrated the first Mass at the Last Supper the night before He died. By His divine power, He changed bread and wine into His own Body and Blood, so that He might institute a sacred rite whereby the sacrifice that He was to offer to the Father on Calvary the following day could be made present through the centuries in a sacramental way. In order that His sacrifice on Calvary be perpetuated, during that same meal He conferred on the apostles the power to effect that same miraculous change. *"Do this in memory of Me"* (Lk. 22:19).

The Liturgy refers to the Eucharist, which is both a sacrifice and a sacrament, as a *"mystery of faith."* We can attempt to explain what Christ did at the Last Supper as described in the Gospels, but it will still remain a mystery that we believe because of our faith in His word. In no way can we come up with a natural explanation of this miraculous change and of His abiding presence which results from it. Nowhere in nature do we find a change similar to this. We will examine briefly the Church's teaching on this central doctrine of our faith.

Doctrine of the Church

Martin Luther admitted the real presence of Christ in the Eucharist. However, he rejected the doctrine of transubstantiation and taught that the glorified Body of Christ is present in the Eucharist along with the bread and wine (consubstantiation); and he restricted the real presence to the moment of receiving Communion. Other reformers held that the Body of Christ is present only as a sign, that the words of

Christ are to be taken in a figurative or symbolic sense, not in their literal meaning.

Confronted with these challenges to the traditional Catholic teaching on the Eucharist by the Protestant reformers, the Council of Trent issued an authoritative teaching on this change of the substance of the bread and wine at the consecration of the Mass.

> Because Christ our Redeemer declared that what He offered under the species of bread was truly His Body, it has always been the faith of the Church of God (and this holy Synod now states it again) that by the consecration of the bread and wine a change takes place in which the entire substance of the bread is changed into the substance of the Body of Christ our Lord, and the entire substance of the wine into the substance of His Blood. This change the Holy Catholic Church fittingly and properly calls *"transubstantiation."*[1]

We are dealing here with something that cannot be verified or even examined by natural science. The nature of the change brought about in the Eucharist, as taught by the Church, lies beyond what chemistry, physics or biology are able to establish. We have it on the clear words of Our Lord, and we can assent to it only through the supernatural light of faith. But it will be helpful to examine a bit in detail various aspects of this doctrine of the Church.

Nothing Remains of the Substance of the Bread and Wine

One thing that might be a source of confusion in this matter is that the Church in the expression of this doctrine uses the word *substance* as it is understood in scholastic philosophy. In everyday communication we speak of a substance as something we can see, or feel, or taste, etc. However, in scholastic philosophy a distinction is made between what a thing is in itself (its substance), and the perceptible qualities or characteristics which exist in that substance (its accidents).

So, in discussing the question of the Eucharist, theologians make the distinction between what they call the *substance* of the bread and wine, that is, the reality underlying all its visible, tangible, measurable qualities of bread and wine, but which in itself is not visible, or tangible, or measurable, for it has no extension in space; and the *accidents* or appearances of the bread and wine in which are included all those outward characteristics which can be perceived by the sense of sight, taste, touch, smell and hearing. All such characteristics in philosophical language are referred to as *accidents* (not to be confused with the common meaning of that word).

At the words of the consecration of the Mass, *"This is My Body,"* in an instant the underlying substance of the bread is changed not only into the Body of Christ, but into the **body, blood, soul** and **divinity** of Christ. And likewise, at the words, *"This is the cup of My Blood,"* the substance of the wine is changed not only into the Blood of Christ, but into His **body, blood, soul** and **divinity**. And only with the second phase of the consecration is the sacrifice of Calvary made present. For in the separate consecration of the bread and wine, that is, the sacramental separation of the Body and Blood of Christ, there is completed the sacramental rite which makes present the sacrifice of Calvary.

While Christ is truly present at the words of consecration, there can be no physical separation of the Body of Christ from the Blood that flows in His glorified Body, nor can there be a separation of His Body from the human soul that gives life to that Body; nor can that human body and soul be separated from the Divine Word with which it was united at the moment of the Incarnation. For this reason the whole Christ (Body, Blood, Soul and Divinity) is present *"by reason of concomitance,"* as theologians call it, at the instant the words of consecration are pronounced.

This is why the faithful who communicate only under the species of the bread receive the whole Christ no less than those who partake also of the chalice. To receive Communion under both species might, for some, symbolize or express more vividly the sacrifice of Christ in which His Blood was shed; but in itself it does not bring more grace. The grace of the sacrament depends more on the openness of heart to the One received, that is, detachment of soul from those things that tend to enslave the heart.

No Parallel in Nature

In spite of the fact that there is a complete and total change of substance of the bread and wine at the words of consecration, the appearances or perceptible characteristics (the accidents) remain the same. What we see, touch and taste, our *senses* would tell us, is bread and wine. But the reality beneath those appearances, our *faith* tells us, is the person of Jesus, Body, Blood, Soul and Divinity. The outward visible characteristics of bread and wine truly continue to exist, so our senses do not deceive us. However, by the power of God those outward characteristics are sustained in existence, without the substance in which they formerly existed, to serve as an external sign for the sacrament of the Eucharist. Pope Leo XIII spoke of this in his encyclical *Mirae Caritatis:*

> This miracle is the greatest of its kind . . . for here all the laws of nature are suspended; the whole substance of the bread and wine are changed into the Body and Blood; and the species of bread and wine are sustained by the power of God without the support of any underlying substance.

St. Thomas Aquinas gives three reasons why it is fitting that God intervenes in this miraculous way.[2] 1) Because it is not customary but horrible for men to eat human flesh and drink human blood; hence Christ's flesh and blood are given to us under the species of those things more commonly consumed by men. 2) Lest this sacrament might be derided by unbelievers, were we to eat the flesh and blood of Jesus under His own proper species. 3) That while we receive Our Lord's Body and Blood invisibly, this may redound to the merit of faith.

Hence there is no parallel to this in all of nature where there is a complete change of substance, while there is no change in the external sense-perceptible characteristics of the original substance. In fact, every time the priest at Mass pronounces the words of consecration there is a *double miracle* wrought by the power of God, miracles not witnessed by the senses, but known only by the light of faith: 1) The miraculous change of the substance of the bread and wine into the substance of Christ's Body and Blood; and 2) The miracle by which God sustains in existence the perceptible qualities or characteristics of the bread and wine, although the underlying substance no longer exists. St. Thomas wrote so beautifully of this mystery in the Eucharistic hymn sung at Benediction of the Blessed Sacrament: *"Praestet fides supplementum sensuum defectui."* Faith supplies what the senses cannot perceive.

In What Manner Christ is Present

As we have pointed out, when we receive Holy Communion, we receive Jesus, the God-man who suffered, died and rose for us. Our Divine Savior is not only present in each and every consecrated host, but in every part of each host. Just as before the consecration each part of the host was bread, and every drop in the chalice was wine, so after the consecration every smallest particle of the consecrated host contains the whole Christ, and every drop of the contents of the chalice contains the whole Christ, Body, Blood, Soul and Divinity. Consequently, Christ is not divided by the breaking of the host.

We must be careful, however, about imagining how Christ could be present in the small host, or in a tiny part of it. First of all, Jesus is not present in the sacred host in miniature, or in a condensed manner. As St. Thomas Aquinas explains, *"Christ's Body is in this sacrament by way of substance, not by way of quantity,"*[3] that is, not by extension in space. The whole Christ is present in this sacrament with all the faculties and characteristics of His glorified body; but it is an entirely supernatural and unique presence made possible by the power of God, and discerned only by the eyes of faith. As St. Ambrose reminds us, *"The word of Christ which could make out of nothing that which did not exist, can it not change things already in existence into that which they were not?"*

Christ is present in the Eucharist as He exists now in heaven, that is, in His glorified body. When Our Lord changed the bread and wine into His Body and Blood at the Last Supper, it was His *mortal* body, for He had not yet died and risen with His glorified body that is *immortal.* If there are on record miraculous cases where the sacred host has bled, that does not change the fact that the presence of Christ in the Eucharist is the glorified Christ. Our Lord could manifest this mark of His Passion in this way to emphasize the fact that the Eucharist is a sacrifice, spiritually made present at Mass, as well as a sacrament. Pope Leo XIII adds another reason:

> In order that human reason may more willingly pay its homage to this great mystery, there have not been wanting, as an aid to faith, certain prodigies wrought in His honor, both in ancient times as in our own, of which in more than one place there exist public and notable records and memorials.[4]

Too, one might wonder how long the bodily presence of Christ in His physical reality remains with us after we receive Him in Holy Communion. He remains with us in His sacramental presence as long as the species of bread and wine retain their true characteristics of bread and wine. Just as true bread and wine can corrupt, or undergo chemical change so that it is no longer bread or wine, so can the species of bread and wine in the Eucharist undergo such a change, as happens when we receive Holy Communion. When the species of bread in the consecrated host changes within the body so that it no longer has the characteristics of true bread, then the sacramental presence of Jesus ceases. The same is true of the species of wine if one received this sacrament under that form as well as receiving the consecrated host.[5] The reason for this is that the sacrament of the Eucharist is the Body and Blood of Christ really present under the species or characteristics of bread and wine. If the characteristics of bread and wine cease to be present, the sacrament no longer exists, and the sacramental presence of Christ ceases. However, His spiritual presence through grace not only remains, but has been increased through the reception of the sacrament.

The Real Presence

Although Christ ascended into heaven depriving mankind of His visible presence, He remains with us hidden beneath the veil of the Eucharistic host to continue the work of redemption, making intercession for us before the Father through the renewal of His sacrifice and His abiding presence. Faith alone makes us aware of His presence, for reason cannot comprehend it. Yet reason knows that what is of divine faith and divinely revealed is infallibly certain. Christ is present in the Eucharist with all the perfections of his humanity, together with the infinite grandeur of His divinity, both of which are hidden under the appearances of bread and wine, as St. Thomas expresses so beautifully in the hymn *Adoro Te:* *"In cruce latebat sola Deitas at hic latet simul et humanitas." (On the Cross was hidden only His divinity, but here lies veiled also His humanity.)*

Our Savior present in the Eucharist in His glorified Body is identical with the Jesus Christ of history, with the Jesus before whom the angels and saints of heaven worship in awe. He is the same Jesus whom Mary brought forth into the world, whom the shepherds found wrapped in swaddling clothes in a manger; the same Jesus who taught the multitudes, who cured the leper, the blind, the lame, and raised the dead; the same Jesus who was transfigured on Mt. Tabor, who received the kiss of the traitor, was scourged, crowned with thorns, spat upon and treated as a fool; the same Jesus who was crucified to redeem us, rose from the dead, and is seated at the right hand of His Father. And to think that at times kneeling before the tabernacle we cannot think of anything to say!

While our reflection on Christ in the Eucharist centers mainly around His sacred humanity, it is a divine Person that we receive in Holy Communion, the only-begotten Son of the Father. Yet, the divine Word is never alone, for the Father abides in the Son and the Son in the Father, and both are united in the Holy Spirit, all possessing the same divine nature (Jn. 14:11). Thus, the divine Trinity of Persons, of whose vision is the beatitude of heaven, abides with the Word in the Eucharistic host.

Yet, our primary attention to Christ in the Eucharist will always be centered on Him in His sacred humanity, precisely because He took on our human nature to live and suffer the torturous death that He did, to show us the love of the Father for mankind, and to teach us by word and example how to return that love. In receiving this sacrament we receive Him who is infinite Love, and all the gifts and blessings of the incarnation and redemption are made available to us in the measure of our eagerness and openness to receive them. That is to say, the love (not necessarily an emotional disposition) with which we receive our Eucharistic Lord will determine the extent to which this sacrament produces its principally intended effect, namely, transforming the soul into the likeness of Christ. Fr. M. M. Philipon, O.P. speaks of this:

> If we wish to make a profound study of the benefits of the Eucharist, the best way is to view them from the perspective of the incarnation, that is, to bear in mind that God became man to make us divine, that the Word was made flesh to make us like Himself. Everything about the Eucharist comes down to this fundamental point; that through love, Holy Communion brings about a union which transforms us in Christ.[6]

Chapter Notes

1. Council of Trent, Sess. 13, Ch. 4
2. St. Thomas Aquinas, *Summa Theologiae,* III, 75, 5, ad 1
3. *Ibid.*, 76, 1, ad 3
4. Pope Leo XIII, *Mirae Caritatis*
5. St. Thomas Aquinas, *Summa Theologiae,* III, 77, 4
6. M. M. Philipon, O.P., *The Sacraments in the Christian Life*, p. 99

Chapter 38

The Mass and the Mystical Body

We can better understand our union with Christ, and especially our union with Him in the sacrifice of the Mass, if we have some idea of the Mystical Body of which Christ is the head and we the members. As the members of our own body constitute a living organism in the natural order, all physically united, so the head and members of the Mystical Body constitute a living organism in the supernatural order, all united through grace.

St. Augustine speaks of the Mystical Body of Christ as the *"whole Christ."* Not that the individual physical Body of Christ was in any way incomplete; but He became man precisely to become one with us, not merely taking on our human nature, but sharing with us His divine life in such a way that we, as members of His Body, share in the fruits of all that He did.

This oneness with Christ in the Mass is not just a figurative or symbolic expression. It is a reality, since, through grace, we share in His divine life, His knowledge, His love, according to the degree of our growth in grace and charity; for only in that measure is the soul open to the influence of the Holy Spirit. To express this in another way, the spiritual effects of the Eucharist are obtained in the measure that we are free from attachment to venial sins; for as St. Thomas explains:

> The fire of our desire or love is hindered by venial sins, which hinder the fervor of charity. . . . Therefore, venial sins hinder the effects of this sacrament. . . . (Yet venial sins) do not completely hinder the effect of this sacrament, but merely in part.[1]

When we receive our Blessed Lord in Holy Communion, we are united with Him in a twofold way: through the substantial presence of His Body and Blood under the species of bread and wine, which is only temporary;

and through the deeper and more intimate and lasting oneness with Him through the grace infused into the soul in the reception of this sacrament. This latter union is by far the more important, for as we saw, it is an increased sharing in the very life, and love, and truth that Jesus is. Thus we are united with Jesus at Mass, both in offering the sacrifice, and in receiving the sacrament. And the more we give of ourselves in union with Christ in the sacrifice, the more the Lord gives of Himself in the sacrament.

As long as we are in the state of grace, Christ lives His divine life in us, we in Him, and He in us. *"He who eats my flesh and drinks my blood, abides in Me and I in him"* (Jn. 6:57). We abide in Him as members of His Mystical Body, and He abides in us through grace. When we cooperate with His graces and inspirations He lives His divine life in us as the primary cause of our good acts; we are but the secondary cause, cooperating with the graces received. We can, of course, fail to cooperate with His graces, preferring our will to His.

Through Him, With Him, In Him

How do we offer adoration and reparation, thanksgiving and praise to the Father during the Mass? The words of the Mass at the end of the Eucharistic Prayer give us the answer. We make this offering *"through Him, with Him and in Him, in the unity of the Holy Spirit,"* so that *"all glory and honor is Yours, almighty Father, for ever and ever."* It is *through* Christ, our Mediator with the Father, *with* Him, as co-offerers of this sacrifice, and *in* Him as members of His Body that we offer the Mass; and this is done through the action of the Holy Spirit, sent by the Father and the Son to continue and bring to completion the work that Christ began. Our Blessed Lord not only paid the price of our redemption, but merited for us every grace the Holy Spirit brings to us. Our offering in the Mass is pleasing to the Father more than we can ever know, for it is offered to the Father by His only-begotten Son, in union with His own total oblation. That is why prayers and petitions to the Father during the Mass are especially fruitful.

Every good act of ours, then, is not ours alone; it is primarily the action of Christ in us. Our main contribution is that we have not let our selfishness stand in the way. Awareness of that should protect us from pride, from attributing solely to our own talents and strength the good that we do, or rather the good that Christ does in us with our cooperation. This is true of every supernatural act of faith, hope, love, contrition, thanksgiving, chastity, fortitude, and so on.

While the sacrament of *Baptism* brings to all the faithful a share in the priesthood of Christ, giving them a special capacity of participating in the sacrifice of Christ through the Mass, only to those who have received the sacrament of *Holy Orders* has been given the power to act in the person of Christ, calling down the action of the Holy Spirit to change the bread and wine into the Body and Blood of Christ. Through that sacrament Christ, the High Priest, empowers the ordained priest to offer the sacrifice of the Mass in His name for the whole Church; while the faithful, along with the invisible High Priest, participate in the offering *"through Him, with Him and in Him."*

The Mass is Our Sacrifice

Because of this wonderful mystery of the Mystical Body of Christ and our oneness with Him as His members, all that He did on Calvary is ours to offer to the Father, and is reputed to us as if we ourselves had undergone the Passion, as St. Thomas explains: *"The head and members are one mystic person; and therefore Christ's satisfaction belongs to all the faithful as being His members."*[2] And again, speaking of the effects of baptism: *"It is clear that the Passion of Christ is communicated to every baptized person, so that he is healed just as if he himself had suffered and died . . . as if he himself had offered sufficient satisfaction for all his sins."*[3]

Consequently, in this sacramental presence of the sacrifice of the cross, we offer, together with Christ, all that He offered for us on Calvary, along with all the good works He enables us to accomplish. Every meritorious act on our part is made possible by the grace won for us by Christ and infused into the soul here and now by the Holy Spirit. That is why the Mass, in addition to adoration and reparation, should also be a fervent offering of thanksgiving to our Blessed Lord who redeemed us, and to the Father who sent Him.

The infinite adoration, reparation and thanksgiving of Christ, offered to the Father on Calvary, is ours, then, to offer along with our own feeble efforts and to make up for our shortcomings. We offer His obedience to make up for our disobedience, His humility to make up for our pride, His poverty of spirit to make up for our attachment to the world, His purity of heart to make up for our attachment to the flesh. Our oneness with Him in the Mystical Body allows us to do this, for all that He did in His sacred humanity is ours to offer to the Father.

This is brought out clearly in the prayer the angel taught to the three children at Fatima, while prostrating before the Eucharistic presence of our Blessed Lord:

> Most holy Trinity, Father, Son and Holy Spirit, I adore You profoundly, and I offer You the most precious Body, Blood, Soul and Divinity of Jesus Christ, present in all the tabernacles of the world, in reparation for the outrages, sacrileges and indifference by which He Himself is offended. By the infinite merits of the Sacred Heart of Jesus and the Immaculate Heart of Mary, I beg of you the conversion of poor sinners.

The Liturgy of the Eucharist

The sacrifice of the Mass in its traditional concept is divided into the liturgy of the Word and the liturgy of the Eucharist. And this latter has three essential parts: the *offertory* — the offering of the Victim; the *consecration* — the immolation of the Victim; and the *communion* — the reception of the Divine Victim under the appearance of bread and wine. We will briefly consider those three essential parts of the liturgy of the Eucharist.

The Offertory

The Mass is the offering of the whole Christ to the eternal Father.[4] Each of us should be offerers along with Christ, not merely in a general way, but through a renewal of the gift of ourselves, the surrender of our will to the Father in all that He asks of us or allows in our life, our burdens, our trials, and so forth. Relying on the help of God's grace, we do what we can to cope with these challenges, seeing them in the light of His guiding and purifying hand. We offer all this along with our good works and prayers, not only for our needs but for the needs of others, to fill up what is wanting in other members of the Mystical Body. The very association of our offering with that of Christ makes our offering pleasing to the Father.

As the priest offers the *host* that will become the Body of Christ, we can, in spirit, place on the paten our own body with its aches and pains, along with the fatigue and hardships we experience in the fulfillment of duty. We can place there our good works in recognition that they were accomplished only with God's help, and in petition that they be purified of their imperfections. We can place there our needs of body and soul, and those of others for whom we pray. The Catechism of the Catholic Church refers to this:

> In the Eucharist the sacrifice of Christ becomes also the sacrifice of the members of the Body. The lives of the faithful, their praise, sufferings, prayer, and work, are united with those of Christ and with His total offering, and so acquire a new value. Christ's sacrifice present on the altar makes it possible for all generations of Christians to be united with His offering.[4]

When the priest offers the *chalice of wine* that will become the Blood of Christ, we can offer in spirit, as spiritual writers suggest, a drop of our own blood; a symbol of the sacrifices we have to make to keep God's commandments, to fulfill our God-given duties, and to bear the crosses He allows.

And if all that Christ did, as head of the Mystical Body, is ours to offer to the Father, so also, and for the same reason, all that the saintly members of His Body did is ours to offer. We can, in a word, offer the whole Church with the lives and good works, the sacrifices and sufferings of all its members, for all its members who are in need. The more all-embracing our offering and concern, the more perfect it is, the more it resembles the all-embracing offering and love of Christ. One may not be able to reflect on all these details each time he attends Mass, but they indicate ways of making one's participation in Christ's sacrifice more complete and more fruitful.

The Consecration

When we refer to the consecration of the Mass as the immolation of the Victim, this does not mean that the sacrifice of Calvary is repeated, that Christ dies again. At the words of the priest, our Blessed Lord becomes present as the risen Christ in His glorified Body, no longer capable of suffering and death. As St. Paul explains: *"Christ having risen from the dead, dies now no more, death shall no longer have dominion over Him"* (Rom. 6:9). The sacrifice of Calvary is not repeated, but is made present, Christ, the High Priest and Victim offering again the same total oblation of Himself to the Father for our sake.[5] As Fr. Marie-Joseph Nicolas, O.P., expresses it: *"The consecration of the two species is a symbolic immolation, but the symbolism is sacramental and contains what it signifies. The Mass is a sacrifice, because it signifies and at the same time contains the whole reality of the sacrifice of the cross."*[6] The Mass does not add anything to the sacrifice of Calvary, but rather applies its fruits to us in the measure that we are open to the action of the Holy Spirit, that is, that we are willing to sacrifice our will that God's will be done.

The Communion

When one receives our Blessed Lord in Holy Communion, there is no limit to the amount of grace that each reception of the sacrament can bring. That is, there is no limit on the part of the sacrament; for in this sacrament we receive Him who is the fountainhead of all grace, whose divine life is infinite love, infinite truth, infinite wisdom. And this divine Guest wishes to share His gifts with us more than we can ever know. That which limits the amount of grace received is the limited capacity of each individual soul receiving Him, depending on the extent that one's heart is free from enslavement by the world and its attractions.

Catholic theologians distinguish two ways in which each of the sacraments gives grace:

Ex opere operato, that is, by its own intrinsic power, independently of the one receiving it. And it does this in the measure that the recipient of the sacrament does not place obstacles in the way. Those obstacles, as we saw above, can be the attachments to worldly satisfactions that can to some extent enslave the heart, keeping it from total surrender to God's will.[7]

Ex opere operantis, that is, according to the disposition of the one receiving the sacrament. To insure this is not neglected, the immediate preparation to receive our Blessed Lord is important, for it gives rise to sincere acts of faith, of contrition and of surrender to God's will. These acts, with the help of actual graces, enlarge the capacity of the soul to receive an increase of the divine life of Him whom we receive.

We can see from this how important it is not to let our reception of our Blessed Lord become mere routine, both as to preparation beforehand and thanksgiving afterwards. Usually if there is little preparation there will be little thanksgiving, with a corresponding little increase of grace.

Left to ourselves alone, all the time allotted to us in this world would not be enough to pay the infinite debt of gratitude we owe to the Father; and an entire eternity will be occupied in thanking Him for the benefits received. Yet, we have in the Mass an adequate means of paying that debt, for Christ offered His sacrifice of reparation and thanksgiving in our place. And this sacrifice can be offered with Christ again and again. We begin to see the infinite riches of the Mass, which is the center around which the whole of our Christian life should revolve, and from which we are meant to receive the strength and inspiration to follow in Christ's footsteps.

Chapter Notes

1. St. Thomas Aquinas, *Summa Theologiae,* III, 79, 8
2. *Ibid.*, 79, 5. ad 1
3. *Ibid.*, 69, 2
4. CCC 1368
5. CCC 1362
6. Marie Joseph Nicholas, O.P., A *New Look at the Eucharist,* p. 60
7. Council of Trent, VII, Can. 8

Chapter 39

Our Encounter with Christ in the Liturgy

The life of Christ on earth has two phases: the redemptive phase, which ended with His death on Calvary; and the second phase, that of His Mystical Body, the supernatural organism of which He is the Head and we the members. In this second phase He continues the glorification of His Father through the liturgy, in which He makes present the mysteries that occurred in that first and redemptive phase of His life on earth. In this way He applies to souls, through their participation in the liturgy, the graces won for mankind through His Passion and death. He continues the glorification of His Father in each of His members, in the measure that He is enabled to live His divine life in them. *"The life I live now is not my own, Christ is living in me. I still have my human life, but it is a life of faith in the Son of God"* (Gal. 2:20).

In the light of this we will examine the presence and action of Christ in the liturgy of the Church. In these reflections we rely much on the encyclical of Pope Pius XII, *Mediator Dei,* and on the Decrees on the Liturgy and the Church of the Second Vatican Council.

Jesus Christ, Our High Priest

Referring to our Divine Savior as the High Priest of the New Law, St. Paul wrote: *"We do not have a high priest who is unable to sympathize with our weakness, but one who was tempted in every way that we are, yet never sinned. Let us therefore approach the throne of grace with confidence, to receive mercy . . . and help in time of need"* (Heb. 4:15-16).

The sin of our first parents had disrupted the relationship between man and his Creator. No longer were they and their descendants heirs of heaven, but rather heirs of the effects of original sin. In the course of time, the Son of the eternal Father came to restore the divine life that was lost, and to reopen to mankind the gates of heaven. He would do this by assuming our human nature, in order that as a member of the human race, He could (as High Priest of the New Law) offer Himself in total submission to the Father, even to death on the cross, thereby paying the debt of mankind and winning for all the graces necessary for salvation.

Jesus Continues to Exercise His Priesthood through the Liturgy

Not satisfied with the sacrifice of His life to the Father on Calvary, our Savior willed, says Pope Pius XII, *"that the priestly life begun with the sacrifice of His mortal body should continue without interruption down the ages in his mystical body which is the Church."* [1] For this reason, the night before He died, along with the sacrament and the sacrifice of the Eucharist He established the sacrament of Holy Orders, sharing with His apostles and those who would be chosen to succeed them, the powers of His own priesthood, enabling them and bidding them to continue that same sacrifice.

Thus, says Fr. Roguet, O.P., the priesthood of Christ did not cease with His death; it continues to function, the only difference being that since the Ascension it is exercised in an invisible way through the ministry of ordained priests who share the priesthood of Christ. *"It is not true,"* he says, *"to say that the priest celebrates his Mass, still less that he gives his absolution, even though we sometimes express it in that manner. He celebrates the **sacrifice of Christ** and of the Church (His Body); he administers the **pardon of Christ** and of the Church."*

Along these same lines we read in the decree on the Liturgy from the Second Vatican Council:

> Christ is always present in His Church, especially in her liturgical celebrations. He is present in the sacrifice of the Mass, not only in the person of His minister, *"the same one now offering, through the ministry of priests, who formerly offered Himself on the cross,"*[3] but especially under the *Eucharistic species.* By His power He is present in *the sacraments,* so that when a man baptizes it is really Christ Himself who baptizes. He is present in *His Word,* since it is He Himself who speaks when the Holy Scriptures are read in Church. He is present finally when the Church prays and sings, for He promised: *"Where two or three are gathered for My sake, there am I in the midst of them"* (Mt. 18:20).

We might add, when the priest pronounces the *words of absolution,* it is Christ who absolves the penitent. When the priest *anoints the sick,* it is Christ who, through the fingers of the priest anointing, brings healing and strengthening grace to the soul, and sometimes to the body.

> Rightly then, the liturgy is considered as an exercise of the priestly office of Christ.... From this it follows that every liturgical celebration, because it is an action of Christ the priest, and of His Body the Church, is a sacred action surpassing all others. No other action of the Church can match its claim to efficacy, nor equal the degree of it.[4]

Our Participation in the Priesthood of Christ

There are three sacraments that we can receive only once, namely, Baptism, Confirmation and Holy Orders, each of which imprints an indelible character or sign on the soul that remains forever. These sacramental characters, theology tells us, are actually spiritual powers, a sharing in the priesthood of Christ, giving one the capacity to participate in Christian worship.

1) This capacity is received initially at **Baptism**, giving the power to participate in the sacrifice of Christ, not as someone who passively looks on, but as one who actively participates in that which Christ does. As the Second Vatican Council declares:

> Incorporated into the Church through baptism, the faithful are consecrated by the baptismal character to participate in

Christian religious worship. Reborn as sons of God, they must confess before men the faith they have received from God through the Church.[5]

Hence baptism confers not only a power, but also an obligation.

2) By the sacrament of **Confirmation**, the faithful are *"more perfectly bound to the Church, and endowed with the special strength of the Holy Spirit. Hence they are, as true witnesses of Christ, more strictly obliged to spread the faith by word and deed."*[6]

3) By the sacrament of **Holy Orders** (priestly ordination), Christ shares His priestly power in a unique way, empowering certain ministers among the faithful to offer sacrifice and remit sin, acting in His Name. *"By the anointing of the Holy Spirit, priests are marked with a special character and are so configured to Christ the Priest that they can act in the person of Christ as Head of the Mystical Body."*[7]

While both the *laity* and the *ordained priest* share in the priesthood of Christ, the difference between the two is an essential difference, not just a matter of degree. The priest receives the power to *"bring about the Eucharistic Sacrifice,"* while the laity receives the power to participate in it. *"The faithful join in the offering of the Eucharist by virtue of their royal priesthood. They likewise exercise that priesthood by receiving the sacraments, by prayer and thanksgiving, by witness of a holy life, and by self-denial and active charity."*[8]

Offering the Eucharistic Sacrifice

Our Blessed Lord shares His priesthood with us precisely that we might be enabled to unite with Him in renewing the oblation of Himself to the Father. Referring to the faithful in that regard, the Second Vatican Council states: *"Taking part in the Eucharistic Sacrifice, which is the fount and apex of the whole Christian life, they offer the Divine Victim to God, and offer themselves along with it."*[9] While there are many things that could be touched on in regard to our participation in the Mass, we will consider only the twofold offering referred to by the Council.

1) Offering the Divine Victim

It is important to keep in mind our unique oneness with Christ as members of His Mystical Body, for this has an important bearing on the proper understanding of our manner of participation in the Mass. Not only can we offer to the Father, along with Christ, the sacrifice of His own Body and Blood, made present by the words of consecration, but we can offer these gifts as *our* sacrifice.

> *"The Head and members,"* says St. Thomas Aquinas, *"are one mystical person, and therefore Christ's satisfaction belongs to all the faithful as his members."* [10] Because of this, he says elsewhere, *"the baptized person, being a member of Christ, shares in the satisfactory value of Christ's passion, as though he had himself endured the penalty."* [11]

Do we understand the tremendous significance of those words? The infinite satisfaction of Christ, His suffering, His total surrender to the Father, are *ours* to offer to the Father again and again, just as if we ourselves had undergone the Passion. One can see how powerful that can make our prayers, how we never need feel we approach God empty-handed when we ask His graces and favors.

Yet, this sharing in the infinite merits and satisfaction of Christ does not automatically follow. As Pope Pius XII wrote:

> That the redemption and salvation of each person ... be effectively accomplished ... it is necessary (by means of the sacraments and especially the Eucharistic sacrifice) that men should individually come into vital contact with the sacrifice of the cross. ... It is not enough to offer the Divine Victim; it is necessary that the people add something else, namely, the offering of themselves as a victim

... so that each can repeat with St. Paul: "With Christ I am nailed to the cross" (Gal. 2:19).[12]

2) Offering Ourselves to the Father

Since Christ exercised His priesthood, offering Himself to the Father for us, we should see in our sharing in His priesthood an invitation to offer our lives to the Father, not through a *physical immolation* as Christ did, but by offering *spiritual sacrifices* of all we do. St. Peter wrote of this in his first epistle: *"You are living stones, built into an edifice of spirit, into a holy priesthood, offering spiritual sacrifices acceptable to God through Jesus Christ"* (2:5).

The Second Vatican Council in its decree on the Church explains in detail these "spiritual sacrifices."

> The supreme and eternal Priest, Christ Jesus, wills to continue His witness and to serve through the laity too ... giving them a share in His priestly function of offering spiritual worship for the glory of God and the salvation of men. For this reason the laity, dedicated to Christ and anointed by the Holy Spirit, are marvelously called and equipped to produce in themselves ever more abundant fruits of the Spirit. For all their works, prayers and apostolic endeavors, their ordinary married and family life, their daily labors, their mental and physical relaxation, if carried out in His Spirit, and even the hardships of life, if patiently borne, all these become *spiritual sacrifices* acceptable to God through Jesus Christ.[13]

Pope Pius XII was referring to this same participation in the Eucharistic Sacrifice when he said: *"Nor should Christians forget to offer themselves, their cares, their sorrows, their distress and their necessities in union with their Divine Savior upon the Cross."*[14]

Each Mass, then, is meant to be an occasion and opportunity of offering to the Father the "spiritual sacrifices" that are a part of each day. *"During the celebration of the Eucharist, these sacrifices are most lovingly offered to the Father along with the Lord's Body. Thus as worshipers whose every deed is holy, the laity consecrate the world itself to God."*[15]

Practical Reflections

1) We see, then, the vocation to which we have been called, that of being incorporated into the Mystical Body of Christ, and sharing in His priestly office. By reason of this, all of our good works, offered up in union with His redeeming sacrifice, have the capacity of *giving glory to the Father,* and of *remitting sin* — ours and those of others.

2) Our sharing in the fruits of Christ's sacrifice on Calvary depends on the degree of our union with Him in the renewal of that sacrifice; and this, in turn, depends not on any emotion or feeling of closeness to Him, nor even on how attentively we follow every action of the Mass, but on how intimately we are one with Him in the *oblation of self.* We are one with Christ at Mass, and share in the fruits of His sacrifice, in the measure that we ourselves are willing to make the sacrifices needed to keep His commandments, to fulfill our God-given duties, and to bear patiently the crosses of daily life.

St. Paul expressed this same thing in terms of obedience. Christ redeemed us by His total obedience to His Father on Calvary, and *"became the source of eternal salvation to all who obey Him"* (Heb. 5:9). The repeated sacrifices that obedience to God demands are the "spiritual sacrifices" referred to above, which we bring to Mass, offering them to the Father along with the infinite gifts of the Body and Blood of His Son.

3) Since the Catholic faith is spread over the whole world, the sacrifice of the Mass is being offered without cease in some part of the globe. Therefore, just as each beat of the human heart sends life-giving blood to every part of the body, so each Mass offered up is as a heartbeat of the Mystical Body of Christ, constantly sending the life-giving grace of Christ the Head to every member of that Body that is disposed to receive it. Each time, at the renewal of the Eucharistic Sacrifice we offer ourselves to the Father along with the Body and Blood of His Son, that accrues *"not only to our own advantage, but to that of the whole Church, where whatever good is*

accomplished proceeds from the power of her Head and redounds to the advancement of all of her members."[16]

Chapter Notes

1. Pope Pius XII, *Mediator Dei*, n. 2
2. Fr. Roguet, O.P., *Christ Acts Through Sacraments*, p. 11
3. Council of Trent
4. Vatican Council II, *Sacrosanctum Concilium,* 7
5. Vatican Council II, *Lumen Gentium*, 11
6. *Ibid.*
7. Vatican Council II, *Presbyterorum Ordinis*, 2
8. *Lumen Gentium*, 10
9. *Lumen Gentium*, 11
10. St. Thomas Aquinas, *Summa Theologiae,* III, 48, 2, 1
11. *Ibid.*, III, 79, 5
12. *Mediator Dei*, 77, 98
13. *Lumen Gentium, n.* 34
14. *Mediator Dei*, n. 104
15. *Lumen Gentium*, n. 34
16. *Mediator Dei*, n. 35

Chapter 40

The Millennium and the Eucharist

The Church founded by Christ has not only endured for 2000 years, but like the mustard seed in the Gospel (Mt. 13:31), has grown to cover the whole world with its branches; and like the leaven put in a measure of flour quickening the whole mass of the dough (Mt. 13:33), it has extended the kingdom of God with its life-giving message to all parts of the world. Yet, this has not happened without opposition of the Evil One who established his kingdom at the fall of our first parents, and whose aim is our eternal damnation.

While both Satan and his kingdom were conquered by Christ through His Passion and death and their ultimate defeat is certain, yet, in the providence of God, he will be allowed to test the souls of men until the end of time. For this reason, today, as with the first Christians 2000 years ago, growth in the divine life of grace won for us by our Divine Savior will not be attained without a price. It is by sacrifice that we share in the fruits of Christ's sacrifice. It is by obedience to His word handed down by the Church He established and by the fervent use of the means of grace He gave us, that we share in the life-giving fruits of His painful obedience to the Father. Such has been the history of the followers of Christ for twenty centuries.

The Great Jubilee

For the second time since the birth of Christ, the Church celebrated the completion of a millennium of the Christianization of the world. Yet, while this past century has seen outstanding progress in the fields of scientific research and technology, it seems that the Church has not been equally successful as to the spread of the message Christ brought to the world. The forces of evil have made better use of modern advances of technology than have the forces for good; that is, they have been more effectively used to spread the spirit of the world, than the spirit and message of Christ. Perhaps it has always been so, for our Blessed Lord declared 2000 years ago that *"the children of this world are more clever in their own sphere than are the children of light"* (Lk. 16:8).

For this reason Pope John Paul II, on the occasion of this "great jubilee," issued a special call for the **evangelization** of those who had not received the good tidings of the Gospel, and for the **re-evangelization** of those who had received it, but because of compromise with the world have not accepted it wholly, or have abandoned it completely. This has caused the Holy Father to declare that *"the more the West is becoming estranged from its Christian roots, the more it is becoming mission territory."* [1]

In keeping with the plan of the Holy Father, the three years of preparation immediately preceding the third millennium were dedicated to each of the divine Persons of the Trinity, with the focus of the celebration of the year 2000 on rendering glory to the supreme Godhead of this great mystery.

From this source everything comes, and to it everything returns. But, as the Holy Father explains, *"since Christ is the only way to the Father, in order to highlight His living and saving presence in the Church and in the world, the International Eucharistic Congress will take place in Rome, on the occasion of the Great Jubilee. The year 2000 will be intensely Eucharistic: in the Sacrament of the Eucharist the Savior, who took flesh in Mary's womb twenty centuries ago, continues to offer Himself to humanity as the source of divine life."* [2]

Christ in the Eucharist

During the celebration of the Great Jubilee the Church focused our attention on the divine source of all things and the ultimate end to which all must return; and since Christ is the only way to the Father as well as the perfect image of the Father (Jn. 14:9), a special emphasis was placed on honoring the Father through the Eucharistic presence of His only-begotten Son. There are many ways in which we can render glory to God by the fulfillment of His will, but a special emphasis was placed on seeking a better appreciation and use of Christ's gift of Himself in the sacrament and sacrifice of the Eucharist.

Christ, the Life of the Soul

True love is a unitive force, and this is especially true of God's love for us. In His infinite wisdom and love He has established through the Eucharist, a means of union between the human soul and Himself so intimate even in this life, that we can never fully understand or appreciate it. It is a union as close as that between truth and the mind conceiving it, between goodness and the will desiring it, for by means of this divine food of the Eucharist, Christ transforms the soul into the likeness of Himself who is infinite Truth and infinite Love. As the Council of Trent explains: *"Christ willed that this sacrament be received as the spiritual food of souls, whereby may be fed and strengthened those who live by His life, who said, 'He that eats Me, shall also live by Me'"* (Jn. 6:36).

It was not enough that He should become one of us by adopting our human nature, but He devised a most extraordinary means of union in which He becomes our food, doing for the soul what ordinary food does for the body. Unlike ordinary food that is transformed into our own flesh and blood, this food causes us to be transformed into Him, that is to say, to share more and more in His divine life, so that more and more we see as He sees, will as He wills, love as He loves. Such a one can exclaim with St. Paul: *"The life I live now is not my own; Christ is living in me. I still live my human life, but it is a life of faith in the Son of God, who loved me and gave Himself for me"* (Gal. 2:20).

He of whom St. John says, *"All things were made through Him"* (Jn. 1:13), the maker and fashioner of the entire universe, has deigned to conceal Himself under the appearance of bread and wine in order to become our spiritual food, filling an ongoing need of the soul with His light and strength and peace. He comes to us in this invisible way known only by the light of faith. While the real presence of the Body and Blood of Christ is only temporary, remaining only until the properties of the bread and wine disappear through the natural process of digestion, there is a deeper and lasting union with Christ by means of grace through our incorporation into His Mystical Body, of which He is the Head and we the members. This incorporation into the Body of Christ through which we live by His life, should increase with each reception of Holy Communion.

The Eucharistic Sacrifice

St. Thomas explains that the Eucharist *"is both a sacrament and a sacrifice; it has the nature of a SACRIFICE inasmuch as it is offered up; and it has the nature of a SACRAMENT inasmuch as it is received."*³ We come to Mass, therefore, not merely to *receive* from the Father the Word of God — both in the liturgy of the word, and as divine food in the liturgy of the Eucharist; but we come to *offer* to the Father: 1) the *divine Victim* who is made present by the words of consecration, and who offers infinite adoration, thanksgiving and reparation to the Father through the renewal of the oblation of Himself made on Calvary; and 2) we offer *ourselves* in the renewal of our resolve to surrender our will to God's. In the measure that our resolve is sincere, in that measure we are united with the divine High Priest and Victim, offering again to the Father, along with His prayers, the sufferings, wounds, insults, rejection, and hatred He endured on our behalf. And we shall see that those two aspects of the Mass (offering and receiving) are intimately connected. The fruitfulness of the second depends on the completeness of the first; that is, on the extent of our union with Christ, and the completeness of our surrender to the Father.

We can never fully appreciate the greatness of the gift we receive in Holy Communion, for that divine food is our Blessed Lord Himself truly and substantially present. Yet, from what we have just explained, it should be clear that the extent that this Eucharistic meal enriches the soul depends in no small measure on the extent that we are one with Christ in the renewal of His Sacrifice, for Holy Communion is the fruit of that sacrifice. For that reason it is important to understand the sacrificial aspect of the Mass and our participation in that sacrifice.

When Christ pronounced the words of consecration over the bread and wine at the Last Supper the night before He died, He endowed us with a twofold wonder. He made it possible for each of the redeemed to share in a unique way in the fruits of His redemptive mission through this sacramental meal. And secondly, He provided the Church with a sacred rite whereby, in union with Him, the Church could continue to offer the Father the infinite adoration and praise rendered to Him during the Passion. It would be a rite which consists in the renewal of the offering Christ made of Himself on Calvary for the glory of the Father and the salvation of mankind.

We are dealing here with a great mystery. Yet, the love, wisdom and power of God have made possible this mystery of the Eucharist in which Christ is really and truly present, and whereby, in the Church, there is made possible a permanent sacrifice that is identical in substance with that of the cross. It is a sacrifice that transcends the limits of time and space, so that the offering of Calvary can be made present until the end of time in the midst of the Church for the salvation of souls. St. Thomas refers to this:

> We do not say that Christ is daily crucified or killed (in the Mass), because both the acts of the Jews and the punishment of Christ are transitory. Yet, those things which carry with

them Christ's relation to God the Father are said to be done daily. These are: to offer, to sacrifice, etc. On that account, the victim is perpetual, and was offered once by Christ in this manner that it might be offered daily by His members.[4]

Various Protestant religions do not accept the sacrificial aspect of the Eucharist, for they say that the sacrifice of Christ that took place on Calvary was all-sufficient, and it is by faith in that unique and perfect sacrifice that we shall be saved. To say that the Mass is a renewal of the sacrifice of Calvary, they claim, is to detract from the efficacy of the Lord's Passion and death.

It was in response to this that the Council of Trent went to great lengths to clarify and reaffirm the traditional doctrine of the Church, namely, that the sacrifice of the Mass is a renewal of the sacrifice of Calvary; for in each Mass there is the same High Priest, the same divine Victim, and the same oblation of Himself for the same purpose, the glory of the Father and the salvation of souls. The main difference between the two is that on Calvary, Christ physically suffered in His mortal Body and shed His Blood; but after His resurrection, in His glorified and immortal Body He can neither suffer nor die. As St. Paul insists: *"Christ, having risen from the dead, dies now no more"* (Rom. 6:19). Yet, in the Mass He renews the outpouring of His human soul in total surrender to His Father's will on our behalf. Too, the Catholic Church teaches that the sacrifice of the Mass does not add anything to what Christ did on Calvary, but that it applies to souls the fruits of that sacrifice. And this it does in the measure that one is united with Christ — Priest and Victim — in the renewal of that immolation. Each Mass the world over bears fruit for every member of the Mystical Body in all parts of the world insofar as one is open to the action of the Holy Spirit. We commented on this in chapter thirty-five, where this is treated in more detail.

Christ in heaven with His glorified Body is the Christ present in the Eucharistic Host, the Christ who in the Mass renews the offering of Himself to the Father. We are dealing here with a supernatural reality made possible only by the power of God, and known only by the light of faith; consequently one must not try to visualize it in terms of a sacrifice in the natural order. Fr. M.M. Philipon, O.P., gives the common theological explanation as follows:

> As the real shedding of the blood of redemption which Christ offered up constitutes the essence of the sacrifice of the Cross, so does the rite of double consecration, which both signifies and effects the sacramental separation of the Body and Blood of Christ, constitute the essence of the Eucharistic sacrifice, which the Church, through her priests, offers in the name and person of Christ.... On the altar, therefore, the same sacrifice of redemption is substantially perpetuated.[5]

Living the Mass

Since the Mass is essentially the renewal of Christ's sacrifice on Calvary, living the Mass throughout the week means living that spirit of sacrifice. It requires a willingness to make the sacrifices required for the observance of God's commandments, for the fulfillment of the duties of one's state in life and for the patient bearing of the crosses that God allows in daily life; for as St. Paul reminds us: *"We must suffer with Him that we may be glorified with Him"* (Rom. 8:17).

All this might be called the remote preparation for our participation in the sacrifice of the Mass, which requires that spirit of self-giving that makes one more united with Christ the Victim, who, at Mass, renews His total self-oblation to the Father.

If one is negligent or half-hearted in his efforts to fulfill his Christian duties throughout the week, he cannot expect to be closely united with our Blessed Lord renewing His oblation to the Father. In other words, the more willingly we make the sacrifices we are called to make to live our Catholic faith in daily life, the more we are living the Mass, and the more fruitful will be our participation in the Mass. The prayers we offer at Mass to prepare ourselves to be more attentive to the great mystery at hand are important, but they will be rather shallow without the remote preparation we have just described. All this is another of way of saying that there must be an abiding *interior* spirit of sacrifice that corresponds to our *exterior* participation in the Mass, if that participation is to bring abundant fruit. In this respect St. Thomas states that *"Christ's Passion has not its effect in those who are not disposed toward it as they should be."*[6]

Since we are one with Christ as members of His Mystical Body, all that He did as Head of that Body is ours to offer to the Father. The angelic Doctor assures us of this:

> The Head and members are one mystical person, and therefore Christ's satisfaction belongs to all the faithful as his members[7].... A baptized person being a member of Christ shares in the satisfactory value of Christ's passion as if he himself had undergone the penalty.[8]

This means that we can offer to the Father not merely all that we suffer, all the sacrifices we make, all the hardships we endure — but also all that Christ suffered — as our own; and this we can do again and again. So when we approach God in prayer we never need to feel that we have little to offer.

Consequently, our Blessed Lord, through the sacrifice of the Eucharist, has placed in our hands the most adequate means of offering to the Father supreme adoration, thanksgiving, and reparation for our sins and the sins of others, that is, of filling up what is wanting in other members of the Mystical Body. And since our Savior offers our prayers along with His own, our petitions offered up in the Mass have a special efficacy, provided what we ask is in keeping with the Father's will.

Ask the help of the Mother of Jesus, who was at the foot of the cross for that first Mass, offering herself and her dying Son for the same redemptive purpose as He. Ask her to assist with you at Mass, and help you to surrender your will to God as she did, no matter how difficult. For God gives Himself to us, especially in Holy

Communion, in the measure that we give ourselves to Him.

Chapter Notes

1. John Paul II, *Tertio Millennio Adveniente*
2. *Ibid.*
3. St. Thomas Aquinas, *Summa Theologiae,* III, 79, 50
4. St. Thomas Aquinas, 4 Sent. vii
5. M. M. Philipon, O.P., *The Sacraments in the Life of the Church,* p. 130
6. *Summa Theologiae,* III, 79, 2, ad 2
7. *Ibid.,* III, 48, 2, ad 1
8. *Ibid.,* III, 69, 2

Chapter 41

The Sacrament of Penance and Reconciliation

All through His public ministry, the message of our Blessed Lord was one of repentance: *"Unless you shall do penance, you shall all likewise perish"* (Lk. 13:5).

The practice of penance that Our Lord was preaching as necessary for salvation, is the exercise of the supernatural virtue of penance, or repentance, as it is perhaps better known. This virtue disposes the sinner to hatred of his own sin because it offends God who is infinitely good, and includes a firm resolve to avoid offending Him.

The nature of this virtue is more clearly understood in regard to grave sin, where the sinner has turned away from God in choosing, in a definitive way, some passing pleasure or satisfaction in opposition to God's will. Repentance involves a conversion, a turning away from the forbidden fruit, and turning back to God. Even in venial sin, where one has not turned his back on God, repentance inclines the sinner to detest his failures in lesser matters because they offend God, and includes a resolve to strive to avoid the wrong action done or the wrong pleasure sought.

Sacrament of the New Law

Because of the importance of repentance in the divine plan of salvation, a necessary condition for the forgiveness of sin, our Blessed Lord, knowing the weaknesses of human nature, not only preached the need of repentance, but instituted a sacrament of the New Law to facilitate it. To this penitential rite He gave special healing and strengthening graces, and a peace of soul from the certainty of forgiveness. *"Whose sins you shall forgive,"* He said to His apostles, *"they are forgiven them; and whose sins you shall retain, they are retained"* (Jn. 20:23). By these words, Christ conferred on them and their successors the power of forgiving sin in His name, a power not given to the angels, whose nature is superior to ours, nor even to the Blessed Mother, the most perfect and exalted person in all creation.

By the above words, Christ conferred on the apostles a power greater than any power conferred on the wonder workers of the Old Testament. And He conferred it, as Pope John Paul II stated, *"as something which they can transmit — as the Church has understood from the beginning — to their successors, charged by the same apostles with the mission and responsibility of continuing their work . . . as ministers of Christ's redemptive work."*[1]

Only God Can Forgive Sin

When Our Lord said to the paralytic, *"Son, your sins are forgiven you,"* the Scribes were murmuring among themselves, *"Who can forgive sin, but only God?"* (Mk. 2:5) They were correct in their statement that only God can forgive sin; but they were wrong in not believing that Christ was God. Their statement is just as true today as it was then, even though Christ said to the apostles, *"Whose sins you shall forgive they are forgiven them."* He conferred on them the power to forgive sin, but to forgive sin *in His Name*. In this sacrament, Christ operates through the priest pronouncing the words of absolution.

Although Christ has taken His place at the right hand of His Father in heaven, He still exercises His priestly power among us for the sake of our salvation. He comes through the medium of the external sacramental rites of the Church, to act personally with His hidden power, to apply to souls the fruits won by His Passion and death. In this sacrament of Penance, then, Christ perpetuates, through the Church, His work of reconciling sinners with God by remitting their sins.

The Three Elements of Penance

We can better understand why the name by which this sacrament is most commonly known is the *sacrament of Penance* when we see the nature of the *virtue of penance*. That virtue, as understood in theology, involves three things: 1) sorrow for sin, 2) acknowledgment of guilt — at least before God — and 3) adequate satisfaction. When Jesus elevated the practice of repentance to the dignity of a sacrament, He retained those three elements. Yet, by His words He specified that confession, or acknowledgment of guilt, be made outwardly before a human minister, as well as inwardly, before God, and that satisfaction be done as prescribed by that minister. Otherwise, why would Christ have expressly granted that power to His apostles?

St. Thomas Aquinas, in speaking of the integral parts of penance in relation to this sacrament, refers to the three parts mentioned above in this manner:

> The first requisite on the part of the penitent is the will to atone, and this is done by **contrition**; the second is that he submit to the judgment of the priest standing in God's place, and this is done by **confession**; and the third is that he atone according to the decision of God's minister, and this is done by **satisfaction**.[2]

We will consider in detail each of these three ingredients of the sacrament of Penance.

A) *Contrition*

Contrition, which the Council of Trent has defined as *"a sorrow and detestation of sin committed, with a purpose of sinning no more,"* is the most essential part of the sacrament of Penance. There can be no valid confession without it. The actual confessing of one's sins can at times be excused, e.g., because of inability to speak, or lack of privacy in a sick room, etc., but never can there be a valid reason for not being sorry for one's sins.

We are all familiar with the distinction between *perfect* contrition and *imperfect* contrition, both of which are supernatural sorrow enlightened by faith. The first is grief of soul because one has offended God who is infinitely good, and a firm resolve to cease offending Him. The second is sorrow for one's sins because of the fear of punishment due to them. In most of us there is a combination of both; but as one grows in grace, love of God grows, with a greater sorrow for having offended Him. While we should strive for *perfect* contrition because of the added fruitfulness of the sacrament, *imperfect* contrition (along with the sacrament) would be sufficient for remitting grave sin. Apart from the sacrament of Penance, however, imperfect contrition would not be sufficient for removing the guilt and punishment for mortal sin.

While it is true that perfect contrition can remove the guilt and eternal punishment of grave sin even apart from the sacrament of Penance, for Catholics who have the opportunity for sacramental confession, that contrition must include a resolve to receive that sacrament at the first opportunity. One very common act of contrition expresses clearly the mind of the Church in this regard: *"I firmly resolve, with the help of thy grace, to confess my sins, to do penance, and to amend my life."* However, even with this perfect contrition, one who has fallen into grave sin may not (except for special circumstances) receive Holy Communion until after receiving absolution in the sacrament of Penance.

The penitent must strive to have true contrition for each and every one of his grave sins insofar as he can. It is not possible to have true sorrow for one mortal sin and not for another. If, for example, out of five grave sins, one has sorrow for only four of them, none of them is forgiven.

Too, this sorrow must not be confused with a mere wish to overcome sin, but must include a firm purpose of amendment. We can hardly be said to be sorry for offending someone if we do not intend to take steps to avoid offending him in the future. Nor are tears always an indication of true sorrow, for one might be unhappy or emotionally upset because he is making a mess of his life, rather than because God is offended.

Mortal sin causes one to lose not only sanctifying grace, but all the supernatural merits stored up for all the good works done in his entire previous lifetime. The question may be asked: After receiving sacramental absolution for grave sin, does one regain the merits for the good works previously performed? Does he return to a degree of grace equal to what he had before the fall? St. Thomas Aquinas answers that after sacramental absolution one can end up with a *lesser* degree of grace and merits, or the *same* degree, or a *greater* degree than before the fall, depending on the sincerity of his sorrow, and the intensity of the fervor of love with which he turns back to God.[3] In this way God can bring good out of evil; for at times, after a serious fall, one will turn back to God with a greater humility, a greater resolve to serve God and to make amends for his sinfulness than he had before the fall. For one sincerely trying to lead a good life, therefore, his very falls can become stepping stones to spiritual growth. It is thanks to the medicine of this sacrament, says St. Augustine, that the experience of sin does not degenerate into despair.

As we saw with grave sins, either all are forgiven or none. With venial sins, however, this is not true. We may obtain remission for some while others remain in the soul, owing to a hidden attachment to something venially sinful. For this reason some spiritual writers recommend that the penitent single out one or two predominant failings, and concentrate his prayers and efforts at correcting them. As a rule, our contrition is no better than our purpose of amendment; and it is not possible to concentrate on the correction of a number of things at the same time. It is true that venial sin can be remitted apart from the sacrament of Penance by an act of charity, or by some other virtuous act performed out of love for God (1 Pet. 4:8). However, when remitted in the sacrament of Penance, additional sacramental graces are given to help overcome sin, and the penitent enjoys a greater peace of mind from the certainty of being forgiven.

B) Confession

We have seen the necessity of *contrition* for every mortal sin for the valid reception of this sacrament, and the fact that in certain rare situations the *confession* of them could be omitted. Outside of those extraordinary circumstances, however, all mortal sins committed since baptism and not yet absolved in the sacrament of Penance must be confessed as to their number, kind and circumstances that change their nature. This is what theologians refer to as *necessary* matter for the sacrament, while venial sins are referred to as *sufficient* matter, i.e., sufficient for absolution.

If, for example, one is guilty of three grave sins and confesses two of them, but not the third, for fear or shame, none of them is forgiven. On the other hand, if, in confessing, one omits to confess a grave sin because it was forgotten, yet would have confessed it with sorrow if remembered, the forgotten sin is pardoned, but should be mentioned at the next confession.

It is not at all certain that one is without grave sin, who fails to confess some deed gravely forbidden by the official teaching of the Church (e.g., contraception), simply because his conscience "allows" it. To such a one, Pope John Paul II answered:

> Ask yourself if your conscience is telling you the *truth* or something *false,* and seek untiringly to know the truth. If we were not to make this necessary clarification, man would risk to find in his conscience a force which is destructive of his true humanity, rather than that holy place where God reveals to him his true good.[4]

While an *examination of conscience* is an important preparation for the sacrament of Penance, no hard and fast rule can be given for the length of time to be devoted to it. For those who are in the habit of examining their conscience regularly, it need not be a lengthy affair. Many of our readers recall the former catechism that instructed us to confess all mortal sins, and as many venial sins as we may wish to mention. We should strive to have sorrow for all our venial sins, but it is probable that we will have truer contrition if we confess just the predominant ones with a firm determination to strive to correct them; for, as we said, it is not possible to concentrate on correcting many faults at the same time.

In order to increase the fervor of our contrition, we should dwell on the goodness of the God we have offended and who suffered so much on our behalf, as well as on the ways we have offended Him. When we speak of the fervor of contrition, however, we are referring not to the feelings or emotions, but to the determination of the will to avoid what offends God.

In chapter nineteen we distinguished between venial sins of *human frailty,* and those that are *fully deliberate.* These latter should receive our first attention, for there will be little spiritual growth as long as they are ignored.

Too, in order that one's confession be not superficial, but a revealing of one's inner self, there should be a humble confessing of one's failings in their root causes. For example, one might simply mention telling lies, but fail to mention the deep pride that caused him to build up his ego by *lies of exaggeration*, or that made him guilty of *lies of excuse* to avoid humiliation.

Those who neglect this sacrament gradually grow insensitive to the little failures of each day that offend God and interfere with the growth of grace. And because of this neglect, they, little by little, become insensitive to greater violations of God's law. For those Catholics who neglect this sacrament, believing they can obtain pardon directly from God, Pope John Paul stated:

> It would be foolish, as well as presumptuous, to wish arbitrarily to disregard the means of grace and salvation which the Lord provided, and, in the specific case, to claim to receive forgiveness while doing without the sacrament which was instituted by Christ precisely for forgiveness.[5]

C) *Satisfaction*

For each sin that man commits, he incurs both *guilt* before God — for every sin offends Him— and a *debt of punishment* to satisfy divine justice. Even after the guilt of sin (mortal or venial) has been removed, most often some debt of temporal punishment remains because of the imperfection of our contrition and the incompleteness of our turning away from sin. For this reason, true repentance brings us not only to detest sin and stop sinning, but to make reparation for it.

Consequently the penance imposed in this sacrament is not a price one pays for pardon, for no human price could ever repair for even the slightest offense against a God of infinite holiness and majesty. Rather, the penance imposed in this sacrament has a special efficacy in paying the debt of temporal punishment due to our sins, recent and past. Our Blessed Lord paid the penalty for our sins, and for that reason a comparatively light penance is imposed compared to the offense forgiven.

The Cleansing Power of the Blood of Christ

The Second Vatican Council stressed that Christ is present and confers grace in all the sacraments of the Church.[6] Those who confess regularly, in order to guard against routine confessions, should strive for a lively awareness in this sacrament of the presence of our Divine Savior who has been offended by our sins, and who shed His Blood that the guilt of our sins be washed away.

One who is aware of this divine presence will not approach this sacrament without humble reflection and a contrite heart. St. Catherine of Siena was filled with gratitude and wonder as she spoke of the mercy of Christ in this sacrament: *"Do not despise the Blood of Christ,"* she exclaimed, *"which has bathed us in order to cleanse the face of our souls from the leprosy of sin."*

Christ atoned for the whole of mankind by His Passion and death. It is the purpose of the sacrament of Penance to apply to us the inexhaustible fruits of His satisfaction. No matter how great, no matter how many the sins, the absolution given by the priest can bring full remission of sin for the penitent properly disposed. This is because the efficacy of the Precious Blood is infinitely greater than the malice of men and fallen angels combined. When applied to the soul of the penitent, it purifies from guilt, lessens the debt of punishment, and restores grace if it has been lost, or increases it if it is already present in the soul; and it does this in proportion to the penitent's fervor and sincerity of repentance.

As to the fruits of this sacrament, they can hardly be summed up better than did Pope Pius XII in his encyclical on the Mystical Body of Christ:

> We heartily recommend the pious custom introduced by the Church, through the inspiration of the Holy Spirit, of frequent confession. It gives us a more thorough knowledge of ourselves, stimulates Christian humility, helps us to uproot our evil habits, wages war on spiritual negligence and tepidity, purifies our consciences, strengthens our wills, encourages spiritual direction and, by virtue of the Sacrament itself, increases grace.

Chapter Notes

1. John Paul II, *Reconciliation and Penance*
2. St. Thomas Aquinas, *Summa Theologiae,* III, 90, 2
3. *Ibid.,* III, 79, 5
4. John Paul II, General Audience, August 17, 1983
5. *Ibid.*
6. II Vatican Council, *Sacrosanctum Concilium,* 7

Chapter 42

The Priesthood of the Laity

St. Peter, in his first epistle, was writing to baptized Christians when he referred to them as a holy priesthood. *"You are living stones, built as an edifice of spirit, into a holy priesthood, offering spiritual sacrifices acceptable to God through Jesus Christ.... You are a chosen race, a royal priesthood, a holy nation"* (2:5, 9).

The Second Vatican Council, in its Decree on the Apostolate of the Laity, speaks in similar language: *"The laity derive the right and duty with respect to the apostolate from their union with Christ their Head. Incorporated into Christ's Mystical Body through baptism and strengthened by the power of the Holy Spirit through Confirmation ... they are consecrated into a royal priesthood and a holy people"* (n. 3).

Ordinarily when we hear the words *"priesthood"* or *"priest,"* we think immediately of those who have received the sacrament of Holy Orders. Yet, the quotations above refer to every baptized Christian. It will be fruitful to discuss a bit what Saint Peter and the Vatican Council meant by those words, to better understand our Christian vocation.

To better understand the priesthood of the laity, which is a sharing in the priesthood of Christ, it will be helpful to consider, first of all, the priesthood in general, and secondly, the priesthood of Christ in particular.

Priesthood and Sacrifice

From time immemorial, the notion of priesthood has been associated with sacrifice. The most ancient and primitive of peoples had a deeply ingrained notion of a supreme being who had an influence over their lives. Consequently they sought the favor or pardon of the supreme being (or supreme beings) by offering sacrifice, a function carried out by a designated one (priest) who represented the community before their god. By their natural religious instincts these primitive peoples saw these supreme beings as in some way having power over them, and thus they offered sacrifice to appease them, or to seek a blessing on their harvest, on their marriage, or to obtain victory in battle, etc. In the most primitive times, this priestly function was carried out by the head of the family; and in more complex communities, by the head of the community.

Priesthood in the Old Testament

In addition to the natural religious instincts mentioned above, God has revealed to mankind the need to offer sacrifice, and has given extensive and minute details in the Old Testament as to how it is to be carried out. It appears, however, that there was no priestly class in the earliest periods of the ancient Hebrews. The Israelite priesthood was established at Mt. Sinai, when Moses was instructed by God to appoint the house of Aaron, of the tribe of Levi, to carry out the ceremonial precepts contained in the Law (Ex. 28:41).

From then on, the priests exercised considerable influence in Israel, becoming its official teachers and interpreters of the Law which regulated the life and worship of the Israelites. Its members being descendants of Aaron, of the tribe of Levi, the Israelite priesthood was hereditary. Lest, however, the service be interrupted at any time in the temple, King David divided the priestly families into twenty-four classes, each class serving for a week, i.e. from Sabbath to Sabbath. Their duties necessitated a knowledge of the requirements of the sacrificial rites, the precepts to be observed, and all the rules regulating the liturgy in the temple. Only the high priest, who became the spiritual leader of the people, was anointed (Lev. 21:10). Sometime after the Babylonian exile in the 6th century B.C., the high priest became the national leader.

The priesthood of the Old Law filled an important role in the divine plan for the People of God before the coming of Christ. It served primarily — as did the whole Old Testament — to prefigure and prepare the way for the royal priesthood of the New Testament.

The Priesthood of Christ

Our Blessed Lord is not simply a priest of the New Law, He is the one and only High Priest of the New Law. He is the one and only mediator between God and man. All other priests of the Christian era share in His priesthood; all other mediators share in His mediation. For this reason St. Thomas Aquinas refers to Christ as the fountainhead of the entire priesthood, for the priest of the Old Law was a figure of Him, while the priest of the New Law acts in His person.[1] Unlike the priests of the Old Law, He was not a descendant of Aaron of the tribe of Levi, a fact that meant the abrogation of the priesthood of Aaron, and the institution of a new order of things, as the Angelic Doctor points out:

> Since the priesthood of the Old Law was a figure of the priesthood of Christ, He did not wish to be born of the stock of the figurative priests, that it might be made clear that His priesthood is not the same as theirs, but differs therefrom as truth differs from figure.[2]

Too, unlike the priests of the Old Law, who had to wait until they were twenty before being admitted to the office, Christ's priesthood began at the moment of the Incarnation, for then the total oblation of Himself to the Father began. St. Paul wrote of this to the Hebrews:

> Wherefore, coming into the world, Jesus said: Sacrifice and oblation you did not desire, but a body you prepared for me. Holocausts and sin offerings you took no delight in. Then I said: "As it is written in the book, I have come to do your will, O God" (10:5-7).

Every act of Christ's entire life on earth was an act of His priesthood, all of which were offered for the redemptive purpose for which He came, and were consummated in His sacrifice on Calvary. There as priest and victim, He offered Himself totally in obedience to the will of the Father for the salvation of the world.

Again, unlike the priesthood of the Old Law, that of Christ *"continues forever"* (Heb. 7:24). His sacrifice on Calvary was of infinite and everlasting value. And now, having ascended into heaven, *"He is able at all times to save those who come to God through Him since He lives always to make intercession for them"* (Heb. 7:25).

Sharing Christ's Priesthood

There are different ways of sharing in Christ's priesthood. To understand this we must first consider some fundamental ideas about the sacraments through which Christ shares His priesthood with others.

There are three sacraments which can be received only once (Baptism, Confirmation and Holy Orders), and the reason why they can be received only once is because each of these sacraments imprints on the soul an *indelible character*, that cannot be destroyed or effaced in this life or the next. *"And therefore, after this life,"* says St. Thomas Aquinas, *"the character remains both in the good, to their glory, and in the wicked, to their shame."*[3] This sacramental character is a spiritual faculty or power to share in the priesthood of Christ. It is a power enabling one to take part in the public worship which Christ offers to His Father through the Church, especially the Mass and the other sacraments.

A) The Ministerial Priesthood:

In order to perpetuate the priestly work He came to do as mediator between God and man, Christ established His Church and gave it a priesthood that would be a continuation of His own.

At the Last Supper, the night before He died, Christ instituted the ritual sacrifice and the priesthood of the New Law. Changing bread and wine into His own Body and Blood, He offered to the Father for the sins of mankind His Precious Blood that would be shed the following day, and His Body that would be so torn and bruised during the Passion. He then said to His apostles: *"Do this in memory of me."* He thereby gave to them the power to effect that same change, to offer that same sacrifice.

Shortly after His resurrection He gave them another priestly power, the power to forgive sins (Jn. 20:22). And before His Ascension into heaven, He gave them the mandate to preach His gospel and baptize in the name of the Divine Trinity, making disciples of all nations (Mt. 28:19-20). Thus they were to continue His priestly redeeming mission. *"As the Father has sent me, so I send you"* (Jn. 20:21). These powers were granted to His Church in such a way that they would be handed down to their successors through the sacrament of Holy Orders, in which the ordained priest, by the anointing of the Holy Spirit, is marked with a special character, and is so configured to Christ the Priest that he can act in the person of Christ the Head of the Mystical Body.[4]

Although the ordained priest is a representative of the community in offering their prayers to God through the *sacrifice*, and in bringing God's gifts to men through the *sacraments*, he is not a representative of the community in the sense that he is chosen by them, or receives his powers from them. He is chosen by Christ through the grace of vocation, and by the Church through its acceptance of him, his powers coming from Christ through the Church He has established.

B) The Priesthood of All the Baptized:

The sacramental character, of which we have been speaking, is received initially at *Baptism,* giving the power to all the faithful to participate in the sacrifice of Christ, not as someone who passively looks on, but as one who actively participates in that which Christ does. As Pope Pius XII explained in his encyclical on the Mystical Body:

> By the waters of Baptism, as by common right, Christians are made members of the Mystical Body of Christ the Priest, and by the character which is imprinted on their souls, they

THE PRIESTHOOD OF THE LAITY 349

are appointed to give worship to God. Thus they participate according to their condition in the priesthood of Christ.

The sacramental character of *Confirmation* brings added power and obligation, enabling the faithful to share in the priesthood of Christ in a more perfect way:

> They are more perfectly bound to the Church, and endowed with the special strength of the Holy Spirit. Hence they are, as true witnesses of Christ, more strictly obliged to spread the faith by word and deed.[5]

In the fact that Christ exercised His priesthood offering Himself to His Father for us, we should see in our participation of His priesthood an invitation to offer our lives to the Father, not through *physical immolation* as Christ did, but by offering *"spiritual sacrifices."* The Second Vatican Council speaks often of this:

> Incorporated into the Church through baptism, the faithful are consecrated by the baptismal character to the exercise of the worship of the Christian religion[6]. . . . The baptized, by regeneration and the anointing of the Holy Spirit, are consecrated into a . . . *holy priesthood,* in order that by means of every work befitting Christian men, they may offer *spiritual sacrifices,* and proclaim the power of Him who has called them out of darkness into his marvelous light.[7]

> Incorporated into Christ's Mystical Body through *baptism* and strengthened by the power of the Holy Spirit through *confirmation* . . . they are consecrated into a royal priesthood and a holy people, in order that they may offer *spiritual sacrifices through everything they do,* and may witness to Christ throughout the world.[8]

The reception of these two sacraments, then, gives to each of the faithful a share in the priesthood of Christ, in the sense that it not only gives them the capacity to participate actively in the Eucharistic Sacrifice, but gives a *sacrificial value* to everything they do in union with Christ the Priest.

The above statements of the Vatican Council help us to understand the admonition given by the Angel to the children at Fatima in 1916: *"Pray a great deal. The Hearts of Jesus and Mary have designs of mercy for you.*

Offer up prayers and sacrifices constantly to the Most High." At this Lucia asked: *"How are we to make sacrifices?"* The Angel answered:

> Make everything you do a sacrifice, and offer it to God as an act of reparation for the sins by which He is offended, and in supplication for the conversion of sinners. Bring peace to your country in this way.... Above all, accept and bear with submission the sufferings sent you by the Lord.

All baptized Christians, then, can exercise their priesthood by offering to God, in union with Christ the Priest, everything they do or endure that is in keeping with the will of the Father. They can place a constant flow of *"spiritual sacrifices"* in the hands of Our Lady, that she may add to them the boundless love of her own Immaculate Heart, and offer them to the Father *"in reparation for the sins by which He is offended, for the conversion of sinners, and for peace in the world,"* as the Angel at Fatima requested.

> During the celebration of the Eucharist, these sacrifices are most lovingly offered to the Father along with the Lord's Body. Thus as worshipers whose every deed is holy, the laity consecrates the world itself to God.[9]

Such, then, is the *priesthood of the laity* derived from the sacrament of baptism, as distinguished from the *ministerial priesthood* derived from the sacrament of Holy Orders. The difference between the two, however, is an essential difference, and not just a matter of degree. We have a parallel to this priesthood of the laity in the Old Testament. Israel, a figure of the Church, was also called *"a kingdom of priests, a holy nation"* (Ex. 19:6). The Israelites were consecrated to God in a special way by the covenant which God established with them as His chosen people, set apart from other men for the worship of God. Yet, the individual Israelites were not priests in the strict sense, and were not allowed to offer sacrifice in the temple, a function, as we saw, that was reserved to the descendants of Aaron of the tribe of Levi.

These considerations on the priesthood of the baptized, and the capacity it gives to each one to share in

THE PRIESTHOOD OF THE LAITY

Christ's sacrifice, and to offer *"spiritual sacrifices"* of all that one does in union with Christ the Priest, should make us recall and respond to the plea of our Blessed Mother at Fatima, so concerned about the souls of her children:

> Pray much, and offer many sacrifices for sinners; many souls are going to hell because there is nobody to offer sacrifices and prayers for them.

Chapter Notes

1. St. Thomas Aquinas, *Summa Theologiae,* III, 79, 5
2. *Ibid.,* 22, 1, ad 2
3. *Ibid.,* 76, 1, ad 2
4. Vatican Council II, *Presbyterorum Ordinis,* 2
5. Vatican Council II, *Lumen Gentium* II
6. *Ibid.*
7. *Ibid., 10*
8. Vatican Council II, *Decree on Laity,* n. 3
9. *Lumen Gentium,* n. 34

PART FOUR
Prayer

Chapter 43

The Lord's Prayer

On one occasion Our Lord was in journey with His disciples, and while on the way He stopped to pray. At the sight of Him praying, they wondered why He had not taught them to pray as John the Baptist had taught his disciples. When He finished, they asked Him: *"Lord, teach us to pray."* In response to their request, He taught them the *"Our Father,"* commonly referred to as THE LORD'S PRAYER, because it was taught by Our Lord Himself.

This prayer has seven petitions divided into two parts. The first part contains three petitions which are an expression of our desire that God's sovereignty and dominion be acknowledged and that His will be done, while the second part contains four petitions as to our needs.

Our Father Who Art in Heaven

This first phrase is an expression of adoration which precedes the seven petitions that follow, and which is meant to put us in the presence of God. Not that we are not always in God's presence, but rather it is to make us mindful of it.

We would never have dared to call God our Father and consider ourselves as His children, if Jesus had not revealed it and told us to pray in that way. Yet, we can see the fittingness of that expression, for the Father has created us in His own likeness and image.

Our Savior speaks of His Father in heaven who shares with Him the fullness of His divine nature. He and the Father are one (Jn. 10:30). Yet, while we too are children of the same Father who shares with us His own divine nature through grace, we are His children *by adoption* through baptism, and not *by nature* as Jesus is. Since both we and Jesus have a common Father, He taught us to pray *"Our Father."*

In instructing us to address our prayers to *our* Father, and not *my* Father, Jesus is teaching us to be mindful of the needs of others as well as our own, namely, all those for whom the Father gave His only-begotten Son. That is why all the prayers of the Liturgy are addressed in the plural. As the new Catholic Catechism explains, the *our* in the first half of the Lord's Prayer, like the *us* in the second half, excludes no one.[1]

But as some saints have pointed out, if we are to call God *"our Father,"* we ought to act as His children, with the love and reverence and obedience that this relationship demands. We should live in such a way that we give witness by our lives of that LOVE and TRUTH that is God, and which He has shared with us (1 Jn. 4:8) (Jn. 14:6).

Hallowed Be Thy Name

To *"hallow"* means to make holy, to cause to be revered. We do not add to the holiness of God's name by our prayers; rather we are asking that His name be revered in us and by us. God is infinitely holy, the source of all holiness. Our prayers add nothing to that.

We pray that we who have been made holy by His presence in our soul through the grace of baptism, may persevere in what He has begun in us. We offer this daily prayer to the Father, that the new life which is ours by His favor may be preserved and grow by His protection.

May His name be revered, for in that name devils are cast out, the lame and sick are healed, etc. (Mk. 16:17; Acts 3:6). May His name be glorified, for at the name of Jesus, His only begotten Son, every knee should bend, in heaven, on earth, and under the earth (Phil. 2:10).

We can speak of God's internal and external glory. His *internal* glory (His infinite knowledge, love, power, goodness, etc.) is limitless and cannot increase. But His *external* glory (the manifestation of His wisdom, love, power, etc..) can and should be better known and loved. May we be instruments of making Him better known, loved and revered.

Thy Kingdom Come

In this petition we pray that His kingdom grow and increase, not only in the world, but *in us*. May He reign in our souls and govern our lives; i.e., may we recognize His sovereignty and dominion over us, and obey His commands.

We ask that the messianic kingdom, the Church of Christ established for the salvation of mankind, spread throughout the world, that the zeal of its members be intensified, that Christ the King reign in all hearts through their obedience to His Church.

Referring to that kingdom, St. Paul warned: *"Do not let sin reign in your body so that you obey its lusts"* (Rom. 6:12). In line with that St. Ambrose says that there are as many kings ruling in our heart as there are sins and vices controlling us. Christ reigns in our heart insofar as, led by the Holy Spirit, we observe His commandments, fulfill the duties of our state in life, and bear willingly the crosses He allows; and insofar as our mind is submissive to His teaching as handed down by His Church. Thus, says St. Thomas Aquinas, when we pray that His kingdom come, we pray that God, and not sin, may reign in us.[2]

We offer this petition, too, for those who do not recognize the Lord's kingdom and His sovereignty over all, and for those who do not recognize His very existence. We offer it also for many within the Church who at times do not recognize its teaching authority and refuse to accept its official teaching.

This petition will find its total fulfillment and glory at the final coming of Christ, when He hands over the kingdom to the Father.[3]

Thy Will Be Done on Earth as it is in Heaven

In this petition St. Cyprian explains that *"we do not pray that God should do His will. How could anyone prevent God from doing His Will? But in our prayer we ask that God's will be done in us."* ⁴

St. Thomas explains that this petition presupposes two things: God's grace and man's will. May our will be submissive to His with the help of God's grace, and with solicitude and effort on our part.⁵

In heaven the rebellion of our fallen nature is completely missing. In this petition we ask that, with the help of grace, every rebellious element of mind or body be removed. In heaven the sovereignty of God is perfectly acknowledged, and His will perfectly fulfilled. We are asking that His sovereignty be acknowledged on earth, and that His children in this world love and revere Him by observing His laws and keeping His commandments.

The Father wills the salvation of all mankind. But He has created us with a free will; so He wills our salvation on condition that, with the help of His grace, we fulfill His will. In this petition, therefore, we pray: Help us to cooperate with Your grace and unite ourselves with the obedience of Your Son, and to bear patiently the trials and crosses You send. *"Thy will, not mine be done"* (Lk. 22:42).

Give Us This Day Our Daily Bread

In the first three petitions we asked for spiritual blessings that begin in this life but are not possessed perfectly until the next life. In this fourth petition we ask for needs of the present life. Those needs can be temporal or spiritual.

A) Bread for the Body

This is a plea to the Eternal Father, the divine Provider, to grant us the basic needs of our livelihood. It is an acknowledgment that He is the source of all that we have, and a plea that He will continue to bless us, our family, our nation, the whole world, with the necessities of life. It is a plea for those who hunger because they lack the necessities of life.

It is a plea also, says St. Thomas, to help us avoid sins which tend to arise from an inordinate desire of temporal goods, such as: greed, fraud, excessive solicitude for the future, and so forth.[6] It is a plea for sharing in keeping with the solidarity of the human family.

B) Spiritual:
1) Sacramental Bread:

This is a plea to receive the *"Bread of Life,"* the Eucharist, which the Church prepares for us for our spiritual nourishment. This bread is not given to everyone, but only to those who acknowledge God as Father, and Christ as His Son, and who accept the full teaching of His Church. It is a plea also that the whole world will some day be able to partake of this divine banquet.

2) The Bread of God's Word:

Just as the body needs to be fed with bread made of wheat, so the soul needs to be fed with the bread of truth, God's word. Just as the body craves and needs material food, so the soul needs the light and guidance of God's revealed word to know Him Who is the Way to the Father. *"Not by bread alone does man live, but by every word that proceeds from the mouth of God"* (Mt. 4:4).

3) The Bread of Divine Grace:

This plea includes all those graces and divine helps necessary for salvation. Each day, each minute of the day, we are dependent on God far more than we realize for the countless graces we receive in every conscious thought and deed.

Forgive Us Our Trespasses as We Forgive Those Who Trespass Against Us

This petition is a plea for mercy; but it is a reminder that God's mercy is conditional, that is, it depends on our willingness to forgive those who have offended us. The Lord spoke of this in the Sermon on the Mount: *"If you forgive men their offenses, your heavenly Father will forgive you yours; but if you will not forgive men, neither will your heavenly Father forgive you your offenses"* (Mt. 6:14).

It is not only a plea for forgiveness, but that we have the charity, humility and spiritual strength to forgive those who have offended us. And we must remember there are subtle ways of not forgiving: for example, harboring resentment, not speaking to someone, seeking to get even and so forth.

Only the Holy Spirit by whom we live can transform our heart to forgive as Christ did on Calvary. *"It is not in our power not to feel or to forget an offense; but the heart that offers itself to the Holy Spirit turns injury into compassion and purifies the memory in transforming the hurt into intercession."*[7]

"Forgiveness bears witness that, in our world, love is stronger than sin. . . . Only hearts attuned to God's compassion can receive the gift of prayer."[8]

Lead Us Not Into Temptation

This petition is an appeal to God's protective providence. We can distinguish two kinds of temptation: those of *solicitation* (inducement to sin), and of *probation* (a testing of virtue). God never tempts in the first manner, but does frequently in the second. He uses persons and situations to test our patience, our humility, our purity, our faith, our hope, our love of Him. Without this kind of temptation or trial there would be little progress in virtue, and we would not be aware of our own weaknesses. Consequently, in this petition we do not ask that we not be tempted, but that we not be overcome by temptation.

Even temptation by the devil, who knows well our weaknesses and how to exploit them, and who wishes only our eternal damnation, God allows at times to test our virtue and to bring about spiritual growth by our resisting the allurements of sin.

We must, then, with the help of the Holy Spirit, discern between trials which are necessary for spiritual growth, and temptation that leads to sin. We must discern, too, between *being tempted* (which is not sin) and *consenting to temptation* (which is sin).

"God is faithful, and will not let you be tempted beyond your strength, but with the temptation will also give you a way out that you may be able to bear it" (1 Cor. 10:13). Yet, one who deliberately walks into a tempting situation must not expect God's protection. He walks into a snare the devil will make good use of. Victory in this battle is possible only through prayer.[9] *"Watch and pray that you may not enter into temptation. The spirit is willing but the flesh is weak"* (Mt. 26:41).

But Deliver Us From Evil

In this petition, evil is not an abstraction, but refers to a person, Satan, the Evil One, the angel who opposes God. We ask to be delivered from the power of the devil whose object is to thwart God's plan of salvation accomplished in Christ.[10] And notice that it is always *"we"* who pray, in common with the whole Church, for the deliverance of the whole human family.[11]

Christ conquered Satan by His passion and death, a victory won for the whole of mankind; but since man is free to obey or disobey his Creator, he can turn from God and come again under the dominion of the Evil One. And thus we are asking to be delivered from the evil of falling into sin, and from failing to cooperate with the graces that accompany every temptation. We are asking to be strengthened and protected from the wiles of the devil who deceived our first parents into disobedience against God's command, and who through the centuries has never ceased to strive to deceive their descendants into choosing their own will and plan in preference to God's.

Our Blessed Lord gave us a warning as to the power of the devil, and a reminder of protective safeguards against his cunning when he cast out the evil spirit from a tormented youth: *"This kind can be cast out only by prayer and fasting"* (Mk. 9:28). Many centuries later Our Savior revealed to St. Margaret Mary: *"The devil is powerless over those who obey."*

NOTE: *Some people ask if the "Amen" is still a part of the OUR FATHER, since it is no longer recited in the Mass. The new Catechism of the Catholic Church makes it clear that this prayer should end with "Amen" whenever it is said outside of Mass* (CCC 2856).

Chapter Notes

1. CCC 2792
2. St. Thomas Aquinas, *The Three Greatest Prayers*
3. CCC 2816
4. *Roman Breviary*
5. *The Three Greatest Prayers*
6. *Ibid.*
7. CCC 2842, 2843
8. CCC 2844
9. CCC 2849
10. CCC 2851
11. CCC 2850

Chapter 44

Ask and You Shall Receive

While prayer may be considered under many aspects, one classical division of prayer summarizes it under the headings of prayer of *adoration,* of *thanksgiving,* of *contrition* and of *petition.* We sometimes hear remarks to the effect that there is something imperfect, something selfish about prayer of petition. Yet, asking God's help is not only not something imperfect, it is something necessary. Was it not Our Lord Himself who said: *"Ask, and you shall receive"* (Mt. 7:7)? And, as we shall see, theologians point out that there are graces that we will not receive if we do not ask for them.

There is no need to justify prayer of petition, for it springs naturally from a growing recognition of our own frailty, and of our dependence on the providence of God.

The Importance of Asking God's Help

St. Thomas Aquinas points out that we ask God's help, not to inform God of our needs, for He knows them before we ask, *"but that we ourselves may be reminded of the necessity of having recourse to God's help."*[1] Our prayer is necessary, then, not to enlighten God, but is needful on our part to express our need of Him, and our trust in His merciful providence.

The Angelic Doctor also points out that we do not ask God's help in order to change the divine will, to bring God to change His mind, but that *"we might ask that which God has disposed to be fulfilled by our prayers. . . . God's providence not only decrees what* **effects** *shall take place, but also from what* **causes,** *and in what order these effects shall proceed."*[2]

What St. Thomas is saying is that, under the providence of God, prayer can be the cause of certain effects, in the sense that when one achieves something by his prayers, he is receiving what God has decreed he shall receive through those prayers. Thus there are certain graces and gifts that we will receive if we ask for them with the right dispositions; and there are certain graces that we do not receive because we do not ask.

This is beautifully brought out in the words of the Mother of God to St. Catherine Labouré. On one occasion when Our Lady appeared to St. Catherine, her fingers were adorned with precious jewels. From some of them fell glittering rays of light that blazed with much splendor. Our Lady explained: *"These rays symbolize the graces I shed upon those who ask for them. The gems from which rays do not fall are the graces for which souls forget to ask."* A failure to ask for God's help through prayer, is actually a form of pride, a belief that we don't need it, that we can manage alone. In His merciful providence, however, God has ways of showing us that we cannot.

God Will Keep His Promise

We have this assurance from our Blessed Lord: *"Whatever you ask in my name, I will do, so as to glorify the Father"* (Jn. 14:13). In the light of this assurance from God's revealed truth, how do we reconcile these words with our own experience; for we know that at times we have asked in prayer for certain things, and have not received that for which we asked. Does that mean that God has not kept His promise, or that our prayers were offered in vain? It happens at times that some, instead of looking within themselves for the reasons why they did not obtain what they asked, blame God, and even cease asking His help.

St. James refers to such people in his epistle: *"You ask and you do not receive, because you have not prayed properly; you have prayed for something to indulge your own desires"* (4:3). Since we know that God cannot go back on His promise, the cause of this failure can only lie with us. Let us try to find that cause by examining the conditions our prayer must have if we are to receive what we ask for. The Scriptures clearly indicate what those conditions should be.

We Must Ask God's Graces and Gifts:
1) In a spirit of resignation to His will.

Our Divine Savior taught us how to pray, both by word and by example. We can and should ask our heavenly Father for all our needs, natural and supernatural, asking humbly, confidently, and with a readiness to accept His decision regarding what we ask. He taught us to say *"Thy will be done,"* before we ask *"Give us this day . . . ."*

What we ask must be beneficial to our soul, or the soul of others—at least not detrimental to salvation. Often we do not know whether something we ask for will be helpful or harmful to the soul. For this reason, when asking for temporal favors, we cannot be certain our prayers will be answered as requested, for we do not know if what we ask is in accordance with the divine will.

We often ask for things of which we do not foresee the possible consequences to ourselves or others, while God, in His infinite foresight, may foresee evil results if this or that be granted. Because of this God at times grants not what we ask for, but something more beneficial eternally.

We may be deeply distressed at times at not receiving the favor we prayed for; but when we reach Heaven, we will see in the Beatific Vision of God how often it would have been detrimental to us had we received what we asked; and we will praise and thank God eternally for granting, not what we so eagerly sought, but something of far greater value.

One suffering from some bodily affliction may pray for good health. But it could be that God foresees that a return to perfect health would result in a slacking off of the practice of his religion, a carelessness that would endanger his eternal salvation. Or it could be that He sees that the sick person in his patient bearing of trials is doing far more to build up the Body of Christ, and gaining far more for eternity, than if returned to good health.

As spiritual writers express it, it is a greater gift of God to receive the grace to bear a cross, than to have that cross taken away. After one has prayed for relief from some trial or suffering, God may leave that person with his cross or affliction, but strengthened to bear it with much fruit. The prayer of such a one was answered, but not as the praying one sought. He received instead the wisdom and strength of preferring God's will to his own, the grace of praying as Our Lord did in the Garden of Gethsemani: *"Nevertheless, not as I will, but as You will"* (Mk. 14:36).

2) With faith and trust in God's Providence.

St. James says of those who ask God's help: *"He must ask in faith, never doubting, for the doubter is like the surf tossed and driven by the wind. A man of this sort . . . must not expect to receive anything from the Lord"* (James 1:6).

Again, Our Savior taught us: *"You will receive all that you pray for, provided you have faith"* (Mt. 21:22).

Even with that faith, we cannot fathom at times why God allows certain situations that involve suffering. We cannot understand the place they occupy in the plan of His providence, in which everything is ordered to our ultimate good. God, who is infinite goodness and love, permits suffering only for this purpose. While we know this in theory, in practice we often forget it, and find ourselves complaining, *"Why does God permit this? . . . Why doesn't He answer my prayer?"*

Our Savior promised before ascending into Heaven that He would not leave us orphans (Jn. 14:18). He has not left us to care for ourselves, but like the most loving of all Fathers provides for our needs: *"Can a mother forget her infant, be without tenderness for the child of her womb? Even should she forget, I will never forget you"* (Is: 49:15). He assures us that our heavenly Father knows our needs, our difficulties, and will not fail to provide for those who trust in Him: *"Look at the birds in the sky. They do not sow or reap, they gather nothing into barns; yet your heavenly Father feeds them. Are you not more important than they? . . . O you of little faith . . . Your heavenly Father knows all that you need. Seek first His kingship over you, his way of holiness, and all these things will be given you besides"* (Mt. 6:30).

How slow we are to truly believe these words of God Himself. We need unlimited confidence when we ask. But His providing for our needs presupposes and demands that we are seeking His kingdom before all else, His way of holiness, trusting that He knows better than we what contributes to our ultimate good.

3) In Jesus' Name.

The night before He died, Our Lord said to His apostles: *"I give you my assurance, whatever you ask the Father, He will give you in My name. Until now you have not asked for anything in My name. Ask and you shall receive, that your joy may be full"* (Jn. 16:23). To ask *in His name* is to ask in view of His infinite merits gained on our behalf, and of the infinite love and total surrender by which Jesus glorified the Father. Liturgical prayer is always offered up in His name, for it is the prayer of Christ united with His members. For this reason prayers of the liturgy end beseeching the Father *"through Jesus Christ our Lord."*

A common and fruitful way of asking Heaven's help in Jesus' name is by offering to the Father the infinite merits of Christ, His Precious Blood shed on Calvary, the sufferings of His passion — the fruits of which, in a true sense, are ours, because of our unique oneness with Christ as members of His Mystical Body. *"The Head and members (of the Mystical Body),"* says St. Thomas Aquinas, *"are one mystical person, and therefore Christ's satisfaction belongs to all the faithful as his members."*[3] Again he says: *"The baptized person, being a member of Christ, shares in the satisfactory value of Christ's passion as though he had himself endured the penalty."*[4] From this there follows this tremendous fact, that we have a claim on all that Christ did in His human nature. We can offer to the Father, as *our* offering, the sufferings of Jesus, His Precious Blood, His perfect obedience, and so forth. We have a claim on these because we and Christ form *one mystical person.* We can see how acceptable to the Father this can make our pleas for help, and how we never need feel that we approach Him empty-handed.

Our Lord, in His revelations to a Spanish nun, asked again and again for this kind of prayer in His name. *"Do not stop uniting your action to Mine and offering my Precious Blood to the Father. . . . Never cease offering My Precious Blood for souls."*[5] Another example from Heaven of this kind of prayer in His Name, was taught to the three children at Fatima by the Angel in 1916: *"Most Holy Trinity. . . . I offer You the most precious Body, Blood, Soul and Divinity of Jesus Christ, present in all the tabernacles of the world, in reparation for the outrages, sacrileges and indifference by which He is offended."*

We should have unlimited confidence in the merits of Christ, which infinitely surpass our misery, our sins, our necessities. In view of those merits, we can never ask too much in His name. It gives glory to our Savior when, confident in the power of His name, we are bold in imploring Heaven's help.

4) With perseverance.

Our Lord stressed the need of perseverance in prayer by His parable of the man who knocks at night at the door of his neighbor and asks for three loaves. The friend, having retired to bed, refused to be disturbed. Yet, after persistent knocking, for the sake of peace, the neighbor finally gets up and gives him what he asks. His persistence is rewarded. As Our Lord points out, if a selfish neighbor will give in to persistent asking, how much more will our Heavenly Father give to those who persevere in asking His help (Lk. 11:5; also 18:1)!

There comes to mind also the persistence of St. Monica, who prayed for years for the conversion of her son Augustine. His conversion was certainly willed by God, yet only after many years did she see her prayers rewarded. God held off the fulfillment of her pleas for years, but then granted her petition a hundredfold, far more than she ever dreamed.

If Our Lord said, *"Ask, and you will receive,"* it may at times take years of asking. We must be prepared to have our faith and trust tested, to be kept waiting. God grants His gifts in His own way, in His own time; yet what He chooses is always to our best advantage.

There are many graces that God will give only to those who truly desire them, and who express that eager desire by generous sacrifices and by perseverance in asking for them. Christ paid a high price to win the graces to redeem us, and we have to pay a price to share in them and to win them for others. However, important as perseverance in prayer is, that alone is not sufficient. What we ask must be, as we have seen, in accordance with God's will. Theologians warn us:

> It is an error to believe that if we persevere in prayer, come what may, we shall always obtain that which we seek. Some things will be granted to us *whether we pray for them or not,* because God has decreed that they shall be granted to us absolutely; some things will *never be granted* to us, no matter how earnestly and how long we pray for them; and still others will be granted to us *only if we pray,* because God has decreed that they will be given only on the condition that we ask for them.[6]

5) With sincerity.

One is sincere in asking help if he is doing what he can in the matter in which he is asking help from God. It would be sheer presumption to ask God to help overcome some fault, if we ourselves made little effort to overcome it, or if we were little concerned about avoiding situations that occasion our failures.

It would be presumptuous to expect God to shower us with His graces if we are not using the means of grace

ASK AND YOU SHALL RECEIVE

He has given, for example, neglecting Sunday Mass when we are able to attend, or neglecting the sacraments — Confession and Holy Communion — when they are available. We cannot expect God to rush to our aid, if we are not doing what we can to help ourselves.

Our asking, then, will be more sincere when accompanied by sacrifice, especially the sacrifices needed to keep the commandments of God and to fulfill the duties of our state in life. As Fr. Gabriel of St. Mary Magdalen says: *"Vain is our prayer, vain is our confidence in God, if we do not add our generous efforts to perform all our duties, to live up to our vocation in life. . . . We can, and should, hope for everything in the name of Jesus, but He expects a constant effort on our part to be entirely faithful to Him. . . . The more prayer is nourished and accompanied by sacrifice, the more efficacious it becomes."*[7] St. Teresa of Avila, echoing the same, warns that *"prayer and self-indulgence do not go together."*[8]

* * * * * * *

Such are the qualities our prayer should have if we are to have a favorable hearing. Prayer is not just a matter of asking, but must be endowed with the dispositions that one should have before God. We may ask for anything that seems good and desirable to us, and which will not hinder our salvation. But all failures to receive what we ask come from our lack of the proper dispositions, or the lack of asking for what is conducive to our salvation, not from any unfaithfulness to His promises on the part of God.

Too, the more we acknowledge our total dependence on Him, our total indebtedness to Him, and our constant need of Him, the more His merciful heart is drawn to care for our needs. *"The prayer of him who humbles himself pierces the clouds"* (Sir. 35:17).

Chapter Notes

1. St. Thomas Aquinas, *Summa Theologiae,* II-II, 83, 2-4
2. *Ibid.*
3. *Ibid.*, III, 48, 21
4. *Ibid.*, III, 69, 2
5. Sr. Josepha Menendez, *Way of Divine Love*, pp. 115, 128
6. Antonio Royo, O.P. and Jordan Aumann, O.P., *Theology of Christian Perfection*, p. 501
7. Fr. Gabriel of St. Mary Magdalen, O.C.D., *Divine Intimacy*, pp. 525, 980
8. St. Theresa of Avila, *Way*, 4

Chapter 45
Giving Thanks

Passing between Samaria and Galilee on His way to Jerusalem, our Blessed Lord was met by ten lepers, one of whom was a Samaritan (Lk. 17:11). Ordinarily a Samaritan would not associate with the Jews, but necessity often makes strange bedfellows, and the hideous disease that afflicted all of them, as well as the requirements of isolation demanded by the law, brought these unfortunates together.

While Jesus was still at a distance, they cried out: "Jesus, Master, have mercy on us." Our Savior did not cure them then and there, but told them to go and show themselves to the priests, for the Mosaic law prescribed that it was the duty of the priest to examine a man suspected of leprosy, and to decide whether or not he had the disease or was cured of it.

With faith in His word all of them left immediately to see the priest, and while on the way their disease disappeared. One of them, the Samaritan, the moment he realized that he had been cured, returned to give thanks at the feet of Jesus. Our Savior was pleased with this action, but sad at the ingratitude of the others: *"Were not ten cleansed? Where are the nine? Was no one found to return and give thanks to God except this foreigner?"* (Lk. 17:17).

Christ was sad, not for His own sake, but for theirs, for He would have given them an even greater gift had they been grateful. Their own self-interest came first in their mind, and once they saw that the leprosy was gone their only thought was their good fortune, and the one who cured them was quickly forgotten; whereas, with the Samaritan, his first thought was the one who cured him. He was delighted with the cure, but uppermost in his mind was a consciousness of his duty to render thanks and praise to the one who had effected that cure. And Jesus said to him: "Rise and go your way, your faith has made you whole." He was not only physically well, but his faith in Jesus' word and his gratitude won for him an interior grace and healing that was not given to the other nine.

The Divine Benefactor

Giving thanks is an expression of gratitude for favors received. When it is sincere, it springs from recognition of a favor or gift to which we have no just claim. One need not be grateful when receiving something that is owed in justice. However, when receiving something not owed, but given out of the goodness of heart of the benefactor, a debt of gratitude is incurred.

With regard to our neighbor, therefore, we can owe him something in strict justice, because of some contract entered into; or we can owe him something out of gratitude, because of some favor received out of the goodness of his heart. In this latter case, if at times the ability to repay in kind is wanting, the expression of a grateful heart suffices. It is, as they say, "a poor man's payment."

But with regard to gifts received from God, we do not have a strict right to them; they are His free gifts. Therefore we have a serious duty to thank God for the countless gifts He has bestowed upon us. Let us examine this duty and the reasons for it.

Our Infinite Debt of Gratitude

Because of the countless blessings God showers upon us, both in the order of nature and in the order of grace, He has a strict right to expect gratitude from us. As St. James reminds us, *"Every good gift and every perfect gift comes down from above, coming down from the Father of Lights"* (Jas. 1:17). And St. Paul asks: *"What have you that you have not received? And if you have received it, why do you boast as if you had not received it?"* (1 Cor. 4:7)

Never in this life will we ever fully appreciate those gifts, neither as to their number nor as to their greatness. God brought us into being, and in every moment of our existence conserves us in being. He gave us a soul made to His own likeness and image, with an intellect enabling us to know Him and a will enabling us to love Him. He gave us all the capacities and talents we enjoy of body and soul. He gave us sanctifying grace that enables us to share in His own divine life, and is constantly giving us actual graces that enlighten the mind and strengthen the will in times of need. All the material goods and the opportunities we enjoy are gifts of His Divine Providence. How often do we stop to reflect on this total dependence on God and thank Him for His never-failing love?

Lack of space does not allow us to consider these gifts in detail, but let us take a brief look at a very basic one, *the gift of faith*. We have no right to this gift, a gift not given to all. It is a mark of God's special favor, but it is a gift that can be lost by those who do not appreciate it and are not grateful for it. Those without this gift grope in the darkness of error and doubt, and have little realization of the peace of mind that comes to those who live their Catholic faith by trusting reliance on the teaching authority of the Church. How often do we reflect on this gift and thank God for it, striving to keep the light of faith as the guiding light of our life? For those whose strong faith gives them a deep insight into God's ways, even crosses and trials can be seen as a gift of God's love bringing spiritual growth. Are we ever able to thank God for them as did the Psalmist: *"It was good for me that I was afflicted . . ."* (Ps. 119:71)?

Too, we can never thank God enough for His merciful forgiveness. In this life we so quickly forget the multitude of our offenses against God and the countless times He has pardoned us. Like the nine lepers who failed to return and give thanks, how easily we forget the leprosy of sin from which we have been cleansed, not once but many times, and sink into a self-complacency which forgets the mercies of the past and the dangers of the present. When we appear before God at the end of our life all will be so clear, and our unpaid debt of gratitude so manifest.

When our first parents rebelled against God in spite of these gifts, the Father gave His only-begotten Son to redeem us, and the Son in turn gave His life in that redeeming sacrifice. Too, before He returned to the Father, the Son not only gave us His own mother as our mother, but also gave us another visible and guiding mother, the Church, as custodian of His message and of the Sacraments, the crowning gift of which is the Eucharist, the sacrifice and sacrament of His own Body and Blood. So bountiful has God been with His gifts that St. Augustine exclaimed: *"He who is infinitely rich had nothing more to give."*

Because of these endless gifts bestowed upon us by our Heavenly Father, adoration and thanksgiving are man's first fundamental duty, apart from any question of sin and satisfaction. Before his fall, Adam was bound to adore and thank God. Even Christ Himself, as regards His human nature, was not exempt from this obligation. It is an essential condition of the relation between creature and Creator. Because of this, the life of the angels and saints in heaven, who are vividly aware of the gifts received, is one of eternal praise and thanksgiving.

Man's Ingratitude

Yet, this duty of giving thanks is so often neglected, even by good people who have been especially blessed with God's favors. So many of us are like the nine lepers who failed to return and give thanks.

So often it is not the most highly favored that are the most grateful, but those who at times are without many of the comforts and conveniences of life, and who have not enjoyed these benefits with sufficient regularity to take them for granted. Those who are well situated,

GIVING THANKS

materially speaking, can grow so accustomed to enjoying plentiful food and the conveniences of life that they forget that there is anything to be grateful for. And the more our modern world supplies us with material comforts and conveniences, and the more medical science succeeds in preventing, or curing, or alleviating pain and disease, the less mindful many seem to be of God's bountiful hand, and therefore of their debt of gratitude. We are more conscious of gifts received from our fellowmen. Yet, not until the next life will we be aware of the constant flow of gifts that God bestows upon us, so many of which we take for granted as though we had a natural right to them.

If one received a miraculous cure at Lourdes or Fatima, he or she would no doubt be everlastingly grateful to God for it. But if we do not need a cure, if we have good health, good vision, good hearing, strong limbs . . . do we just take all this for granted? Does one have to lose these gifts, or see another lose them, before he becomes mindful that God is their source and express heartfelt thanks? We might enjoy good reading, listening to good music, etc. Do we ever reflect that the very capacity to enjoy these things is a gift of God, a gift that could be lost, a gift that some people are born without? We read of the millions upon millions throughout the world who are undernourished. Do we remember to thank God for the plenty we enjoy, and resolve to share some of God's blessings with those who have been less fortunate?

God gave us a human body so wonderfully made that only gradually are the natural sciences, with their advanced technology, discovering its wonders and the natural safeguards with which it is endowed. And yet, so many take it all for granted, and render praise to science for discovering these things, instead of praising God who made them, and who gave man the very capacity to discover them.

God is so prodigal with His gifts that we forget the immense debt of thanksgiving that we owe for them. We forget that they are gifts, and not something for which we have a right. God's infinite generosity should not cause us to be forgetful of His loving concern, but fill us with a humble acknowledgment of our total dependence on Him.

Ingratitude Brings Spiritual Loss

We know from our own experience that we enjoy giving to one who is sincerely grateful, and we feel somewhat upset towards those who are ungrateful for what we have done for them, and less inclined to continue our giving. In this painful disappointment that we feel at the ingratitude of others, Our Lord is allowing us to experience a small portion of the pangs of His own Sacred Heart when we are not grateful for His gifts, when we do not return His love. He is more generous with His gifts to those who are humbly grateful for them, those whose heart is ever mindful of His endless favors. For this reason it has been said that *"gratitude is the best means of petition."*

In spite of our ingratitude, God, who knows our weaknesses, still does not withhold His gifts from us entirely. Yet, God's patience should not make us forget that our ingratitude will lessen the frequency and the extent of those gifts. If we feel hurt at the ingratitude of others, we should be all the more careful not to fail in that manner towards God, who is a benefactor to us infinitely more than we are to others. In this regard St. Bernard wrote,

> Blessed is the soul, who every time he receives a gift of grace from God, returns to Him who responds to our gratitude for the favors we have received by giving us new favors. The greatest hindrance to progress in the spiritual life is ingratitude, for God counts as lost the graces we receive without gratitude, and He refrains from giving us new graces.

If the multitude of divine gifts we have received do not produce in us proportionate fruits, one of the reasons probably lies in our want of gratitude. And if we would look more deeply for the root cause of ingratitude, almost always it will be found to be a lack of humility.

Only the Humble are Truly Grateful

The proud person robs God of His glory, seeing himself as the principal cause of his accomplishments. Unmindful of his dependence on God, he seldom asks God's help, and if he does it is mainly from the lips and not from the heart, for he attributes to his own merits any graces received. Seldom, therefore, is he conscious of his duty of giving thanks to God. The humble person, on the other hand, is fully aware of his dependence on God and of his incapacity apart from God. When he does some good work, or practices some virtue, he sees it as the fruit of God's grace, and is constantly thanking God whom he recognizes as the source of all good. For the truly humble person gratitude is spontaneous and natural.

Working as a missionary in a remote area of Central America, where a considerable percentage of the population are descendants of the Mayan Indians, I encountered natives whose culture and living conditions were very primitive. Many of them lived in huts made of clay, with the bare ground as the floor. A fire built in the middle of the hut served as the stove to cook their tortillas, or whatever other simple item they might have to eat. The material poverty and lack of sanitary living conditions was extreme. Other than their simple dwellings, they had few possessions with the exception of a few tools with which they obtained a meager return for the grain they planted in the small plot of land allotted to them.

Most of these natives are Catholic, and when they came to the parish church to pray they often prayed aloud and in their own native tongue. I recall that on one occasion, an elderly native woman came to the church to pray. A daughter of hers was dying of tuberculosis. I could not help noticing her prayer. It was almost like a litany of "thank you's." Again and again, *"Thank You, Lord."* Here was one who had so little materially speaking, but who was truly rich with the riches of the soul, so aware of God's providence, and so grateful for the simple blessings He provided.

Sacrifice of Thanksgiving

As we have already indicated, we are so indebted to God for all His gifts both in the natural and supernatural order, that if it depended on ourselves alone the whole of eternity would not be sufficient to pay the debt of gratitude. Yet, God has not only provided us with His gifts, but has also provided us with an adequate way of rendering thanks. In the sacrifice of the Mass we can completely satisfy that debt, because in that sacrifice Christ offers Himself in our place, adding our prayer of thanks to His. In fact, the very word "Eucharist" means thanksgiving, so that the expression "Eucharistic Sacrifice" literally means *sacrifice of thanksgiving.* As Abbot Columba Marmion, O.S.B., expressed it, *"Christ Himself becomes our thanksgiving, our Eucharist."*[1]

Before the institution of the Eucharistic sacrifice at the Last Supper, our Blessed Lord *"gave thanks"* to His Father (Mt. 26:27). And in every Mass, before the Consecration, the celebrant, following the example of Christ, reads or sings a hymn of thanksgiving — the Preface: *"Father, all-powerful and ever-living God, we do well always and everywhere to give you thanks through Jesus Christ Our Lord . . ."*

As we have pointed out in chapter thirty-five, thanksgiving is one of the four ends of the Mass: adoration, reparation, thanksgiving and petition. The Mass does not automatically fully pay our debt in these regards, but does so in the measure that we are united with Christ renewing His oblation. And we must express our gratitude by our lives, as well as by our words. If thanksgiving means anything at all, it will show itself in some tangible form in leading a better life, in a more faithful service, in fewer lapses into sin. The real proof of gratitude to God is a more fervent love in His service.

Chapter Notes

1. Abbot Columba Marmion, O.S.B., *Christ, Life of Soul,* p. 279

Chapter 46

Understanding the Rosary

We have come across some Catholics who do not pray the rosary because, as they say, they find it too difficult to think about two things at the same time, namely, the *Hail Marys* and the rosary mystery. As a result, these people of good will have given up praying the rosary because they do not understand how the rosary should be prayed. Then, too, after the Second Vatican Council there were some who downgraded the rosary, claiming that this devotion was not in keeping with the spirit of the Council.

Misunderstandings

The first objection mentioned above stems from a misunderstanding of what the rosary is and how it is to be prayed. The rosary is a combination of *vocal* prayer, the *Hail Marys* and the *Our Fathers,* and of *mental* prayer, namely, the meditation on the various incidents or mysteries in the life of Our Lord and His mother. Yet there is no conflict in this combination, but rather a blending of one with the other, for while the lips pronounce the words of the *Hail Mary*, the mind should reflect on the mystery of the rosary that has been announced. The repetition of the 10 *Hail Marys* is used as a measuring device to determine the length of time to meditate on the mystery at hand.

As one might use an hourglass to measure sixty minutes, or a three-minute glass to cook an egg, so one uses the ten *Hail Marys* to measure the time to reflect on each mystery of the rosary.

We are told that in parts of Ireland in times past, if someone lived near, it might be expressed as *"about five or six Hail Marys down the road."* Or like the young nun who used to walk from the convent to the school each morning with her superior. When asked how far distant was the school, she responded, *"About three admonitions away."* So there are many different ways of measuring time or distance.

The very fact that the words of the *Hail Mary* are so well known that their recitation becomes mechanical is an asset, for then they require no attention of the mind. The mind is thus free to reflect on the mysteries of the rosary. As Pope Paul VI expressed it, *"The litany-like succession of Hail Marys . . . constitutes the warp on which is woven the contemplation of the mysteries."*[1]

This combination of mechanical action and mental activity is also seen when women are gathered in a sewing circle. The activity of the fingers which becomes mechanical, does not interfere with the mental activity of conversation; in fact it seems to stimulate it.

So there need be no opposition or conflict between the lips pronouncing the words of the Hail Mary, and the mind reflecting on the mysteries of the rosary. On the contrary, these two actions are complementary to each other.

As regards the claim that the rosary devotion is not in keeping with the spirit of Vatican II, that Council clearly stated in the decree on the Liturgy that *"popular devotions of the Christian people are warmly commended, provided they are in accord with the laws and norms of the Church."*[2]

And the fact that Pope John XXIII who called the Council, Pope Paul VI who presided over its sessions and conclusion, and Pope John Paul II in his Apostolic Letter on the Rosary, all so highly recommended this devotion, is clear evidence of mind of the Church in this regard.

In his Apostolic Letter, Pope John Paul II testified:

> How many graces have I received in these years from the Blessed Virgin through the Rosary. *Magnificat anima mea Dominum!* I wish to lift up my thanks to the Lord in the

words of His most Holy Mother, under whose protection I have placed my Petrine ministry: *Totus Tuus!* [3]

Just a few weeks after he was elected to the papacy, Pope John Paul II declared, *"The Rosary is my favorite prayer."*

Pius XII and the Rosary

Not only were the above-mentioned Popes great lovers of the rosary, but so was the Pope who preceded them, Pope Piux XII, who wrote in an encyclical on this prayer of Mary: *"We well know the Rosary's powerful efficacy to obtain the maternal aid of the Virgin."* And speaking of the vocal and mental prayers that make up the rosary, he said:

> What prayers are more adapted and more beautiful than the Lord's prayer and the angelic salutation, which are the flowers with which this mystical crown is formed? Adding to the vocal prayers the meditation on the sacred mysteries, there emerges another great advantage, that all—even the most simple and least educated—have in this a prompt and easy way to feed and keep their own faith.[4]

More Divine Than Human

The rosary is not only an important means of instruction in the truths of our faith, but also an important means to bring Catholics to love and to be loved by Mary who gave this form of prayer to the Church. As Pope Pius XII points out, its very origin and the wisdom of its composition are *"more divine than human."*

The Mother of God is so desirous that her children pray the rosary because it focuses one's attention on the redeeming life and death of her Son. It is a devotion that leads one to the divine Trinity of Persons through the hearts of Jesus Incarnate and Mary Immaculate. It is Mary's instrument to bring us closer to her divine Son and to become more involved in our lives as her children.

One is often saddened by the number of children and adults who do not know how, or do not care, to pray the rosary; for when it is understood and prayed with devotion, it is a celebration of faith, of confidence and of love for the Most Holy Trinity.

Compendium of the Gospel

The rosary, in the words of Pope Paul VI, is a compendium of the Gospel. It is so devised that it helps us to reflect briefly on the principal events of our redemption. If some find it difficult to meditate on these mysteries, either because of lack of instruction, or because of fatigue, or some physical or mental difficulty, the rosary will not be without its fruit, if they do the best they can, keeping in mind that involuntary distractions do not detract from the value of prayer. What we want to do and try to do is more important before God than whether or not we actually succeed in doing it. Those fifteen minutes, more or less, given to this prayer, doing the best we can, are very pleasing to the Mother of God and the source of much fruit, even it they might leave us without much personal satisfaction. We do not measure the value of prayer by the lift we get out of it.

As Pope Pius XII wrote, speaking of the rosary:

> The recitation of identical formulas, repeated so many times, rather than rendering the prayer sterile and boring, has on the contrary the admirable quality of infusing confidence in him who prays, and causes a sweet compulsion towards the maternal heart of Mary.[5]

The Body and Soul of the Rosary

It will be helpful to see how the vocal and mental elements of the rosary blend together to form the body and soul of this prayer so dear to the Mother of God. The following are a few examples of similar blending.

After World War I, shell-shocked soldiers were introduced into a therapy that helped them deal with tensions. Doctors discovered that the art of knitting greatly relieved tensions. Somehow the fingers are the little avenues relieving anxieties for restoring natural calm. Perhaps one of the reasons why people love to smoke comes down to the pleasantness of touching the cigarette or pipe.

In a similar manner, the purpose of beads in any religion that uses them, is to boost the art of concentration.

The mere fingering of the beads has an effect of calming the mind, while the frequent repetition of the Hail Marys is a quasi-hypnotic attempt to further increase the attention span, helping to shut out distractions, something like the soft murmur of the flow of the stream helps to drown out competing noises.

As we have already indicated, the fingering of the beads while repeating the angelic salutation and the Lord's Prayer is the body of the rosary; but it is a body that needs a soul, and its soul is the successive reflection on the joyful, luminous, sorrowful and glorious events or mysteries in the life Our Lord and His Mother.

Rosary Meditation—Limitless in Scope

Nineteen of the twenty mysteries of the rosary are directly from the New Testament, while one, the Assumption, comes from Tradition.

The fifth glorious mystery, the Queenship of Mary, many think has its basis in the book of Revelation (Ch. 12). The woman of the Apocalypse, according to most scholars, seems to refer to the universal Church. However, as it is customarily thought in the Church today, whatever perfections are attributed to the whole Church, reside in their perfection in Mary and are attributed to her, the one individual member of the Church other than Christ without stain.

These mysteries of the rosary are like high points of the New Testament that contain explicitly or implicitly all the fundamentals of our faith. For that reason, the more we are familiar with the content of these mysteries as interpreted by Sacred Tradition and the living Magisterium, the more profound will be our use of the rosary. Our meditation on the mysteries of the rosary might bring us to reflect on a wide variety of themes, such as: God the Father, His will, His love, His wisdom, the incarnation of His divine Son and the major events in His life, Heaven, Mary, Joseph, and so on.

School of the Christian Life

All of us can reflect on the various virtues of Jesus, Mary and Joseph that we contemplate in the Gospel story, and strive to apply these lessons to our own lives. Pope Pius XII stated in the above-mentioned encyclical how efficacious this can be.

> "From the frequent meditation on the mysteries," he said, "the soul draws and imperceptibly absorbs the virtues they contain . . . and becomes strongly and easily impelled to follow the path which Christ Himself and His Mother have followed." For this reason, he declares that "the Holy Rosary will . . . form the most efficacious school of Christian life."[6]

Pope John XXIII spoke in similar terms:

> In reciting the Rosary, the thing that matters is devoutly mediating on each of the mysteries as we move our lips. Therefore, we are sure that our children and all of their brethren throughout the world will turn it into a school for learning true perfection, as, with a deep spirit of recollection, they contemplate the teachings that shine forth from the life of Christ and of Mary most holy.

Antidote for the Ills of Life

It was yet another Pope, Leo XIII, the rosary Pope of the nineteenth century who wrote nine encyclicals on devotion to Mary through the rosary, who expressed the theology of this prayer so simply. He spoke of the *Joyful Mysteries* as an antidote for the boredom and tedium of ordinary life; the *Sorrowful Mysteries* as an antidote for those who feel suffering has no meaning; and the *Glorious Mysteries* as an antidote for those who forget their real homeland. And to that we might add the *Luminous Mysteries* given to us by Pope John Paul II as an antidote to our forgetfulness of important events in the life of our Savior.

Looking at a Mystery in Depth

One can pray the rosary privately, or in common with others. Praying it privately one can determine his own pace, spending as long as he wishes on one decade, or if one's time is limited he can skip along at about three minutes a decade, which is equally legitimate as long as one lovingly considers the mystery under some aspect.

If one is praying alone and time permits, it can be helpful to pause a bit after declaring the mystery under consideration. Let us take, for example, the mystery of the Annunciation. As you announce this mystery, you can pause as long as you wish, putting yourself and your problems into your reflection on the mystery. Since there are many different types of prayer, such as prayers of petition, of thanksgiving, of praise, of repentance, of faith, of trust, and of simple love, we can begin to look at the Annunciation from any of these angles.

We can, for instance, pray for the gift of faith and confidence, as Mary consented to a most difficult assignment from Heaven with faith and confidence in God. Or we can thank Mary for having consented to be the mother of God on our behalf, welcoming the Savior of the world. We can also praise the work of the Holy Spirit for creating in the womb of Mary the human body and soul of the Word. We might simply express to God the Father, or to the Son, or to Mary, our sorrow for those who refuse the gift of human life and have aborted it; or for those who refuse to accept God's revealed word, or have doubted it.

Then again, we might be rebelling against some necessary decision either for ourselves, our family, or our work that will entail personal pain or difficulty. Reflect on this in the light of Mary's trusting and total surrender. Or we may be fascinated with the Angel Gabriel, and think of the many times we have either listened to or rejected the suggestions of our guardian angel. Or we might just be wrapped up in loving wonder of the Trinity, that the Divine Persons would plan such a mystery of love, the Word becoming flesh through the love of the Holy Spirit. For some, these considerations might hold their attention for a considerable time, and while they finger the beads their whole personality could experience a deep and trusting surrender to the Divine Trinity.

From all this, we can see there is no limit to the extent of the depth and breadth to which one's rosary meditation can lead. Its freedom within the consideration of the mysteries gives a structure to our meditation, and yet will let the inspiration of the Holy Spirit lead one towards those meanings which are more helpful for stirring up love and devotion to the Holy Trinity. In each mystery we are considering lovingly a different aspect of the merciful love of God. Thus, through it all, while fingering the beads, we are trying to imitate Mary's spirit of reflection, of which St. Luke says: *"His mother meanwhile kept all these things in her heart"* (Lk. 2:51).

Do Whatever He Tells You

What we are doing in the rosary is recalling the chief mysteries of our faith, in a manner taught us by a living mother, Mary, the Mother of Jesus and of us all. And the love of this mother does not stop with her, for her role is to lead us to her Son. Mary's last words recorded in Scripture at the marriage feast of Cana summarize well her whole concern in our regard: *"Do whatever He tells you"* (Jn. 2:5). She leads us to her Son, not only by her words, but especially by her example, for more perfectly than all others she mirrors His virtues.

May the rosary bring an increase in the prayer life of each one who takes up his beads seeking union with the Divine Trinity through the perspective of Jesus and Mary. When we reflect on these mysteries, we ask that Mary help us to *"imitate what they contain, and obtain what they promise."* She not only reflected on those mysteries in the past, and had an intimate part in them, but she prays along with us now, and helps us to understand them and to live them.

Chapter Notes

1. Pope Paul VI, *Marialis Cultus,* 49, c
2. Vatican Council II, *Sacrosanctum Concilium,* n. 13
3. Pope John Paul II, *Rosarium Virginis Mariae,* n. 2
4. Pope Pius XII, *Ingruentium Malorum,* n. 8
5. *Ibid.,* n. 9
6. *Ibid.*

Chapter 47

Some Objections to the Rosary

In spite of the great emphasis placed on praying the rosary by the Mother of God at Lourdes and Fatima, and by practically all the popes in the last century, there are many Catholics who do not pray the rosary regularly. When asked why, there is a variety of reasons or excuses given. Our purpose here is to consider some of those objections. If we can induce some to pray again this prayer so dear to the Mother of God and so efficacious a means of obtaining heavenly aid, our efforts will be worthwhile. These are some of the excuses given:

1) I Can't Keep My Mind From Wandering

Due to the weakness of the human mind, distractions are something that we cannot entirely avoid; but we must try, and that very trying can be a source of merit. Whether we are beginners or advanced in prayer, distractions in some degree will be present. So the first rule is, don't get upset about it, nor think that your prayer is not fruitful. To understand these matters, we must keep in mind the difference between distractions that are *voluntary,* and those that are *not voluntary.*

Distractions can be:

a) Voluntary — if one deliberately entertains thoughts not in keeping with prayer. For example: picking up a newspaper to read during Mass; or if while praying the rosary one is constantly looking out the window to follow the progress of a ball game. Such prayer would merit the rebuke of Our Lord against the Pharisees: *"This people honors me with their lips, but their heart is far from me, and in vain do they worship me"* (Mt. 15:8).

OBJECTIONS AGAINST THE ROSARY

b) **Involuntary** — when distractions come in spite of one's efforts to avoid them. Because of the limitations and weakness of the human mind the field of our awareness is in a constant state of flux, readily shifting from one thing to another. This is due in part to what psychologists refer to as the association of images and ideas. It often takes only an image in the imagination to divert our attention off in a completely different direction. Let us take an example: One might be meditating on the third joyful mystery of the rosary. In his mind he sees the divine Infant in the crib, Mary and Joseph, the shepherds and sheep; and then before he realizes it, that reminds him of the sheep on his uncle's farm. That reminds him of the vacation he spent on his uncle's farm with his cousin, and that in turn reminds him of the vacation he and his cousin spent at the beach, and so the mind travels. It is all a joyous experience, but not the third joyful mystery of the rosary.

This is but an example of how the mind works, and how easily out attention can be drawn away from the starting point of our reflection. Add to this the fact that the devil has the power to place images in our imagination, and we can see how readily distracting thoughts can gain entrance into our mind, especially at times of prayer.

Yet all this should not breed discouragement, for as we said, our very efforts to bring our mind back to the point of our reflection can be a source of merit.

In these matters it is also important to understand the distinction between the *attention of the mind,* and the *intention of the will.* The *attention* has to do with the fixing of the mind on what we are doing, the focusing of our consciousness on something; while the *intention* involves one wanting to pray well, trying to pray well, wanting to help souls, determining to persevere in spite of difficulties encountered, and so forth. If at times the attention of the mind may wander, the intention of the will does not necessarily falter; and it is this latter that has more to do with the fruitfulness of our prayer.

As regards the attention of the mind, people vary in their capacity to concentrate. Speaking of this one theologian comments:

> In most people, even under favorable circumstances, there will be some fluctuation of attention, and few can fix their minds for an extended period without some deviation from a proposed train of thought requiring mental effort. Even those with well disciplined minds find it difficult, or even morally impossible, to sustain attention when they are weary, uncomfortable, or situated in a noisy or disturbing environment.... Much distraction, therefore, is involuntary.[1]

The basic reason why we pray is to please God, not ourselves, and to fulfill our obligations to Him. While involuntary distractions detract from the satisfaction we derive from prayer, still our divine Savior is pleased with our efforts, if we are doing the best we can. Our efforts may not always bring us the satisfactions that give us a lift, yet they are a reaching out for God; and what we want to do and try to do in these matters counts much before Him, who sees the aspirations of the heart of those who seek Him.

Saintly souls and distractions:

Lest we think that distractions in prayer are proper only to beginners, or the undisciplined, we have the testimony of advanced souls in that regard.

- **The Little Flower** at times experienced almost constant distractions in meditation from someone near her in chapel; but in her effort to keep recollecting her mind, she felt that those meditations were as fruitful as any she ever made.

- **St. Bridget** suffered much from distraction, and on one occasion Our Lady appeared and said: *"The devil is wont to torment anyone who prays, and to send him as many distractions as he can. But be not troubled on that account, my daughter, for though you may suffer from distractions, you can always have an earnest desire to pray well, and then your prayer will be pleasing to My Son."*

OBJECTIONS AGAINST THE ROSARY

-**St. Francis de Sales** wrote to one of his spiritual children: *"When your heart is wandering and distracted, bring it back gently to its point . . . and if you did nothing the whole of your hour (of meditation) but bring your heart patiently and place it near Our Lord again, your hour would be well employed, and you would perform an exercise very agreeable to Him."*

-**Fr. Faber:** *"As the Eucharist is the testament of Jesus, so the Rosary is Mary's testament to us. In consequence of its blessings the devil makes the Rosary a special object of temptation, weariness . . . and such like. Persevere in it, and it will itself be the chain of your final perseverance."*

-**St. Louis de Montfort:** *"Of course, you cannot possibly pray your rosary without having a few involuntary distractions, and it is hard to pray even one Hail Mary without your imagination troubling you a little, for our imagination is never still. The one thing you can do, however, is to pray your rosary without giving in to distractions deliberately. . . . Even if you have to fight distractions all through your whole rosary, be sure to fight well, arms in hand: that is to say, do not stop praying your rosary even if it is hard to do so and you have no sensible devotion. . . . If you put down your arms, that is, if you give up the rosary, you will be admitting defeat and then, having won, the devil will leave you alone."*[2]

2) I Find Constant Repetition Monotonous

It is not difficult to understand someone saying that who does not understand the nature of the rosary, who sees it merely as a repetition of the same vocal prayers over and over again. But as we saw, those prayers are accompanied by the reflection on the mysteries of our redemption. *"Without that reflection,"* wrote Pope Paul VI, *"the rosary is a body without* a soul, and its recitation is in danger of becoming a mechanical repetition of formulas,"* and would merit the warning of our Blessed Lord: *"In praying do not heap up empty phrases as the Gentiles do, for they think that they will be heard for their many words"* (Mt. 6:7).

Without doubt, if someone speaking to another repeated the same thing fifty times, it could well become boring, both for the one speaking and for the one listening. But in the rosary there is something vastly different. Those who are listening are our Blessed Lord and His Mother; and they never tire of hearing again and again those most perfect prayers — even when said mechanically — while we meditate on the great events of their life on earth. Besides, they are listening not so much to the prayer of the lips as to the prayer of the heart, the aspirations that flow from our reflection on the mysteries of the rosary.

With these thoughts in mind, even if we have to struggle with distractions or discomfort, or with little feeling of devotion in praying the rosary, we know that our efforts are most pleasing to those heavenly listeners and fruitful for our own soul. At such times St. Louis de Monfort recommends that we keep in mind that *"Our Lord and His Blessed Mother are watching you, and that your guardian angel is standing at your side, taking your Hail Marys — if well said, and using them like roses to make a crown for Jesus and Mary."*[3]

Even if in praying the rosary there is little variation, prayer is meant to be a language of love; and that does not need endless variation. If a suitor tells his lady friend of his affection for her, she does not demand that he always express it in a different way. In fact she does not mind if he always uses the same words, as long as he says it often, and sincerely means it.

3) I Seem to Get in a Rut as Regards My Meditations

In our meditations, we form certain images in the imagination to aid us in the reflection on the mystery in question; and it can be that the same images come to mind again and again. This need not worry us, as long as they give rise to aspirations of love, of trust, of thanks to Our Divine Savior who gave His life to redeem us, and to our Blessed Mother who gave us this beautiful and efficacious form of prayer.

We can, however, bring variation to our rosary meditations, by applying the lessons of each mystery to the changing needs and problems of our life.

We can bring variations to our reflections by viewing the various mysteries through the eyes of Our Lady. As Pope Paul VI wrote: *"By its nature the recitation of the rosary calls for a quiet rhythm . . . helping the individual to meditate on the mysteries of the Lord's life as seen through the eyes of her who was closest to Him. In this way the unfathomable riches of these mysteries are unfolded."* [4]

We can bring variation to our rosary reflections by doing some spiritual reading relating to those mysteries, such as the Scriptures, a life of Christ or of Our Lady, and booklets on rosary meditations.

Finally we can bring a most fruitful variation in our rosary meditations by relating them to the changing themes of the liturgy. Pope Paul VI, while discouraging the use of the rosary during Mass, saw the rosary as a good preparation for it.

> Once the preeminent value of liturgical rites has been reaffirmed, it will not be difficult to appreciate the fact that the rosary is a practice of piety which easily harmonizes with the liturgy. In fact, like the liturgy, it is of a community nature, draws its inspiration from Sacred Scripture, and is oriented towards the mystery of Christ. The commemoration in the liturgy and the contemplative remembrance proper to the rosary, although existing on essentially different planes of reality, have as their object the same salvific events wrought by Christ. The former (the Liturgy) presents anew, under the veil of signs and operative in a hidden way, the great mysteries of our redemption. The latter (the rosary), by means of devout contemplation, recalls these same mysteries to the mind of the person praying, and stimulates

the will to draw from them norms of living. Once this substantial difference has been established, it is not difficult to understand that the rosary is an exercise of piety that draws its motivating force from the liturgy and leads naturally back to it.[5]

Practical Reflections:

1) If while praying the rosary involuntary distractions drag your attention away from the mystery at hand, do not repeat the decade or any part of it. Bring your awareness back before our Blessed Lord and His Mother, ask pardon for whatever fault might have been yours, and go on from there. They understand the problem better than you.

2) *"Before beginning a decade,"* suggests St. Louis de Montfort, *"always be sure to ask of Almighty God, by this mystery and through the intercession of the Blessed Mother, one of the virtues that shines forth most in this mystery, or one of which you stand in particular need."*[6]

3) Involuntary distractions are a form of temptation, a trial that God allows to test our patience, our perseverance, our trust. He wishes too, to keep us from depending too much on interior satisfactions, and from judging the value of our prayer by their presence. The presence of involuntary distractions, or the lack of interior satisfactions is not a sign that our prayer is not fruitful. He who ardently wishes to pray well, and tries to do so, prays well.

4) Keep in mind that when one tries to put aside thoughts that intrude in prayer, that very effort, regardless of how successful, is loving God. It is not the kind of love that brings interior delights, but the kind that delights our Blessed Lord; for if the mind is momentarily distracted, the heart is at work trying to make room for Him.

Chapter Notes

1. C. I. Litzinger, *New Catholic Encyclopedia,* 4,912
2. St. Louis de Montfort, *The Secret of the Rosary,* pp. 89, 91
3. *Ibid.,* p. 89
4. Pope Paul VI, *Marialis Cultus,* p. 47
5. *Ibid.,* p. 48
6. *The Secret of the Rosary,* p. 92

Chapter 48

St. Dominic and the Rosary

Most of us are familiar with the tradition that goes back many centuries, and which has been accepted in the writings of many popes, as to the connection of St. Dominic with the beginnings of the rosary devotion. According to tradition, the occasion was the Albigensian heresy which ravaged Christendom, particularly in southern France during the latter part of the twelfth and the beginning of the thirteenth centuries. St. Dominic was distressed at his lack of success in his preaching in countering this heresy, and in his desperation turned to the Mother of God for help. According to the tradition she appeared to him and told him to use *her Psalter* in conjunction with his preaching of the mysteries of our salvation, as an instrument in combatting the great heresy of his day.

We have no historical documents dating from that period expressly referring to St. Dominic and the rosary. We will endeavor to show, however, that a number of things could be responsible for that silence.

The Evolution of the Rosary

We have to keep in mind that over the centuries there has been a considerable evolution in the form that this devotion called the rosary has taken. We have to remember that in the time of St. Dominic:

1) The **Hail Mary** did not exist as we pray it today. Only the first half of it was then used. The word JESUS was not added until the fourteenth century, and the second half of the prayer came later still.

2) The **Our Father** and the **Glory be to the Father** were not then part of the rosary.

3) The *mysteries of the rosary* were not fixed as they are now. Even in the fifteenth century in the time of Alan de Rupe, O.P., who was responsible for the revival of the rosary devotion 250 years after the time of St. Dominic, the rosary he preached was the Marian Psalter of 150 Hail Marys and 150 mysteries. These were divided into three groups of fifties dedicated to the joyful, sorrowful and glorious mysteries. The fifteen mysteries in use for centuries were officially established by Pope Pius V in 1569. Pope John Paul II added the five luminous mysteries in 2002.

4) There was no *pendant* (the cross and five extra beads) as we have now.

5) The very word *"rosary"* taken from the Latin word *"rosarium"* meaning rose garden, or bouquet of roses, was not used in the time of Dominic as applied to this devotion. So obviously there would be no reference to that term in documents of his time.

The Marian Psalter

The custom of counting repeated prayers by the use of a string of beads or knots, or pebbles in a bowl was prevalent long before the time of St. Dominic. This was common among the Muslims, the Buddhists, and other non-Christian religions as well as among Christians.

From time immemorial the *150 Psalms* of the Bible comprised the most important part of the official liturgical prayers prayed by the clergy and the monks in monasteries. Since, however, many of the common folk were illiterate, there was an attempt to offer those who could not read (especially the Latin) a substitute for the 150 psalms. The practice arose of substituting 150 *Our Fathers* in place of the Latin psalms, using a string of beads to count them, dividing them into *"fifties."* This chaplet, or string of beads, came to be known as *"Paternoster"* beads.

Little by little, the *Hail Mary* took its place along side the *Creed* and the *Our Father* as a standard prayer. But still, it was only the first half that was used. In the course of time there came to be a parallel Psalter, i.e., one of 150 *Hail Marys* known as the *Marian Psalter.*

The Albigensian Heresy

The Albigensian heresy that plagued southern France in St. Dominic's time was based on a dual view of the world similar to that of the Manicheans of the third century, namely, that there are two supreme beings, a good God who created the spirit world, and an evil god who created the material world. The spiritual world is essentially good, and the material world (including the human body) is essentially evil. The evil god (Satan) imprisoned spirits in material bodies, so whatever one can do to be released from that prison (including suicide) is good. Since matter is evil, marriage and the procreation of mankind is evil. The proponents of this heresy rejected Catholic belief regarding the Trinity, the Incarnation, the sacraments, hell and purgatory, but believed in the transmigration of souls. Christ was not truly a man, nor, therefore, was Mary truly the Mother of God. The crucifixion, death and resurrection of Christ were only illusions, and the whole concept of the cross in the Christian life was rejected.

This heresy was deeply rooted in southern France in the first part of the thirteenth century. Its rapid growth was nourished, among other things, by the moral laxity and worldliness of the clergy. In addition, most of the nobility fostered the heresy because of their hope to take over the lands and goods of the Church.

This is the situation that St. Dominic encountered when he began his missionary labors in southern France. This was the situation, according to tradition, that occasioned a special intervention on the part of the Mother of God. In view of Our Lady's apparitions at crucial times in the centuries that followed, would not the intervention of our Blessed Mother at this period in history seem most likely, when the Church in Western Europe was so seriously threatened? How fruitful would be the introduction of the *Marian Psalter* in conjunction with preaching to those who denied the Incarnation of the Word, the motherhood of Mary and the sanctity of marriage. For mingled with the explanation of the mysteries of our salvation would be the prayerful repeating over and over: *"Blessed art thou among women, and blessed is the fruit of thy womb."*

Cardinal Luigi Ciappi, O.P., who for many years was the theologian of the papal household (the pope's personal theologian), in 1975, a few years before he was made a cardinal, published an article entitled *A Deepening of the Faith By Means of the Rosary.* In that article he referred to St. Dominic as an ardent promoter of the *Marian Psalter,* for he preferred a form of instruction in which he alternated his preaching on the mysteries of the life, passion and death, and resurrection of Christ, with the Psalter of *Hail Marys.*

The Bollandists

The tradition of St. Dominic and the rosary was more or less universally accepted, especially in documents of many popes, until the work of the *Bollandists* in the seventeenth century. This was a group of learned scholars (Belgian Jesuits) who were charged with the work of publishing the *"Acta Sanctorum"* covering the life of Christ and of the saints included in the liturgical calendar. These were men of undeniable scholarship who set out to rewrite the lives of the saints, so as to preserve in them all that could be established by historical sources, and to weed out legends that surrounded the lives of many saints.

This group concluded that there was not sufficient evidence to support the tradition of St. Dominic and the rosary, that this tradition stemmed only from the testimony of Alan de Rupe, O.P. (d. 1475), and that his claims, written 250 years after St. Dominic, cannot be substantiated by any documents dating from the time of St. Dominic.

Yet, it appears that this *argument of silence* put forth by the Bollandists did not seem to outweigh, in the mind of succeeding popes, the impact of the centuries-old tradition concerning St. Dominic and the rosary; for popes coming after the 17th century continued to refer to St. Dominic in connection with the beginnings of the rosary.

Around the beginning of the twentieth century an English Jesuit, Herbert Thurston, a prolific writer and for many years a member of the staff of the English periodical *The Month*, followed the lead of the Bollandists. Through the medium of that publication he published many hundreds of articles, and had more than 100 entries in the original *Catholic Encyclopedia*. Among the topics he wrote on some dealt with the rosary, its history and origin. Looking at the origin of the rosary from the viewpoint of scientific research, the lack of documents dating from the time of St. Dominic linking him with the rosary led him to the conclusion that this tradition had no historic foundation. His conclusions have influenced many of the writers since his time dealing with this topic.

While documents from St. Dominic's day expressly linking him with the rosary are lacking, there are many things pointing in that direction that taken together tend to substantiate that tradition.

The Militia of Jesus Christ

Fr. Francis Willam, in his book *The Rosary, Its History And Meaning*,[1] speaks of the *"Militia of Jesus Christ"* founded by St. Dominic, the members of which recited daily the *Psalter of Our Lady*. He refers also to the *"Confraternity of Prayer"* founded by the Dominicans in Piacenza in 1259, 38 years after the death of St. Dominic, the members of which also prayed the 150 *Hail Marys* daily. Fr. Benedict Ashley, O.P., in his book *The Dominicans*, speaks of this Militia as having been founded by a Dominican bishop of Breganza who died in 1271.

At any rate, we have the Marian Psalter actively employed during the life of St. Dominic and shortly after. In this we have the 150 *Hail Marys* which constitute the *"body"* of the rosary, i.e., the vocal prayer. What is wanting is the *"soul"* of the rosary, i.e., the praying of these *Hail Marys* joined with reflection on the mysteries of our salvation. And yet, as Fr. Ciappi pointed out, a common method of preaching of St. Dominic was to preach on the life of Christ, interspersing his reflections with the Marian Psalter.

So it seems that the heart of what the rosary is (the combination of vocal and mental prayer) was practiced by St. Dominic, not as we have the rosary today, but in such a way that *what he did then* in time evolved into *what we have now;* i.e., that his form of preaching interspersed with prayer eventually evolved into what the rosary is today.

We know from his biographers that St. Dominic had a great devotion to the Mother of God. And it could well be that the inspiration to preach as he did came from her, as tradition says it did, i.e., the combining of her prayer (the *Hail Mary* as it existed then) with the reflection on the mysteries of our salvation. Pope Pius XII, in his encyclical on the rosary, seems to imply this when he states that this devotion *"in its origin and the wisdom of its constitution is more divine than human."*

Alan de Rupe

History well documents the fact that Alan de Rupe, also known as Alan de la Roche (1428-1475), was a great apostle of the rosary. There must be some basis for his claims that St. Dominic's connection with the rosary is proved *"both from tradition and from the testimony of writers."* I find it hard to believe that he just made it up. He was not a dreamer. He was a Master of Sacred Theology, wrote a commentary on the Sentences of Peter Lombard, lectured in Paris, was visitator of his Order in central Europe, wrote his *Apologia* for the rosary, and preached in widely spread places. He founded the Rosary Confraternity in 1470 in Douai, and did much to popularize the rosary.

It could well be that sources to which Alan de Rupe had access did not exist in later centuries. Even if documents did originally exist connecting St. Dominic and the rosary, countless religious houses and convents were destroyed (with their libraries) in the wars of religious persecution that ravaged Europe over the centuries.

We find this thought clearly expressed by John S. Johnson in his book *The Rosary In Action*.

> The critics relied mainly on the argument of silence to question the ancient tradition that the Blessed Virgin gave the rosary to St. Dominic. They should have known that many documents referred to by Alan de Rupe may have existed, but did not survive the burning scourge of the Huguenots, who destroyed convents, monasteries, libraries among the countless institutions they committed to the flames. The critics went so far as to say that Alan had invented the rosary devotion... and had attributed it to St. Dominic to tie it in with a famous name. But the two persons Alan relies on for his story of the origin of the rosary had their "Mariales" preserved at the Convent of Gand; which library was burnt during the wars on religion. There are other documents which have been discovered in later years which were from before Alan de Rupe's time. The long poem *Rosarius* antedates him by 100 years or so, and clearly refers to St. Dominic and the battle of Muret. This removes Alan from all suspicion of inventing his sources. The elements were all in place at the time of St. Dominic; how did they get together in the rosary?[2]

We might put this question in another way: Were these elements brought together by the preaching of St. Dominic? We cannot prove with certainty *that they were;* but neither does the lack of documents prove *that they were not*.

Maisie Ward further undermines the *"argument of silence"* when she writes in her book *The Splendor Of The Rosary*: *"Discussions of what happened in the Middle Ages are apt to be obscured by the fact that so many documents have been lost, especially during the ravages of the Black Plague."*[3]

Fr. Guy Bedouelle, O.P., in his book *St. Dominic, The Grace and the Word*, includes this important comment about a contemporary of St. Dominic:

> Blessed Romee of Livia, one of St. Dominic's companions, Prior of the Convent of Lyons, France in 1223, and later

Provincial of Provence, was said to have died, according to the medieval chronicler Bernard Gui, holding tightly in his fingers the little knotted cord on which he counted his AVES. Historians regard this as one of the earliest texts describing our present rosary in its embryonic form.[4]

Fr. Ludovicus Fanfani, O.P., states in his book *De Rosari B. M. Virginis* that some years after the death of St. Dominic, the devotion of the rosary (as he promoted it) began to decline. Among the causes of the decline were the great plague of the Black Death which swept through Europe, wiping out great portions of the population, and the great Western Schism which split Europe into various factions. The devotion did not completely disappear, however, as traces of it remained among the people; and, says Fr. Fanfani, documents are not wanting to establish that the devotion was kept alive in England during the thirteenth and fourteenth centuries.[5]

Testimony of the Popes

Pope Benedict XIV (1740-58) was a renowned scholar and a promoter of historical studies and research. When he was an official of the Sacred Congregation of Rites, he was asked about the tradition of St. Dominic and the rosary. The following is his response, a century after the work of the Bollandists:

> You ask whether St. Dominic was the first institutor of the rosary, and show that you yourselves are bewildered and entangled in doubts on the matter. Now, what value do you attach to the testimony of so many Popes, such as Leo X (1521), Pius V (1572), Gregory XIII (1585), Sixtus V (1590), Clement VIII (1605), Alexander VII (1667), Bl. Innocent XI (1689), Clement XI (1721), Innocent XIII (1724) and others who unanimously attribute the institution of the rosary to St. Dominic, the founder of the Dominican Order, an apostolic man who might be compared to the apostles themselves and who, undoubtedly due to the inspiration of the Holy Spirit, became the designer, the author, promoter, and most illustrious preacher of this admirable and truly heavenly instrument, the rosary.

After quoting the above, Fr. Anthony N. Fuerst, in his well documented book, *This Rosary*, states: *"To reject this tradition in its entirety, without strong arguments, would be very rash."*[6]

To the above list of Popes accepting the tradition of St. Dominic and the rosary could be added many more coming after the time of Benedict XIV. But this is not the main argument supporting the tradition. It is the coming together of many pieces of a puzzle pertaining to the essentials of the tradition as handed down. For example, given the following facts:

1) The members of the *Militia of Jesus Christ* founded by St. Dominic or by a Dominican of his day, prayed the 150 *Hail Marys* daily...

2) St. Dominic's devotion to Mary and his ardent prayer in combatting the great heresy of his day, along with the testimony of Alan De Rupe that St. Dominic did receive some communication from the Mother of God as to how to combat the errors of his time...

3) Some of his biographers explain, a common manner of Dominic's preaching was the frequent alternating of his instruction on the mysteries of our faith with the Marian Psalter...

4) The first beginning of this devotion in the time of Dominic was vastly different from its present structure, for then there was no set sequence of the mysteries, and even the name (rosary) had not yet been established...

5) Many convents with their libraries were destroyed in the religious persecutions that followed the thirteenth century...

... it seems to me that the **negative argument,** the absence of documents, is outweighed by the presence of the essential components that constitute the heart of what the rosary is. It seems to me, not merely possible, but very probable, that the Mother of God, as Alan de

Rupe testified, did use St. Dominic in some way to give this devotion to the Church. One source of misconception in this regard is religious art, which portrays St. Dominic receiving from Our Lady the rosary such as we use today. This would not have been. But then, if artists are to portray this tradition, how else would they do it?

And too, what Dominic did could have been done in such a way that it did not stand out as an innovation, as something new; for it was simply taking the Psalter of Our Lady, already in existence, and using it as a means of making his preaching fruitful. It could be that for this reason it was not commented on by the chroniclers of his day. And yet, the combining of the *Hail Mary* with reflection on the life of Christ is the essence of the rosary devotion.

If Our Lady at Fatima gave us a remedy in this past century for overcoming *Communism* and attaining peace — which remedy included the rosary — does it not seem probable that she would have intervened in the thirteenth century, offering a means of combatting the devastating heresy of *Albigensianism,* as tradition assures us she did?

Chapter Notes

1. Francis William, *The Rosary, Its History and Meaning*, p. 26
2. John S. Johnson, *Rosary in Action*, Ch. 3, p. 26
3. Maisie Ward, *The Splendor of the Rosary*, p. 34
4. Guy Bedouelle, O.P., *St. Dominic, the Grace and the Word*, p. 254
5. Ludovicus Fanfani, O.P., *De Rosarie B. M. Virginis*, p. 27
6. Anthony N. Fuerst, *This Rosary*, p. 20

Chapter 49

Weapons from Heaven

When the Mother of God appeared to the children in Fatima, the First World War was still in progress. In the first of those apparitions, May 13, 1917, she told the three children: *"Pray the Rosary every day, in honor of Our Lady of the Rosary, to obtain peace and the end of the war."* In each of the following five apparitions she repeated her request for the daily rosary, and twice again repeated the phrase *"to obtain peace and the end of the war."* In the light of those requests, it will be helpful to recall how, through the centuries, the rosary has proven a powerful weapon against the forces of evil, a weapon from heaven for the attainment of peace. Almost half a century before, Pope Pius IX had asked, *"My children, help me combat the evils of the Church and society, not with the sword, but by the Rosary."*

The Feast of the Rosary

The feast on which we honor Our Lady of the Rosary (Ocober 7), was instituted over four centuries ago, after the historic victory of the Christian forces over the Turks in the Battle of Lepanto. That was a crucial victory in the history of the Church, for if that battle had been lost, it could well be that today all or most of Europe would be Muslim, not Christian.

Pope Pius V, who sat on the throne of Peter when that battle was fought, had asked for public processions in Rome, during which the faithful sought the aid of the Mother of God through the public praying of the rosary. *"They formed bands of supplicants,"* wrote Pope Leo XIII, *"who called on Mary again and again in the words of the Rosary, imploring her to grant the victory to their companions engaged in battle."* At a crucial moment the galleys of the Turks, through a sudden change in the winds, were thrown into disarray, enabling the outnumbered Christian forces to gain a decisive victory.

In thanksgiving to the Mother of God, Pope Pius V instituted the feast of *Our Lady of Victory,* issued an Apostolic Constitution *"that the remembrance of the great victory obtained through the merits and intercession of this glorious Virgin, may never be forgotten,"* and granted additional indulgences to members of the Rosary Confraternity.

The immediate successor of Pope Pius V, Gregory XIII, changed the name of the feast to that of *Our Lady of the Rosary.* About a century and a half later, the Christian forces were again victorious over the Turks at Temesvar in Hungary, and at Corfu; and in both cases these victories coincided with feasts of the Blessed Virgin, and with public praying of the rosary. In memory of this, Pope Clement XI extended the feast of Our Lady of the Rosary to the universal Church.

In the above instances, and others which could be enumerated, the victory, in the eyes of those involved, was due to help from above, help sought through public and fervent recitation of the rosary. For centuries, as Pope Leo XIII pointed out in several encyclicals, the rosary has brought *public* as well as *private* blessings from heaven.

David's Slingshot

To some, this question will come to mind: Does not all this seem rather preposterous, when one thinks of the superpowers of today, with war machines that defy the imagination as to their powers of destruction? How can we with our rosaries, so insignificant, be of any consequence in the face of all this?

A similar question might have been asked when David, with his slingshot and a few pebbles from the stream, went forth to meet Goliath armed with sword, shield, and his protective armor for battle. Yet, David was not alone, for the powers of heaven were with him, and that made the difference.

The rosary is like the slingshot of David. It is the weapon that Our Lady has chosen. She chose this instrument, so insignificant in itself, precisely that the power of God behind it might be all the more manifest. God chooses the weak to confound the strong (1 Cor. 1:27). He chooses insignificant instruments, in preference to those the world relies on, to make it more clear that the end result is more the *hand of God* than the *work of man*. As Pope Pius XII wrote in his encyclical on the rosary:

> Place great confidence in the Holy Rosary. Use this most powerful form of prayer with the utmost possible zeal, and let it become more and more esteemed and more fervently recited daily . . . It is not with physical force, not with arms, not with human power, but with the divine help obtained through this prayer, that the Church and all its members, strong and undaunted like David with his sling, will be able to confront the infernal enemy.

A Prophecy, A Warning, A Promise

When the Mother of God at Fatima asked for the daily rosary as an instrument of peace, she meant the rosary to be not merely prayed, but also lived; and not by just a handful of people, but by a considerable portion of her children living its message. It was an appeal for men to amend their lives in keeping with the message of the Gospel. Her message included:

1) A Prophetic Warning:

> The war (World War I) will soon end, but if men do not cease offending God, another and more terrible war will break out during the pontificate of Pius XI. . . . If my requests are not granted, Russia will spread her errors throughout the world, fomenting wars and persecutions against the Church. Many will be martyred, the Holy Father will have much to suffer, various nations will be destroyed (July 13, 1917).

How truly this has come to pass. Reflect for a moment on the significance of those words: The Second World War could have been prevented and the spread of atheistic Communism could have been prevented, if her requests had been heeded. And when we look at the world today, not only have men not ceased offending God, but their disregard of His laws seems to have increased since 1917. What is more, as recent popes have pointed out, so many have lost the sense of sin, and this makes repentance very unlikely unless the necessary graces are won for them by others.

2) A Warning of God's Justice:

During the apparition of July 13th Our Lady revealed: *"The world, on account of its innumerable crimes, will soon be punished by war, famine and persecution against the Church and the Holy Father."*

After showing the children a vision of hell: *"You have seen hell, where the souls of poor sinners go"* (July 13). *"Pray, pray very much, and make sacrifices for sinners. Many souls are going to hell because there is no one to offer sacrifices and prayers for them"* (Aug. 19).

Fr. Thomas Mc Glynn, O.P., the artist who carved the large statue of Our Lady above the main entrance of the basilica at Fatima, and who has written a book entitled *Vision of Fatima*, had several prolonged conversations with Sr. Lucia, a Carmelite nun, the oldest of the three children to whom Our Lady appeared at Fatima. Sr. Lucia asked: *"In your writings, please stress the spiritual meaning of things . . . so that all may understand the true meaning and purpose of the coming of Our Lady to earth, which is to bring souls to heaven, to draw them to God."*

In the above-mentioned book, Fr. McGlynn, after referring to the sufferings caused by World War II and the worldwide scourge of atheistic Communism, wrote:

> From the words of Our Lady we must fear even greater afflictions unless there is a change in human conduct. But we definitely miss *"the spiritual meaning of things"* if we think that Our Lady came to Fatima to tell us how to keep out of a third world war, or how to convert Russia, or to achieve tranquility in our earthly existence. She came to tell us how to keep out of hell. . . . All the bleeding, dying and despair of a thousand wars cannot equal the disaster of a single soul being damned. . . . War can come or not, it is evil in the final

analysis in the measure that it brings about the final evil, the loss of souls.

Even though Our Lady foretold that Russia would spread her errors throughout the world, resulting in wars and persecution of the Church, Fr. McGlynn wrote:

> This does not mean that Russia is the enemy of peace; it means that Russia, unwittingly, indeed is the instrument of divine justice. The enemy of peace is not Russia, but sin, which abounds within all borders.

3) **A Message of Mercy and Hope:**

> To save souls (from Hell) God wants to establish throughout the world the devotion to my Immaculate Heart. If people will do what I tell you, many souls will be saved, and there will be peace (July 13). I promise salvation to those who embrace this devotion (June 13).
>
> If my requests are granted Russia will be converted and there will be peace. . . . In the end my Immaculate Heart will triumph. The Holy Father will consecrate Russia to me, and it will be converted and some time of peace will be given the world (July 13).

How to Heed Our Lady's Requests

1) by praying *the rosary* daily, reflecting on its mysteries, striving to apply its lessons to our lives, and adding after each decade: *"O my Jesus, forgive us, etc."*

2) by *Communions of reparation* (and confession) especially on the First Saturdays, with the intention of making reparation to the Immaculate Heart of Mary.

3) by *offering the sacrifices, trials and crosses* of life, especially those involved in keeping God's commandments and fulfilling the duties of our state in life, offering them through the Immaculate Heart of Mary in reparation to the divine majesty so offended by sin, and for the conversion of sinners.

Sr. Lucia, the Carmelite nun referred to above, related that Our Lady had revealed to her that she had accepted the consecration of the world to her Immaculate Heart made by Pope John Paul II as a fulfillment of her request. Yet we should continue to offer our prayers and sacrifices for a continuation of that restoration of world peace. In any case, whatever the world situation, we can and should take steps to insure the triumph of her Immaculate Heart in our own individual souls.

Root Cause of Today's Ills

From Our Lady's words, we can clearly see that the lack of peace, the threat of war and actual wars in various parts of the world can be reduced, in their roots, to man's disregard for the laws of God. The root cause is spiritual. The economic and political disorders simply flow from that. That is why the Mother of God is calling for spiritual weapons, such as the rosary.

Our Lady's Antidote for Today's Ills

Let us reflect for a moment on why the Mother of God has singled out the rosary as an efficacious antidote to the ills of human society:

1) Because of the pressures of everyday life, man tends to get so immersed in the things and cares of this world, that he easily loses sight of and concern for things more lasting. The rosary helps us, for a brief while, to reflect on the realities that are all-important as regards our eternal welfare, realities that are meant to give direction and motivation to our life.

2) In the materialistic culture in which we live, so many rely solely on material means to attain their goals, even the goal of world peace. Blind as to eternal and revealed truths, so much of their planning ignores God and His laws. When this happens, as history proves, and as Scriptures testify (Ps. 81:12), God leaves man to his own devices, to his own self-destruction. In the face of this blindness, this reliance solely on material means, the Mother of God offers her children a weapon that is entirely spiritual, the rosary, so that the final outcome can be clearly seen as more the *hand of God* than the *work of man*.

3) Another reason why Our Lady emphasized the rosary is because it keeps before us a *pattern of life,* a model of what our life must be if it is to be truly Christian, truly fruitful. Therein we reflect on the JOYFUL mysteries, the beginnings of the mystery of our redemption, the early life of Jesus in Nazareth; the LUMINOUS mysteries which single out key events in His public life; the SORROWFUL mysteries culminating in His passion and death on Calvary, fulfilling the will of His Father; and the GLORIOUS mysteries of His resurrection and ascension into heaven, and the assumption and coronation of His Mother.

In family life we find a parallel pattern to the above. In the beginning there are deeply satisfying and joyous years; but as time rolls on, suffering of various kinds enter in. It may be sickness, poverty, opposition, misunderstanding, rejection, etc. The *joyful* mysteries of life have become mingled with the *sorrowful,* in some more than in others. To some Jesus gives a greater share of His cross. And why all this? Because our true homeland is not in this life, but in the next, where we will share the *glory of Christ* in the measure that here and now we willingly share in His Cross.

This pattern of life is repeatedly kept before us in the rosary. And as Pope Pius XII explained, the rosary not merely points out the way in which to follow Christ, but helps us to follow in His footsteps.

> From the frequent meditation on the mysteries, the soul draws and imperceptibly absorbs the virtues they contain ... and becomes strongly and easily impelled to follow the path that Christ Himself and His Mother followed.[1]

4) There is one final and key reason why Our Lady singled out the rosary, and asked for it daily as an instrument of peace. That is because, ultimately, the enemy we are confronted with is not a political power, not a foreign nation; it is an infernal power that is superhuman, both as to strength and intelligence, against whom only spiritual weapons will avail. St. Paul referred to this:

> Our wrestling is not against flesh and blood, but against the principalities and the powers, against the world-wide rulers of this darkness, against the spiritual forces of wickedness on high . . . Therefore take up the armor of God that you may be able to resist in the evil day (Eph. 6:12).

Only spiritual weapons will avail against this enemy.

Under Mary's Banner

The ultimate forces of evil behind the strife, the conflicts, the immorality of today, are such that no human power can match them if man is left to himself alone. Yet, this is the enemy that Our Lady has been designated in God's plan to conquer (Gen. 3:15; Rev. 12). The Immaculate Virgin is *"the woman"* who will be God's instrument in crushing the head of the serpent. To her God has entrusted the war against Satan and his seed. She is, so to speak, the Commander-in-Chief empowered with the strategy of the war. And she has made known that strategy at Fatima, and the weapons we are to use.

The Song of Songs, which the Church applies to Mary in a figurative sense, refers to Our Lady as *"terrible as an army in battle array"* (6:4). Commenting on this passage, St. Augustine wrote:

> Even St. Michael, the prince and leader of the heavenly army, and all his angelic militia take orders from Mary in defending the souls of those who have placed themselves under her banner, and in leading them to final victory.

By ourselves alone, we are quite helpless against the infernal powers. But under Mary's banner, and using the weapons she asked in union with countless thousands of others, it is a different story; for she can accomplish what no earthly power can accomplish. As she revealed at Fatima:

> Continue to pray the rosary every day, in honor of Our Lady of the Rosary, to obtain peace for the world, and the end of the war, because only she can bring this about (July 13).

If the above was true in 1917, it is equally true today. All of Mary's powers come from Christ. But He has designated her as the instrument through which the victory over Satan will be accomplished; so that, as St. Louis de Montfort says, the defeat of the proud Evil One will be all the more humiliating, all the more painful, having been accomplished by a humble virgin.

All of us, then, should answer Mary's call to arms. Join her army, enroll in the Rosary Confraternity if you have not already done so. Become one of her soldiers, following the strategy she outlined at Fatima, using daily her weapon the rosary, trying to live what it recalls, and placing in her hands the fruits of all your prayers and sacrifices.

Chapter Notes

1. Pope Pius XII, *Encyclical on the Rosary*

Index

ABORTION
The Slaughter of the Innocent 193
   God, the Author of Life 193
   Abortion — An Abominable Crime 194
   God's Unfailing Intervention 195
   God's Providential Safeguards 196
   A Cry for Vengeance 197
   The Signs of the Times 197
   Under Our Lady's Banner 199
   Pro-Choice Catholics 207
   Cafeteria Catholics 160
   Worldliness 169
   Secularism's Impact on Education 212
   The Tactics of Satan 221

BEATITUDES
Blessed are the Meek 111
   The Virtue of Meekness 111
   False Concepts of Meekness 113
   The Meekness of Christ 114
   The Passion of Anger 115
   Remedies for Anger 116
   Importance of Meekness 118
Blessed are the Merciful 120
   God's Merciful Plan 120
   Conditions of God's Mercy 121
   Repentance and conversion 121
   Works of mercy 122
   Mercy Involves Sacrifice 123
   Mercy Enriches 124
   Divine Mercy and the World's Misery 125
   Seeing Christ in His Members 126
Blessed are the Clean of Heart 128
   They Shall See God 129
   Vices that Impede Spiritual Vision 132

BODY
This Body of Ours 43
   Dependence of the Soul on the Body 44
   Like Two Different Persons 45
   How the Passions Affect Our Judgment 46
   The Morality of the Passions 48
   Body-Soul Relationship 33
The Body Before Original Sin
   Immortality of the Body 4
   Loss of Bodily Immortality 9

INDEX

CHARITY
- **Loving is Self-Giving** 69
  - Loving is Giving 70
  - Perfect Loving is Total Giving 71
  - Love has Many Facets 72
  - Practical Reflections 75
- **Two Kinds of Self-Love** 95
  - True Self Love 96
  - Love of Self and Love of Neighbor Inseparable 97
  - False Self-Love 98
  - Love or Hate 99
  - Today's Confused World 99
  - Love Your Neighbor as Yourself 100
  - How Sloth Opposes Charity 185
  - The Joy of Charity 186
- **Envy & Jealousy, Enemies of Charity** 226
  - Hidden Vices 227
  - Enemy of Charity 228
  - What Envy is Not 228
  - A Capital Sin 230
  - The Grave Evil of Envy 231
  - Countering Envy 232

CONSCIENCE
- **Conscience Our Guide:**
- **Its Difficulties** 12
  - What is Our Conscience? 12
  - Not an Infallible Guide 13
  - Conscience Needs Training 14
  - The Sensitivity of Conscience 14
  - The Seared Conscience 15
  - Wishful Thinking 16
  - Conscience Becomes What We Make It 17
- **Its Formation** 20
  - The Voice of God 20
  - The Law of God Written in the Heart 20
  - Conscience and Freedom 21
  - Conscience Alone is Not Sufficient 21
  - The Role of the Holy Spirit 22
  - The Need of Discipline 24
  - Beware of Presumption 24
  - Conscience — Not Always a True Guide 203

EUCHARIST
- **Holy Eucharist, Part I: A Sacrifice** 285
  - The Last Supper and the Mass 285
  - The Sacrifice of Calvary and the Mass 286
  - The Same Priest 286
  - The Same Victim 287

The Same Oblation 287
　　The Same Effects 289
　　The Ends of the Mass 289
　　Adoration 290
　　Reparation 290
　　Petition 290
　　Thanksgiving 291
　　The Heartbeat of the Mystical Body 291
Holy Eucharist, Part II: A Divine Banquet 293
　　The Eucharistic Meal 294
　　It Nourishes and Causes Growth 294
　　It Restores Our Daily Losses 296
　　It Diminishes Concupiscence 298
　　Preparation for Holy Communion 299
　　A Pledge of Future Glory 300
Transubstantiation 302
　　Doctrine of the Church 302
　　Nothing Remains of the Substance 303
　　No Parallel in Nature 305
　　In What Manner Christ is Present 306
　　The Real Presence 308
The Mass and the Mystical Body 310
　　Through Him, With Him, In Him 311
　　The Mass is Our Sacrifice 312
　　The Liturgy of the Eucharist 313
　　The Offertory 314
　　The Consecration 315
　　The Communion 315
Our Encounter with Christ in the Liturgy 318
　　Jesus Christ, Our High Priest 318
　　Jesus Continues to Exercise His Priesthood 319
　　Our Participation in the Priesthood of Christ 320
　　Offering the Eucharistic Sacrifice 321
　　Offering the Divine Victim.. 322
　　Offring Ourselves to the Father..................................... 323
　　Practical Reflections 324
The Millennium and the Eucharist 326
　　The Great Jubilee 326
　　Christ in the Eucharist 327
　　Christ, the Life of the Soul 328
　　The Eucharistic Sacrifice 329
　　Living the Mass 332
　　The Mass Continues Christ's Forgiveness 104
　　Eucharistic Reparation 149

FAITH
　　The Gift of Faith 161-167
　　Today's Crisis of Faith 249

INDEX

Safeguarding the Gift of Faith 255

FREEDOM
    Conscience and Freedom 21
    True Freedom Requires Discipline 24, 40, 79
  Freeing the Heart 77
    Attachments are Unavoidable 78
    The Need of Mortification 79
    God Takes the Initiative 80
    The Role of Divine Grace 82
    Letting Go 84
  The Truth Will Make You Free 242
    Two Opposing Concepts of Freedom 38, 77, 242, 247
    The Scriptures and False Freedom 244
    False Freedom Leads to Slavery 244
    We Cannot Serve Two Masters 245
    The Fruits of These Two Freedoms 246
    Further Contrasts of These Two Freedoms 247

FORGIVENESS
  The Love of Forgiveness 103
    True Love is Forgiving 104
    The Mass Continues Christ's Forgiveness 104
    The Power of Forgiveness 105
    The Obstacle of Pride 106
    Confused Notions of Forgiveness 107
    The Extent of Forgiveness 108
    The Fruit of Forgiveness 109

HOLINESS
  The Call to Holiness 62
    The Attainment of Holiness — A Command 62
    Sanctity, the Normal Development of Grace 63
    The Garden of the Soul 63
    Holiness is Perfect Charity 64
    Holiness and God's Will 65
    Does Not Require Extraordinary Achievements 66
  Loving is Self-Giving 69
    Loving is Giving 70
    Perfect Loving is Total Giving 71
    Love Has Many Facets 72
    Practical Reflections 75
  Blessed are the Clean of Heart 128
    They Shall See God 129
    Vices that Impede Spiritual Vision 132
  Monica's Wayward Son 235
    St. Monica 235
    St. Augustine 236
    How Some Saints are Made 237
    God's Mysterious Ways 237

Filling Up What is Wanting 239
A Reason for Hope 240

HUMANE VITAE
Humanae Vitae Reviewed 201
    The Basis of the Church's Teaching 201
    Peter, the Rock 203
    Conscience — Not Always a True Guide 203
    The Garden of Eden Today 205
    The Tree of the Knowledge of Good and Evil 206
    Pro-Choice Catholics 207

INDULGENCES
Indulgences 258
    What is an Indulgence? 258
    A New Norm of Measurement 260
    Three General Grants of Indulgences 262
    To Gain an Indulgence 264

MAGISTERIUM
Sacred Tradition 268
    What is Sacred Tradition? 268
    Public Revelation Ends with the Apostles 269
    Christ Commissioned the Apostles to Preach 270
    Christ Established a Living Teaching Authority 272
    The Development of Doctrine 274
    The Unity of Sacred Tradition and Scripture 275
Feed My Lambs, Feed My Sheep 277
    Christ, the Good Shepherd 277
    Peter, the Supreme Shepherd Under Christ 278
    The Roman Pontiff – The Supreme Shepherd Today 279
    Our Need of the Supreme Shepherd 280
    Wandering Sheep 280
    St. Thomas Aquinas and the Magisterium 282
    The Obedience of Faith 282

MERCY
Blessed are the Merciful 120
    God's Merciful Plan 120
    Conditions of God's Mercy 121
    Repentance and Conversion 121
    Works of mercy 122
    Mercy Involves Sacrifice 123
    Mercy Enriches 124
    Divine Mercy and the World's Misery 125
    Seeing Christ in His Members 126

MODERNISM
Today's Crisis of Faith 249
    Not the Fruit of the Council 249

INDEX

The Remnants of Modernism 250
Neo-Modernism 251

MODERNISM (cont.)
The New Morality 252
Safeguarding the Gift of Faith 255

OBEDIENCE
Obedience to the Church 25
"Yes, Father" 86
God's Will is Our Sanctification 86
The Divine Physician 89
God's Way Makes Us More Human 90
A Marvelous Exchange 91
Transformation in Christ 92
The Obedience of Faith 282

ORIGINAL SIN
First Sin in Human History 3
Before the Fall 3
The Fall of Our First Parents 5
We Inherit Fallen Human Nature 6
Loss of Sanctifying Grace 7
Loss of Integrity 7
Loss of Bodily Immortality 9
Loss of Impassibility 10
Dogma of Faith 10
The Wounds of Fallen Human Nature 55
The Body Before Original Sin
Immortality of the Body 4
Loss of Bodily Immortality 9

PEACE
Perfect Harmony Within Man 4
Loss of Integrity 7
Peace of Christ 111
Effect of Charity 120
Christian Notion of Freedom 247
Attaining Peace 405

PENANCE
The Bishops' Report 154
Is Lent Dead? 178
The Spirit of the World 179
The Need of Self-Discipline 180
We Can't Serve Both God and Mammon 180
The Full Meaning of Penance 181
Pope John XXIII and Penance 182
The Conflict Within Man 183
Sacrament of Penance/Reconciliation 335

Sacrament of the New Law 335
Only God Can Forgive Sin 336
The Three Elements of Penance 337
Contrition 337
Confession 340
Satisfaction 341
The Cleansing Power of the Blood of Christ 342

PRAYER (see also Rosary)
The Lord's Prayer 354
    Our Father Who Art in Heaven 354
    Hallowed Be Thy Name 355
    Thy Kingdom Come 356
    Thy Will Be Done on Earth as it is in Heaven 356
    Give Us This Day Our Daily Bread 357
    Bread for the Body 357
    Sacramental Bread 358
    The Bread of God's Word 358
    The Bread of Divine Grace 358
    Forgive Us Our Trespasses 358
    Lead Us Not Into Temptation 359
    But Deliver Us From Evil 360
Ask and You Shall Receive 362
    The Importance of Asking God's Help 362
    God Will Keep His Promise 363
    We Must Ask God's Graces and Gifts 364
    In a spirit of resignation to His will 364
    With faith and trust in God's Providence 365
    In Jesus' Name 366
    With perseverance 367
    With sincerity 368
Giving Thanks 371
    The Divine Benefactor 372
    Our Infinite Debt of Gratitude 372
    Man's Ingratitude 374
    Ingratitude Brings Spiritual Loss 376
    Only the Humble are Truly Grateful 377
    Sacrifice of Thanksgiving 378

PRIESTHOOD
The Priesthood of the Laity 344
    Priesthood and Sacrifice 344
    Priesthood in the Old Testament 345
    The Priesthood of Christ 346
    Sharing Christ's Priesthood 347
    The Ministerial Priesthood 347
    The Priesthood of All the Baptized 348

INDEX

REDEMPTION
- **Redemptive Suffering** 135
  - The Need of Redemption 135
  - Why the Passion? 136

REDEMPTION (cont.)
  - Our Sharing in the Redemption 137
  - Filling Up What is Lacking 138
  - Embrace the Cross 139
  - Testimony of the Pope 140
  - Mary's Role 141
  - Not My Will... 141
  - Sharing Christ's Work of Redemption 146

ROSARY
- **Understanding the Rosary** 379
  - Misunderstandings 379
  - Pius XII and the Rosary 381
  - More Divine Than Human 381
  - Compendium of the Gospel 382
  - The Body and Soul of the Rosary 382
  - Rosary Meditation — Limitless in Scope 383
  - School of the Christian Life 384
  - Antidote for the Ills of Life 384
  - Looking at a Mystery in Depth 384
  - Do Whatever He Tells You 386
- **Some Objections to the Rosary** 388
  - I Can't Keep My Mind From Wandering 388
  - Saintly souls and distractions 390
  - I Find Constant Repetition Monotonous 391
  - I Seem to Get in a Rut 392
  - Practical Reflections 394
- **St. Dominic and the Rosary** 396
  - The Evolution of the Rosary 396
  - The Marian Psalter 397
  - The Albigensian Heresy 398
  - The Bollandists 399
  - The Militia of Jesus Christ 400
  - Alan de Rupe 401
  - Testimony of the Popes 403
- **Weapons from Heaven** 406
  - The Feast of the Rosary 406
  - David's Slingshot 407
  - A Prophecy, A Warning, A Promise 408
  - How to Heed Our Lady's Requests 410
  - Root Cause of Today's Ills 411
  - Our Lady's Antidote for Today's Ills 411
  - Under Mary's Banner 413

SANCTIFYING GRACE

Sanctifying Grace 4
Loss of Sanctifying Grace 7
The Need of God's Grace 37
Sanctity, the Normal Development of Grace 63
The Role of Divine Grace 82
The Bread of Divine Grace 358

SIN

First Sin in Human History 3
  How the Passions Affect Our Judgment 46
Why Are We Tempted? 51
  Apparent Contradictions 51
  Temptations of Probation 52
  Temptations of Solicitation 53
  The Devil 53
  Other Sources of Temptation.. 55
  The Wounds of Fallen Human Nature 55
  Temptations of the World 57
  The Overall Picture 57
  Doing What We Can 58
Freeing the Heart 77
  The Obstacle of Pride 106
  The Passion of Anger 115
  Vices That Impede Spiritual Vision 132
Reparation for Sin 143
  Breaking Through the Barrier 145
  Sharing Christ's Work of Redemption 146
  Meriting and Atoning for Others 147
  Two Consoling Thoughts 148
  Eucharistic Reparation 149
What Has Become of Sin? 151
  What Has Brought This About? 152
  Social Sin 153
  The Bishops' Report 154
  The Nature of Sin 155
  Sin and Divine Friendship 158
  Concupiscence of the Flesh (Lust and Gluttony) 173
  Concupiscence of the Eyes (Greed) 174
  The Pride of Life 175
The Vice of Sloth 185
  How Sloth Opposes Charity 185
  The Joy of Charity 186
  The Oppressive Sadness of Sloth 188
  The Capital Sin of Sloth 189
  Remedies for Sloth 190
Our Adversary the Devil 217
  The Kingdom of Satan 217
  The Kingdom of God 218

INDEX

    The Fall of the Angels 218
    The Arch-Enemy of Christ 219
    The Smoke of Satan 220
    The Tactics of Satan 221
    The Devil's Subtle Suggestions 222
    Call Upon Mary 224

SIN (cont.)
  Envy and Jealousy, Enemies of Charity 226
    Hidden Vices 227
    Enemy of Charity 228
    What Envy is Not 228
    A Capital Sin 230
    The Grave Evil of Envy 231
    Countering Envy 232

SOUL
  The Human Soul 27
    Made to God's Image and Likeness 28
    The Soul — The Source of Life 29
    The Soul and Its Faculties 30
    The Soul Created by God 31
    The Spirituality of the Soul 32
    Body-Soul Relationship 33
    The Soul — Temple of God 33
    Dependence of the Soul on the Body 44
    The Garden of the Soul 63
    The Divine Physician 89
    Christ, the Life of the Soul 328

SUFFERING
    Loss of Impassibility 10
    The Need of Mortification 79
    Mercy Involves Sacrifice 123
  Redemptive Suffering 135
    The Need of Redemption 135
    Why the Passion? 136
    Our Sharing in the Redemption 137
    Filling Up What is Lacking 138
    Embrace the Cross 139
    Testimony of the Pope 140
    Mary's Role 141
    Not My Will... 141

WILL
  Our Free Will 35
    The Key Faculty In Man 36
    Two Notions of Freedom 38
    A Union of Wills 39

True Freedom Requires Discipline 40
Cafeteria Catholics 160
   The Gift of Faith 161
   The First Dissenters 162
   Today's Dissenters 163
   Theologians and the Magisterium 165
   Where Some Have Gone Astray 165

WORLDLINESS
   Temptations of the World 57
   Today's Confused World 99
   Worldliness 169
      Pilgrims on the Way 170
      Sources of Worldliness... 172
      Concupiscence of the Flesh (Lust and Gluttony) 173
      Concupiscence of the Eyes (Greed) 174
      The Pride of Life 175
      The Spirit of the World 179
   The Fruits of Secularism 209
      Secularism's Impact on the Individual 210
      Secularism's Impact on the Family 211
      Secularism's Impact on Education 212
      The Need of Evangelization 214